WOMAN

Woman

A Contemporary View

by

F. J. J. Buytendijk

Translated by

Denis J. Barrett

NEWMAN PRESS
Glen Rock, N.J.   New York, N.Y.
and
ASSOCIATION PRESS
New York, N.Y.

A Newman Press Edition, originally published under the title *De Vrouw* by Uitgeverij Het Spectrum N.V., De Meern, Netherlands

Library of Congress
Catalog Card Number: 68-16676

Published by Newman Press
Editorial Office: 304 W. 58th St., N.Y., N.Y. 10019
Business Office: Glen Rock, New Jersey 07452
and
Association Press
291 Broadway
New York, N.Y. 10007

Printed and bound in the
United States of America

Contents

v

Foreword

Philosophy in the present generation, in some places, is making a determined and largely successful effort to overcome the drawbacks inherent in that necessary tool of thought, abstraction. The Middle Ages were very much aware of the concrete significance and application of their metaphysics and philosophy of essences, but in the centuries that followed, the historical origins of the terminology employed came to be forgotten, and thought withdrew more and more into the region of pure abstract speculation. This led eventually to the complete hiatus between philosophy and the "exact sciences" characteristic of the early years of this 20th century.

In the awareness that progress in the perfection of knowledge is to be found somewhere between the practical study of particular things on the one hand and speculation about things in general on the other, several lines of development have emerged. Common to them all is the fundamental understanding that generalized or abstract statements about reality have constantly to be tested against concrete and particular realities, and that study of the particular is a chief source of knowledge of the universal.

Perhaps the most popular of the new developments is the Existentialism developed mainly by French thinkers during and after the 1939-1945 war. It is wholly in keeping with the efforts made that this Existentialism was, and is, developed through the medium of the novel and the theatre, for these provide a context of immediate contact with reality not readily available in the medium of the philosophical treatise. The pendulum of human reaction, rather than defects inherent in Existentialism itself, has drawn the main exponents of this line of thought even further into abstract generalization than the old philosophies had dared to go. Thus Sartre can say, *"l'enfer, c'est l'autre."*

Another of the new developments took place in England, where contact with reality was sought first of all through the immediacy of words, thus giving rise to a concentration on linguistic analysis.

1

A third new development, and one that will possibly prove to be the most significant, has its roots in Germany and Holland, and has come to be known as Phenomenology. It is perhaps more a method of investigation than a philosophy in the usual sense, for its basic aim is to let reality "speak for itself."

The aim of the scientist is to get to know as much as possible as profoundly as possible about his world, his cosmos. All that is to be known is already somehow contained within the given universe of which human beings are a part. As the universe appears to us, so it reveals something of its knowable content to us. In this sense, the universe is an appearance, a *phenomenon,* and all its parts are interrelated phenomena. Knowledge is our consciousness becoming aware of whatever appears to us, but the fallibility of human knowledge consists in the fact that we are able to separate our knowledge from its roots in phenomena and arbitrarily to "construct" upon this knowledge in the abstract. Therefore, progress in knowledge requires that a careful check be kept on the fallibility of knowledge, which is to say that our conscious awareness must constantly be kept in touch with the world of phenomena in which we have our being and of which we ourselves are a part.

This aids progress in scientific knowledge for two reasons. Firstly, it keeps us in touch with things as they are, and not as we would perhaps be inclined to imagine them to be. Secondly, it makes us return to the same thing again and again. A reality cannot reveal its entire knowable content in one appearance—we cannot know the whole truth of any matter "at a glance." As we return again and again to the same phenomenon, it becomes more and more "familiar" to us. The phenomenon reveals more to the penetrating glance than to the cursory glance, more still to the familiar penetrating glance, and even more to the methodically controlled, penetrating and familiar glance, and this calls for a Phenomenology—a highly methodical study of the actual appearance of things, to discover the *"eidos,"* the essential reality of what is appearing in its place in and relationship to the rest of the world of reality.

Phenomenology, then, strikes the desired balance between abstract thinking which tends to stray from reality, and "departmentalized" awareness of things, which may take the form of scientific specialization like nuclear physics, or of utilitarian practicality, like trade, neither of which makes life in this one world any more *human* if they are not freed from their own limitations and really related to all other aspects of the world and of life in it.

Although phenomenology itself is not a "philosophical system," it makes itself felt most clearly in those sciences which have customarily been built upon a philosophical system, such as theology, sociology, ethics, anthropology and psychology. It is not mere coincidence that fellow countrymen of Dr. Buytendijk are among the foremost writers in these fields to-day. This book represents the highly fruitful application of the phenomenological method, not only to one particular problem in psychology, but to psychology as a whole. Moreover, the immense experience and wisdom of the author is revealed perhaps above all in the essential simplicity of his style and approach. Reflecting on my own experiences in translating the book, it brings not only a much deeper understanding and appreciation of Woman, our fellow human being whom we take so much for granted, but also much valuable light to bear upon our own presuppositions about ourselves.

D. J. BARRETT

A Word of Explanation

This study is based on the fact that woman is human. Starting from this point, therefore, we have tried in our *theoretical* investigation to grasp the connection between woman's *nature,* and the *way she manifests herself,* and her *existence,* for these are the three aspects of all being that is human.

1. By *nature* we mean all that can objectively be ascertained concerning woman: the characteristic qualities which, like any other "thing," she possesses, and which may be discovered by observation and experiment in the manner of procedure employed by the physical sciences.

The characteristic qualities of woman, by which her "nature" is *defined,* can be divided under two headings: physical and psychological. This reduces quite simply to a distinction between anatomical-physiological structures, and the structure of behavior and capabilities. As far as the former are concerned, and according to the current view, a scientific understanding of the human body can be achieved only in the comparative study of human and animal bodies. Thus, we have gathered the most important data concerning the distinction and relation of the sexes in the animal kingdom in a special chapter, in order to enquire whether the nature of woman is perhaps to be understood in terms of its biological basis.

In psychology too, efforts have already been made to find an intelligible correlation of a multiplicity of phenomena by means of genetic investigation. As far as the psychological characteristics of woman are concerned, pretensions are made to the achievement of an explanation of this kind particularly in the field of psychoanalysis. It therefore seemed good to us to pay critical attention to these psychoanalytic views.

2. The *way* in which woman *manifests herself,* or, her *appearance,* refers simply to the phenomenological aspect of her physical reality as expression, inasmuch as a woman is met in this face, this

5

figure, this attitude, this voice, and, in these, precisely as an exteriorly manifest "interiority."

3. By the *existence* of woman, we mean the *manner* in which woman finds herself physically in the world; the *manner* in which she is conscious of her nature and appearance, and also of the world, her fellow human beings and herself; the *manner,* too, in which she chooses to take notice of all this, to perceive and take her place in it, to observe it, to feel it, to present it, to judge, love, hate it, etc. This awareness which she has of herself, of the world and of the meaning (intentionality) of her own conduct can be non-reflexive, and can arise spontaneously out of her involvement in situations in which she becomes engrossed almost to the point of being wholly unmindful of herself. Or this awareness can come about in the manner of a perception of all that actuality of which one is the witness, and upon which one thinks, but in which one does not take part oneself. This conscious reflection on those things in the presence of which one stands but in which one does not play a part, belongs in the existence of woman as well. All that woman is conscious of, whether reflexively or not, belongs to the world of woman. She discovers and forms (projects) this world by directing herself toward it, and this always takes place in a determined manner, this being the sense of her intentional acts.

Every act is chosen by man, and thus by woman, on the basis of a motive. Motive is not a cause, but an antecedent which is operative exclusively in virtue of its *meaning*. However, the validity of the motive is founded on the decision, and the decision at the same time confers its dynamic effect on the motive. Thus, in an onflowing stream of existence upon which there is no reflection, it is not possible to suppose a connection of plans and executions.

In relation to the *fore*casting character of the projection of a situation, it is the act itself which always creates its own motive. Merleau-Ponty is therefore very right when he notes, "Motive and decision are two elements of a situation. The former is the situation as produced; the latter is the situation as assumed".[1] Thus, the world and existence in their relation and opposition are formed in a history of meanings (Sinngeschichte) which begins for every

---

[1] *Phénoménologie de la Perception*. Paris (N.R.F.) 1945, p. 299. English translation by C. Smith, *Phenomenology of Perception*. New York (Humanities Press) 1962.

man from his very birth, and which is none other than his own personal history.

We know human beings by their world and their behavior, and thus, this is the way we come to a knowledge of woman. The *ground-plan* of the world in which existence is couched, and the basic *structure* of conduct, bring us to a knowledge of that which is characteristic (typical) of a person (or a group).

The world of woman, as we shall see, may be characterized as a *world of care;* that of men may be characterized as a *world of labor.* We recognize the origin of these worlds in the earliest experiences little children encounter: the little girl forms a world of qualities through a dynamism which is predominantly adaptive; the little boy comes across a world of resistances through a dynamism which is predominantly expansive and aggressive.

Thus, through this "dynamism," which is the basic structure of her conduct and which is physically determined, the little girl involves herself in a reality that is "other" from the very beginning, and that becomes manifest in situations formed in a meaningful way.

Relation of Woman to Her Own Body

However, the body is the first—and the last—situation which every human being comes across in his existence and to which he gives meaning. It is clear that woman takes more notice of her own bodily nature and appearance than man of his, and in this measure she finds it the more difficult to forget her own body, and she becomes proportionately engrossed in the external world. Therefore it is necessary for us to give attention to the *relation of woman to her own body*.

Finally, it is our view that the essentials of nature and of the mode of appearance in the medium of feminine existence can be gathered together in the idea of woman's *quality of "motherliness."*

Having in the above given an explanation of the basic intent and the division of this existential, psychological study of woman, we may now refer briefly to the results of our investigation, and do this to some extent in connection with the many practical questions that arise in many different ways in society.

Woman differs—so our conclusion will read—from man in a

bodily way, in her "nature", her inborn characteristics and qualities. Besides an anatomical and physiological difference, there is an aboriginal difference in the dynamic structure of all conduct.

Because of this difference, the content as well as the forms of behavior develop in a manner of their own, and thus, there is at the same time a special development of the choice of intentional acts and of the project, the structure, of the feminine world.

The difference is already present in the baby at the breast, and it is, in our culture, strengthened by education and *"used"* in order to make feminine existence develop in the direction that agrees, partly, with woman's inborn qualities, but that agrees above all with traditional views. These views are generally looked upon as something indicated by the "being" of woman, by genuine, absolute and eternal femininity. In this, however, there is the failure to see that woman's being is identical with human being, and there is a confusion of what is essential with what is characteristic and typical and peculiar to the nature of woman as such. Woman has an ordinary human soul. Her *essentia concreta* (the nature of her existence) develops out of her human possibilities (the *essentia abstracta*) in connection with her encounters in the world.

Because every existence is a being-bodily-in-the-world, and because the difference between the body of a man and the body of a woman is more important than we are accustomed to think, the nature of her existence is always typically feminine, and differs from the manner of a man's existence, however much the structures of society may change and whatever educational norms are followed. This difference remains, even when a woman does the same work as a man. For she is indeed *able* to work, and it is quite certain that she can work just as well as a man. The years of the war taught us this, but not only this.

Experience shows just as clearly—and it is our view that we can now understand this more fully—that woman always works in a way that is *different* from man's way. And it is precisely this fact that has given rise to a series of practical questions. Does this "difference" mean, perhaps, not quite as well after all, or does it mean, in many cases, better? Does it mean that, in our culture, it is undesirable that women should exercise certain professions? In our view, these questions are inadmissible in such general terms, —unless, as is only too often the case, the questioner has certain ulterior motives.

For indeed, if our explanations hold any truth, it is clear that the "genuine" woman will bring an element of *care* to development in the labor she undertakes in the community, and it is obvious that this can be of much value in many professions and functions. But we have pointed out a contrast in the dynamism and in the worlds of the sexes, and from the *relativity* of the sexes it follows that a number of women will be able to develop a masculine (for example, a technical) grasp of things.

However, there is one fact that must not be forgotten in the problematic of the work of women. Women, just as all human beings who are weaker or who have less power of endurance, are inclined to demand too much of their powers and to overwork themselves, or else they are inclined to choose passivity and impotency as a means of self-protection. That this last is the less common occurrence is something that is connected with social circumstances. Moreover, women are more inclined to overwork because they have a higher sense of duty—this was noted already by Heymans, and it is explained in our theoretical investigation.

On the matter of woman's work, an important question is asked: is it not detrimental to the development of "genuine femininity?" There is a touch of irony in the fact that it is never asked whether certain work is conducive to the development of "genuine masculinity." Clearly it is judged that of the two, genuine femininity is the more endangered. This is understandable, for we have seen that "the genuine" in this case is something artificial, and it does not uphold itself of itself by its nature, but only by means of "the rules."

The things that are considered to be the most endangered are certain spiritual qualities of great value that are customarily thought of as specifically feminine. We name three of these: gracefulness, meekness and humility.

Concerning the first of these, it is clear that many traditional views play a predominant role in the formation of the concept of gracefulness: traditional views of beauty, charm, elegance of dress and manners, and, particularly, of the relationship of the sexes. Nevertheless, gracefulness is a spiritual quality which is essentially important to woman's social position and above all to family life. It is quite certain that this kind of "gracefulness" can be threatened just as much by faulty education as by unfavorable social circumstances.

Circumstances of this sort are clearly the result of the kind and the length of the labor undertaken by women—including the labor of household tasks. These circumstances therefore are not merely economical; of their nature they are also psychological. One needs only for a moment to think of the way children in school are sometimes badgered, the impersonal and unfriendly atmosphere in some offices, the disparaging remarks passed by men in charge (surgeons and others), the way women are sometimes passed over in decisions regarding salary and promotion, the lack of recreation in the housewife's routine, etc. Even an "angel" could lose her gracefulness in circumstances like these more easily than she would in working 8-hour days in a factory or by doing back-breaking labor on a farm.

Every social group has and appreciates its own particular type of gracefulness, but invariably in all groups there is one special quality that is demanded of a woman. This quality is variously indicated by words and expressions like friendliness, good humor, "she doesn't get angry," vivaciousness, sunny disposition. If this quality is lost, the woman is thought of as unwomanly, and the underlying intention is to say that she is *unattractive.* It seems that only a man can permit himself his outbursts of "anger" or un-pleasantness, because all that the community expects of *homo faber* is his work—and this is often all that woman expects of him.

But what then is the position as far as meekness and humility are concerned?

The notion that these are specifically feminine qualities must be rejected emphatically. For these are in fact the *highest* moral attitudes which any *human being* is able to adopt in his relationship with his fellow human beings and, indeed, in his relationship to all that exists.

We need to give some explanation of the reasons why we chose, as the motto of this book, the meekness and humble lowliness of him who is able to bring man to the fulfillment of his essential destiny.

The choice was not decided on the grounds that these words were addressed to women. It was decided on the grounds that they were addressed to all human beings, *including* women, and that women know themselves confronted by these words more than men do.

Men in their sphere generally give the words meekness and humility or lowliness a limited, "Sundayish" kind of meaning, to such an extent that very little can be found to which the words might apply in the every-day world of business and work. But at the same time meekness and modest humility are demanded of women —especially by men—always and everywhere—even in a matter like trying to get onto a crowded bus.

Now in our view, theoretical investigation shows that, in actual fact, the *possibility* of developing the highest moral values is more open to women than to men, and that the reasons for this lie in that mode of existence which is typically feminine, and, more fundamentally, in the basic dynamism of behavior which is the source of this mode of existence. There is however a reason why the realization of this possibility is often retarded. The customary demands in terms of which women are evaluated give occasion for unfaithfulness to reality, and give rise to the danger that the perfection of genuine humanity will be betrayed—especially by those women who think mainly of winning the "marriage stakes."

Under pressure of the demands made on her, many a woman has developed the rather tragic art of appearing to be the very picture of meekness, whereas in fact there is nothing more in her than shyness, docility, sentimentality, ingratiating affection or exaggerated friendliness—in keeping with her age and circumstances.

In the place of modesty or humility, there is often something that is not much more than subjection, accommodation of self to circumstance because it cannot be avoided, camouflaged cowardice, tacit suppression.

There is nothing mysterious about all this. It is a pity, but human beings are like that. Those who are called to reach the heights, have also the possibility of betraying the heights.

Of this we are convinced, that the world which is so much in need of care, the world which is found and formed in the womanly mode of existence, is ever and again a call upon woman to represent the perfection of genuine humanity. The measure of the hearing given to this call, the depth of understanding and of the response to it, is something that is left to the decision of each woman —a decision taken in the secret of her own heart.

The appearance of a new printing of this book gives me a valued opportunity to fill out this general and impersonal "explanation" and address myself directly to my readers. I am moved to do this, not only by the critique offered in many reviews, or in letters or through verbal report, but also by an "atmosphere of emotional doubt" about the validity of my investigation and explanations, sometimes manifesting itself in silence, sometimes in hesitant, searching expression.

Toward an Understanding of Women

An uncertainty of this kind can arise on various levels, and it is usually found very difficult to formulate exactly. On the scientific level,[2] the uncertainty rests chiefly on the question of method: *in what way can we come to an understanding of woman?*

On the level of day-to-day life, emotional doubt arises—and condenses sometimes into a rain of protest and indignation—if the image of woman as presented does not agree with affective personal experience and its interpretation, or if it does not agree with traditional views which, in the popular mentality, seem to be the very foundation of society and civilization.

The reaction to my discussion of the characteristic quality and nature of woman—a reaction which the seemingly unquestionable certainty of every-day experience can elicit—is expressed in the following questions:

Is not the picture of woman too highly idealized?

Is the difference in innate aptitude between man and woman in fact a difference that is exclusively physical?

Is not woman "wholly and entirely" different from man?

1. The question about the way in which the most fundamental understanding of the nature, mode of appearance and existence of woman can possibly be achieved is but a part of many methodological questions that have arisen out of the renewed correlation of psychology with the philosophical investigation of human reality and of man himself. It is possible to hold a variety of views about the mutual connections of science and philosophy, but in the last analysis it is only an evaluation of the results actually achieved

[2] After I had written this, Prof. Révész's extensive review of my book appeared in the *Ned. Tijdschr. voor Psychologie*, 1952, VII, p. 98-114, giving critical attention in particular to the methodology.

that can decide the question of the efficacy of a methodological approach.

Psychology used to aim chiefly at the gathering of as large as possible a collection of facts. Nowadays the conviction is gaining ground, that the facts are scientifically valuable only if it is possible to understand the *significance* which these facts possess on the concrete level of human existence. Now this existence cannot come to be known by means of a discursive analysis proceeding from a basis of hypotheses; this existence can only be known by taking part in it, and each man's part in it takes the form of an immediate directing and applying of himself to the world in which his existence is concerned. This is of course what is meant when it is said that *a man is known by his world.*

By "world," then, we mean all that man "inhabits;" all toward which he directs himself in his acts of perceiving, feeling, thinking, presenting, remembering, etc.; all that he relates to himself as friend or enemy; all in which he feels at home and all that is foreign to him. Man is involved in his own particular way, through his ensouled or animated corporeality, in *situations,* which are parts of the world defined by structures of space and time. The world is the recorded witness of a person's life history, of all that he encountered and all to which he gave stature, meaning and value; of all that elicited his passivity and thus formed him, or of all that was formed *by* him through his own initiative.

The orientation of a psychological investigation into the world of man is at the same time a directing of the investigation toward the *evidence* provided by modes of behavior and conduct, in the conviction that these reveal their own significance, if they are seen in the context of a "fundamental projection" of the mode of existence.

It is clear that, according to the principles of its approach, the science of psychology differs in its method from the physical sciences. The basic standpoint of the physical sciences is "objective," and called purely scientific, and it means that these sciences observe the laws of reality and describe them in terms of universally valid concepts that as far as possible are mathematical concepts. Psychology, on the other hand, arrived at the conviction that man, in his humanity, is not an "object," not a thing with properties, but a "subject" whose experiences and activities are knowable only to the extent that we make them our own experiences and activities by taking our own part in existence.

This participation is made possible on the basis of that which unites all men, and this uniting factor is a great deal more than exclusively the faculty of intelligent judgment. This we learn from life itself, from encounters and connections with others, from mimicry and gesture, dialogue, sympathy, and so on. Psychology is thus able to develop as a science, by a *methodical* application of those same means that make an understanding of our fellow man possible in all daily, normal inter-personal relationships of the kind that we do not usually submit to reflexive analysis.

This application is methodical, if the psychologist does not allow his participation to flow without reflection upon it, but continually directs his conscious attention to the *actual* (essential) significance of each experience. Moreover, psychological insight will be the richer and the more certain, the more the circumstantial character and partiality of the understanding of man brought by ordinary life is able to be superseded by a certainty and exactness. This will be all the more convincing if the immediate evidence of the insights can be tested against a wide and deep field of actual experience.

Psychology has abandoned the ideal of knowledge as this is presented in the physical sciences, because of the conviction that we can come to know our fellow man only in personal connection with him, and indeed heart to heart connection—in listening to him and conversing with him, and also by following closely his personal development from stage to stage, by sharing his acts and their fulfillment, and by inhabiting his world together with him. In this way psychology has entered into the *spiritual climate* in which, from time immemorial, art has been developed.

However, it is quite clear that this sharing of the same climate does not imply any identification of science with art. However divergent the knowledge of man achieved in art may be from that achieved in science, the fact remains that art, in its essence, is "putting the truth to work," and also that all genuine scientific knowledge is "to have *seen,* in the broad sense of 'to see,' and this means, to accept and understand reality present as it is in itself".[3]

2. I can very easily understand that ordinary daily experience should incline a person to say that the picture of woman that I

[3] Heidegger, *Vom Ursprung des Kunstwerkes,* in *Holzwege,* Frankfurt, 1950.

have drawn is idealized. However, could we not expect similar remarks if we confront daily experience with a treatise on the essence of man? If one reads, "man is characterized by intelligence, a moral consciousness and a free will," one might scornfully remark that in "practice" very few people actually bear out this description. In the same way, there are many sentences in this book that will give occasion for ironical and even sarcastic remarks that are based on less pleasant encounters with women, "in actual fact." We might expect that the experience of such encounters would be exclusively man's experience, but it has become clear to me that quite a number of *women* find an unallowable idealization of woman in what is said later on: "In the element of caring, in feminine existence, we find the moral requirement of selfless love, self-giving and sacrifice".

Many readers seem to have missed the point that my investigation concerns *femininity in women* according to the way it *can* be developed in a favorable milieu and *can* become the ground-plan of a mode of existence. In many places, moreover, I have stressed the point that woman's encounter with the world, and care-full sojourn with that which is in need of care, is *human* and thus, that "every man possesses the freedom to dwell on the essential value of things." A discourse on the meaning of humanity in human beings would not give attention in great detail to the many forms of irrationality, immorality and unfreedom. It would not be expected to. In the same way, I have referred only cursorily to the *decay* of femininity, and thus to the degeneration of woman, her characteristic offenses, maliciousness and ridiculous failings.

I have also left a special chapter on these out of this edition (the 1958 edition of the original), my reason being that, in my view, this existential psychological study ought to be limited to theoretical investigation. So, the many questions that arise in actual situations in society do not come within the actual subject of this study. Those who are interested in these questions will find a large collection of data in numerous works, among them the second part of Simone de Beauvoir's book, which is subtitled *"l'expérience vécue"*—"experiences from life." It will however be remembered that many of the views of this French authoress relate to the state of relationships in her own country, and even, in part, relate only to one small Parisian milieu.

Aspects of "Genuinely Feminine" Evil

We see, therefore, that all forms of the degeneration of human being are sociologically defined in such a way that a scientific investigation of them is possible only if it is based on a meticulous analysis of concrete situations, and thus, if the forms of degeneration are understood in an historical context. We do not yet know of any investigations of this kind, and their absence explains the great diversity of judgments on womankind that one comes across in the literature of the world's nations, some examples of which will be found in the chapter on "The intuitive concept of the essence of woman."

However, if feminine existence is grasped as a being-in-the-world in a manner that is different from that of masculine existence, it can certainly be seen that woman's mode of existence is able to degenerate in a way that is different from man's. Every-day experience bears witness to this, most typically in the terms of abuse that are aimed exclusively at women. The language conventional among teachers can teach us just as much, in this regard, as the spontaneous imagery that adds fire to an argument between husband and wife. Every country, and even every region, city, social stratum and professional group, has to some extent its own vocabulary of terms of abuse. A linguistic investigation of this fact could produce results of great interest to social psychology, even though it would surely be found that the selection of certain terms is determined by history. In the meantime it is not possible to see why someone who in Holland would be called an "owl," is referred to as a "camel" in France.

However varied the expressions may be which point specifically to the degradation of femininity, there are some words which are (internationally) popular, and which are used to represent an aspect of "genuinely feminine" evil; think, for example, of witch, vampire and snake.

This fact could form the basis of an analysis of the degeneration of femininity. But one would at the same time have to take account of the range of experiences that have given rise to the use of the words. It is noticeable, for example, that a witch is always a woman, and that we do not have male witches, but wizards and magicians. This is evident, not only in fables and fairy-tales, but also in the world's great literary works. In Shakespeare's works and Goethe's *Faust,* covenants with the powers of darkness and the inscrutability of material things can be achieved by women only, sealed in turbid brews and sinister cauldrons. Poison, the evil eye and fatal vengeance, besides, are imputed to a being whose shape is bent and whose features are wrinkled and sharp and pointed.

It is no less remarkable that the actual idea of the witch is one that does not permit of any diminutive. In literature, there are indeed occasions when witches appear in forms of youth and great beauty, and a pretty young girl can indeed be a witch just as a young man can be the "devil incarnate." But when we speak of "little devils" we do not actually relate our meaning to the genuinely diabolical in the way we refer to the angelic when we speak of "little angels." In an analogous way it is possible to speak of "little witches" (*heksje, la petite sorcière, la diablesse*), where again the words refer to a mode of being that actually has nothing to do with evil witchcraft and witches as such.

However, let us leave this problem aside. The picture of woman that I have drawn is not an idealized one. Here and there the reader will find remarks on the common or garden way in which it is possible for feminine existence to fall into degradation. Many authors have sketched (generally in caricature) the pitiful, scrupulous, self-important, envious, face-saving, self-satisfied and fastidious woman always concerned with putting other people's houses in order. Women will not find it easy to recognize themselves in the image of womanhood that this book presents. It could even prove annoying to them, but then, perhaps, this reaction is precisely an indication of a confrontation with the *possibility* open to every woman in her own nature, mode of manifestation and existence.

3. I have noticed that it is a matter of fairly widespread opinion that the difference in inborn aptitudes between a man and a woman is not only physical, but also "psychical." In saying this, it is intended to convey that woman possesses a number of inborn qualities of character which are taken to be the distinguishing marks of a mysterious "interiority." In the chapter on the psychological characteristics of woman, I have discussed this opinion, but in order to eliminate any misunderstanding it is good to state now that, by a physical difference we mean a great deal more than an anatomical difference. The concept, animated materiality (en-

souled body), points more clearly to the fact that a human being, from the earliest moments of his life, comes across his own body as the preliminary sketch of his existence and as the means by which he relates himself to the world. I see the difference in animation above all as a difference in the encounter with the world outside and with fellow human beings, noting that it is through this encounter that *all* manifestations of the person are given their own special characteristic qualities of *form* and *mode*.

There is certainly a profound difference between characteristic qualities of the male and those of the female, but in every man and in every woman both male and female can manifest themselves. One can speak of a complete distinction of man from woman only in terms of the physical organism in the narrow sense of anatomical and physiological sexual differences. These differences manifest themselves in specifically sexual relationships and, in general, in the mutual encounter of the sexes. In a certain sense these differences also determine one's relationship to one's own sex, to all fellow human beings, and to children (for example, in motherhood and fatherhood). The problems that arise in this connection have not been discussed at any length in this book, because the relationship of the sexes and the question of the forms of human love demand such an extensive investigation that this could not responsibly be undertaken within the limits of this study.

In the important work recently published by Dr. Ruygers,[4] a consideration of the physical reality of man has been worked out philosophically in two directions. In the first place, he has shown that the relation of the sexes as it exists in the animal world is not applicable to the human relationship of man and woman. In the second place, he has shown that in ensouled or animated materiality, the differences between man and woman give to human beings the possibility of experiencing, through these differences, that love which more than any other "comes closer to the love of God," as Vondel says.

If we are to aim at an insight into the relationship of man to woman, it is of essential importance to see that the body cannot be taken to be a completed and perfected organism, but something that reveals its significance only in encounters between human beings. It is this fact that in principle lays down the *normative*

---

[4] Dr. H. J. C. G. M. Ruygers, *De beide geslachten* (sketches for a philosophical study of sex), J. J. Romen en Zn., Roermond, 1952.

directions for the conduct of the body, for the body is indeed a preliminary sketch of existence, but then, at the same time it is one that comes as a gift and that sets a task to be fulfilled. This task is possible of fulfillment, only because the actual choice of existence as projected is not quite as free a choice as the French existentialists think. The norms of existence are made known to a man in inscrutable ways, and a "knowledge" of them is written, not only in the heart, but in the whole body, and it is often vague and ambiguous.

In agreement with this view, Gabriel Marcel writes in *Du Refus à l'Invocation* that being-in-a-situation (or being-in-the-body or being incarnate) actually becomes *meaningless* (unintelligible, unthinkable) if I try to think of it as a relation between two terms and thus speak of "having" and "existence." [5] And yet, we cannot quite escape the need to speak in this way. But still, the way in which we speak must not be allowed to make us forget that we can neither distinguish ourselves from our own body, nor can we identify ourselves with it. For this reason, we cannot approach the materiality of human existence as a problem to be solved by reflexive thought; we have to acknowledge it, and that it is a "mystery."

The extent to which man is dependent on the condition of his body in every one of his functions and in all of his manifestations is something that is also made clear on the level of analysis in the physical sciences. We can think, in this connection, of the significance of hormones precisely in relation to the differentiation of the sexes. However, there is always the liberty to give a chosen meaning to the bodily factor or condition, even if this condition as it is found can prove to be a compulsive motivation of the choice in one direction or another.

4. The remark about the completeness of the differentiation of the sexes that reaches me now and then, is based to a fairly large extent on the romantic approach, which is still widely accepted, and which is defined in Feuerbach's words quoted later on in this book. Clearly it seems that the most widespread opinion still holds woman to be "wholly and entirely" different from man. This view

[5] *Du Refus à l'Invocation*, Paris, (Gallimard) 1940, p. 31. "To be incarnate is to appear as a body, as this body, without being able to be identified with it, and equally without being able to be distinguished from it—identification and distinction being correlative operations that can be carried out only in the sphere of objects."

is contrary to the one developed in this study. Occasion for misunderstanding is given by the fact that people usually do not make the distinction clearly enough between the *mode* in which a person manifests himself and the *content* of the manifestation.

I have tried to clarify the point that, in the sphere of our culture, a very large number of actions, ways of thinking, expressive gestures and movements can be found to have typically feminine and typically masculine forms. In spite of this, however, it is obvious that the meaning of an act, the logical structure of a thought or the significance of a gesture or a feeling can in either form be largely the same. Nevertheless, the more a mode of conduct is meant to be the expression of a personal relation to the world, the more its general significance will be permeated by that which is characteristic or typical. Thus, for instance, it is possible to find a kind of sorrow that is specifically feminine.

This additional explanation, which is also intended as a brief reaction to the uncertainty and doubt in which the book has left a number of readers, will undoubtedly leave many questions still unanswered. This is understandable. For our social relationships are so strongly differentiated that many different and divergent types of problems arise from the various situations in work and family, suburb and city in which woman can find herself in any one of the many conditions that fall to her lot. It is not possible to formulate this problematic clearly enough to be able to work toward its solution, if we do not first understand the general psychology of woman, and thus, understand her nature, the way in which she manifests herself, and her existence. This book is an attempt to contribute toward such an understanding.

I
The Problematics
of Feminine
Existence

The Problematics
of Feminine Existence

> Scientific psychology is always based on "an" anthropology, for it is not possible to investigate the particulars of human existence without some general concept of man as a whole.
>
> P. HÄBERLIN [1]

Many centuries ago, Aristotle included some brief and matter-of-fact remarks on the less fortunate characteristics of women in his descriptions of nature.[2] In modern times, Simone de Beauvoir [3] found it not quite possible to hide her very understandable womanly indignation at the myth of "eternal and absolute femininity," in spite of the shrewdly masculine guise of her comprehensive protest. In the years between, very many works indeed, some more scientific than others, were written on woman—and hardly any on man.

There is another fact, no less remarkable. In the ordinary course of life, and in the literature which reflects this life, just as much is said about men as about women, as individual personalities, in the concrete detail of their character and career, but "generalizations" almost always concern woman, and these generalizations are numberless, and not always very profound. When on occasions we hear or read a woman revealing her thoughts "about men"—usually with a sigh—it usually appears that she is more clearly telling us about the "genuine" womanliness that gives direction to her own

[1] *Der Mensch.* Zürich, 1941, p. 91.

[2] *Historia Animalium,* LIX. Woman is more sympathetic. She weeps more easily, is more inclined to jealousy, complaining and scolding. She easily becomes prey to despair and she is less sanguine than man; she is more unashamed and less ambitious, fickle, more quickly disappointed; she has a better memory. She is more prudent, more shy, more difficult to encourage to act, and she needs less food.

[3] Simone de Beauvoir, *Le Deuxième Sexe* I & II, Paris (Gallimard) 1949. (English translation, *The Second Sex,* published by Jonathan Cape, London, and Knopf, New York, in 1953. Volume II only published as a Four Square book in 1960).

acts and thoughts and feelings, than she is telling us about the nature of men.

Now why should this be so? Why have so many philosophers, psychologists, essayists, moralists, theologians and poets throughout the ages written about *women* and not about *men?* Why is it that the authoresses of our own day who are scientifically inclined do not write about the sex that to them is the *other* sex? Is it because they—Gina Lombroso, Viola Klein, Margaret Mead, Georgene Seward, Helene Deutsch and others [4]—hold the view that the problem lies in their own existence, played out against the background of the human world, and that this world is masculine? However, if the identification of human with masculine that we can find in popular opinion at present, turns out to be something determined on historical and sociological grounds only, it would mean that people, in some past or future "matriarchal" culture, would get excited only about the "problem of men" and become all thoughtful about the "mystery" of masculinity.

The historical and sociological perspective of the question of femininity is certainly not a brand new invention. Mathias and Mathilde Vaerting [5] in their generation had already defended the view that woman, as manifesting herself in the concrete in our society, is the "product" of man's domination, and that it was only this dominance that made a problem of feminine existence.

The historical picture that Simone de Beauvoir gives, is drawn from the same viewpoint.

"The problem of woman has always been the problem of man," because the history of women has been determined by men. It was men who, because of their physical prowess, dominated in the primitive hordes of prehistoric times; who created the values, the morals and the religions that regulated human relationships. The world was always something that belonged to men, because in principle bringing forth children and feeding them remained within the functions of nature. The male is "homo faber," the inventor, who wants to control nature and hammer out his own future. He

[4] Gina Lombroso, *L'âme de la Femme,* Paris (Payot) 1947. Viola Klein, *The Feminine Character,* London (Kegan Paul) 1946. Margaret Mead, *Male and Female,* London (Victor Gollancz) 1950. Georgene H. Seward, *Sex and the Social Order,* New York and London (McGraw Hill) 1946. Helene Deutsch, *Psychology of women.* I, New York 1944, II, 1945.

[5] *Die Weibliche Eigenart im Männerstaat und die weibliche Eigenart im Frauenstaat,* Karlsruhe 1923.

chooses not to live within his nature as the animal, but to transcend his life toward an existence which will be determined by *raisons de vivre,* purposes for which to live, and thus, which will be constituted as a value. Man raises himself above the level of the animal, not by repeating himself from one generation to the next and so offering only life to his progeny, but by staking his life upon an "idea": "this is why, among mankind, superiority is accorded, not to the sex that gives birth to life, but to the one that *kills.* Here we have the key to the whole mystery".

It is woman's misfortune that she is biologically predisposed to repeat life. Men have at all times had the fate of women in their hands, and settled it in terms of their own plans, their needs and their fears. The invention of tools of bronze made it possible for men to assert themselves over women entirely, and to establish the patriarchal society. When they settled as tillers of the earth, it was man's mind applied to his existence and world that gave rise to law and custom and founded the relationship of family to society that ruled the position of woman. In the course of history she has been despised and she has been honored, but she has always been in all circumstances the subordinate—*the second sex*—and still is. This is the picture as drawn by Simone de Beauvoir.

Now, undoubtedly it is right that man is "an historical idea" and not a "natural species," as Merleau-Ponty [6] superbly formulates the fundamental concept of the modern philosophical approach to man. But this does not mean that the *past* alone holds the key to the explanation of the way man manifests himself, to the explanation of his characteristic qualities, emotions, tendencies, mental images, value-judgments, the mode of his existence and the world formed in this existence.

Every history, whether of a nation or of an individual person, differs in principle from a natural continuity precisely in that each moment of the history is the *projection* of a future, on the free initiative of the human being, by means of a motivated choice. Motive, however, is not a cause. It is something that comes before a decision, but it does not operate with inevitability; no necessity is inherent in the concrete nature of the motive. A motive precedes every historical development, but it is operative exclusively in virtue of the *significance* which it holds for man. A motive for action

[6] *Phénoménologie de la perception,* Paris (N.R.F.) 1945, p. 199 (*Phenomenology of Perception,* New York (Humanities Press) 1962).

can be found in any event and in any fact—including the fact that
women and men exist. But the significance of any fact is determined by two factors together: by conscious or even non-reflexive
participation in a past which is the history of the genesis of a scale
of values; and by the image man forms of himself, of his physical
presence-in-the-world and of his moral obligations, whether this
image is an original or the traditional one.

For these reasons, it is a noteworthy fact that man's "dominion"
over woman is not confined to cultures in which physical strength
was a decisive factor for existence. It is precisely in the higher
cultures that one often finds the male dominance in a much
stronger—and more refined and absolute—form. Even a superficial acquaintance with popular opinion in our own day will show,
convincingly, that women's existence is governed to a very large
extent by the *rejection* of an historical and sociological determination of the relationship of the sexes.

The "Essential" Differences

It is our judgment that there is an "essential" difference between
men and women, a difference in nature, capabilities, inborn qualities, abilities, talents and character, and *therefore* a difference in
vocation, mission and destiny. Whether the difference between the
sexes is real or a supposed one, an imagined one or a hoped-for
one, the significance that is attached to it is itself determined by an
interplay of motives. However, it is quite certainly not the power
of tradition alone that governs the view of the capabilities and the
destiny of woman. In every period of history every tradition receives a new formulation and is presented anew, and this is true of
every word of even the strictest dogmatic formulae of faith and the
so-called unmistakable facts of physical science. Thus we can say,
quite simply, that the problematic of feminine existence is always
inherent in humankind's knowledge of itself. There are many sides
to this knowledge.

There is an approach to the study of man, an anthropology, in
which man is examined from all angles as a "thing" to be measured and analyzed. His properties and his interaction with other
things (and people) are carefully described. This is valuable
knowledge, and to gain it belongs to the task of the biologist, the

medical man, the psychologist, the ethnologist and the anthropologist in the narrower sense, who are all chiefly concerned with investigation into the physical characteristics of the human race. The scientific knowledge of man gained in this way is called empirical and objective, and itself gives rise to certain problems concerning "the nature of woman."

On the other hand one can approach the study of man in terms of the question of what precisely is human in man, and thus in woman as well. "Precisely human" in this context does not mean, therefore, the actual, objective and thus coincidental characteristics of body and psyche, circumstantial social relationships and manner of living; it means rather, that which in all of this is essentially human, that which belongs to the invariability of human *being,* and which reveals itself in human existence. The science achieved in terms of this question ought, in contrast to the physical kind of anthropology, to be called the essential science of man, genuine anthropology.

The study of the human being in his humanity can take place either on the philosophical level or on the level of empirical science. It is not possible to divorce the one manner of approach from the other, and it is very difficult always to distinguish the one from the other.

We do not want to become involved in the dispute about the limits dividing philosophical and scientific anthropology, but rest our position on reference to the quotation from Häberlin at the beginning of this chapter. Along with this, it will be remembered that psychology cannot confine itself to a description of all that is experienced subjectively, or to a description of the "regularity" of psychic functions, but that its object embraces all man's behavior and thus also the world to which this behavior relates.

Thus we understand why the psychologist must pay attention to the problem of human existence as such. However, this orientation of psychology toward existence has strengthened the bond between the science of psychology and philosophy. The result of this is that in our time a very important modification is taking place in the scientific view of man, and it is going to exercise an ever increasing influence on popular opinion and on the practical judgments that are based on it.

Simone de Beauvoir's book is convincing proof of this. Her book is the *most important* so far written on woman, because it is more than a scientific description of the characteristics of woman as she is found in our society, and it is more than a general review of views on the feminine character or an exposé of a one-sided psychoanalytic approach. It is also far in advance of the stream of more or less popular writings in which psychological and sociological facts are used to defend tendentious ideas.

Her study is based entirely on the anthropological-existential psychology we have mentioned, the fundamental thesis of which correctly holds that there is no essential predetermination in man whatever, apart from the predetermination inherent in his materiality, and that even this is subject to the reservation that the physical predetermination itself is given meaning only by the existential projection of the person. The personal quality of the projection is never quite independent of a "norm," that is to say, of a rule according to which the person judges himself to be obliged to regulate the choice of his behavior. If one asks where this "norm" comes from, it seems as though Simone de Beauvoir thinks exclusively of traditions. In this, she is neglecting the "mystery" of human materiality.

Man's bodily being is not coincidental, but significant in itself, and therefore the body itself is an appeal to the human person to seek and develop the projection of his existence in a *determined* direction. For example, the structure of the human hand calls for things to be grasped hold of, and, more generally, evokes the many-sided human "handling" of things. In the same way, every part of the body is a reference to an attitude toward the world. The eye is aimed at light, as Goethe [7] well knew.

This view of materiality helps to bring much light to an understanding of the development of feminine existence. For it is indeed clear that woman discovers the *significance* of her own materiality only in the most important encounters which are made possible precisely by this materiality—the encounters with the opposite sex and with children. In the same way, the male comes to know the significance of his *specifically* masculine body only in his relationship to woman. This relationship is only occasionally sexual (in

[7] Wäre nicht das Auge sonnenhaft wie könnte es das Licht erblicken? Lebte nicht in uns des Gottes eigene Kraft wie könnte uns Göttliches entzücken? (If the eye were not sunny, how could it catch sight of the light? If the power of God himself did not live in us, how could Godly things enchant us?)

the narrow sense). Normally it is brought about through word and attitude and glance and gesture.[8]

The *value* of this realization of the significance of sexually differentiated materiality must not be overestimated (or underestimated). The blind man or the cripple is not deprived of the full dignity of his own humanity. In the same way, men or women who come across the significance of material sexual differentiation only fleetingly in their lives, can be free human beings.

But it is necessary to state clearly the respect in which our view of freedom differs from that accepted by Simone de Beauvoir in agreement with Sartre.

If the human being must be declared to be free of all *subjective* essential predetermination or of all necessitation arising from nature, it must on the other hand also be acknowledged that every human, existential project is in the very nature of the case designed in inevitable orientation toward an order of *objective* values which are normative in an absolute way.

The basic fault of the Sartre school of existentialism lies in this, that it presents human freedom not only as a freedom from any essential subjective predetermination, but also as a given task to remain free in the face of any objective and absolutely normative value. Simone de Beauvoir and Sartre do not notice that, although a subjective predetermination would indeed exclude freedom, the recognition of the absolute validity of the objective norm actually implies the freedom of the subject, even if at the same time it demonstrates the fact that the subject making the recognition is not self-sufficient. Nor do they notice that this very recognition can be made only in the exercise of freedom itself.

Essential and Accidental Knowledge

It is perhaps likely to be thought that this philosophical judgment is of no importance for an answer to the question, "What is woman?" and that, at the very most, it can have meaning only in conjunction with the determining of what woman *ought* to be. There is certainly a difference between a factual and a normative judgment, but in anthropology (and thus in psychology) they cannot be separated. As far as an understanding of human being is

[8] On shaking hands, for example.

concerned, Kierkegaard speaks truly when he says: "The knowledge that relates essentially to existence is essential knowledge . . . The knowledge that does not refer to existence in the mode of a reflection of interiority upon itself, is essentially accidental knowledge, its degree being essentially equal in validity to its extent. For this reason, ethical and ethical-religious knowledge is essential knowledge".[9]

In the existentialism of Simone de Beauvoir too, the identity of essential and ethical knowledge is accepted; however, her standpoint differs from that of Kierkegaard in that she denies the possibility of a reflection on interiority. In her view such a reflection would be meaningless, because a human being is simply what he does, and thus because nothing can be found in the so-called interiority that has not been done, thought, etc., by the human being himself. Thus man can find nothing in himself that does not belong to his existence in the world. An encounter with an essence of man, preceding his existence and determining and limiting his existence, is simply impossible.

But Simone de Beauvoir neglects an element of experience, and it is the existence of *rest*. This neglect is precisely the consequence of her view of the human being, in which there is no place for immanence. It appears already in the first of her philosophical studies—*Pyrrhus et Cinéas*—that she acknowledges man only as the eternally restless, *"un être des lointains"* (Heidegger), the one who is always *elsewhere,* who is himself only in his relationship to something else. But the incompleteness of her investigation makes her miss the point that this relationship to something else does not necessarily need to have the character of an intentional relation or a project. In rest or leisure as in every form of happiness there is a non-intentional being-together-with, an encounter, a discovery of self with the other (other person), a *"Wirheit"* (no longer I but now *we*), which reveals its fullness and its essence as the basic form of human *"Dasein"* only in love (*Binswanger*).[10]

If existence were really characterized by an undefined and unlimited transcendence from one project to the next, then it could never be fulfilled. Man would then be understood as an *"exister"*

---

[9] *Philosophische Brocken* I. Teil W, Band 6, p. 255. (quoted by Binswanger, p. 546: see the following note).

[10] L. Binswanger, *Grundformen und Erkenntnis menschlichen Daseins,* Zürich, 1942.

(act of existing) without any *"existant"* (existent subject),[11] "or, according to Heidegger's teaching, as a being-cast-into-the-world, as an anxious providing-procuring existence, and as a being that includes death within itself as a possible impossibility of existence. The concept of a genuine transcending of what is human—in Pascal's words, "man infinitely surpasses man"—must be understood in a sense that is entirely different from the notion as the basis of restlessness lasting until the moment of fortuitous death.

What Pascal intends is a transcendence in the direction of an existence which, outside of the *dimensions* of earthly reality and of all intentionality, can only be called an existing with the absolute Existent in a "peace that surpasses all understanding." Simone de Beauvoir finds the idea of such peace, which at the same time would be perfect happiness, scandalously foolish. Every paradise—she writes—is "quiescence, transcendence abolished, a given state of affairs from which it is not possible to escape. . . . Inalterable paradise promises us nothing more than eternal boredom . . . Since man himself is project, his good and his delight cannot be other than projects".[12]

It would all be true, if human existence were wholly and entirely *of* the world in which it is encountered. If it were so, rest and peace would indeed be nothing more than ennui—or sleep. But if the *fundamental* form of the reality of human existence, *"Dasein,"* is in fact existence in the mode of "We," *"Wirheit,"* something not for me alone but for *us,* that is in-the-world but reaching-out-beyond-the-limits of the world, then human existence is not only something more than a mere progression in space and time, but it must also be defined in some other way than merely in terms of what man does.

Since we find the particular form of existentialism which Simone de Beauvoir chooses as her starting-point critically unacceptable, we cannot accept the view of man, and thus of woman, that is founded on *that* existentialism either. This means that in our view this authoress has not taken the phenomenological analysis of the facts themselves far enough. For, like Simone de Beauvoir, we take it for granted that the question, "What is woman?," can never be answered unless we proceed from a consideration of the (pure) phenomena.

[11] See E. Lévinas, *De l'existence à l'existant,* Paris (Fontaine) 1949.
[12] *Pyrrhus et Cinéas,* Paris (N.R.F.) 1944, p. 27-28.

Thus, our existential consideration of woman will not be able to be determined exclusively by the historical actuality of her existence in the world, and neither will it be able to be determined exclusively by the actuality of her "nature." Through and beyond all detail of actuality, we will have to direct our attention to the femininity that is manifested in woman, and that makes her manifest herself to us as woman. We must concern ourselves with the phenomenon of "femininity" itself, regardless of the manner in which it comes into being, and this means quite simply that we must develop an awareness and description of the expression and character of the manifestation of femininity just as it is encountered and understood in our society. The mode of this manifestation determines not only the image that another—man, woman or child—forms of woman, but also the view that woman takes of herself, and thus, the manner in which she approaches her fellow human beings, the manner in which she projects her own existence and in so doing discovers and gives form to her own meaningful world. Therefore the problematics of feminine being are connected in the closest possible relation to the most important questions of sociology, and also to those of psychopathology and applied psychology in general.

We know well enough that by far the greater part of normal and also neurotic conflicts take their rise in the sexual differentiation of human beings, and so, in the mutual relations of the sexes, and thus, in the manner in which man and woman experience and discover themselves in the world they have projected. An existential and psychological investigation of the female world can put us in a position to be able to understand how an actual woman in a particular milieu actually lives in herself, how she finds her own bodily reality, how she evaluates it, and how she bears herself in relation to the opposite sex.

Thus, a careful and detailed phenomenological analysis of feminine existence can undoubtedly help toward an insight into the difference between the sexes. It seems, however, that every approach to this difference draws the limelight once again to the *problematics* of feminine being. Masculine existence seems to be unproblematical, familiar, transparent, free of mystery—not only in every-day life and on superficial consideration, but even throughout the history of science. The mystery of masculine existence, insofar as it is noticed, is identified with the mystery of humanity itself, and understood as the mystery of man's consciousness, his freedom, his physical dependence, his social relationships, language and culture.

It is a simple fact that the problem of sexual differentiation and of the psychology of the sexes is presented almost invariably as a search for the nature of feminine existence, in which search masculine existence is regarded only as the background against which the existence of woman is manifested. This fact in itself is important.

We may perhaps best understand this view of the relation of the sexes by becoming aware that the human physique, precisely as *human* and in contrast to that of the lower animals, always strikes us as a stand, taking an upright position, and so, as the manifest expression of the free, the steadfast, the purposeful and the right. We do not require any more power of imagination than we already possess as a result of our daily experiences of the sexes, in order to be able to understand that precisely this generalized image of the human physique, the upright being, fluidly confronted with a world that takes the form of an opposition, is identical with the image of a being who strides forward from project to project and possesses unlimited prospects. It is easy to see that *this* image of man is none other than the image of the "homo faber," the conqueror and reshaper of recalcitrant nature—the image, thus, of the *man*.

So it is clear—and not on historical grounds—why the problems to which masculine existence gives rise are not different from those to which human existence gives rise. The identification of the male with the human has pervaded all philosophical and every-day thinking, right down to the last nuance of detail. Languages themselves prove it: *"homo," "l'homme," "man,"* mean both "human being" and "the male, man."

The "herrlicher Mensch"

There are a number of expressions in every-day usage in which the same identification crops up. Max Scheler once wrote rather amusingly on the point. In his still very readable work, *Zur Idee des Menschen,*[13] he says: "Ladies of the most highly cultivated type sometimes say, of another woman, that she is an *'herrlicher Mensch.'* They deny her sex, and set up pure humanity as their

[13] *Abhandlungen und Aufsätze* I, Leipzig, 1915.

target." It is not absolutely certain what refined ladies who speak
other languages say among themselves. Probably they would call
another a "wonderful person," but there is some question as to
whether the words, used in reference to another *woman,* are used
with precisely the same special affectivity as their German equiva-
lents. But, to let Scheler continue: "They forget that 'Mensch'
(person) is derived from 'männisch' (mannish)." The idea of man
(human being, person) which is supposed to include both men and
women, is actually a masculine idea.

In a feminine culture, the idea "man" would never have arisen.
It is only because the man is so spiritualized, so dualistically inclined and at the same time so childlike that he is able to miss
altogether the *profundity* of the difference between the sexes. This
failure to grasp the true difference is what gives the concept "man"
its neutral applicability. "The ladies who call each other *'herrlicher
Mensch'* are actually saying that they are not genuine ladies, and—
since it is of the *essence* of human being always to be either man
or woman—that they are slightly less than human."

In Dutch, the expression *"dat mens"* is familiar, and, as in
German, it refers to a woman who does indeed show human characteristics, but not feminine ones, to such an *exclusive* degree that
she is judged unfavorably. The individual so referred to is female,
a being that looks like a human being but is not human because it
is neither feminine nor masculine. It is an in-between *thing.* Hence
the use of the objective, neuter article. It is remarkable, however,
that an unmanly man is not regarded as a thing (an "it") to which
the term *"dat mens"* can apply. In the common estimation, he is a
degenerate, an "old granny." Scheler concludes his discussion as
follows: "A woman who wants to be a *'prachtvoller Mensch'* never
in fact gets beyond the point of aping man. This is 'all too
human,' and here we leave it."

Scheler gets this off his chest in a typically masculine way, but it
contains a portion of the problem that we have to study step by
step. One fact is however quite clear. Whatever the approach to
the psychology of the sexes, even if it leads ultimately to regarding
the "mystery" of woman as a "myth," as with Simone de Beauvoir, the existence of the man is *never* regarded as a mystery. The
man exists as man in his freedom of initiative and in his grasp on
the world. His general dependence on the physical apparently also
explains his sexual behavior. But when one begins to consider the

specifically feminine, one approaches the *profundity* of the sexual differentiation in all living beings and in the specifically human sphere, and one comes up against the inscrutability of so many experiences and expressions of daily life and of science too. One becomes *conscious* of the opposition of the sexes as an opposition of man and woman—which of course does not necessarily mean that this is a true opposition. Clearly, it is not a true one.

No one would maintain that woman is not a "genuine" human being, but still woman is somehow regarded as an *"homme manqué,"* an unfinished man, as St. Thomas appears to call her in one place—probably more on theoretical grounds than out of concern for the mystery of her existence.[14] Simone de Beauvoir sums up the basic thought of her book by saying; "The second sex is the *Other"*—the Other, and nothing but the Other. The man constitutes himself as man, and thereby regards woman as the Other.

For the time being, we do not want to consider how this is to be understood. But it may be remarked that it is not only the man who experiences an opposition between human existence and feminine existence. Woman, too, repeatedly regards herself as the Other, or at least as human "by exception," playing out her role against the background of universal humanity which is something that becomes manifest in the man. Elizabeth Barrett-Browning, a woman of fine sensitiveness, once wrote:

> *Most illogical*
> *Irrational nature of our womanhood*
> *that blushes one way, feels another way*
> *and prays, perhaps another!*

Is this not the existential picture of a person whose "nature" differs in the deepest sense from that of the male and from the "animal rationale"—man in the strict sense?

We are still engaged in a preliminary survey of our field, but already an examination of the spontaneous feelings expressed above show to what a great extent the problem of sexual differen-

[14] In Latin, "femina est mas occasionatus"; cf. *Summa Theologiae* I, q. 92, a. 1, and *ibid.* q. 99, a. 2 ad 1. Thomas took the thought from Aristotle, *De Generatione Animalium* II, 3. It rests on the notion, common in antiquity and in later ages, that the natural result of mating would be a male offspring, female offspring being the result of some deficiency in the mating.

tiation is evident when we see through to the hidden meaning of the things woman says about herself and the things man says about woman. In these expressions, the most remarkable thing, and the thing that is constantly recurring, is the *uncertainty* of the judgment on woman and on her existence, an uncertainty in which the living experience of the problem of feminine existence is revealed.

Woman is constantly being compared to man, and not man to woman. Masculine existence is the norm and the measure, even in those cases where the intention is to judge factually. For example, when it is said that woman is more emotional than man, or that man is less emotional than woman, there is tacit appreciation of the lesser degree of emotionality as "normal," and feminine sensitivity is pointed up as a deviation that needs to be explained.

Why is the contrary not the case? Why does one not find the higher degree of sensitivity normal, and the lower, masculine degree of emotionality the deviation? In the comparison of the sexes, normal does not mean that which is statistically average, or that which is most efficient. Normal in this context means that which is ideal and typical for man, and thus, it means that which is most perfect for human existence. The general practice nowadays is to regard woman as indeed different from man, but as having an "equal value" in her own way. But even where this is meant in all seriousness, the way in which judgments are formulated still shows how ineradicable the opinion that feminine existence is a problematical existence has become.

It may possibly be thought that normative judgments have little worth, or at least that they are unscientific, and that we should try to eliminate their sociological influence. Should we not confine ourselves to the establishing of factual characteristics in society just as we do in science? Methodologically, this would appear to be a most acceptable procedure.

However, it is possible to establish factual characteristics only with regard to *things* such as they appear to us in the world in relation to other things. But a person is not a thing, for a person establishes himself in relation to *his own* world. A person can only appear to us as a thing when we no longer regard him in his humanity, but as a dissectable anatomical organism, a physiological event to be analyzed, a set of functional patterns of reaction, or a structure of characteristic qualities and properties.

If one does approach the person in this way, one will in fact find "objective" differences between the man and the woman. Some of these differences (for example, the anatomical ones) are absolute; most of them are relative. From practically every aspect, there are fluidly transitional regions between the so-called pure extremes of manly men and feminine women, and these make it possible to describe any particular person as a mixture and combination of feminine and masculine characteristics, the actual distribution of these characteristics being merely a statistical problem.

Modes of Existence

It is important to know all this, but the knowledge can do no more than point to the direction in which to seek an answer to the main question: *what* actually is the feminine mode of existence in the world? For example, the question is not answered by the discovery that the majority of women are more emotional than men, or by the discovery that their interest is directed more toward human relationships in their immediate surroundings than toward mathematics.

Science, and society as well, want to know the *meaning* of these facts in relation to the actual mode of man's existence and woman's existence. However, these are modes of human existence, and they can only be *discovered* through an immediate participation in the intentionality that characterizes them. Now, this intentionality always involves a choice, a giving of meaning, and thus, an evaluation. Woman directs herself to a particular aspect of the world, and in so doing, chooses to exist for herself and for others in a particular manner, and develops herself in situations which she, existing as a woman, has called into being and accepted.

Every mode of existence consists not only in an objective relationship to things, but above all in human relationships which, together with the relationship of each person to himself, determine the *ethical*-social structure of society. It therefore follows, necessarily, that knowledge of the feminine form of existence always implies knowledge of woman's normative relationships and judgments.

Thus, if one aims to achieve an *insight* into the factual differences of the sexes, it means that one has to reach a judgment concerning the humanity of each. This is possible only in terms of a philosophical view of human existence. So, as we have said, it is anthropology that makes psychology possible as a science. Sartre understood this very well, when he wrote: "Psychologists do not take account of the fact that it is in fact entirely impossible to attain to the essence by making a compilation of accidents. . . . If we want to establish a psychology, it is necessary to reach back, further than the psychical structures, further than the situation of man in the world, to the very source of man, world and psyche".[15]

However, what is it that we discover of the source from which man as he exists and his world and the reality of the psychical all spring? Present in this source there is undoubtedly an engaged consciousness, *"la conscience engagée"* (Merleau-Ponty), a *"conscience témoin,"* a consciousness bearing witness to itself, and not purely being-for-its-own-sake, *"être pour soi"* (Sartre). By this, we mean that man as a conscious being (a being who knows) does not merely know existent reality from the outside, but directs himself to reality manifesting itself, that he is with this reality and is part of it, that he can even become wholly involved in it and so become entangled thoughtlessly or thinkingly in the world thus projected. But this reality manifesting itself, to which consciousness can direct itself, is at the same time existent reality, in which consciousness is anchored. Thus, man always discovers himself as existent *together with* that which consciousness is conscious of.

It is necessary to refer to these fundamental phenomenological relations in order to be able to understand why the study of human reality cannot be divorced from the study of living nature with which man knows that he is connected. For this reason we meet the problematics of feminine existence, in science as well as in the unscientific judgments of society, in close connection with the sexual differentiation of plants and animals that we can observe objectively. If one takes due note of this in one's investigation, one sees feminine existence in quite a different light.

In the first place, in nature it is the male sex that presents itself as problematical, in contrast with what people think they must accept about the relative positions of the sexes in man. While human history is something that men have made, the biologist understands the "history" of living nature as a continuity of gen-

---

[15] *Esquisse d'une théorie des émotions*, Paris (Hermann) 1939, p. 5 and p. 8 (*Sketch for a theory of the emotions*, London (Methuen) 1962, cf. p. 17 and p. 22).

erations determined by the fertility of the female. In living nature, the male appears as the adventitious element, generating life indeed, but not bearing or propagating it. The functional significance of the male, whether pollen or the male animal, is of only short duration. In the highly individual organic connections of living nature, the male appears to have the significance of a momentary activity, called for and ultimately determined by the fruit as holding the promise of the preservation of the species.

It is only recently, however, that an irreducible expression of expansivity has been discovered in the original mode of being of the male in the manifold ways of nature—later we will examine this in detail—and the variegated colors, the manes and the antlers are no longer explained,[16] as Darwin explained them, in terms of sexual selectivity and breeding. Biology, having abandoned the Darwinian view, regards the typology of male animals as an "irreducible natural phenomenon," that is, as something for which neither causal nor teleological explanations can be given.

The Polarity of the Sexes

In the second place, biology provides an irrefutable foundation for the thought of a complete opposition in the polarity of the sexes in man. This thought is as old as human thinking. Aristotle saw woman as passive being, in contrast to the active being, man. In popular as well as scientific expressions, this image recurs in innumerable forms.

The opposition in polarity of the sexes finds expression in many other ways besides; we will mention a few of them now. A sharp contrasting of the sexes is always represented or expressed in practically every mythology, in the cosmogonies and in ancient religions. It is present in Chinese thought in the image of a circle with equal divisions of light and darkness, Yang and Yin; in the gnostic idea of a male and female world principle, the opposition between creation and redemption; in Babylonic and Egyptian culture in the dual sexuality of the primordial ground of all being; Ischtar is morning star and evening star, in the morning a man, and in the evening a woman.

We often come across the thought of a primordial connection

16 A. Portmann, *Die Tiergestalt,* Basel (Reinhardt) 1948.

which is still reflected in everything: for example, the connection between earth, darkness, chaos and woman, and the connection between the air, light, order and male humanity. All these at the same time express the supposed inscrutability of woman. These mythological and cosmological views of antiquity are regarded as worthless speculations by the rational and empirical science of our day.

But in contrast to this, the psychologist Jung who applied the principle of polarity in so many ways, recognizes a positive value in the archetypal forms of human thought about the sexual difference, and thus he says, "Our aim is to preserve the living core of sexual symbolism, not to confine ourselves to the outer shell of its varying historical presentations." It is necessary clearly to distinguish the wording of myth and mythological presentation concerning woman from the truth they can contain. Not even the famous platonic myth about the origin of the sexes can be regarded as wholly valueless to scientific thought.

In the *Symposium*, Aristophanes tells of the original double beings created by Zeus who were man and woman at the same time (androgyns). They had two faces, looking in opposite directions, four ears, four hands, two sets of pudenda, "and so with all the rest, as one may imagine. . . ." These beings possessed tremendous power and in their rebellious excess of self-assurance tried to fight even against the gods, and so Zeus decided to weaken them by splitting them in two "as one splits fruit to get it ready for the pot, or divides an egg with a horse-hair." This is how human beings came to be, and down to our own day they have been trying to join themselves together again. Love for one another is therefore inborn in man, and through Eros people strive toward their undivided unity and the conquering of their weakness. Part of the basic idea of this myth recurs in the Jewish *Midrash:* man and woman originally had one body with two faces, but God divided them and gave each a backbone. There is even some question as to whether the story of the creation of Adam and Eve in paradise does not bear some relation to this ancient myth. But we have referred to these imaginary pictures of the origin of the sexes only to show that the idea of the opposite polarities of man and woman is as old as human thought.

In psychological writings, the idea of the opposed polarity of man and woman occurs in many forms, most extensively in the work of Klages.[17] To come to a deeper insight into the problematics of feminine existence, we will have to examine Klages' views, however extraordinary they may be. Klages seeks the basis of the polarity of the sexes that manifests itself in a particular manner in man, and he looks for this basis principally in symbolic thought on the opposition of cosmic polarities. "In symbolic thought, there are two series that run parallel: ability to conceive, downwards, rest, darkness, earth, space, night, dying, slowing down, interiorizing, "heart," left;—and: ability to generate, upwards, movement, light, sun, time, day, origin, impulse, "head," right.

It does not matter whether we choose to follow the distinguishing characteristics of behavior in the process of copulation or any other differences of behavior in the two sexes, for there will always be a predominance of movement, an out-going-ness, waste of strength, on the part of the male, and a remaining in rest, a receptivity and a conservation of strength on the part of the female. In keeping with this, revealing clarity, motility, push, an upright attitude, heraclitan "movement upwards," and giving shape to the future respond to the male pole, while on the contrary concealing darkness, rest, power to attract, a supine attitude, heraclitan "movement downwards," and desire for the past correspond to the female pole. If we regard each side as a pole and not as an independent half, then we must see the existence of man to which symbolism refers as saturated with the feminine, and the existence of woman as pervaded by the masculine".[18]

According to Klages, woman is mainly animated materiality and man is mainly "spirit." Woman sacrifices herself more, is more inclined to go by impressions, and is less objective than man. The important thing is that Klages did understand that every characteristic must be understood in a negative and in a positive sense. What do we mean by this? The masculine characteristic of being governed by concepts means, on the positive side, a greater ability to abstract, a stronger tendency to make abstractions, more self-assurance in acting, greater openness to alternatives in rational

[17] For a very good outline of Klages' views, see E. M. J. Breukers, *Levensvormen*, Roermond 1947, chapter XII. See also Seifert, *Geschlechterpolarität als psychologisches Problem*, Neue Psychol. Studien 12, II (1934) p. 69-81.
[18] *Der Geist als Widersacher der Seele*. Leipzig 1932, III, 2. p. 1316 and 1317 (quoted by Breukers—see previous note—p. 131).

combinations, a more pronounced analytic ability and awareness of logical norms. On the negative side, however, this attachment to concepts brings along with it a limited sensibility in the world of feelings, a narrowness of perspective, an underestimation of the imponderable and of the delicate nuances of things, a crudity in dealing with the concrete, a lack of personal approachability and a tendency toward illusions instead of genuine emotions.

On the other hand, the feminine characteristic of being governed by impressions means, on the positive side, a certainty of instinct and feeling, an explicit sense of reality, vitality in the choice of an attitude in human situations, intuition and a sense of relation to totality. From the negative aspect, the attachment to impressions is coupled with a state of spiritual dependence, a certain absence of principle, the lack of a stable pattern of behavior, partiality and blindness to universally valid norms, and along with this an irresistible revulsion for purely objective and impersonal concerns.

Although Klages' views have certainly helped to deepen our grasp of the problems of the psychology of the sexes, it is still necessary to approach his intuitive symbolic explanations with a sober and critical sense of judgment, and all the more so because the connection of his views with romanticism and with Bachofen's speculations on matriarchy (Mutterrecht) serves to warn us to be careful in our evaluation.

Von Humboldt writes: "Everything masculine signifies mainly independence, self-sufficiency; everything feminine signifies mainly passive receptivity",[19] and Bachofen writes: "There the woman, here the man; there the primordial ground of matter, here life developed; there the concept of material fullness, here the concept of powerful action and dominion; there the concept of rest and conservation, here that of acquisition and struggle, of increase and combat both offensive and defensive". One may well ask whether sentiments such as these amount to anything more than a formulation of the obvious difference between the *cultural* images of man and woman well known to all of us.

An anthropologically orientated psychology, however, has the task of explaining this pheno-typical image of woman, and it must be explained precisely in terms of our knowledge of human possibilities, of the significance of physical aptitudes and of the influ-

---

[19] W. von Humboldt, *Ueber den Geschlechtsunterschied u.s.w.* (Neudruck Fr. Giese) p. 35.

ence of the social milieu. Bachofen again says: "Just as the moon can do nothing of itself, but eternally following the sun obtains from it the radiance with which it shines in silent glory, so does woman attain only in the union of marriage with man to that higher beauty through which her human materiality is able to unite itself to a more spiritual being".[20] Does this sort of thing help to clarify our insight in any way?

Feminine Existence Problematical

Is it however possible to get altogether out of the way of thinking in terms of opposition of polarities? Surely it is possible, and can be done by giving our whole attention to an existential psychological analysis of *one* of the sexes, and the one we chose for this is the female sex. As we have said, there are many reasons both practical and theoretical for this choice. We encounter feminine existence primarily as a problematical existence. Moreover, there is a complex ethical and practical feminine problem but no masculine problem in practically every culture. For instance, in our country we have a considerable body of literature on the working woman and on women's studies. We still seem to be awaiting the necessary emancipation of women, but we hear very little about the emancipation of men. There is thus every reason for concerning ourselves with the problematics of feminine existence, to lay a solid foundation for social and psychological questions.

Our investigation will have to show whether, besides the problems, there is also a "mystery" inherent in this mode of human existence—a position that Simone de Beauvoir energetically opposes. In her view, the core and the wellspring of all poetic and prosaic fantasy and of the chief myths about women is the masculine opinion that woman is a *mystery* and not merely a partially solved enigma. Man does not look upon woman as partially incomprehensible, but as silent and secretive, "a stammering presence that cannot quite manifest itself." [21]

Naturally every person is in some sense inscrutable to another, but then everyone finds the other inscrutable as well. Man, how-

[20] Quoted by Lersch, *Vom Wesen der Geschlechter*, Munich, 1947, p. 115 and 119.

[21] *Le Deuxième Sexe*, Vol. I, p. 388. (*The Second Sex*, Knopf N. Y. 1953, p. 257)

ever, who considers himself as the absolute, as *the* human being, looks upon woman as a *"mystère en soi"*, a mystery-in-herself. It is not possible for a man to say what woman is; she is indefinable, a fundamental ambiguity, and she herself can no longer tell what she is. According to this authoress, therefore, any opposition of polarity between man and woman is secondary, that is, it is something that is determined socially. Thus, her view is opposed in principle to that of Klages, and we will have to consider hers more closely as well.

There is only one thing that man is of himself alone, only one thing that he is—independently of the milieu in which he exists— and that is his animated materiality. But this materiality becomes a situation only through the manner in which man grasps it in intentionality. Regarding man in this way, Simone de Beauvoir comes to the logical conclusion that *the only way* in which woman can differ from man is in her materiality and in the (psychical and physical) functions which it determines. "Thus it is quite true that woman differs from man, and the difference is concretely experienced in desire, embrace, love. . .".[22]

Thus there would be only a sexually erotic difference between man and woman, who meet each other as two "freedoms" in a reciprocal relationship, "a contest of consciousnesses each of which regards itself as essential, a recognition of freedoms confirming each other, an indefinite movement from intimacy to complicity." The French existentialists look on this as the only form of love that is not "dupery" (Sartre), thus, a form of relatively reciprocal benevolence.

Simone de Beauvoir does not see woman as the opposite of man, but as an "ordinary" human being just like man, nothing derogatory being intended by the word "ordinary." Woman however is a human being with a troublesome body, a body that is a burden to her, from which she is always in some sense "alienated," for woman's body, unlike man's, is not exclusively an efficient instrument for "taking a hold on the world," it cannot be wholly understood and formed as a grasp on the world, but remains partially ordained to a natural process and subject to the function of childbearing. Woman is condemned to live with this body, a body from which she is to some extent alienated, and, of all the things that take place inside of it, only some are meaningfully involved in

[22] *Le Deuxième Sexe*, Vol. I, p. 383. (Knopf ed. p. 253)

her free human relationship to the world. The rest concern a natural event that "happens" of itself and in which she does not *need* to play any personal part. By her material body she is ordained to two functions: to be man's sexual partner, and the possibility of becoming a mother. There is nothing mysterious in either of these. Hence it follows that the actual vocation of woman is to endure her body and to make as much use of it as possible as a "hold on the world" in the ordinary human sense.

If we go into the views of Simone de Beauvoir a little more deeply, it becomes clear that the anthropology that forms the basis of her study of "the second sex" teaches that man *is* nothing else than what he *does*. "An existent being is nothing else than what it does; the possible does not exceed the real, essence does not precede existence: in his pure subjectivity, the human being *is* nothing".[23]

A "Statue in Black and White"

This short passage is the key to the work of Simone de Beauvoir. It opens up the way to the answer to the capital question, what is woman? Woman is what she does in her freedom. She is measured according to her acts. Of a farm girl one may say that she works well or she doesn't work well; of an actress, that she is talented or not as the case may be. If one wishes to say anything about a woman in her apparently mysterious immanence, one would still be referring to her transcendence, her acts, intentions, tendencies, her judgments and so on. If not, one is being poetically imaginative, making a myth.

Thus there is no immanent mystery in woman! The only people who think there is a mystery in her are dreamers and poets and men who have the time to try to project their own desires and anxieties into a woman. For them, femininity is a statue in black and white, *"une statue noire et blanche de la fémininité."* A genuinely healthy relationship with a partner would teach them to know woman in her freedom. The comrade, the colleague, the fellow worker is never a mysterious person. But on the other hand a "youngster" might well appear mysterious in the eyes of an old man or an old woman, might appear "inessential" to them.

[23] *Le Deuxième Sexe,* Vol. I, p. 388. (Knopf ed. p. 257)

When a man is dubious about why a woman whom he has "taken" but whom he does not know, "gave" herself, it can make him imagine that she is a mystery. Then he is inclined to say that he does not know what he sees in her. In the same way, the colonist might say that he does not know what he sees in the ever-lastingly grinning natives. Many women do nothing, and thereby make themselves inscrutable. In vain they ask themselves, what in fact am I? "A consciousness alienated to the extent that it is consciousness, in its pure immanent presence, would obviously be a mystery." [24]

The more superficial the *personal* experiences of a man are, the more inclined he is to form a *generalized* image of woman. "The appetite for a cheap eternity, for a pocket edition of the absolute, which one encounters in the greater part of mankind, satisfies itself on myths." Contrastingly, the periods when women were most deeply loved were the periods when men saw women as their equals. To regard woman as human, as free, as a person able to reach her own decisions on herself—this does not mean the suppression of poetry, love, adventure, happiness or dreams: "it is simply to demand that conduct, sentiment and passion be grounded in the *truth*".[25] Labor, therefore, is not something that diminishes woman's attractiveness.

We have gone rather fully into the main thoughts of Simone de Beauvoir's extensive and important study, not merely because we will often be returning to them, but mainly because in her book she poses the problem of feminine existence very decisively in a way that has nothing to do with the romantic idea of the opposite polarity of the sexes. It is interesting, finally, to see the conclusion at which Simone de Beauvoir arrived. "A new aesthetic has already been born." The days when the fashion of narrow hips and flat chests was appreciated have gone by. But—let us add—we have by no means gone back to the luxuriant forms of the Reubens ideal, or to the voluminous raptures of the Arabs and Negroes. What the Renaissance delighted in as luxuriance, is today called fat.

But let us hear Simone de Beauvoir further: "We demand of the female body that it should be flesh, but discreetly so; it must be svelte and not ponderously fat; it must be delicately muscled, sup-

[24] *Le Deuxième Sexe*, Vol. I, p. 390. (Knopf ed. p. 259)
[25] *Le Deuxième Sexe*, Vol. I, p. 392. (Knopf ed. p. 261)

ple and strong; *it ought to signify transcendence"*—thus woman's body too ought, in the whole sphere of her manifestation, to be involved in her transcendence over nature. So it is that in our day we want neither man nor woman to be pale as a hot-house flower but "burned like a laborer's back," bronzed in the universal sun that shines on good and on bad, women as well as men. However attractive many may find this picture, we ought to notice quite explicitly that the "ideal" it defends as the ideal of feminine existence is in fact none other than that of *homo faber,* the workman. It would mean that woman, the human being "by exception," would be able to attain once more to the full dignity of humanity only to the extent that she attains to that mode of existence which, on good grounds, is called *masculine.*

This solution to the feminine problem is received with some doubt. Is this, as Simone de Beauvoir thinks, just another expression of the male desire to dominate? Or does the reality of being-in-the-world in the body of a woman in fact present other possibilities, beyond those of being man's partner in sex, being mother to children, and being fellow worker in society? *Is there not a specifically feminine human relationship to the world,* which is the wellspring of a large part—the most important part, perhaps—of our civilization?

These questions express the most *essential* issues in the problematics of feminine existence. We should now be able to see this quite clearly, having just discussed the contrast between the romantic views of Klages and the existentialist views of Simone de Beauvoir. We want to add yet another question, a question of methodology.

According to a very widespread opinion, man is *not* able to understand woman, but woman is able to understand man! There are many women who say that they can see through man quite clearly. Man's existence—as they encounter it—is transparent, because all the elements of his behavior are directed toward ends that can be easily established. It is easy to understand man, easier than to understand the behavior of an animal or a child. Man is as strong as an ox, he eats like a wolf, works like a horse, sleeps like a log, growls like a bear, fights like a lion and, to the woman's eye, he is "by nature" as dirty as a pig. Where is there any problem in all this? Perhaps in his childishness, his naïve pride, his triviality in domestic life, his hobbies and his games? But woman also finds all these things so simple and transparent that, at the very most, she can confess an inability to understand why man does not see through his own childishness.

In man's existence there remains, then, only one obscure patch which woman acknowledges she finds unintelligible. It is his wanderlust, his drunkenness, his will to dominate, his ambition, his desire to destroy and to kill. But we are inclined to label all this sort of thing "abnormal," so that the "normal" man appears to woman's eye as an energetic, intelligent and pretty good sort of animal with the shape and temperament of a great big baby. Why would anyone—even Simone de Beauvoir—want to write a book about him?

But woman! What does woman really do? What does she really want? What is the purpose of her notorious cunning (it only looks like the cunning of the serpent) and of her famous innocence (it only looks like the innocence of the dove)? At a later stage we will have much more to say about woman's mysteriousness. All we want to do here is to note that the general opinion—as popular among women as among men—which holds that man is not able to understand woman is itself a part of the problem of feminine existence and an aspect of the problematical character of feminine being.

It is not only a matter of popular opinion that man is not able to comprehend woman. Science too upholds the notion, and it does so on the grounds that it is actually not possible to comprehend any individual. Naturally all agree that all the determinable facts of woman's life can be established by objective observation, and that the laws and constants of systematic investigation can be discovered. But if one imagines that the entire task of science consists only in doing these things, then science can do no more than collect material facts, and an anthropology of male and female and psychology are impossibilities.

It does as a matter of fact appear as though psychological investigations into the difference of the sexes, such as those undertaken by Heymans and Terman and Miles, are no more than an objective establishing of facts. But when we look a little more deeply into the matter, we discover that it is possible to establish a fact like, for example, the fact that woman is more emotional or more anxious than man, only if the whole investigation is done in relation to the question: in what, precisely, do typically feminine emotions and characteristically feminine anxiety consist? The attempt to answer such a question, however, will meet with success only if it is grounded in a thorough knowledge of the feminine nature.

Insight Required

Therefore, the scientific knowledge of woman demands an *insight* into the foundation, being and significance of feminine characteristics, a knowledge of the manner in which woman exists for herself and of the manner in which she exists in her world with other people. We need above all to know the feminine world, and then, in terms of the feminine world, we need to know the order of importance and the purpose of feminine value-judgments, the way woman lives in and through the most general and elementary conditions, experiences and events concerning things like climate, comfort, health, and her own bodily nature.

It is all a question of gaining an insight into woman's attitude toward her lot in life, toward happiness, sorrow, ideals and expectations, toward the perspective of past and future. It is above all a question of the way woman views herself and of the way she is conscious of herself, taking this to mean the way she is aware of "finding herself," of the way she feels, of the way she lives in terms of her own bodily reality and of the possible meanings she could give it. It is a question of insight into the continuity of existence as projected being and being subjected and of experiencing for oneself the nostalgia (longing for home, but what "Home"?) in which woman finds fulfillment.

This kind of knowledge of woman does not merely *explain* facts in their interconnections. It is just not possible to establish any fact or observe any fact or even to formulate a question for a questionnaire, without already having some "idea" of the *meaning* of the fact established or observed or asked about. But a fact acquires its meaning only in the existence in which it occurs as a fact. Thus, the facts concerning woman acquire their reasonableness, that is, their scientific value, only through an insight into the idea of femininity and the way femininity gives a special form to human existence.

To acquire this insight, it is not necessary to appeal to the judgment of a woman. There is no reason to suppose that a woman knows herself better than "another," for example a man, can know her. Why should women be supposed to understand each other so well? Often enough there are men who can see through a woman and understand even her "most illogical" caprices. The best proof of this lies in the fact that no psychiatrist or clinical psychologist finds it more "difficult" to get to know the interiority of women patients than of men patients.[26]

It is always possible to gain an insight into a particular form of existence insofar as that form of existence is given as a potentiality in our own actual reality. This is the required condition for all participation, empathy, sym-pathy, sharing the taking of decisions and sharing reactions, even with regard to "other" peoples (and with regard to animals too). The criterion of the correctness of such knowledge, for instance of woman, is mainly found in the illumination it can bring to her "being herself" in the world, to her existence. But besides this, it is found in the evidence of coherence among the material facts that can be established.

Man is able to understand woman and woman is able to understand man, and the ability of each to understand the other comes through what they have in common. Besides everything human, they also have the specifically feminine and the specifically masculine *action* they take in common. For a man is very well able to do a thing as a woman would do it, and vice versa. For this, it is not necessary to be a talented actor, nor is it necessary to be an effeminate man or a manly woman. And even if the body refuses to adopt the other sex's manner of executing an act, a gesture or an expressive movement, it can still be done in the imagination— although only to a certain extent. When one sees a juggler continuously in quick time tossing three different objects up into the air and catching them, one understands what is happening to the extent that one is able to copy in imagination the manner of watching and moving and rhythmic alteration in the control of the body. In a dynamic sequence of this sort, there will be moments that we cannot understand at first, but long observation under varying conditions together with illuminating explanations will make them

[26] On the theoretical problem of the psychological understanding of man, see Dr. D. J. van Lennep, *Gewogen—Bekeken—Ontmoet in het psychologisch onderzoek;* my own *Kennen van de innerlijkheid* and the works quoted in it, especially the important book by L. Binswanger, *Grundformen und Erkenntnis menschlichen Daseins,* Zürich 1942.

more and more clear to us. It is even possible to learn to juggle in this way (insofar as one has the *aptitude* for it, that is, is actually able to do what one would like to do).

We apply these experiences to our problem of the sexes understanding each other. Any form of behavior becomes possible in the first instance through a particular attitude toward the world, a manner of finding oneself, through a particular intentionality and a control of the means of execution. The human body is very "willing." A man can learn any of woman's occupations, and a woman can learn any of the affairs of men except those that require exceptional physical strength and which most men in any case are therefore not able to carry out.

The Plasticity of Human Nature

Now, does this apply in the same degree to gestures, mime, inflections of the voice and so on, which are specifically characteristic according to sex to a much greater extent than actions? People generally do not *want* to adopt this sort of thing from the other sex, because they choose to behave in a way that is "genuinely" the way of their own sex. The meaning of the words "want" and "choose" in this context does not refer to any decision based on reflection, but signifies a connection with an historically formed basic personal sketch of existence. Moreover, experience teaches that—when this existence has formed itself differently (as for instance in the case of some homosexuals)—the characteristic expressions of the opposite sex can be assimilated very well indeed. A study of the influence of education and milieu on the manner of expression will reveal the tremendous plasticity of human "nature." Some peoples and some periods of history are feminine, others are masculine.

A man, thus, is certainly able to understand the character of expression in woman's behavior and in her movements and attitudes. But does this bring him to a knowledge of what is essentially feminine existence? Surely it does not. But then, neither does woman have this knowledge. There is however one sphere which is known to woman and not to man. This is the sphere of living in and through her own bodily reality in the specifically feminine way, both in itself and in relation to the bodily reality of the other sex.

As to this, there is most definitely a limit set to the power of imagination. It is quite impossible merely to imagine what tooth-ache is or what the flavor of an oyster is. It is equally impossible for a man to imagine what the physical feelings of a woman are at the time of menstruation or during pregnancy or when she is feed-ing her child at the breast, or for him to imagine how she experi-ences the sexual relation. Nevertheless, the subjective character of these sensations is of little importance for our problem. But the analogy of sensations that every person is able to experience in his own body is important.

Naturally, no-one can know exactly how piercing is the pain another feels or precisely how some flavor tastes to him, but we do see that reactions and impressions can be communicated and these recall to our memory similar pains and similar flavors. Woman's "secret" physical sensations are neither more nor less secret than those of any person. Each one has his own pains and his own delights, and the sensations of no two are the same.

The awareness of these sensations is in itself a simple "appre-hension" or perception, free of intentionality and without meaning, a mode of the existence of consciousness, a manner in which con-sciousness exists physically. What Sartre wrote about *"douleur pure,"* pain simply borne, is true of all these physical sensations, and they must be clearly distinguished from *"objet-douleur,"* sen-sations projected through and beyond the immediate. Like pain pure and simple, every physical sensation "belongs to the species of the indefinable and the indescribable which are what they are".[27] The way in which many women speak of their physical condition, their pains, their weariness and so on, has however been an important contributory factor in man's regard for woman as the inscrutable, "strange" being who must be handled with care. But this, at least fairly often, was the whole purpose of their confidences.

When we speak of woman, we are usually thinking of the women in our immediate circle. An investigation into feminine existence must escape from the narrowness of this way of thinking.

---

[27] *L'être et le Néant,* Paris (N.R.F.) 1943, p. 398. (*Being and Nothing-ness,* New York (Philosophical Library) 1956, p. 333).

We have to pay as much attention to the hard-working country-woman in her silent, awkward simplicity as to the "plumed serpent" who never turns a hand to any task, and as much to the women citizens of our cities as to the women in primitive cultural circumstances. We will have to make a selection among the very many practical and theoretical contributions to the work on the problem if we are aiming exclusively at a phenomenology of feminine existence. But still, it will very often be necessary to concern ourselves with the details of woman's world for in them we are concerned with the projection of feminine existence. And always, along with this, there is the question to face: is a man able to do what has to be done?

We have already in part given an affirmative in answer to this question. But, if we want to understand the ways of children, we must let children speak, or if we want to understand a primitive way of existence, it is necessary first to hear what primitive man has to say for himself. Clearly, above all we are obliged now to listen to what woman wishes to say about herself.[28] We are therefore grateful for the works many women have written about their own feminine existence and about the being of woman in general,

[28] "How can a man know what a woman is? The life of a woman is wholly different from man's life. God made it so. Man is the same from the day he is circumcised until the day of his death. He is the same before he has sought a woman for the first time as he is afterwards. But from the day when a woman enjoys her first love, her life splits in two. After his first love, a man is just the same as he was before. But from the day of her first love, a woman becomes different. Throughout life it remains so. A man spends a night with a woman and goes away. His life and his body are always the same. Woman conceives, As a mother, she is not the same as the woman without child. First she carries the consequences of the night in her body for nine long months. She waits for something. She waits for something to come out of her life, something that does not lessen her life by coming out of it. Then she is a mother. She is mother and remains mother even if her child, all her children, should die. At first she carried the child under her heart. But later, when it is born, she carries it in her heart. And never does it ever leave her heart again. Not even when it is dead. Man feels nothing in all this, he does not know it. He does not know the difference between before love and after love, before motherhood and after motherhood. He cannot know it. That is why we do not let our men interfere in our affairs. For a woman can do but one thing. She can take care of herself. She can keep herself respectable. She must always be as her nature is. She must always be both maiden and mother. Before every love she is a maiden, after every love she is a mother. In this you may see whether she is a good woman or not." (Words of an Abyssinian noblewoman, reported by Frobentius, in *Der Kopf als Schicksal, Munich,* 1924, p. 86).

although we do not think that Simone de Beauvoir's remarks about the fellow members of her sex can be applied to every woman: "And yet we know woman's world more intimately than men, because it is there that we have our roots; we grasp more immediately what the fact of being a woman means for a human being; and we take pains to know it all more fully."

II

The Intuitive Notion of the Essence of Femininity

The Intuitive Notion
of the Essence of Femininity

M. de Roannez said: "The reasons occur to me later, but at first I find a thing agreeable or offensive without knowing why, and I say I find that offensive for this reason, although I discovered it only afterwards." But I believe, not that that is offensive to me for these reasons which I discovered afterwards, but that I discovered these reasons because that was offensive to me.

PASCAL [1]

There is a certain stature of truth in poetry and literature and in the spontaneous activity of the emotions, and a wisdom welling up from man's religious awareness that has come down to us through the ages. We have already seen that we may not disregard this entirely in a scientific discussion of feminine existence. We can sum it all up, and call it the intuitive notion of the essence of woman—a concept which reflects the immediacy of experience, without any reflection or critique or analysis, without asking whether the experience is accidental or essential. The things that have been said about woman give us, therefore, a multiplicity of possible subjective experiences of her, and the fact that these are so often contradictory is convincing proof of the falseness of the idea of an unchangeable, eternal and absolute essence of woman, an essence preceding her existence in the world and determining, or at least supposed to determine, that existence.

It is naturally quite impossible to gather together everything that has ever been said about woman. "Of women, one may say whatever one likes; it will all be equally true" (Jules Lemaître). The intuitive concept of the feminine nature is reflected with extreme variability in myths and fairy tales and sagas, almost in the same way as it appears in the works of philosophers and writers of antiquity and of later ages. Woman may be sibyl, muse or prophetess; it is apparently just as easy for her to be temptation and

[1] Pensées, Fr. 276.

disaster as it is for her to be redemption and wisdom; she is shown uplifting and ennobling life and she is shown endangering and demeaning it. She is held to stand decisively for fidelity, and just as decisively for treachery; she is called a living lie, and she is called the purest truth; she appears as the complicity of darkness or as the perfection of light and simplicity; shameless, or chaste; docile, or quite untamable—and so we could go on.

If we listen to the conversations round about us, we see that they project an image of woman that is every bit as variable. There is not any schoolboy or professor, laborer or ruler, man or woman, who does not feel called every now and then to say, "Actually, a *woman* is. . . ." More often than not, these generalizations are little more than an emotionally tinted view based on some coincidental experience that has touched the speaker personally. Thus, John Stewart Mill had grasped a good deal of the truth when he wrote: "One can, to an almost laughable degree, infer what a man's wife is like, from his opinions about women in general." [2] Literature too is full of this kind of subjective judgment, and if we want to know the actual state of public opinion or what it is that people like to hear repeated, we have only to look at the cartoons and jokes and aphorisms in popular magazines which have to do with "woman," some with gentle humor, some with acid sarcasm.

And yet, the ultimate responsibility for this opinion does not lie altogether with the men, who hold a leading function in society, and neither is it wholly determined by traditional views that have grown from historical roots. Within the objective situation of woman's existence in our cultural history, there must be a reason for the endless rash of negative judgments, on the nasty mother-in-law, the finicky schoolmarm, the sneaky secretary, the nagging housewife, on spring-cleaning fever, on cosmetics and fashions, and so on.

One can find something of the same kind of judgment in the most ancient writings of our civilization. We can say that woman at almost all times has been judged unfavorably more often than favorably, and that it still is so today. Even if only one so-called fact is being considered, it can easily be judged in a negative way, and thus we can understand how Aristotle, who did not stop at simply noting down the passivity of woman, could go on to say that woman is therefore inferior and defective. And Plato, who

[2] *The Subjection of Women,* 1869.

thanks the gods that he was not created as a slave or a woman, does not have many good things to say about the "other" sex in the fifth book of the *Republic,* and writes in the *Timaeus:* "Of all who are born as men, those who lack courage and those who have passed their lives in injustice will, in all probability, when they come to be born again, change into women."

From these and many other quotations (for instance, Vergil's *"varium et mutabile semper femina"*) it is more than clear that we can infer no more than that feminine existence more often than not appeared in a form that elicited certain unfavorable modes of human behavior. In addition, writers delight in being "entertaining," and this usually takes the form of ridicule or casting suspicion or exaggeration. But still, it is not difficult to see that there is a deeper reason yet for man's negative judgment on woman. Man will almost invariably experience the power which woman exercises over him as irresistible and thus as a humiliation of his dignity as a man, for it means an abrogation of his freedom. So we can understand why the wicked woman who misuses her power should be thought of as the most hideous and diabolical being there is. Thus every age repeats Homer: "There is no more vile and devilish creature than a woman whose heart is bent on evil."

It is not an easy task to represent in a true light the intuitive concept of the essence of woman as it was developed in the early centuries of Christianity and as the writings of that time have helped to maintain it down to our own day. In any case, we cannot agree that it is characteristic of the Christian tradition to look on woman as inferior—the contention of Simone de Beauvoir.

The Old Testament held the good woman in high honor, and we find no trace in it of the morning prayer of the Jews, in which they thank God that they are not women. The significance of Eve's role in the origin of mankind's sufferings during his earthly life is in a totally different order from that credited to Pandora in the legend. Nor is it admissible that the words of St. Paul, in which he likens the relation of man and woman to that of Christ and his Church, are an eruption of "the Jewish tradition, ferociously anti-feminist," no matter how true it may be that this text is still, today, being misused in an anti-feminist way.

Kierkegaard shows that it *is* possible to understand the Apostle's thought in an entirely different way. Woman has an inborn talent, an absolute virtuosity "for making sense of finiteness. . . . And the scripture is right: insofar as woman gives finiteness to man, she is stronger than he, she is his refuge. It is a great happiness to me to understand the meaning of woman thus; to me she becomes the symbol of the congregation. . . . For the congregation, of which the Spirit demands that it should be at home in finiteness, there is indeed no more beautiful symbol than woman." [3]

However, Kierkegaard's thoughts on woman are of a highly unusual kind, and when he writes, "of a hundred men who lose their way in the world, ninety-nine are saved by woman, and one by an immediate grace of God",[4] the sense intended is wholly different from that of the Christian tradition, when it calls the "blessed among women" the "gate of heaven." In any case, the intuitive concept of woman in Christian civilization too is formed more by the concrete manner in which feminine existence is made manifest than by the *possibilities* inherent in woman's being.

Undoubtedly the troubadours and a number of poets and the philosophers of romanticism have secularized the veneration of the Mother of God, and we find, for instance, in Claudel a modern poet writing in praise of the redeeming power woman possesses. All of this gives us a picture that is not like the one Simone de Beauvoir claims she finds in the writings of the Church Fathers. However, it appears that the texts she quotes are not all translated properly, and that some of them come from sources other than the writers she names.

Tertullian writes: "Every one of you should be clothed in mourning and tatters. . . . God's judgment on your sex continues to live in the present; thus it can not be otherwise than that your guilt is still alive. You are the door that gave entrance to the devil . . . you too are the one who persuaded him whom the devil was not able to attack. . . . As a result of your guilt, the Son of God had to die." [5] The quotation from St. Ambrose—"Adam was induced to sin by Eve, and not Eve by Adam. It is just that woman should receive as her sovereign him whom she induced to sin"—is indeed found in the patristic tradition, but it is highly probable that in this form it comes from some other source.

[3] Kierkegaard, *Entweder Oder* (überschr. van Christoph. Schrempf), Leipzig 1939. p. 422ff.

[4] *Entweder Oder*, p. 291.

[5] *De Cultu Feminarum*, I, 1.

The same is true of the extremely unkind words attributed to St. John Chrysostom, which Simone de Beauvoir stresses when she quotes ("among all wild beasts, there is not one that is more harmful than woman").[6] The words Simone de Beauvoir quotes as St. Augustine's, "Woman is an animal who is neither steady nor steadfast," are certainly not Augustine's words. In the 16th century, the text appears to have been used to maintain guardianship over married women.

It cannot be doubted that Christianity, in upholding the sacramental dignity of marriage and respect for motherhood, has proclaimed evangelical compassion with *all* who suffer and are oppressed, among whom woman is clearly included. This has helped to improve woman's social standing, and it has also brought about changes in the intuitive concept of woman's existence, although views like the ones quoted above continued, in slightly altered forms, to work their mischief in our thinking. This was so, not because such views were directly or indirectly known and their authority accepted, but because, on account of the stability of social structures and of the relationship of the sexes, the manner in which woman has been experienced through the ages has maintained a general uniformity.

Women in Other Cultures

It is quite remarkable how little our social structure differs in principle from that of other cultures—so little, that we often find the same things said about women in other cultures that we find in our own. By way of example, let us give some impressions of the Islamic view of woman.[7] We can begin with a number of proverbs

[6] But compare this with the following passage which is certainly from John Chrysostom: "Love therefore is an affair of men, patient endurance is woman's affair. . . . Therefore God made her subject to you (men) so that she would be loved all the more. Therefore he devised you, Woman, with love, so that you might bear subjection the more easily. Subject yourself without fear; for there is no hardship in subjection to him who loves us. And have no fear in showing all love to your wife. For she repays you with docility. You possess the mastery which must needs be yours by nature; possess then also the bond which is the fruit of love" (*Comm. in Col. 10*). The passage however does show clearly that Chrysostom adheres to the opinion that woman ought to be completely subject to man.

[7] The data presented were generously made available to me by Dr. Hoeben, S.J., of Maastricht.

which do not sound too unusual to our "Christian" ears: "Women are a scourge in the devil's hand"; "Never trust a king or a horse or a woman"; "Obey a woman, and you will regret it later". One could compare these with the sigh in Vondel's line: *"Een vrouw is duizend mannen t'ergh"*—it would take a thousand men to keep up with one woman's wiles.[8] The Koran preaches, just as Christianity preaches, that woman has a soul that stands in direct relationship to God, and there is a saying that tradition ascribes to Mahommed which agrees with the Proverbs of Solomon: "The world and all things in the world are valuable, but a virtuous woman is more valuable than all the rest." But even though the doctrine of Islam regards woman benevolently in many respects, the practice of Islam has certainly not accorded her the place its founder intended her to have. It is certainly a shameful reflection on the existing system, that the worth of woman is set so low, and that the ancient heathendom of Arabia has in fact been able to influence Islam so strongly. The fault does not lie with the Prophet; it lies in the customs of pre-Islamic times that have continued to hold sway.

Mahommed looked on women as attractive beings though the devil had made them a temptation to the faithful. Women are ornamental and useful in the home, they are lovely to play with but difficult to tame. Mahommed does not seem to have had the idea that woman could be man's adviser and companion. But he did have great respect for his first wife. However, this does not seem to have had any influence on his attitude to other wives. But it is a fact that he did much to improve woman's position in many respects: he limited the legal number of wives to four, most strictly forbade all incest, forced men to support their divorced wives for the four months of the trial period, and demanded four witnesses to give validity to an accusation of adultery.

There is enough source-material for an extensive study of woman's existence and of the judgment accorded her in Oriental religions and among primitive peoples, but just now we want to confine ourselves to the more important of the views that have arisen intuitively in Western culture and that find their expression

---

8 Or with Victor Hugo's: *"Une femme est un diable très perfectionné"*— woman is a highly accomplished devil.

in our society.[9] Among these, we can distinguish a number of main general tendencies:

- *a.* the presupposition of woman's inscrutability;
- *b.* an underrating of woman, even to the point of contempt;
- *c.* an overrating and adulation of woman;
- *d.* the rationalized explanatory schemes of "feminists";
- *e.* the more or less humanistic opinion that woman is neither higher nor lower in value than man but has a value that is *other* than his, and that many of the noticeable differences between the sexes have been produced by social circumstances.

To quite a striking degree, the presupposition of woman's inscrutability is something that we find chiefly in the poets. It seems they all experience woman as Shakespeare did: "Who is't can read a woman?" It would be interesting to make a closer analysis of the poetic view of woman. It certainly proceeds from quite another source than the prosaic view, expressing scandal at the apparent unpredictability of woman and her unintelligible behavior. The thing that strikes the poet is a hidden and phenomenal interiority which seems to point to an indefinable bond with the very foundations of human existence: with love, suffering, and death.[10] The poet also sees woman as his inspiring muse and as a promise ever unfulfilled. Her very inscrutability is significantly expressive of the unbridgeable abyss between the poet and woman; it is the sign of the impossibility of ever possessing her fully and discovering her as something of the world one grasps by one's understanding. In the Shakespearian sonnet:

> *When my love swears that she is made of truth I do believe her, though I know she lies*

[9] It would be a very important work, carefully to trace the history of the manner in which woman has manifested herself, of woman's existence, to study the forms taken by the structure of woman's world and by the aesthetical and ethical appreciations of woman's being during the course of history. If we want to understand present attitudes well, an insight into those that prevailed in the past century can be very helpful, even if we cannot go further back than that. What the attitudes of the last century were, we can best learn from the literature of the time. There is however no room to go into the actual historical data here.

[10] Woman herself perceives this, as we can see from the deep feeling of George Sand's words: "Woman! O woman! You are an abyss, a mystery, and he who believes he knows you is mad, thrice mad!"

there is a clear echo of the discovery of this inscrutability, and rational judgment is transcended in the direction of a faith that is identical with love and that attains to an order beyond the conceptual.

We will have occasion to speak more at length on woman's mysterious interiority, and for the moment go no further than to point out that in the aesthetic and romantic approach, the whole of nature, particularly living nature, possesses the characteristic of inscrutability, and that there is even an evident regularity in it that is understood as a revelation of a "mysterious commandment", a *"geheimes Gesetz"* (Goethe). And because woman bears in her very body the signs of her inward, impersonal, unwilled bond with nature, and because in her, as Rilke says, "Life tarries and dwells, more immediately, more fruitfully, more full of trust",[11] we can understand why it is that an artistic person has such an experience of her inscrutability.

As the second of the tendencies that we find generally recurring in the intuitive concept of woman, we mentioned the tendency to underrate and even to condemn the "weaker sex." It is not surprising that, of those who can hardly be said to hold woman in high esteem, many are found mainly among the philosophers—or among those who would like to be called philosophers. Veneration of the rational, and admiration for high intellectual talent and for a moral order liberated as much as possible from subjective evaluations, will probably have helped to bring this about. But many a sage has become estranged from life through taking but little interest in the concrete, being only too eager to call it the accidental, and so has become estranged from human existence insofar as it is discovered in and involved in and gives meaning to its soul-enlivened bodiliness.

Philosophers and "Woman"

The "genuine" philosopher is interested in the absolute, in Being as such, in consciousness, knowledge, reality, truth, goodness and beauty—and so it does not surprise us in the least when we read, in the *Anthropologie in pragmatischer Hinsicht* by the great Immanuel Kant, sentences on woman that do not differ in

[11] *Letters to a young poet.*

the least from the most banal of street-corner generalizations. "Intellectually, woman is the less gifted," morally, women are inferior, because they want men to "pay homage to their charms." Moreover, they are vain, and fashion displays, not good taste, but their pointless vainglory. "Man himself has taste, but woman makes herself an object of taste for another, it does not matter whom. . . . Man is jealous when in love; woman is just jealous, even when not in love, for she regards every lover won by another woman as lost to her own circle of adorers".[12] In the chapter on the imagination, where Kant speaks of the use of intoxicating drink, we read: "Women, ecclesiastics and Jews hardly ever get drunk, or at least they avoid very carefully any appearance of drunkenness, for their civil status is insecure and it is necessary for them to be reserved (hence they always promote sobriety). For any outward esteem they enjoy depends entirely on the *credence* others give to their chasteness, piety, or separatist adherence to the Law." [13]

Undoubtedly, Kant discovered that women have a few good qualities as well, such as patience and thrift and so on, but he sees no more than the most simple woman-hater could observe without the benefit of philosophical training. If this is Kant's view, what can we expect of other philosophers? The majority remain silent on the matter of the difference between the sexes. However, the way Schopenhauer attempted with anger and affectation to describe and explain woman's inferiority is fairly well known. It was he who called woman the *"sexus sequior,"* from every aspect a backward sex, very much the "second sex," whose shortcomings one must disregard but not respect. "The veneration of woman," he says, is the "perfect flowering of germanic-Christian stupidity" which has led to only one result, to "make women so arrogant and disrespectful that one is reminded at times of the sacred apes of Benares which, knowing their own holiness and invulnerability, permitted themselves any and every excess." An end must be put to the "ladies of scandalous conduct" of Europe, and only housewives and girls who want to become housewives allowed to exist.

In his *Metaphysics of Sexual Love,* Schopenhauer explained that woman is nothing more than a natural trap who as a girl "captures" a man by her beauty, and after two children loses her

12 Ausgabe van Dr. R. Schmidt. Reclam 1942, p. 277.
13 *Ibid.,* p. 86.

beauty apparently for the same reason that a queen ant loses her wings after mating—for they serve no function in caring for the brood.

This of course is not an example of the intuitive concept of feminine existence like the previous ones; what Schopenhauer is doing is developing a theory of sexual differentiation applicable to the world of animals, and of the significance of this in human existence. His views did carry weight in the 19th century, and their effect can be seen in the effort to explain human reality in terms of lower nature, under the influence of a naturalistic anthropology.

A good example of this is found in the work of Weininger,[14] from which we may quote just one sentence: "The mind of woman is neither profound nor exalted, neither acute nor direct, but rather the contrary of all these; she is, as far as we have been able to see up to now, without mind; she is as it were senseless, a complete non-sense." The author was twenty-three years old when he wrote this, and within ten years his book had been re-printed twenty-five times besides being published in practically all the other European languages.

Considering these facts, they do prove to what a great extent disdain—one could even say, contempt and hatred—had taken hold of spontaneous opinion concerning women almost everywhere, and they show how attempts were made to justify this opinion of her on (pseudo) scientific grounds.[15]

Even today, man is very prone to trot out *"cherchez la femme"*,[16] a cliché in every language, his intention being to say that woman is the cause of all the difficulties he is involved in and of all the vices he discovers in himself. This opinion is stubbornly irrepressible, but still, at least in our country, it is possible to notice an important shift in public opinion. Thus the following anthology of derogatory views is important as history rather than as an echo of the living present. We list a number of spontaneously expressed judgments, well known as having found their way into

[14] *Geschlecht und Charakter.* 25. Aufl. 1923.

[15] For example, Möbius, *Ueber den physiologischen Schwachsinn des Weibes,* 1908; "proofs" were also quoted from the book by Lombroso and Ferrero, *Das Weib als Verbrecherin und Prostituierte,* 1894.

[16] Originally from Alexandre Dumas, *Les Mohicans de Paris,* although we find, as far back as Juvenal, *"nulla fere causa est, in qua non femina litem moverit"*—there is practically no dispute in which the argument was not started by a woman.

literature, without commenting on them, for they relate in any case more to the psychology of their authors than to the psychology of woman. This applies to Nietzsche's often-quoted "woman is God's second mistake" and also to Milton's, woman is "a pretty defect." [16a]

Derogatory Comments on Women

Quite remarkable, too, are the number of derogatory sayings that are English in origin: "Women were liars since the world began" (Masefield); "No is no negative in a woman's mouth" (Sir Philip Sidney); "I expect that woman will be the last thing civilized by man" (Meredith); and, "Every woman should marry, but no man" (Disraeli). It is not difficult to surmise the nature of the social and psychological grounds that gave rise to these views. In any case, in 1947, Richard Curle, more or less in agreement with the D. H. Lawrence of the "Plumed Serpent", wrote: "Women have an unpleasant habit of playing up their sex in order to justify behavior that is not really excusable." [17] Dr. Johnson too is true to the type when he writes—as it seems, in the name of all the Johnsons, Jones and Smiths—"nature has given women so much power that the law has very wisely given them little."

We do not depart from the genre of these views when we come to the deed of sale of a married woman from a workhouse in Surrey in 1815 cited by Viola Klein,[18] and it is she who tells us that in 1856, R. W. Emerson wrote, in his *English Traits,* "The right of the husband to sell his wife has been retained down to our times." The British Government approved the "Sex Disqualification (removal) Act" in 1919, but in 1944, equal wages were still refused.[19] G. W. Curtis is indeed right when he says: "The test of civilization is the estimate of woman."

In French literature, or at any rate in modern French literature, positively derogatory judgments on woman are less frequent. Even Simone de Beauvoir was able to cite only Montherlant as an out-

16a Although the author usually quotes English texts in English, he has quoted a Dutch translation here, and I cannot trace the original (Translator).

17 *Women.* London 1947. p. 149.

18 *The Feminine Character* (History of an ideology). London 1946. p. 8.

19 Viola Klein, *The Feminine Character,* p. 28.

spoken anti-feminist among the French. In opposition to him are
Stendhal ("the fantasy of truth"), Breton ("or poetry") and
Claudel ("and the handmaiden of God"). Quite certainly, in France
too the concept of woman is determined partly by the dominance
of man's status, but this does not eliminate a greater nicety of
awareness or a more loving attitude or a greater purity of feeling
for relationships. Dufresny says: "One cannot speak of women
with justice and moderation. Always, one says either too much or
too little."

It would certainly be possible to find unfavorable judgments on
woman in French literature too, but in most cases their sting is
drawn by a measure of benevolent humor. La Rochefoucauld still
lives in the spirit of France, and it could equally well be said today
that "the probity of women is often love of their reputation and of
their tranquillity"; "the majority of honest women are hidden trea-
sures whose only security lies in the fact that they are not sought
after." Or, "most women give themselves through weakness rather
than through passion."

What might most strictly be called the veneration of woman is
expressed most strongly in German romanticism, and its influence
is felt down to our own time.[20] Naturally, romanticism is not the
only source of this glorification of woman. For instance, Kamp-

[20] We find a lofty admiration of women in very many passages in Von
Humboldt, Goethe, Schiller and others. Stress is laid particularly on the
moral worth of the feminine character. Note for instance Von Humboldt:
"To see the female sex from the aspect which is most properly its own,
one has to approach it in terms of its *moral* character. Just as spirit in man,
the most lively and active thing in woman is intention." (*Plan einer
vergleichenden Anthropologie,* Werke I, p. 406). There is a critical discussion of many passages in the (unpublished) thesis of Dra. J. Kunze (*De
psychologische opvatting betreffende de relatie der sexen in de Duitse
Romantiek*). It is important to note that Goethe, who was no romanticist,
sought the idealization of woman in the fullness of her worth as a human
being, and Dra. Kunze remarks, correctly, that the Leonore figure in *"Tasso"*
shows that Goethe regarded it as a weakness in a woman to "shut herself
up in her femininity with too much self-satisfaction, submitting to her
feelings too much, and directing herself too little toward her surroundings."
Goethe did not find the "eternal feminine" in woman's sex, and neither did
he find it in woman as more or less misfortune by the social position forced
upon her or by her own passivity. He saw the "eternal feminine" much more
as an eternal idea, a form in which the human spirit could express itself
just as it can in masculinity. French romanticism too did not miss its op-
portunities, as we may see from the following line from Lamartine:
"Women, mortal angels, divine creation, only ray to brighten a moment of
life."

mann shows how Bergmann,[21] following Bölsche, starting from biological and zoological premises, arrived at psychological, sociological and even metaphysical and theological conclusions. One could summarize these conclusions like this: man is the inferior, the secondary, adventitious sex—the drone in the beehive—and he is moreover the cause of all crime, confusion and misery in society. Woman is altruistic (the opinion of Gina Lombroso too, and many others), she is the "primordial spirit" of society, she is good, she heals and saves. Bergmann says it is true of all of us that "the nostalgia in our soul for the divine Origin is a longing for our mother's breast." One would think that a disciple of Freud was speaking.

However, the best expression of the intuitive notion that woman represents and protects and brings forth and offers what is noblest in humanity is preserved in the words of Schiller. And the best known are his lines in the poem, *The dignity of Women:*

> *Hold women in honor! They plait and weave*
> *roses of heaven into this earthly life.*
> *They wind us about with love's happy bond,*
> *chaste-veiled in grace, their hand so fond*
> *and holy to tend the undying fire,*
> *feeding its flame with beauty's desire.*[21a]

Women Are "God's Flowers"

The idea inspiring this verse has spread perhaps as far as the United States, where there is a women's club with the motto: "Men are God's trees, women are his flowers." Still closer to Schiller's model of the veneration of femininity are Ernest Renan's words: "Woman brings us back to the eternal source where God contemplates himself." This source springs abundantly on earth, reflecting not only the supreme spiritual reality, selfless love be-

[21] Ernst Bergmann, *Erkenntnisgeist und Muttergeist*, Breslau 1933.
[21a] *Ehret die Frauen! Sie flechten und Weben*
Himmlische Rosen in's irdische Leben.
Flechten der Liebe beglückendes Band
Und in der Grazie züchtigem Schleier
Nähren sie wachsam das ewige Feuer
Schöner Gefühle mit heiliger Hand.

come a person, but also that this love would become fruitful and be encountered in human shape in woman. Thus, the veneration woman is accorded rests mainly on the opinion that she possesses by nature a more intimate bond with the purity of love than man.

This thought finds the most varied expression. Mme. de Remusat comes to this conclusion about the members of her sex: "To get them to do anything, it is almost always necessary to ask them in the name of another's happiness." [22] The judgment of Gertrud von le Fort is similar in tenor: "Wherever woman is most deeply herself, she is not herself, but given to another." [23] This self-giving, which is essentially the union of love and sacrifice, lies in the willingness of the heart to participate more deeply than the intellect in the mystery of existence, and therefore in its more intimate bond with the truth. Thus, when Kampmann calls woman "the Genie of Love," [24] he fittingly quotes in the same passage the sensitive thought of Theodor Haecker: "Amare means to love, amare means bitter: amare, amare, who can yet distinguish you"? [25]

The veneration of woman thus expressed is actually respect for the most elevated of human potentialities. It suggests, then, that the longing to realize these potentialities is more alive in woman than in man, and this longing is none other than the longing for salvation. Kampmann sees even in the simple fact that woman weeps easily a telling proof that she experiences herself as not yet in the bliss of salvation but as longing for it, and he adds: "In this view, is woman the more perfect being? I believe surely she is at least the more human." [26]

In Rilke's letters to a young poet,[27] with sensitive perception and truth he says that life dwells in woman more immediately, more fruitfully and with greater confidence than in man. "Life," in this context, means more than that unknowing nature in which man participates through his physical reality. Rilke is thinking much rather of that intangible goodness and perfect innocence to

[22] *Essai sur l'éducation des femmes,* Paris 1841, p. 37, quoted by Heymans.

[23] *Die Ewige Frau.* Munich 1934. p. 18.

[24] *Die Psych. des Frauenwesens,* Paderborn 1947, p. 183.

[25] *Satire und Polemik,* Innsbruck 1922, p. 60.

[26] *Die Psych. des Frauenwesens.* Paderborn 1947. p. 183.

[27] P. 41 of the Insel-Bücherei edition No. 406.

which nature seems to bear witness, just as much as it bears witness to its origin and its quiet search for its destiny.

This life, made present to us in the "lilies of the field" which "care not," and in the wholly unambiguous aspect of an earnest animal, is the life that is raised to the dignity of humanity in woman, "who must therefore basically be a more mature, more human person than man who, easy-going and inclined to be dense and hasty, and not knowing any bodily fruit of suffering, is held down below the upper level of life and is inclined to underestimate what he thinks he loves." It could not be better or more simply expressed. For, to mature "basically" to the perfection of human dignity, to mature in the very foundations of existence, to mature in that which provides the ultimate basis of all the manifestations of existence, man has to abandon the superficial frivolity and the self-satisfied attitude of a hurriedly-moving existence, and in the fruitfulness of sorrow discover what it means genuinely to love.

As a human reality, this sorrow is engendered by "life," and not by an enlightened and enlightening consciousness of it. For sorrow is indeed a fruit of life, but in the same way as death is a fruit of life, and every sorrow is a sign of death—a darkling, heavy fruit that ripens in the intimacy of loneliness for the "more human" person who does not live in the superficiality of conceited haste. Only then will "woman's humanity, gestated the full term in sorrows and humiliations," be revealed.

This is woman's promise, and the mission she has the power to fulfill. "One day (in northern lands especially there are already clear and telling signs of this), one day the girl and the woman will have come into their own, their names no longer meaning merely an opposite of the masculine, but something in themselves, something that no longer conveys the thought of complement or limitation, but of Life and Presence: the feminine human being."

The feminists' esteem for woman is something of an entirely different order. In the first place, it takes the form of a reaction, sometimes exaggerated although not always as excessively so as Emerence M. Lemouche's "The lowest prostitute is yet better than the best of men." The more normal feminist view is reflected in Elisa Burt Gamble's rather effusive texts, for instance, "The female among all the orders of life, man included, represents a higher stage of development than the male" (1893), or in the opinion of Mabel Powers (1914) that "The best man is 49 per cent feminine, the best woman 49 per cent masculine."

In her review of the history of the problem of women, Simone de Beauvoir cites many examples to persuade us that from as early as the 15th century, French women have been protesting against existing social relationships and showing a desire to take their part in their country's cultural and political development. In the 16th and 17th centuries, a fair number of writers argued vigorously for or against the emancipation of women. The work of Poulain de la Barze is important. In 1673 he published his *De L'égalité des Deux Sexes*, in which we find the excellent observation chosen by Simone de Beauvoir as the motto of her book: "Everything written about women by men ought to be suspect, for these men are at the same time judge and litigant."

In spite of all this, even in France the intuitive concept of the essence of woman has remained practically unchanged, and public opinion agrees with the traditional view that woman is destined "by nature" to fulfill the function of housewife, and that in any case she ought to render obedience to man. Rousseau thinks that "All the education of women ought to be in relation to men"— "Woman is made to give way to man and to put up with his injustices," [28] and, in the words of Balzac, "The destiny and the sole glory of women is to excite the heartbeat of man"—"The married woman is a slave whom one ought to know how to put on a throne," [29] and these sentiments are still shared by conservative (and "gallant") Frenchmen today.

These views are not however felt to be at odds with the opinion that woman is neither a higher nor a lower kind of being than man, but that she has a value that is quite other than man's, and that the many differences of behavior and "character" between the sexes are the result of education and social circumstance. Nevertheless, there is such a strong attachment to the conviction of a connection between this "other" value and an essential difference between man and woman that, even where there is all readiness to approach woman in a friendly and humane fashion, and to grant her certain rights and privileges, we still find people thinking that, from

---

[28] Quoted by Simone de Beauvoir, *Le Deuxième Sexe* I, p. 181. (Eng. Tr. Knopf, N. Y. 1953, p. 107)

[29] *Psychologie du mariage,* quoted by Simone de Beauvoir, *Le Deuxième Sexe* I, p. 188. (Eng. Tr. Knopf, N. Y. 1953 p. 111)

the social point of view, woman's *fundamental* position *must* remain unchanged.

But *what* is to be regarded as fundamental? And *to what extent* is woman *obliged* to undertake or avoid certain lines of action? And *what* authority is competent to define the limits of her freedom? All these questions continue to be disputed questions, and they are the very heart of the feminine problem. The solution to this problem cannot be provided by any intuitive concept of the essence of woman.

III

Woman's Nature

Introduction

In the language of science as well as in ordinary conversation we speak of a person's "characteristic" properties, and in both usages the term refers to his diligence, his love of neighbor, his devotion to duty, his enthusiasm, his perseverance, his reliability, his stability, his sensitivity and so on, or it refers to the opposites of all these, more or less in the same way as it is possible to sum up the valuable or unfavorable points of a thoroughbred horse, a fruit-tree or a sample of ore. The concepts delineating the character of a thing relate in all cases to properties of the thing that can be directly observed, or that are not immediately evident but can be inferred. The observable properties comprise the visible shape of the thing, those qualities which are evident on the surface, and everything that the thing can be seen to do. By the properties which are not immediately evident, we mean all those things the thing should be able to do, all its potentialities—its capabilities (such as explosiveness, or the ability to grow, or intelligence), structures that are discovered only when the thing is analyzed, its reactions to various stimuli and conditions, and finally, the "forces" and the fundamental hypotheses which help us to understand why it has these actual qualities or to understand how they arise.

A study of this kind applied to a human being, investigating, analyzing and describing him, is considered to establish the *nature* of a human being. Thus it is possible to speak of woman's nature in the context of this kind of study, and in science this is done on several different levels. Firstly, it is done in the biological investigation of woman, with comparative reference to female specimens of "other" species of animals; secondly, it is done in establishing woman's specific physical characteristics as contrasted with those of man; thirdly, it is done in investigating woman's actual psychological characteristics; and finally, it is done in seeking for the causes of woman's behavior in the fundamental interiority of her person, attempting to establish woman's *"characteristic"* or *"actual"* nature in the manner known as that of depth-psychology. We will follow each of these four ways in the scientific approach to woman's nature, and consider first of all its biological basis.

1. The Biological Basis

> If our body does not impose on us definite instincts
> from birth, as the body of an animal does, our body does
> at least give general form to our life and stable continuity
> of disposition to our personal acts. . . . The body is the
> universal means by which we possess a world.

MERLEAU-PONTY [1]

If it is true that the difference between man and woman affects
the whole personality and the whole of existence, and that it can
be traced in all functions and habits, in temperament and in inclinations, one might well ask why this complete contrast of the sexes
occurs among human beings precisely and not among animals. It is
possible that the separation and contrast of the sexes in man is
most certainly not "the zenith of organic development" as Goethe
thought, and it is possible that the distinction of which Feuerbach
speaks, a "distinction having no point of beginning and no definable end, more universally present, more infinite, more penetrating
of marrow and bone" than any other distinction, does not rest on
any inborn difference, but is the result of education and milieu,
and must therefore be regarded as a cultural phenomenon. For
man, says Merleau-Ponty, is "an historical idea" and not "a natural species." But still, man does belong to nature, even in his
animated materiality.

Hence, we obviously need to study sexual differentiation in the
world of plants and animals, for the objectivity of the facts we can
find there will be likely to provide helpful indications for an insight
into the psychology and the existential status of woman, or at least
into the "nature" that forms the basis of her psychology and existence. This must not be taken to mean that we will be able to find
some causal connection between animal and human behavior. A
causal connection would be possible only if man and animals were

---

[1] *Phénoménologie de la perception.* Paris (N.R.F.) 1945 p. 171. (*Phenomenology of Perception,* New York, Humanities Press, 1962).

natural beings in the same sense, whereas man precisely is set apart by his peculiar characteristic of being able to take up a position with regard to his own nature. This emancipation, this potential freedom, is the essence of human reality and is decisive for human existence.

This means that man in principle develops himself, his world and his existence freely and without any predetermination. That this freedom is not mere arbitrariness—certainly with regard to the biological actuality provided by the body—does not need any further explanation. Nevertheless, and before all this, it is clear that we can never regard the "natural" in man as a series of invariable characteristics. Man's naturalness is always something he forms, and his body is at his disposal—even if not perfectly—like the material from which he manufactures his tools, his dwellings and all cultural objects.

But there is no material which is quite as properly man's own as his body, and so there is nothing else that limits him to such an extent in his choice, or that is able to compel him, apparently so completely. Thus we need to know the biological basis of woman's nature as it actually is, and this is the reason for our taking a close look at the polarity of the sexes in the world of plants and animals.

However, when we do this we are immediately struck by one of the *mysteries* of life, for science is certain that the division of organisms into two sexes is something for which it knows no explanation. If by explanation one means an indication of the causes that have produced this division, there is simply no biological explanation to be found. We will therefore have to approach the phenomenon in some other way—by application of the phenomenological method, this method being needed in biology besides that of causal analysis. In this method, we ask nature the question: what is the "eidos," the idea, the essence and the significance of the primordial phenomenon of sexual differentiation? This will at the same time help to make another irreducible fact more clear. All living beings have a finite existence, and all living beings manifest growth and expansion. This expansion is something that extends beyond the limits of the individual. We cannot think of it as a transcendence, for the concept of transcendence is most definitely reserved for an exceeding of the limits of nature as it is in itself, an overstepping of these limits such as takes place in intentional consciousness. Yet, in a certain sense the expansivity of life is an *image* of transcendence; it is transcendence in appearance. We will frequently have to use this additional qualification, "in appearance," when we speak about living being. It was first used by Schiller—and the meaning he attaches to it is most clear— when he spoke of living nature as "Freiheit in Erscheinung," freedom in appearance. In actual fact, a bird is not genuinely free, even though it flies high in the air without compulsion and sings its exuberant song. It is the image of freedom, freedom in appearance. It is certainly possible to recognize many characteristics of freedom in this freedom-thus-appearing, but this does not mean that it is genuine freedom. In the same way, we are able to recognize the self-multiplying characteristic of living being as such in the expansivity of the individual living thing. This self-multiplication is simultaneously self-maintenance and the conquest of opposing factors, and it shows us the directedness of living being toward overstepping its own given limits. In this there is no manifestation of genuine transcendence however, for nature does not ever overreach itself. Nature exceeds itself only in human consciousness. Man exists in fact beyond the borders of his own limitation, and thus man exists not merely *in* the world but also *toward* the world, sharing through his consciousness in a manner of being that is not nature's manner of being.

The phenomenon of reproduction can be meaningfully understood in terms of the essence of living being as finite and overcoming this finiteness through expansivity. But does this phenomenon of reproduction in turn make the division of the sexes intelligible? It surely does not. Reproduction could just as well take place as it does in certain kinds of plants and lower animal organisms, through fission, budding, etc. For reproduction means only that a new organism has come to be, and, granting the structural differentiation of the organism, this is intelligible only in terms of an originally more or less amorphous status of the new organism, when it is still imperfect and unable to support itself. Yet this does throw light on a particular aspect of the phenomenon of reproduction. The imperfect, unself-sufficient and amorphous state of being is necessarily a state of being which is not wholly protected against those factors of the milieu to which the adult, reproducing organism has adapted itself and against which it has protected itself.

Preservation of the Species

Reproduction thus always implies a certain special "precautionary care" for the coming generation. We can grasp, from the *idea* of reproduction, that there *must be* some kind of precautionary care. But in nature the precaution is not genuine care and foresight, it is not an *act,* whether deliberate or undeliberate, based on a status of knowing. This precautionary care is merely "care in appearance," a care which can be called care only metaphorically, but which is called care precisely because it makes the meaning of genuine human care and precaution phenomenologically visible for us. This is why man from ancient times has spoken of *nature's* care for the preservation of the species. The intention is not to suggest, for instance, that the hard shell of the egg was produced on the hen's initiative. We speak this way because the eggshell does demonstrate the meaning of precaution, even though the demonstration consists wholly in the naturalness of an event which itself can certainly not know of anything at all.

However, when we examine animal species in the order of their development from lower to higher, it is remarkable that it is only in the lower species that the care of which we have been speaking must be seen as something taking place in nature itself, and so, as something that cannot be called care, but only care in appearance. Among the higher animals, care for offspring takes on the clear image of an act performed by a subject.

Let us however examine plant life first. The term *increase* is aptly used in this connection. Expansion takes place in a plant by repetition of part after part, leaf after leaf, stalk after stalk. Like this, the event appears to us to be wholly enclosed within the inward nature of the plant. This mode of being alive is called the lowest form of life, and it is conceived of as a closed existence, an existence which in virtue of its nature does not direct itself *toward* a world and thus does not maintain a structured interaction through sensation and self-movement. It merely undergoes, like any object, an accidental and external encounter with the world round about, which is thus not an encounter in the proper sense. The plant is essentially a pseudo-subject, an always incompleted form-producing form which is a "self" only to the extent that it appears to us as a *shape* subsisting in itself. That is to say, the plant does not consist in activity related to itself as an animal does, nor does it exist in the proper sense as a man does, who can genuinely be a self, for himself and by himself, but it manifests immanence and interiority "in appearance."

All the basic facts which we can learn from plant-life can be understood in the light of this idea of vegetable existence. The plant is not an individual in the proper sense; from point to point in contact with light, oxygen, and so on, it is delivered over to the material elements and the forces it meets on its concrete surfaces. The interaction between the plant and the world round about it is in principle quantitative and unformed. Just as the whole plant is itself an incomplete form, the functions of a plant are an incomplete form. In its bud and blossom a plant tends—but only *tends*—toward the closed completeness of form of animal existence, but it never entirely *reaches* this completeness. A flower may appear to us as something clearly formed, to which nothing either can be added or needs to be added, and thus as a completed form, but still it is completed form always in the mode of immanence that belongs to plant-life, and this is not immanence properly speaking.

Therefore it is not possible to say, except metaphorically, that in the flower the plant has achieved something that could be a *means* of taking care of a coming generation. Of itself a plant is not able to produce a means, but nature, being what it is in the plant, establishes one form after another and so manifests "care in appearance." Fruits ripening on the plant look as though they are things made, and even made in a subtle way, with tough shells, with little hooks on them, or with other devices—taking the milieu and local animal life into account—efficiently related to the distribution of the seed and the development of new generations. It is possible to describe all this as if it belonged to the animal order, but in fact it does not belong to that order of being.

Whatever happens in the plant is in perfect continuity with what will soon happen in the earth when the seed, as it is said, is "entrusted to the earth," the soil from which the plant will spring and once again multiply itself in endless repetition. This phenomenological view of plant-life does not elicit the thought of sexual differentiation and even renders it meaningless. We could ask whether and to what extent nature is still a perfect unity in this? The principle of the division of individuals into two sexes is contradicted by the close relation connecting plant and soil and connecting plant and all that lives with it.

Henderson's book, *The Fitness of the Environment,* explains at some length that we ought to extend the notion of purposiveness which we are accustomed to limit to living nature, and make it applicable to non-living nature as well. As actual chemical and physical properties, many qualities of ordinary matter, such as carbons, water and carbonic acid, are meaningfully related to vegetable and animal life. It is possible to speak of an unconscious purposiveness in non-living nature for the sake of living nature. Henderson's book is not very widely remembered, and neither is that of Erich Becher, *Ueber individuelle Zweckmässigkeit der Pflanzengalle,* in which we find once more the notion of unconscious purposiveness. Both of them mention the gall-nut, and Becher shows that this strange excrescence, which grows on a plant as a result of the sting of a gall-nut fly, is purposive even in its minutest details, not indeed with regard to the plant, but for the sake of the larvae which develop within the gall-nut. We will not follow this line of thought any further, but turn now to the lower animals, in whose order the plant-like immanence-in-appearance can still clearly be seen.

Distinction between Plant and Animal

The distinction between plant and animal is most certainly an essential distinction. The idea realized in the plant is wholly different from that realized in the animal, although in fact there seems to be an area in which the two orders overlap. We saw above that the flower appears as a completed form, in contrast with the plant which manifests the image of uncompleted form. We are generally familiar with the spores of ferns which move themselves like little animals but which do not actually have any self-movement. Theirs is a movement like all movement in the vegetable order—including that of flowers and tendrils—wholly determined by a quantitative and unformed interaction between the vegetable organism and the forces operative in its environment. Thus, the moving plant manifests an animal quality in appearance only. But in the animal, we always find qualities of the vegetable order in reality. Animals share in the vegetative order of existence. The expansive tendency (Scheler speaks of the "ecstatic urge") [2] of the plant is always observable among animals. But in the animal order of existence, an entirely new relationship to the environment emerges. Even the lower animals reveal a system of behavior; they do something, and their action is primarily concerned with food, that is, with *something* in particular, and thus with a *quality* and a *form* of the environment which the animal discovers. Among the lower animals, however, the obtaining of food is still entirely enclosed within the pseudo-immanence of the vegetative system, as it is in plants.

Now we may ask whether the precautionary care for the coming generation, which we met in plants as an unconscious purposiveness, becomes an actual care in the animal order. Even among the lowest animals, we can observe a seeking out of the best environment and a maintenance of the best conditions for living. For instance, these animals avoid danger and flee from it. Normally we refer to this as their "struggle for survival," but in a certain sense we can look on it under the aspect of taking care of themselves as well. Among animals, however, this struggle takes on the fundamental form of avoidance or overcoming of opposition according to fixed laws of reaction to a predominant degree, and it is clear that the care they take of themselves, and likewise their struggle for survival, is more an appearance which we so interpret than the actual reality of care and struggle. There is genuine care only when the subject intentionally carries out the relevant action. Men are able to do this, and the higher animals are probably able to as well.

From this brief examination of animal behavior, it may have become clear to us that the unconscious preservation of the individual and of the species can take place on the level of an *act* presupposing another mode of being, that of conscious being. From the given fact of reproduction, which is something that must be found in all living being, it *is possible* that the actuality of care in the animal order of being can become care properly speaking, although in the vegetable order it cannot. It can be a real care for the new generation, to the extent that the new organism, the egg or

[2] *Die Stellung des Menschen im Kosmos.* Darmstadt 1928.

the new-born offspring, takes on the meaning of an *object* to be cared for by the subject, and is no longer merely committed to the efficiency of the structures of the living organism or of the milieu.

It need hardly be said that this care for the offspring or the egg certainly does not yet signify any consciousness of the care itself. Consciousness of care is possible only when the subject reflects upon the act precisely as an act of care. Animals take care "naturally," which means that they do it from positional awareness, without deliberation, from an immediate sense-perception of the significance of the situation in which the subject finds itself and in which it is completely enclosed.

If we want now to draw any conclusion from this phenomenological investigation of the vegetable and animal orders of being, it is clear that the fact of reproduction cannot help us in any way to an insight into the division of the sexes. It helps us to understand only that the principle of care as care in the proper sense for the new generation *can* and *must* be manifested in the animal order, and that this follows necessarily from the *idea* [2a] of reproduction.

Let us now turn to the facts, in order to take our lead from them in attempting to come to a more far-reaching insight into the division of the sexes. One of the basic facts is that fertilization takes place in such a way among plants and animals that a minute and generally motile microgamete or spermatozoon reaches and penetrates a larger macrogamete or egg-cell. We find the motile type of microgamete already in certain plants (such as ferns and mosses). Thus, the new organism is always produced out of the union of differing and unequal individuals, considering each independent cell, and thus the microgamete and the macrogamete, may be considered as separate individuals, as we are fully justified in doing.

Activity and Passivity

There is a fairly extensive literature on the philosophy of nature, speculative in character, in which attempts have been made to show that the image of the essential difference between man and

---

[2a] "Idea" is used here, and throughout the chapter, in the technical sense of the term as defined by the phenomenologists (Husserl, Max Scheler, Merleau-Ponty etc.), *i.e., eidos,* "essence," the concrete meaning of a thing (Tr.).

woman is already present in the microgamete and the macrogamete, or at least to show that this difference is already prefigured in the gametes. This line of thought goes as far back as Aristotle, who held that the contrast between the sexes was the contrast between activity and passivity. The receptive macrogamete with its large supply of protoplasm is taken to be identical in principle with female nature, whereas "that which engenders the new in others," as Aristotle says, is male nature, and thus seems to be represented already in the microgamete or spermatozoon which penetrates and fertilizes the ovum or egg-cell. There is a question which may seem unimportant, but which must be asked here. The phenomenological method likes to take a lead from the intuitive usages of language, and so we ask why it is that even in the botanical order the microgamete is called the male sex cell and the macrogamete the female sex cell? We might be inclined to think that the influence of Aristotelian natural philosophy is behind this, or that it reflects a very simple application of our experience with higher organisms in which we have found that female individuals produce the macrogamete and male individuals produce the microgamete.

Yet it is equally possible that the speculative philosophy of nature is right to the extent that there is a direct phenomenological relationship between the motile, "aggressive" microgamete and man as he is pheno-typically known to us, and that there is the same relationship between the "passively awaiting," bulky macrogamete at rest in its enclosure and woman as she manifests herself to us. In practically all organisms, reproduction takes place through the fertilizing of a macrogamete by a microgamete, but this fact does not yet provide any explanation of the sexual differentiation of the individuals producing the ova or spermatozoa. Would it all not be equally possible if all plants and animals occurred in only one sex? In her book, Simone de Beauvoir even says that it would be quite imaginable to have only one sort of human being, and thus no men or women but only hermaphrodites. There are in fact types of animals that are hermaphrodite, and in plants the microgametes and macrogametes are more often than not present in the same individual.

It is only in the context of the closed forms of animal organisms that we can understand that sex cells have to be developed in particular organs apart from other body-cells. In some higher forms of plant life there are sex organs analogous to these, but the differentiation of the tissues does not always exclude the possibility of other parts of the plant developing into a complete new individual in favorable conditions (the leaf of a begonia planted in the soil produces a new plant). An animal, however, is a closed form and it is not constructed in such a way that each part sums up the whole; each part of the animal—as an integral aspect of the total stature—has a proper function to perform. It is therefore understandable, in terms of the idea of the animal mode of being, that in an animal the reproductive cells will be different from those that have their specific function within the organism. But even though this is the case, the sexual differentiation of animals remains wholly obscure.

Amphimixis and Rejuvenation

Two attempts have been made to find a teleological explanation for sexual differentiation. These have produced the theory of amphimixis and the theory of rejuvenation.

The notion of amphimixis traces back to the work of the biologist Weismann (a late contemporary of Darwin). Among other achievements, he deserves credit for having clarified the principle of the continuity of the germ plasm. The fertilized ovum forms the animal body by a series of cellular fissions, and at the same time it forms new cells of germ plasm. The young organism carries these within itself until it reaches maturity and forms new organisms in its turn. The organisms die, but the germ plasm continues through one generation after another. The continuity of life, so Weismann taught, is nothing else than an uninterrupted series of germ cells, while the individuals that are formed from these merely fulfill the function of securing the continuity of the germ plasm.

But it is possible to fulfill this function only if the organisms vary quite strongly among themselves, their variety enabling a number of them to survive in spite of changes in their environment. And it is the intermingling or amphimixis of two sex cells that establishes the possibility of variation, and even gives rise to the possibility of new species developing. This is Weismann's train of thought, and it certainly expresses a principle correctly, but, like most teleological explanations in biology, it is clear that it proceeds simply on the basis of the given fact.

What assurance have we that variants can arise in no other way than by amphimixis? The discovery of mutants, which are so much more important than variants, has shown us that it is indeed possible for entirely new types to appear as a result of a spontaneous change in the germ plasm or gene. Amphimixis is an efficient means toward the production of variants and toward the adaptation of a species to changing circumstances, when the division of the sexes already exists. But amphimixis does not provide any explanation of this division itself.

The second teleological theory proposed by biology is that of rejuvenation. Woodruff undertook a program of research on which this theory is based. He experimented with one of the unicellular infusorians, the slipper-shaped paramecium, that could multiply itself quickly (several times a day) by fission. When these animalcules are bred from a single specimen in a drop of water, it is possible to isolate the individuals after each division. Thus, in the space of seven years, Woodruff followed twenty thousand generations in isolation without permitting any commingling of cells or "copulation." For these unicellular organisms too, left in their natural condition, display a kind of copulation after a number of cellular divisions. This is called endomixis, because, among other effects, there is in fact a fusion of nucleic substance when these outwardly identical cells coalesce. Woodruff established that when endomixis is prevented over a long period, the cells degenerate. Thus he came to take the view that the process of fertilization is the actual cause of the rejuvenation and of the continuity of life. This is a fact related to the real requirements for the existence of these protozoa. But it throws no light on the fact of sexual differentiation; it merely establishes that, given a certain differentiation, endomixis has a certain rejuvenating effect on these unicellular protozoans.

We may therefore conclude that no empirical explanation has been found for the division of the sexes. We know neither the cause of the division nor its ultimate purpose. For this reason we called the division of the sexes a biological *mystery*.

We have to ask once again, then, whether it is likely that we will be able to understand sexual differentiation phenomenologically, proceeding from the *idea* of living being.

Sexual Differentiation

We have noted that, proceeding from the idea of reproduction as such, no insight is to be gained into the division of the sexes. Neither is it possible to understand the division in terms of the idea of living being itself. Hegel did attempt to do so in a speculative way. In his *Philosophy of Nature* (III) we find this thought: Through sexuality the subject in itself reaches an existence as a species. In the sexual union, the individual finds his proper fulfillment in another individual. Sexual differentiation must therefore be understood as a condition for a possible copulation.

This is clearly established and demonstrated, but it is certainly not a clear insight gained through phenomenological investigation of the idea of life as self-sufficient and expansive being. Let us turn once again to the facts.[3] There are hermaphroditic types of animals, but animals are mostly of either one or the other sex. An actual biological investigation reveals the following:

1. All ova would be capable of developing into a male or a female specimen or an hermaphrodite. (In general, sex is determined by a particular chromosome, a particular factor present in the microgamete).

2. In every order of animals—and so in every extensive class of animals—the hermaphrodites belong to the lower species (for example, flatworms, and the lower kinds of gastropoda; some snails and molluscs).

3. The individuals of all the higher classes of animals are divided into two sexes. This is true of the higher species of worms as well as of molluscs and of the vertebrates classified as chordates.

4. Although all higher animals appear in two distinct sexes, hermaphrodites do occur as very rare exceptions, and there are occasional examples of a change of sex in such a way that an animal which was male before maturity later becomes female.

However, the impression one gains from an over-all view of the whole animal world leads to one conclusion: *sexual differentiation and the higher stages of development belong together*. Thus, sexual differentiation is not something that must be present in the lower orders of nature either necessarily or to further the purposes of lower nature, but it is indeed *suggested* in the lower orders of

[3] Taking our lead from Portmann, *Die Tiergestalt*, Basel 1948.

nature as a fact that becomes clear and a pronounced reality only in organisms of a higher order. We find the same with regard to many other phenomena as well.[4]

Now, in what does the difference between the sexes consist? Sometimes the difference is confined to the sexual organs alone, and sometimes there is a great difference between adult organisms of one sex and those of the other. There are lower animals, such as a particular species of marine worm, the male of which lives as a parasite in the female. There are examples of deep-sea fish, the male of which lives in symbiosis with the female, losing his individuality entirely, his blood-vessels becoming integrated into the circulatory system of the female, and so becoming nothing more than a breeding gland vegetating on the female and carried by her. It is important to note these facts, in order to avoid the mistake of taking schematically for granted that human relationships are already prescribed in nature. It is a mistake we do tend to make: how ready we are, for instance, to point to the care little birds take of their eggs, and hold it up as an example to women that they should care for their little ones in the same way.[5] But there are many sides to nature, and no-one likes to uphold the total independence of some male animals with regard to the females of their kind as an example to be followed in the human relationship of the sexes.

In the animal world, there are other extreme differences between the sexes, besides the ones mentioned. There are sometimes enormous differences, for example in some insect species. The male of the stag-beetle, a fairly well-known example, possesses large antlers. Tropical species of the same class of insect also have excessively large appendages (horns) which certainly do not serve any purpose. On the other hand we sometimes find such a great similarity between male and female vertebrates, even among mammals, that it is difficult to recognize which is which. A famous case is

[4] The point is dealt with at greater length in *Rangorde der organismen in de biologie;* Tijdschrift voor Philosophie, Vol. 3, No. 1, 1941; and in *De schaduwen van het kennen,* Tijdschrift voor Philosophie, Vol. 1, No. 1, Feb. 1939.

[5] Oswald Schwartz perceptively remarks: "This comparing or contrasting of men with animals is the wrong way to find out what is 'natural' for men and recourse to the *Origin of the Species* does not lead to the discovery of the Origin of Morals." (*Psychology of Sex,* Pelican Books A 194, p. 30).

that of the hyena. It had already become legendary in olden times, and was thought to be hermaphrodite because its sex could not be determined. The female hyena has an appendage that looks exactly like the male scrotum. These variations indicate that, where the differentiation of the sexes is a *given fact,* there are all sorts of peculiarities that may well be significant for a particular species but that certainly have nothing to do with relationships among human beings. The variations that occur in nature may be explained partly by the effect of hormones on the external and other characteristics of the individual.

The influence of hormones on the constitution is one of the important facts that physiological and clinical research has brought to light. We all know that the constitution of male and female human beings is also dependent to a very large extent on these internal secretions, not only during the years of the body's growth but also throughout the individual's later life.

If we look into the influence of hormones on sexual differentiation in animals, it becomes clear that there is a very great deal of variation. Neither is it easy to gain any general insight into the matter which would be helpful toward a better understanding of human nature. Let us mention a few facts.

If a cockerel is caponized, the result is a bird with a number of feminine characteristics. But the spayed hen develops an identical constitutional image. There is very little difference between the capon and the de-sexed hen. We may be inclined to conclude from this that the female hormones alone are responsible for the feather development typical of the hen. On the other hand it is clear that the male hormone in these birds exercises a strong influence on behavior, aggressivity, and on the production of sounds, such as crowing. But in the same zoological class, the effect of castration on species such as sparrows and starlings is entirely different. It seems to have little influence on their outward appearance. Their feather development is thus determined much more by heredity, that is, by the presence of the chromosomes that determine sex in the fertilized cell. Development is even independent of the influence of hormones at a later stage. In some birds, some characteristics are clearly hereditary and others are determined by hormones; for example, the color of the beak may be hereditary and the feather-pattern the result of hormone activity.

Hormones

Data that vary to such a degree provide little prospect of being able to understand human phenomena on the basis of biological facts. But we do know that the influence of hormones on pubescence among the higher mammals and man is exceptionally strong. We know too that young male castrates, whether higher mammals or human, undergo a clear femininization, their external appearance and behavior becoming effeminate; but, on the other hand, spayed females do not take on a masculine appearance but show an arrested development, retaining youthful or immature external characteristics and behavior.

It is also generally known that hormones have a strong influence on the development of the secondary sexual characteristics in women and in female mammals, and that the sexual behavior, expecially of the lower mammals, is dependent on hormone activity to a very large extent, although in man sexual behavior is very much less influenced by hormone secretion. There is a fairly wide experience of castration in many countries, and it shows that sexual behavior is not always affected in the same way by castration.

This fact reminds us once more that, when we are speaking of sexual differentiation in human beings, we must not lose sight of the reality: man meaningfully accepts or rejects his physical constitution as an experienced situation, and man always projects his physical constitution as an integral part of his existence in the world, for it is always a physical existence. If a human being is castrated, his bodily reality is indeed changed, but what meaning will he give this changed reality in relation to his grasp on the world and as a means toward relationship with other people? This always remains on open question. There is also much uncertainty, therefore, with regard to the actual influence of hormones on homosexual or heterosexual development.

We possess some data on the hormone composition of the blood in children between the ages of 3 and 10, and these data have an important bearing on our problem. Both male and female hormones are found in each sex, although in different proportions. The quantity of male hormones (androgens) occurring in boys is about double that found in girls. Yet the quantity of female hormones (estrogens) occurring in girls is 40 to 50 times as much as that found in boys. The fact that both male and female hormones play a part in the development of the human constitution, whether male or female, is confirmation of the already ancient idea that both male and female characteristics are physically and therefore psychologically present in every man and woman, even though the proportion of male to female hormones is variable and is very clearly different in the two sexes. More research is needed to discover the influence of hormones on the physical build and on the temperament of men and women. There is also the question of whether and to what extent the projected existence is able to influence the internal secretion of hormones. Whatever the case, the human being is not merely an animal, and the biological study of animal life provides no certainty concerning the influence of hormones on the sexual differentiation of man and woman.

Being interested in animal biology, it is obvious that we will be concerned above all with mammals. Mammals are not only the highest order of animals, but they are distinguished from all other animal orders in that the female organism is involved in the production and care of the next generation to a much greater extent than in any other animal order.

Concerning mammals, if we begin by considering once more the anatomical facts, we see clearly—as Portmann explains—that the more ancient forms, the prehistoric forms discovered by paleontologists, manifest a greater similarity between male and female. We see this similarity disappearing in the mammals found in later, historical times, and for a number of reasons we refer to these later species as higher forms. A differentiation evolves, in which the *males* show peculiar characteristics, often in the shape of a marked development of a part of the jaw or the development of antlers or horns—thus, of bony attachments to the head—and sometimes, finally, in the shape of differences in the outward aspect of the anal region of the body.

First we will look at the development of eye-teeth and incisors. We have clear examples of a sexual characteristic of the male animal in the powerful development of the elephant's incisors into tusks, in that of the eye-teeth of the wild boar, and in similar developments of large teeth in several kinds of prehistoric ungulates. It is pretty certain that canine teeth were primarily weapons in the struggle against rivals, and thus they are basically an expression of the characteristic *aggressivity* of the male mammal. But here again, as so often in nature, we see that the requirements of efficiency have been grossly exceeded. And so the science of zoology can point out that these fangs take on a *demonstrative* function rather than that of a weapon, as in the wild boar of Celebes whose canines curve so far back that they are completely useless in a fight and even prove a hindrance to the boar. We see that the canine tooth has become the *sign* of maleness as such, and this simple fact is of the greatest importance in our effort to understand the connection between the physical build of an organism and its manner of existence.

Physical build is clearly not only functional. It is also involved in the form of existence, as expressive of this form, and the aggressive, expansive mode of the male mammal's existence is manifested demonstratively in many ways in the shape of his body. Mammals which lack fangs or tusks as a sexual characteristic of the male, have very often developed horns. Occasionally we find animals with both horns and tusks; the yak-deer has large eye-teeth and small antlers as well. Two demonstrative "styles" are found in this one animal.

In general, the more recent and more highly developed forms of animals are characterized by the development of the frontal organs, the sign of masculinity being antlers or horns. Lower forms on the other hand are characterized by development of the teeth. As Portmann remarks, when we speak of higher and lower forms in this context, we are actually referring exclusively to greater or lesser development of the brain.

As we follow the phylogenetic order—the consecutive arrangement of species according to development—we notice that among the ungulates the eye-teeth gradually get smaller and even disappear while horns or antlers develop more and more strongly. These male sex characteristics, carried in front and at the top of the head, are actually still more demonstrative than tusks placed lower down in the skull, and so we find too that there is more emphasis on the development of horns or antlers in animals whose sense of sight takes primacy over their sense of smell, while it is precisely in those animals whose sense of smell is stronger that we find tusks and canine teeth highly developed. Now, in the matter of brain-development and behavior, the animals that depend on the sense of sight more than on the sense of smell are certainly superior to those who depend more on the sense of smell.

The facts concerning the sexual differentiation of mammals are not yet exhausted, however. There are two important rules that still must be noted. The first is that a characteristic formerly belonging exclusively to male individuals, for instance, horns or antlers, appears also on *female* individuals at a later stage of evolution. One has only to think of many types of antelope, of gazelles, goats, chamois, ordinary cows, and some types of deer, of which both male and female animals have horns or antlers. Here we see that as development progresses, the original difference between male and female is levelled down by the female individuals taking on the same characteristics as the males.

The second rule is this. A characteristic that at first was determined by hormone activity and that therefore would not be manifested by a male castrated early in life (such as horn or antler growth), will be determined by *heredity* in a higher and later development of the form, and will therefore be independent of the composition of the hormone-content of the organism. There is a farm-yard illustration of this rule, familiar to everyone; the ox, a castrated bull, not only has horns like a bull, but its horns more often than not are bigger than those of a bull. The striking fact is this: the higher we ascend through the stages of development, that is to say, the higher we follow the cephalization index (index of head and brain development), the more we find the sexes becoming alike and the more we find the female animal taking on a shape typically the same as that of the male—a shape that in its appearance manifests a whole existence actively directed toward the external environment, overcoming opposition, maintaining itself and struggling for its preservation.

Besides tusks, horns and antlers, I mentioned a third biological fact: the development of the anal region in the higher mammals. This too is mainly demonstrative in character and, as Portmann says, the most striking phenomenon in this regard is the development of the external sexual parts of the male animal. These external sexual parts consist of the male member and the scrotum. Quite remarkably, the scrotum is found only in the higher mammals. It is simply not possible to explain this in terms of purpose. The descent of the male sex glands (testes) from the abdominal cavity to the scrotum is a process that takes place in every individual mammal male, including the human boy-child. It is not possible to imagine that this process could have any selective value in the struggle for survival. From Darwin's standpoint, therefore, the descent of the testicles is a fact that simply cannot be explained. We do know that sperm is formed at temperature slightly lower than normal body temperature, but this is a consequence and not a cause of the testes being in the scrotum. Once the external siting of the scrotum with the male sex glands inside it is given, it is clear that the germ cells will have to develop in the cooler temperature of this site.

Now paleontology and zoology show that in those forms of prehistoric animal life which still survive, the male sex glands are situated internally. There are a number of examples of this; we see it for instance in the very interesting primitive forms found in South America, the insect-eaters and toothless species. We see it also in paleontologically ancient forms, such as the elephant. The absence of a scrotum in the whale could be explained in terms of the whale's habitat and its swimming, circumstances which provide a real purpose for the body to have a perfectly streamlined shape. The remarkable fact is that in all these primitive forms an internal descent of the testes does take place. Thus, the same sort of process is found in these forms as well, but it is not continued in them as far as it is in the higher mammal forms.

Demonstrative Characteristics

Portmann drew up a comparison of the various kinds of mammals, and it demonstrates convincingly that the most highly developed forms, which are also those in which the strongest sense is the sense of sight, are those in which the scrotum is developed to the greatest extent. We can see this in the predators, in the cloven-hooved ungulates and in the apes. Along with this, a number of visible, ornamental male characteristics are developed in the posterior region. These may take the form of a special conformation of the fur round about the anus, mostly a lighter color than the fur on the rest of the body, and sometimes too the tail has a particularly lively color or, as in some apes, the hide of the buttocks is very brightly colored. The conclusion which Portmann therefore draws is that the scrotum is a semantic characteristic, that is, a characteristic in the nature of a sign, and thus a *demonstrative* characteristic serving to distinguish the male from the female in an obvious and striking way among those animals that depend most on the sense of sight. The development of the scrotum is very often coupled with semantic-ornamental conformations on the head, such as antlers, horns, and manes. In the same species there is a parallel development of the frontal organs of the brain and of the power of optical perception.

Naturally it would be highly contentious to claim a connection between these phenomena and various aspects of human culture, but even so, we cannot fail to notice that the external male sex organs play a particularly demonstrative role in social relationships within primitive tribes, and that they do so because their visibility is accentuated beyond the biological level in an artificial way.

Let us sum up the actual data on the physical difference between males and females among mammals. We have noted that male characteristics arise which do not serve any purpose in the struggle of the individual or of the species for survival, but which possess a strongly demonstrative quality. Further, we have noted that as the upward development proceeds, the same characteristics appear in the female organism—as far as possible, and thus naturally excluding those characteristics based on the primary sex organs of the male. Now it is generally known that the demonstrative physical characteristics of the males of very many species are accompanied by other demonstrative expressions as well. For example, among birds we find song, erectile and highly developed tufts of head feathers, or the display of brightly colored tails as with the peacock and pheasant. Among fish and salamanders we find intense coloring, usually red and yellow, and patterns of energetic movement at mating time. In various mammal species we find things like the expressive agitation of the mane, and so on. It is a general rule that the more highly an animal is developed, the greater the differentiation and variety of the expressive characteristics will be.

If we look at it in terms of the male mode of existence in the animal world, it is understandable that these demonstrative characteristics in the male animal are of the type described. Among mammals and birds too, it is precisely the male whose activity is directed more toward the outward environment, and who is more aggressive and more inclined to take possession of his world. This attitude toward the environment and toward other animals is manifested by the male in all his expressive behavior. His physical build develops in accordance with this expressive character of his behavior. Attempts have been made more than once to use this coincidence of phenomena as the basis of an explanation of the demonstrative expressions that accentuate the differences between the sexes in human beings. It has been noted that in the more primitive tribes, it is almost exclusively the men who display an exorbitance of demonstrative expression, manifested partly by their dress, partly by pomp, partly by tatooing or other ornamentation. It has been noted that in the more advanced cultures the demonstrative characteristics are wholly taken over by the women and more and more reduced among the men, until the men in our time have become very dull birds in comparison with the ladies in their bird-of-paradise adornment. Naturally it is open to question, whether we can admit this kind of biological comparison, and above all whether the manner in which the sexes manifest themselves in our culture does in fact reveal the highest development of expression.

It is not such a very long time ago that the position even in cultured Europe was not as it is now. But it is indeed remarkable that in the unconsciousness of living nature, the "demonstrative values of being" (as I named them in a previous work),[6] or the "exhibiting values" as Portmann calls them, are found exclusively in the male individuals of the lower forms of animal, whereas in the higher forms they occur in both sexes. Man is conscious of the demonstrative significance of his physical appearance. During the middle ages, the most flourishing period of our European culture, and in the aesthetic culture of the Renaissance and even through the 17th and 18th centuries, both men and women shared the demonstrative values of dress and ornamentation without restraint. But at the same time a higher degree of civilization demands a proportionally more inward realization of the values of human existence. This above all is the reason why no comparison with purely biological reality is possible.

[6] *Anschauliche Kennzeichen des Organischen.* Philos. Anzeiger II (1927-1928), p. 391.

We will now examine one last group of phenomena in the animal world, concerning the relationship of the sexes from a sexual point of view.

Individual Existence a "Background"

As we have already seen, we do find an occasional uniting of cells among the unicellular organisms, but this can hardly be called a mating, for there is no clear difference between one cell and the other, and it is not possible to speak of them as male or female individuals. As a rule, lower organisms are fertilized from without. In whatever way this might take place, one thing is clear: in all species at the bottom of the scale of animal life, the existence of the individual is so very much a background affair in relation to the survival of the species, that numerous cases can be pointed out in which either the female or the male or even both, with regard to their physical build and behavior, are not much more than producers of the next generation. Along with this their independent being-in-the-world is markedly reduced.

We have already remarked that, in general, the female animal is more valuable in nature than the male. We can find famous illustrations of this among the lower forms of animal life (notably in many insect species). The best known is the destiny of the drone in the beehive—tragic, from a human point of view. Another very familiar fact is that in the nests of ants and termites the queen (a tremendously swollen egg-sac with a tiny little head in front) is the focal point of the whole colony and is cared for as such. Also, everyone knows the story of the kind of lady spider who eats up the male with which she mates, and of the no less dramatic existence of the praying mantis (mantis religiosa) of southern France and northern Africa—among these, it is the female and not the male that lives with a genuine "grasp on the world." The male creeps up shyly, is mated with, and eaten. Naturally, these are examples which show only how important the female organism is for the survival of the species. The female usually lives longer than the male, but only in order to produce eggs. In most cases the male has more autonomy and is more directed toward the outside world. In some species of butterfly, the female has no wings, and even no mouth, while the males have wings of colors even if they are very short-lived.

Simone de Beauvoir also mentions these facts in her book, and adds, in this connection: "The life of the male is gratuitous and useless," and "The species which holds the females in slavery punishes the male that pretends to escape it; it suppresses him brutally." [7] This may well be quite correct. Nevertheless, even in many of the lower animal forms, nature usually shows the male as displaying a luxury that is certainly "gratuitous" but that the female in most cases does not possess, although the male, whatever the length of his life, is relatively unimportant to the species. However, this gratuitous luxury represents a demonstrative value of being, and this is one of the ways in which living nature differs from a merely efficient machine.

As far as care for the young is concerned, we do not find the female organism taking any care of offspring in lower nature, although there are some exceptions to this rule. In some cases it is the male organism that looks after the young. Perhaps the most picturesque example of this is a certain type of frog (alytes obstetricans), the male of the species having little hollows in the hide of his back in which the young are carried while they are still developing. Here it is the male animal that looks after the offspring. Among the birds, the males help to build the nests and share the work of feeding the unfledged chicks and sometimes take turns in incubating the eggs.

But the dependent status of the female in the matter of reproduction is most marked in the order of mammals. Among the mammals, the dependence of the female contrasts most strongly with the "freedom" of the male. The life of the female is almost wholly absorbed in caring for the offspring. Mating is something the female has to undergo more or less passively. Outside of the sphere of reproduction, the female animal is the male's equal in hunting, fighting and in speed of movement, but once she had conceived—and her destination is to conceive—the female animal appears to become of a piece with nature in which all kinds of events take place and which is subjected to their happening. We may say, then, that the sexual life is something that the female undergoes.

[7] *Le Deuxième Sexe,* I, p. 54. (Eng. Tr. Knopf, N. Y. 1953, p. 19)

The independence of existence which is characteristic of the animal as an individual is suspended by the process of mating and reproduction. However much the male mammal too may be confined within his nature, he stands in contrast to the female in that his sexual life is part of his activity. That is to say, the male's sexual life is *mediate*—as all activity through the means of an animated body—and realized as an action and reaction. In the male mammal there is already a certain distance between desire and satisfaction, as there is in every initiative. The male seeks and pursues the female, he sniffs her and touches her, immobilizes, seizes and possesses her. Thus Hegel said that the subjective element, meaning being as a self, was a pronounced manifestation in the male, while the female appeared much more as the representation of the species. The species dominates the female mammal and absorbs a large part of her individual existence as a subject. We cannot fail to see that the animal world does show this to us, and that it shows it precisely in its highest forms, the mammals.

These facts also throw some light on the demonstrative characteristics of animals. They help us to understand why the male sex, which in actual fact has more initiative and a greater grasp on the world, and thus lives more expansively, seems to go beyond its own limits in all its activity, and why this sex also *demonstrates* a "grasp" on the world in its physical appearance, in its expressive motion and vocal expression, and even in the vigor of all its movements and in the aggressiveness of its actions.

We have gone into the facts relating to the development of sexual differentiation in organisms of higher and lower orders at some length, in order to discover to what extent the biological basis of feminine nature is able to help us to understand this nature.

If one looks on man as the highest animal species—and this seems to be admissible "in a certain sense"—it is only to be expected that one will compare woman with a female animal, and by preference with a female mammal. Now it is perfectly obvious that woman bears and feeds her children as the higher animals do, but we have seen that even the mammal female animal is something more than a mere "reproductive apparatus" at the service of the species—an ovary with some overgrowth, as some have even called woman. Virchow says, *"Propter solum ovarium mulier est, quod est"*—for the sake of the ovaries alone a woman is what she is—although he probably borrowed the expression from some ancient author. As we have seen, living nature teaches us two basic facts; in the first place, sexual differentiation is most pronounced in the higher animals, but we cannot discover any fact causing it or say why there should be sexual differentiation, and in the second place, the essential quality of expansiveness inherent in the idea of living being is demonstratively manifested primarily by the male animal, in his physical build and behavior. In the highest stages of development, these semantic characteristics are hereditary in the female as well as in the male, although they continue to be *predominant* in the male, partly owing to the influence of hormones.

Credit is due to the outstanding research and theoretical investigation done by Portmann for the most important result of this enquiry: confirmation by the facts of the idea that life does not find the fulfillment of its meaning in the efficiency of form and function. Living organisms are not machines. Purposive efficiency in nature is merely a necessary condition for the overabundant values of demonstrative being which constitute the proper meaning of living nature, which is "transcendence in appearance."

Females of the higher animal species too have these "exhibiting values" in their characteristics; they are subjects with initiative, just as much as the males, at least to the extent that they are not passively subject to the process of reproduction. Nor is this the whole picture: *precautionary* care, which is implicit in the idea of reproduction, is displayed by the mammal female beyond the requirements of the unconscious efficiency of lower nature and manifested in her *active care and protection* of the offspring.

If one sees the image or the foreshadowing of humanity phenomenologically already present in animal life, then the biological basis of woman's nature does in fact reveal something of her meaning. But we can understand this revelation properly only if we take into account the essential difference between man and animal just as much as we take into account the connection between human and animal life. Doing this, we can learn from biology that woman is able to direct herself to the world as freely as man, and that none of her physical characteristics, not even her "aptitude" for bearing and feeding children, inevitably determine her lot in any way. All human beings, men as well as women, *must* always grasp their physical characteristics meaningfully as a part of their existential situation and thus accept them or not as the case may be.

2. The Physical Characteristics

> In a general way it is her sex itself, and all that follows
> necessarily upon it, that subordinates woman through the
> situation—I will not call it the inferior situation, for there
> is nothing of moral inferiority in it, and in some respects
> it is a situation of superiority—but, through the disad-
> vantageous and dependent situation in which it places her.
>
> HENRI MARION [8]

After having looked at the differences between the sexes in the
animal world, the better to understand the biological basis of
woman's nature, we now want to turn to woman's particular mode
of physical appearance, and once again we will turn first of all to
the relevant facts. This is by no means an easy task, because in the
nature of the case all our cultural values and cultural evaluations
give a particular bent to the view we take of another human being,
evoking associations of meaning that cause our view to go beyond
what is pure fact in the appearance of the other.

When one speaks of woman *"as such,"* one is usually thinking
above all of the pheno-typical image of adult American or European women (the image of the women we know as they manifest
themselves to us), and actually one is usually thinking of the
women of a particular social group within one's own cultural
sphere—as it may be, those of the so-called intellectual and more
well-to-do group. It is clear that we will have to bear in mind the
particular bent of our own view.

We have two aims in considering the physical characteristics of
woman. In the first place we want to discover in her stature those
qualities which characterize her and to see how these are related to
a woman's mode of existence in her social relationships. Whether
we have here to do with an original and inborn sexual differentiation or with a differentiation that has developed on the basis of an
hereditary aptitude in the course of cultural history, is of course a
question inherent in the realities we aim to consider, but we will
not be going into it.

[8] *Psychologie de la femme,* Paris (A. Colin) 1925, p. 50.

The second aim in our consideration of woman's physical reality will be to discover what is "genuinely" feminine in the image of her bodily being, setting aside the question of whether this "genuinely feminine" is not perhaps mere appearance. There is more than a mere theoretical value in the discovery of what is phenomenologically genuine femininity in the observable appearance of woman as we know it from day to day. For value-judgments and norms play a leading role, for instance in education and in very many social questions, and it is clear that we can understand these judgments and norms only with the help of that kind of discovery and phenomenological appreciation of essential femininity.

Of the questions we could ask about the pheno-typical image of woman's body, the most obvious is this: to what extent is this image the result of selective breeding, of sexually selective breeding? Above, in our consideration of the biological basis of woman's nature, we pointed out that Darwin thought that all secondary sexual characteristics existed for an efficient purpose and were therefore the result of selective sexual breeding. We could not accept this view because of the insights gained by modern advances in zoology, but nevertheless it is clear that a genuine sexual selective breeding is a possibility among human beings, because in fact the choice of a marriage partner is to some extent dependent on normative views that are cultural in origin.

A choice of this kind exists, however, only when an individual has the real opportunity of selecting one partner from among many possible partners, and this opportunity is actually realized only in a particular group of some standing. Among primitive peoples there will of course be some few cases of extreme deviation from the appreciated norm, and these will be barred from taking any part in the reproductive process, but this certainly does not amount to a practice of selective breeding. In the upper social levels, "selective breeding" is known, taking the form of a choice of marriage partners, and following the example of the appreciation and judgment of the upper levels, it is known to some extent in the lower levels too, for in every society the lower levels aspire toward the higher. Literature provides us with an incident which is interesting in this connection. Jenner, the inventor of cow-pox vaccine and vaccination, as a country doctor noticed that the nobility of his time often married smooth-cheeked farmers' daughters in preference to the pock-marked heiresses of their own class. This moved him to look into things more closely, and he discovered to his astonishment that farm-girls were hardly ever infected by outbreaks of small-pox, at least, certainly not as often as others. But from the point of view of our problem, the interesting thing that comes out so clearly in his story is the extent to which a particular social class could possess a schematized image of the "ideal" woman.

Women of course are equally inclined to possess a schematized image of man. Now these schematic images do play a role in the choice of a marriage partner, and because of this they will have a notable influence on the typological appearance of the sexes in the course of a number of generations. The significance of these schemata in the cultural life of a group is a very important factor in the development of the physical and psychological characteristics of a nation. With regard to woman, the accepted schemata have undergone many variations and changes. There was a time when an hour-glass figure and a wasp-waist were very much sought after, and there was a time when luxuriant bosoms were the appreciated thing—these things strike us as much less strange than the misshapen feet the Chinese used to appreciate in their women. The same can be said of the image of "genuine" manliness. With regard to at least one group, for instance, the German nobility liked to cultivate the "eagle eye," though the desire was not confined to the nobility.

In all of this, the question is to what extent the schemata that are appreciated are *hereditary*. It is quite clear that the constricted Chinese foot was just as little an hereditary characteristic as the wasp waist, but it is probable that the tendency to run to fat and the development of large breasts are based on hereditary character-istics, at least to some extent. This is indicated by a phenomenon found in only one primitive people. Among the Southern African Bushmen and the related Hottentots we find a characteristic known as steatopygia. This is the name given to the fact that the normal outward and backward curve of the buttocks, present in every human being and a little more pronounced in women, is very highly exaggerated in the women of these tribes and accompanied by a gross accumulation of fatty tissue on the buttocks. As far as can be established, this is very probably a "cultivated" product. It does indicate an actual possibility that the image we call the pheno-typical image of woman's appearance has, at least to some extent, been developed in the course of human history, and that it is thus not based on a "natural" difference between man and woman.

The finer details of the form and features of the human body are *always* manifestations of a culture. In general it is simply not possible to determine the characteristics in which the primordial reality of "race" consists, or the nature of those that are "typical" of a given people. Nevertheless, this question is an important one for our problem. It would be making a mistake to imagine that we could discover *the* typical characteristics of femininity simply by analyzing the manner in which modern woman manifests herself. One glance at a primitive tribe is enough to convince us that the difference between the sexes in a different kind of society is a different kind of thing altogether. Stratz, well-known author of a number of popular books on the physical appearance of women, points out that mammae are the only secondary sexual characteristic that is constant, but among peoples known for having very little body and facial hair there are still unmistakable differences between the features of men and women—unmistakable at least for those peoples themselves—although the differences in the structure of the physiognomy are not the same as they are in America and Europe.

"Natural" Physical Characteristics

After these introductory remarks, we want to look into the matter of the physical characteristics of American and European woman, and see which of these must in fact be considered to be "natural" ones. We can sum them all up in the following four classes of phenomena:
1. all phenomena connected with reproduction;
2. the lighter development of the muscles and the stronger development of the fatty tissues;
3. the lability of the vegetative (sympathetic or autonomic) nervous system. (Here we should remark that there is still much dispute as to whether this lability is not the result of cultural influences);
4. life-expectancy and sensitivity to disease and all that is connected with these.

From each of these four aspects we can speak of woman's natural, physical characteristics, paying attention to her positive characteristics as well as to her shortcomings in comparison to man. At the same time, we can open a question. Is it not possible for a "natural" inferiority of development to be a cultural advantage, and conversely, for a natural superiority to be a cultural disadvantage? In any case—to repeat this once again—the factual structure of the physical reality is always given a personal value in a social situation, and consequently, physically weak can mean personally strong, and physically strong can mean personally weak.

We must certainly not regard the contrast between man and woman as a contrast between the active and the passive. The contrast between man and woman is much rather the contrast between relative unfreedoms: each person is to some extent physically subjected to an impersonal force. This "alien" force can be called the power of the "species," and it manifests itself in woman through her sexuality. This brings us to the *first* problem, the problem of woman's physical reality inasmuch as this is determined by the requirements of reproduction.

The contrast between more free and less free is meaningful only to the extent that the various human physical aptitudes are related to human existence. In his physical reality, man *represents* his attitude toward the world; in his body he *represents* his consciousness, his being awake to the possibility of taking action. He exists over against the world and finds in this differentiation of himself from the world the grounds on which he is able to transcend his own nature by means of the freedom of his action. We have already remarked that the characteristics we think of as typically human are equated in our consciousness with the typically masculine. We will discuss this at greater length when we come to speak of woman's physical appearance as having the character of an outward expression of her interiority, but for the moment we will confine ourselves to the actual facts of the characteristics of the female body.

We cannot fail to see that there are processes in a woman's body which do not have to stand in any relation to the existence she freely chooses as a human being in the world, and that can even conflict with this freely chosen existence. Simone de Beauvoir deserves credit for having pointed this out. Very early in the history of literature, we find the thought that woman is more essentially sexual than man, and that the species resides in woman's body, but no-one has understood more deeply than Simone de Beauvoir what this actually means. "Woman," she says, "the most female of all females, seems also to be the most vulnerable . . . she who lives out her destiny more dramatically than any other, and who is more profoundly distinct from her male than any other." This is entirely in keeping with what we find in romanticism, and following its lead, in the writings of philosophers and poets; the general impression is that woman's bodily reality saturates and determines the whole of her existence even to its smallest detail, and that it makes her existence deviate from the simple and clear position comprised in the idea of the male stature.

Man's sexual life is integrated into his existence over against the world and along with it. In the desire and in the act, man objectively overcomes the limits of his existence in the line of reproduction and the survival of the species. Overcoming his limits in this way is explicitly identified with the subjective choice of this transcendence. In this respect we may say that man *is* his body and that he *possesses* his body. Woman, says Simone de Beauvoir, *"est son corps, mais son corps est autre chose qu'elle même"*—woman is indeed her own body, but her own body is something other than she herself as a human being. Hence the problem to which the actual facts concerning the bodily reality of women give rise.

Earlier writers have expressed the position somewhat more crudely. We have already seen Virchow's well-known line: "Woman is an ovary with some overgrowth." The meaning of this is, woman is in fact nothing more than a female. Some say the same thing in slightly more polite terms, and speak of woman's being "destined" for motherhood. However, we must decisively reject all expressions of this kind as incorrect. Woman *is* a human being, and the facts of her bodily reality receive a meaning only *in* her human existence, and thus, only in her own mode of existence and through her own initiative, even if the meaning they receive may be a problematical one. There are some statistical data that suggest that women do give their bodily reality a problematical significance.

Gynecologists estimate that 85% of their patients have disturbances connected with their menstruation. It is also remarkable that the mortality rate between the ages of 14 and 18 is higher among girls than among boys, the proportion being 128 girls to 100 boys; between the ages of 18 and 22, the proportion is 105 to 100. Everyone knows that childbirth is a very dramatic event. Simone de Beauvoir says that women have *"des maladies dans le ventre,"* "illness in the belly"—there is an inimical element in their body. We can note, too, that the English refer to menstruation as "the curse." Possibly this reflects some connection between experience and a last vestige of an ancient mythology concerning the periodicity of woman's life as bound up with the cosmological event of the moon's twenty-eight day cycle. If there is any connection between woman's cycles and the moon's cycles, it certainly does not hold any significance for woman as a human being; it is "nature" grasping and pervading her existence as an individual.

As a human being, woman must in some way find and maintain an independent attitude of her own in the face of these natural facts, and she does this precisely through her humanity. As a rule, her attitude is a good deal less dramatic than Simone de Beauvoir supposes. Predominantly it is one of resignation, although it very seldom appears that this resignation is entirely free of a touch of annoyance.

Man does not find the sexual phenomena in himself alien to him, nor is he annoyed by them. He can give them a clearly-defined place in the pattern of his existence. It is quite true that a man can become the slave of his sexual appetites, but then he is equally able to become enslaved to any other appetite. Thus, in the existence of a man, the sexual phenomenon is not something that is *in principle* able to continue apart from the pattern of his existence. But in contrast to this, woman as a subject can be "more profoundly alienated" (from the objective events in her nature) than any female mammal, alienated from herself, and as a *human being* woman is "the one who most violently refuses to be alienated in this way."

This rejection of physiological events can take the form of the resignation with which very many women bear many small ailments. Menstruation however is not an illness, but this fact points up more clearly the problem that arises because of the nature of woman's body. Objectively the physiological event *can* have an important significance for a woman. This is obvious. For when a woman becomes a mother, the event in her body is meaningful, not as a series of acts freely chosen, but in terms of what is happening in her and to her as a result of her own possibly free decision.

One thing is certain. This subjection by nature which operates regularly in woman's body and which Simone de Beauvoir calls "dramatic", actually is "dramatic" only if a woman refuses to accept the cyclic subjection as the invariable and objective reason for a difference of sexes. As a human being, woman is never an unchangeable reality; she is not a thing with fixed properties or characteristics, but, just like man, she can be defined in her humanity, and thus psychologically defined, only in terms of the *possibilities* open to her and in terms of the existence she has chosen.

"Not a Thing . . . a Situation"

Thus we may take the words of Merleau-Ponty as a lead in the next stage of our discussion: "The body is not a thing, it is a situation." We ought to make this thought entirely our own, but this will be possible only if we thoroughly understand what is meant by a situation. Whenever we take up an attitude toward our own existence, we discover ourselves and surrounding reality in relation to ourselves. Thus we give a certain meaning to ourselves and to our surroundings. All that we discover in the act of discovering is made into a situation by the act of giving meaning to what we discover. For instance, if we find ourselves depressed, our depression will make being in a room full of people an oppressive situation. But our understanding of the concept must be much wider than it normally is in the every-day way. Our body too is a situation, because we give it a meaning, and because the meaning we give it is not always the same meaning. To some extent the meaning we give it depends on the basic design of our manner of existence.

There is a general meaning which a human being always gives to his body. The body is a medium, linking everyone to the world, and thus it is everyone's means toward a possible grasp on the world in relation to space and time and objects. Now among women this grasp is less firm and less decisive—and this brings us to the *second* of her objective characteristics: woman's less powerful muscular development.

The characteristic we dealt with first (the processes involved in reproduction which take place in woman's body) may be called a *gift* of nature involving a *task* to be taken up by woman as a human being. Exactly the same may be said of the comparative weakness of woman's muscular system, the characteristic we are considering now.

Weakness can be defined in a physical sense and in a physiological sense. But what does weakness *mean* for a human being? The answer to this question depends upon a person's culture. If an attack upon the "weaker sex" is taboo, the meaning that woman's weakness has for herself and for man is something else than it would be if the taboo did not exist. The particular meaning that weakness has in terms of the taboo (or in terms of its absence) affects not only the mutual social relationships of men and women, but also every detail of each individual's personal experience and self-awareness.

Small deviations in aptitudes can bring about far-reaching changes in the pattern of existence. A child born with a hunched back or a squint, or someone who has developed a defect of this kind very early in life, becomes a different kind of person than one of "normal" build. If someone blushes easily, his existence is quite different from that of a person who does not blush. Grünbaum, a psychologist whose work places him among the most brilliant thinkers, who was himself a very short and very fat man, once said, "If I had been 5 centimeters taller, I would have become quite another person." He was right; he was 5 centimeters too short. The comparative weakness of the little girl's muscular system in relation to that of the little boy has the same effect.

Man's constitution is determined to some extent by hormones, just as the constitution of animals is. By examining the changes in the hormones during growth or illness, or by experimenting with the effects of administering preparations containing hormones, it is possible to establish that male hormones give strong muscles and female hormones produce more fat. But the strength of a muscle is not a characteristic of the muscle alone; it depends above all on the distribution and supply of nerve stimulation to the muscle. The physiologist can calculate, for example, that the theoretical maximum pull of the biceps is 600 kilograms if a simultaneous innervation of all its tissues could be developed, though such a force would of course tear the muscle apart. In fact, the innervation of the muscle is such that this force never is developed. As innerva-

tion varies, the effective strength of one muscle can be quite different from the effective strength of another in which the muscular
development is identical. And everyone knows that under the
stress of extreme emotional upheaval, the muscles can deliver
more power than usual—sometimes astonishingly much more than
usual.

Thus the fact that the girl's muscles are weaker is based, not on
muscular development alone, but to a large extent on the innervation of her muscles, and thus on her way of moving. The feminine
pattern of movement may be intended to compensate for a consti-
tutionally lesser muscle strength, or, on the other hand, it may be a
constant demonstrative expression of a lower measure of strength.

Some have maintained that a girl's comparatively lesser strength
of muscle is shown clearly by the way she throws a stone. Everyone knows the difference between the way a boy throws a stone
and the way a girl does. There is a threefold principle behind the
boy's method: firstly, he builds up a tension to be released in the
throw as a bow is tensed and released to shoot the arrow; secondly
he flexes his reach as far as possible in the line of the throw before
throwing; and thirdly, the whole thing is done in a way calculated
to manifest most clearly his intention and his daring. Thus the boy
is not merely throwing a stone; through the demonstrative quality
of his movements he is displaying the "manliness" of his action.
One need only recall a little of one's own ordinary experience, and
one will realize how different the whole pattern of the act is when
it is done by a girl. There are two entirely different structures of
meaning in the two patterns of the same simple act. In this we
have a demonstration of the existential significance of weakness in
relation to strength.

As measured on a dynamometer, women certainly have weaker
muscles and lower muscular power on the average than men,
everywhere in the world—even according to tests in India where
the heaviest labor is customarily done by women. Naturally there
are important individual variations from the rule, and many a
woman is stronger than many a man. But a much more important
fact is this: a girl who happens to be stronger than a particular boy
is nevertheless still the representative of a group that is weaker,
that loses every race, that is always on the receiving end of pushes
and punches. She "belongs to" her own group, the girls. This

"belonging" shows that the concrete facts of the build of a person's body are constantly subordinated to the meaning that a human being, as an individual and as a social being, chooses to give them. The girl knows herself to be weaker than the average boy, and she represents this knowledge in her projection of herself in relation to all situations. *As a girl* she simply does not do what she would if the need arose to be able to do as an individual. She bears the *sign* of the weaker sex in the way that a person bears the sign of his social standing.

Now it is very interesting that of all muscles, those that show the greatest comparative weakness in women are the muscles of the arm. The greatest degree of comparative weakness is found not in the thigh, but in the arm, that is to say, precisely in those muscles that are constantly in play, in every action and in every gesture, in every greeting and handshake, in all the affairs of cultural life and in every kind of work known to man. It is precisely with respect to the muscles of the arm that woman is conspicuously the weaker in comparison with man.[9] Such is the fact, but the question that arises is this: how does woman herself face up to the fact, accepting or rejecting it? Is the fact not already compensated for in the way the child develops her existence in a manner typical of her group? In some or other book we can read, "Little girls are weaker, and *therefore* they stick their tongues out more often". There is perhaps a good deal of wisdom behind that "therefore"!

[9] The muscles of a woman's arms are naturally weaker than those of a man's arms, and the extent to which this quite literally means that woman has less of a grasp on the world may be seen most clearly in the fact that woman's motor-reflexes are insufficiently adapted to the demands made on a person's activity by a society designed by men for men—demands such as those that occur in the flow of traffic, in industry, etc. We need only to note how "clumsy" women are in trains, trolley cars, buses. The inward confusion they evidently experience in such circumstances, and that they manifest outwardly by their hesitancy, cannot be ascribed exclusively to their so-called emotionality. It appears that a startlingly large percentage of women are not quick and sure in movements requiring manual dexterity. Presenting a ticket in a train or a coin on a bus is a weighty task. Naturally the experience of this lack of adaptation and more particularly the experience of the cheerful sympathy with which most male officials regard it give rise to an "emotionality" which is much more deep-seated and so has a much greater effect than is often supposed. Fortunately a more open and active education is able to improve the control efficiency of movement to an important extent, and consequently we are able to see that the behavior of the younger generation of women is more on a par with that of men in this respect.

Vegetative Lability

We come now to the *third* of the four objectively determinable characteristics of the female body: its vegetative lability.

A little explanation might be in place here for the sake of those who have no medical training. All functions of the internal organs of the body come under the influence of the vegetative or autonomic nervous system without any noticeable connection with human existence. By this we mean that these functions take place unconsciously; they are not "for us," that is, not under our voluntary control, and thus we can exercise no influence over them. We are however able to observe them indirectly, and we simply undergo their effects, for example, the swelling of an organ. But by becoming aware in some way of the autonomic functions within the body and of their effects, it is possible to represent the bodily condition more or less clearly as a situation, and thus indirectly to control the autonomic functions.[9a] Hansen, in this connection, speaks of "ideogenetic reactions," and the term is well-chosen.

To a great extent the influence of the autonomic nervous system can be seen in the effects it produces on the skin. Changes in color, changes in temperature and perspiration are all outward manifestations of the vital functions of the autonomic nervous system. It also makes itself felt in changes in the frequency and intensity of the heartbeat and in the movement of the intestinal canal and in the secretion of gastric fluids.

Now, when we speak of a vegetative lability, we mean that all these influences do not remain constant within the small variations of organic function ordinarily accompanying life, but that their reaction to these variations is changeable and irregular. Thus a person who is vegetatively labile is one who colors quickly and easily becomes pale, whose pulse is caused to quicken or to slow down by very slight changes in situations and so, by mild emotional changes. Although such a person is quite unconscious of the actual processes inside his body which constitute the lability of his autonomic nervous system, he does notice the changes in the rate of his heartbeat and in his surface temperature, in the contraction

[9a] The autonomic nervous system and its functioning does not impose a given *meaning* on us; we impose a freely-chosen *human* meaning on them while they retain their *natural* autonomy (Tr).

and tension of his skin, and he experiences all these as the outward signs of emotions that seem to overwhelm him from within.

In this way, woman, who manifests a vegetative lability, knows that she can become quickly and disproportionately confused, deeply moved, "stirred up"—the term is graphic and significant—and she knows that these things happen to her *in* her bodily reality and thus *in* the way she manifests herself. This lability is most evident in the majority of women at the time of puberty; at this time especially, lability has an important bearing on the development of personal existence. Its bearing is very important, because puberty comes at a time when a young person is at the threshold of social life, and it is at this time that a young woman begins to have experience of herself as stigmatized in her flesh, vegetatively labile. This is how she sees herself, and this is how she is seen by others, and she knows she is seen in this way. This makes her even more uncertain, and her uncertainty in turn intensifies her lability.

This is the beginning of one of the many conditions of interaction between culture and nature. Every human being is caught up in these interactions, but women are caught up in them in a way peculiar to woman. She may try to withdraw from her lability by seeking support in and adopting the behavior and consciousness of a "group," but this makes her manifest herself as impersonal and "artificial" in her actions. She can choose simply to undergo being "like that," visibly stirred up and confused, on the one hand either accepting it and constituting herself as confused, disturbed and emotional for herself, or on the other hand merely being so in the view of others. This is what is called "genuinely" feminine. Of all the characteristics of woman mentioned in literature, it is precisely this emotionality that is most constantly presented as "genuinely" feminine. We will discuss this point at greater length, but for the moment note only the fact that vegetative lability causes woman to experience her bodily reality in every situation in a way that differs from man's way.

Many of woman's emotions relate less to external circumstances than they relate to factors in her own body, and this is why it is *easy* for them to appear "false" in woman's own self-awareness and to others as well. Emotionality is therefore not a factual characteristic, to be understood in the same way as we understand muscular weakness. With regard to emotionality, if we want to be able to know the dividing line between culture and nature, and between genuine and false, we will first have to undertake extensive investigations in various types of populations and in primitive civilizations.

For it is not impossible that vegetative lability is to some extent the result of education, or that it has been greatly intensified by education. We already know that it varies among women individually and that it also varies according to the social milieu, and we know that it can be lessened considerably by a well regulated physical education in youth.

Woman's Life Expectancy

Coming finally to the *fourth* point, we want to see what is known of woman's life expectancy and sensitivity to illness, as compared with man's.

There have been many who hold the opinion that woman's weakness is actually a myth, but one that woman finds pleasant and that she therefore perpetuates. Whatever the case, woman has the greater life expectancy, and she is less prone to fall ill, and on these counts she ought to be called the "stronger sex." Thus we might speak about the *"stronger* weaker sex," meaning that woman is in fact stronger than man in relation to the biologically determined span of life and in relation to susceptibility to illness, but that she is weaker than man in relation to her subjection to the biological processes of sex and in relation to muscular strength and the lability of which we have been speaking.

Of the total number of births, the proportion of boy babies to girl babies is 105½ to 100. This proportion appears to be very constant, and to be the same in all countries.[10] The reason for this is thought to be that there is more chance of fertilization being brought about by a spermatozoon containing a Y-chromosome than by one containing an X-chromosome. In every cell of the human body there are many chromosomes, and in the nucleus of the cells of a woman's body, 2 of these are X-chromosomes, arising from one X-chromosome from the mother and one X-chromosome from

[10] These and many other data are taken from the summary presented in Amram Scheinfeld, *Women and Men*, New York 1943.

the father. The cells of a man's body each contain one X-chromosome deriving from the mother, and one Y-chromosome deriving from the father. There are thus two sorts of spermatozoa, produced by fission from male cells in the testes. One sort contains an X-chromosome, and the other contains a Y-chromosome. Now if the spermatozoa containing a Y-chromosome have a greater vitality than those containing an X-chromosome, there will be more chance of fertilization being the union of an X-ovum (always X) and a Y-spermatozoon (more lively), which means, in germ, a greater number of boys. Now it seems very likely that this actually is the case. It appears so, above all from the greater number of male births in spite of the fact that the prenatal mortality rate is higher among unborn boys than among unborn girls. On an average, 25% more boys than girls are stillborn. Statistics even show stillbirths in the fourth month of pregnancy as 100% boys.

The most remarkable thing is that this higher mortality rate for males is also found in those animal species in which it has been investigated; in cattle, pigs and rats. Now these are species in which the male also has the X-Y chromosome pattern. But in these species too, in spite of the higher mortality rate among males, male individuals *are more numerous* than females. Thus the immediate result of fertilization is much more often the conception of a male than of a female. More males are stillborn, but they still maintain a small majority in the number of live births.

The position with chickens is just the other way about, but then the X-Y chromosome pattern is characteristic of the female bird while the male bird has the X-X combination. It is also found that the mortality rate among unhatched chicks is higher for the female embryo than for the male embryo.

After birth, boy babies are weaker than girls. This is true especially during the first year, during which 27% more boys than girls die of various illnesses. There is some explanation for this in the fact that girls develop more quickly (for instance, bone-formation in an infant girl is a month in advance of that of a boy of the same age). Another suggested explanation of the higher mortality rate of boys in the first year is that a greater number of boys are injured, perhaps fatally, in birth itself; it is pointed out that the skull of a male infant is larger and thus runs a greater risk of traumatic delivery—this opinion is particularly popular among midwives. Now, the average measurement of a boy infant's skull is only a half-centimeter larger than a baby girl's, and, moreover, the skull of a new-born child is quite plastic, and so this explanation does not seem to be a very likely one. Nevertheless some statistics show that fatalities at birth are 54% more frequent among boys than among girls.

As far as sensitivity to sickness is concerned, the difference between the sexes is remarkable. There are some defects, such as hernia or defects of the urinary passages, which occur more frequently in boys for understandable reasons (partly medical reasons). But according to the data compiled in the United States by Scheinfeld, mortality in cases of "convulsions" is 50% higher among boys than among girls. This is a children's disease which can have a number of causes (intestinal disturbances, etc.), and it is not possible to say why more boys die of it than girls do.

Diseases of the circulatory system are also more frequent among boys than among girls. Hospital records, for instance those of the gigantic Bellevue Hospital in New York, show that the number of boys treated is 15% higher than the number of girls. If we look at statistical tables of the incidence of various diseases in the two sexes, we find, for example, that asthma is twice as frequent in boys as it is in girls. Stuttering (not of course a fatal disease, but a disturbance) is 8 to 10 times more frequent in boys than in girls. The only disease that is more frequent in girls is chorea (St. Vitus dance). Dislocation of the hip is 8 times more frequent in girls, for anatomical reasons.

Thus, important facts can certainly be found in these statistical data on illness. As we have seen, the mortality rate during the years following on puberty is higher among girls than boys.

Now, according to statistics compiled in the United States but confirmed by data gathered in other countries, as far as the average life expectancy is concerned, women live longer than men. In 1900, the average life-span for men was 48 years, and 51 years for women; in 1942, 63½ years and 68½ years; in 1946, 65 years and 70 years. Thus, on the average, woman lives 5 years longer than man in our generation.

These figures gave rise to a rather amusing popular publication in America on the "weaker sex," meaning the men. It was pointed out that heart-ailments were the most frequent cause of death. In the Netherlands too, the highest percentage of deaths are due to heart conditions. Women were therefore advised quite literally to take care of their husband's heart, and in general to give their seats in buses to the men. In this book we do not quite follow the same line, but there is one fact it is well worth while to think upon.

The Life Span of the Sexes

The length of life appears to be no more than a simple natural fact—one lives so many years more or less and that is all. Yet it is also a fact that a man can have experience of and give meaning to in various ways. The probable length of life forms the perspective of personal existence, and Scheler, in his discussion of the essence and meaning of death, *Wesen und Sinn des Todes,*[11] has given a phenomenological analysis of the way the probable life-expectancy plays a rôle in the whole project of human existence. Age, as everyone knows, is not counted in years alone.

The process of becoming old consists, properly speaking, in an alteration of the attitude toward the past and the future, and in a certain withdrawal from the immediate situation. The aged person is less involved in things; in a literal sense he has become gray, colorless, and reciprocally he is no longer colored by the world, and his world becomes more and more misty. This characteristic of the process of aging, which is manifested in many different ways and can also be seen in monotony of movement and loss of motorial coordination,[12] is something that can appear fairly suddenly; after a deep sorrow or some other climactic personal experience, a person can even become old overnight. But it is more usual for a person to be able to present himself as young or as old for a considerable period, and to choose to live either youthfully or as an old person.

This is an important point. The average life-span of woman is longer than that of man. There is a greater chance of a wife outliving her husband than of a husband outliving his wife. Woman faces the probable prospect of a number of years of loneli-

---

[11] *Aus dem Nachlass.* I.
[12] Cf. my *Algemene theorie van de menselijke houding en beweging,* Aula 175, p. 541.

ness. It is extremely unusual to find a woman who actually *counts* on this and deliberately plans for it, but even so the prospect makes itself felt unconsciously, as for example some always live in the prospect of remaining poor and others in the prospect of being well off. Every prospect, like every possibility and every expectation, plays a part in constituting the present. The way in which man perceives and experiences his own life, and the way that political, social, cultural or religious factors can change his perception and alter his experience radically in the space of one generation, depends to some extent on the perspective of his life-span and the meaning man gives to this.

In an earlier generation, when the average life-span was considerably shorter and thus when a person discovered himself in an existential era different from the present one, the graph of life was quite different too, the curve for men and the curve for women each being peculiar to that time. When a man reached the age of 40, he did in fact "feel" an old man, and no doubt the same would have applied to a woman at that time. At that age, people were accustomed to manifest themselves as old people; those of us who can remember our grand-parents and great grand-parents can confirm this. This simple example shows us once again how a natural fact had a determinative effect on human existence only through the meaning that is given to it.

And now, what is the position with regard to the fact that there are more women than men? This is a problem that has an important bearing on the whole social psychology of woman.

There are at present more women than men in practically every country. In America in 1930, the proportion of men to women over the age of 21 years used to be 102½ to 100. In 1940, the number of men was more or less equal to the number of women. After the second world war, in 1945, there were more women than men, and their majority was increasing. In 1940, there were twice as many widows as widowers under the age of 30 years; between the ages of 30 and 40, 0.4% of the population were widowers and 2.1% widows—thus about 5 widows to every widower; above the age of 40, 5% were widowers and 17% were widows. The Central Bureau of Statistics in the United States calculated in 1945 that 33% of married women are widows by the time they reach 60 years of age, and 55% by the time they reach 64 years. Above 65 years old, two women out of every three are "alone," whether as widows or because they have never been married or through divorce. Thus, on the average, adult men and especially older men die earlier than women.

The statistics show that the causes of death are very varied, and that only a very few diseases cause more fatalities among women than among men. As examples we could mention Basedow's disease, a form of pseudoparaplegia (apparent paralysis of the lower limbs) caused by an indirect hyperstimulation of the thyroid gland, in which emotional factors play an important part (other disorders of internal secretions, for instance of the hypophysis or pituitary gland, are also more frequently found in women), and a few diseases relating to the metabolism, such as the formation of gall-stones (for which all sorts of organic causes are recognized), and diabetes (sugar diabetes), which occurs 64% more often among women than among men. All other diseases are more frequently found in men. Mental illness occurs 10% more frequently among men than among women.

It is clear that the above statistical data have been compiled from case records of death. But the causes of death do not provide us with what is needed in order to gain a complete insight into the *fragility* of life as life. If, from the statistics, one wishes to draw the conclusion that woman is stronger than man, and indeed, biologically stronger than man, one must be careful to add that her comparative strength in this sense refers exclusively to the length of her life-span. But there is one thing that does not appear in the statistics, and that would be extremely difficult to compile statistically. What of the very many little illnesses with which woman's longer lifetime is filled? Any general practitioner, any doctor, will tell us that it is mainly on account of these little diseases that women take up a far greater part of his practice than men do. Thus, even though women in the long run are "tougher," their life is much more of a struggle! And this has a very important bearing on existence as experienced, and on the personal view a woman takes of herself, that is to say, in her being-for-herself in relation to her body as a situation.

Therefore, if we want to come to an understanding of feminine existence through an understanding of woman's physical nature, we need to consider not merely the perspective of her life expectancy, but also the fact of her being perpetually aware of her own sensitivity and vulnerability. According to the modern views of the science of medicine, very many organic diseases, and most certainly the "little" illnesses, are *psychogenetic* in origin, that is, they arise from a reaction of what is human in man, as he finds himself in the world, to the difficulties and the conflicts of life. Knowing this, the question we clearly must ask is, whether woman's frequent illnesses are to be explained as purely biological and somatic or not.

If they are purely biological and somatic, they are unchangeably woman's lot. If they are not, they are a cultural phenomenon which certain circumstances will be able to alter. And if this latter is the case, then resignation and silent suffering are not woman's only answer, but we may also weigh up the moral requirement of alleviating woman's "weakness" for the sake of her personal happiness and for the sake of society, just as we feel obliged to alleviate poverty and disease.

In thinking over the chief physical characteristics of woman and the meaning these have for woman herself, we have emphasized the point that the objective facts take on a meaning and thus a value only in social relationships, and only through these social relationships, the most important of which is surely the relationship of woman's existence to the existence of man. Now there is also a question as to whether there is some "natural" basis to these social relationships as well.

In this question, we are not thinking of sexual relationships in the narrower sense, but of encounters between men and women in which the strictly sexual plays no part. A mother sees her son as a male person; a brother sees his sister as a girl or a woman. Their views are formed primarily on the bodily mode of manifestation of the son or the sister; they are thus based primarily on stature, features, voice, glance, gesture and so on. All of these constitute the animated materiality of the person, and we understand them as psychological characteristics of the person's sex. With regard to the physical characteristics of sex, the question arose: what elements of these characteristics have developed reactively in the history of life, and why or how have these developments given rise to the difference we can actually observe between adult men and women? The same question arises with regard to the psychological characteristics of sex, but here it has an even more important bearing on our problem. In order to be able to answer this question—it is a question of the genesis of these psychological characteristics—we will first have to learn to know these psychological characteristics of woman as they are in objective fact, according to the various phases of woman's life.

3. The Psychological Characteristics

> And so this is what woman is? Just so much breadth of awareness, so much emotionality, activity, sense of duty, and so on—is this all there is to the typical feminine soul? Surely not; no more than the mere botanical characteristics of the rose are all there is to the typical rose.
>
> G. HEYMANS [13]

In the whole life of society, we quite rightly take woman's psychological characteristics to be more important than her physical characteristics, and normally when we speak of the peculiar nature of woman, we are referring above all to her behavior, her inclinations, her feelings, her capabilities and all those things that are reckoned to be basically psychological. Education in all its phases, home training, the free formation of youth, the choice of a career, commerce and industry, the outlay and policy of newspapers and magazines, advertising in all its media, the propaganda of political parties, the combatting of crime—all of these have to take the psychological difference of the sexes into account. Thus it is quite understandable that responsible people in these fields do not simply follow the intuitive concepts of which we spoke in a previous part of this book, but try to base their approach on knowledge that is scientifically grounded.

For this reason the number of investigations into observable psychological differences in various age-groups has become so vast in the past few decades that it is not possible to take account of them all. In any case, it is not necessary for our purposes to refer to them all. We have a number of modern studies in which the hundreds of different investigations and experiments are summed up,[14] and there are also a number of monographs avail-

---

[13] G. Heymans, *Die Psychologie der Frauen*, Heidelberg 1924, p. 270.

[14] Catherine Cox Miles, *Sex in Social Psychology* (in *A Handbook of Social Psychology*. Worcester. Clark University Press 1935, p. 683-797); Lewis M. Terman, *Psychological Sex Differences.* (in *Manual of Child Psychology* edited by L. Carmichael, New York and London, 1947); A. Scheinfeld, *Women and Men.* New York 1943; T. Kampmann, *Anthropologische Grundlagen ganzheitlicher Frauenbildung* I & II. Paderborn 1943.

able in which the results of one extensive and thoroughgoing investigation are set out.[15]

It is obvious that there can be some practical importance for establishing certain psychological characteristics, such as for instance the *interest* shown in particular careers, school subjects, types of literature, games and occupations; or the powerful *tendency* to dominate, the tendency to rebel, the need for friendship; or *behavior* in emotional situations; or mental *aptitudes* like memory, verbal expression, general intelligence, and so on. However, it would be theoretically insufficient merely to establish what are the (pheno-typical) characteristics of woman in our present society. This would provide no solution to the question of what is to be considered "genuine" and inborn (geno-typical) from the psychological point of view, and must thus be considered as "natural."

Attempts have in fact been made to find a solution to this question. One of the first was made by Heymans, who thought that a solution could be found by comparing the results of his investigation of adults with the results of his investigation of schoolchildren. But more recent research has proved that the formative influence of milieu and education is felt from the very beginning of life and usually even determines the basic pattern of behavior, inclinations, etc.

It is not easy to learn to know a human being, because his observable behavior depends not only on variable circumstances that are known only in part, but also very often has the undeliberated—usually called the unconscious—intention of manifesting the person as other than he actually is, to hide a feeling or a desire, or to express it indirectly in a modified form. Moreover, modern psychology is becoming steadily more critical of the value of tests and of the accounts people can give of their own experiences and inclinations and feelings and so on. Tests can certainly play an important part in establishing elementary functions, such as perception, movement, memory or mathematical ability, but even in these cases it is obvious that the results obtained under experimental conditions may be used only with the greatest caution to draw conclusions regarding the same functions in conditions of "real"

15 Terman and Miles, *Sex and Personality.* New York 1936; Margaret Mead, *Male and Female,* London 1950; Heymans, *Die Psychologie der Frauen,* Heidelberg 1924.

life. People have tried to establish a closer approximation of the real value of the tests by statistical methods, but the uncertainty increases when under test conditions one tries to determine qualities of character and to gain an insight into the "mental-emotional" life of a person.[16] And it is precisely this insight that we wish to gain, for practical as well as theoretical reasons.

Now, if it is already difficult to understand a single individual through the application of experimental methods, or, if not to understand him, at least to form some image of his personal psychic structure, it will be all the more difficult, from the methodological point of view, to investigate and try to understand a whole group of individuals—in the present instance, woman. Even when dealing with a whole group, it is a fairly simple affair to apply a number of tests relating to elementary functional performance. If the results of these tests are compiled statistically, they do give some impression of the average achievement of the female person. Thus various tests have shown that girls have a superior general memory, but on particular matters like remembering a series of numbers and comprehension of sentences, no difference could be found between girls and boys. In tests based on the ability to remember stories, the difference between boys and girls has been shown to be dependent on the material used and the various degrees of its power to hold the interest of boys or girls. Up to the age of puberty, girls in general have a better memory than boys, but the material to be remembered and the manner of its presentation is always an important factor in a girl's memory. Girls and women are usually best at remembering things learned by heart or at remembering details concerning people or social life. Emotional appeal always plays an important part in this. Without exception, women are better than men at remembering facts and events with a strong emotional content.[17]

The results of investigations show clearly that, even in tests relating to an apparently elementary function such as the memory,

16 For a worthwhile critical discussion of the matter, cf. D. J. Van Lennep and others, *Psychotechniek als kompas voor het beroep*. Utrecht 1949.

17 These and other data are taken from an unpublished study of the literature on the subject of the psychological differences between men and women, done by R. H. Houwink as an assistant at the Psychological Laboratory, Utrecht.

the entire situation has to be taken into account. Now, the situation is constituted, in general, by the meaning given to himself and to his world by the person being tested, and in particular, by the meaning this person gives to the test itself, its possible results, its circumstances, and to the conductor of the test. Since this is the case, all these meanings should be known before the results of the test can be judged and evaluated.

But, knowledge of all these meanings is the same thing as knowledge of the existential project of the person undergoing the test, together with knowledge of that person's world. Therefore, the investigations carried out by means of so-called "elementary" tests achieve nothing more than a quantitative result relating to a selected function (e.g., "memory") regarded as an isolated phenomenon for the purposes of the test, or else the investigator is interpreting the results he obtains in terms of his own "intuitive" notion of the mode of existence and of the world of the person being tested.

If any test is to have any important significance, it must be coordinated with a phenomenological analysis of the whole situation of the investigation. This alone will give the investigator some idea of the value of his experiments and of the meaning of the reactions of his subjects. Only on these terms can he know what is mere detail and what is main issue and why.

In spite of these methodological difficulties of the investigation, a wide and varied experience does permit us to say several things: girls are inclined to have a better memory than boys; in the matter of general intelligence there is very little difference between girls and boys; when it comes to the more complex kinds of calculation and mathematical reasoning, girls achieve slightly lower results than boys; and the difference between the sexes usually widens as they get older.[18] This is understandable, for two reasons. In the first place, a slight psychological difference will become more clearly noticeable as the relevant patterns of existence become more differentiated. In the second place, a girl's education, and more importantly, the demands made on her and the demands she makes on herself, are usually based on her given aptitudes, and this promotes a one-sided development.

[18] Lipmann, *Psychische Geschlechtsunterschiede.* Zeitschrift für Ang. Psych. Beih. 14. 1917.

Development of Interests

Although the investigation of functions and abilities is important
for a knowledge of woman's psychological nature, the investigations aimed at establishing the direction of her interest during the
course of her development are even more important. Data on the
direction of interest are provided in very many publications in the
field of child psychology, but as a matter of fact these agree so
completely with what we already know or could easily suppose as
a result of daily experience that we find none of them surprising
at all.

Actual investigations of the behavior of small children have not
always produced the same results, but it is quite certain that girls
between the ages of 2 and 4 years have a better memory for
pictures than boys of the same age-group; girls show more interest
in colors, they learn to speak sooner and better than boys, they
play more with dolls, they are handier at dressing and undressing
themselves, and they are more anxious and more excitable than
boys. If building-blocks are given to 1½ year olds, the boys build
more towers (that fall over), and the girls build lower and wider
buildings. The games boys choose and the games girls choose differ
widely, but, as Scheifler has pointed out,[19] girls certainly do not
always prefer to play with dolls nor the boys with toy soldiers. The
same author also found that girls show a stronger inclination
toward detail and care in their play which is often an adaptation of
situations of domestic life. Girls find quiet games (for instance, in
a small group) more attractive than the active and sometimes
rough games of boys. Girls also usually prefer the "more temperamental" games involving chance to tinkering with things or building them.

Another well-known difference is the difference of the type of
literature boys and girls choose. Generally boys prefer books of
adventure or books that deal with scientific subjects; girls however
show a unanimous preference for books on family life or school
life, or stories with an emotional coloring. In general, girls read
more than boys. This is not surprising, when we consider that
reading is very much a sedentary occupation which can easily

[19] *Zur Psych. der Geschlechter: Spielinteressen des Schulalters.* Zeitschrift für Ang. Psych. 8. 1914. p. 124-144.

conflict with the urge toward activity that is always typical of the boy.

We have known about the typical choice of reading matter for a long time, but what we knew has recently been confirmed by an investigation carried out in youth-clubs in England. The results of this investigation show an order of preference among books chosen by boys, detective stories and books on sport being the most popular categories, with adventure stories in the third place. Practically all of the girls voted in favor of one kind of book that did not get a single vote from the boys—romantic novels and love-stories.

The choice of subjects for essays agrees with the choice of reading matter. It has been established that boys generally prefer to describe actual events, or to write about famous people, machines, industry, and so on. Girls on the other hand almost always base their essays on children, home life, personal experiences, religion, art or an emotion. Boys are better at objective descriptions, while girls display a greater richness of feeling and have a more subjective interest. Concerning the attitude of the writer to the object of his writing, boys show a marked preference for the universal and for hidden structure, while girls concentrate rather on the particular and the outward appearance.

A great number of studies have been published, which concern the preferences of boys and girls for various school subjects. The type of teaching given, the school, and the teachers themselves cause small variations in the typical choice, as is only to be expected. Disregarding these small variations, it appears that boys mainly prefer courses in the physical sciences, mathematical subjects, and history, while girls mainly prefer languages, drawing, music, drama and similar subjects.[20] We should expect the prefer-

[20] It is not difficult to deduce woman's lesser interest in abstract lines of thought and particularly in *mathematics* from the basic structure of woman's existence. The same thing can be found in the existence of a man when his world embraces chiefly those concrete phenomena that can be appreciatively seen and touched. The aesthete, as Spranger describes him, is no lover of mathematics. When the world a person chooses to live in is filled with the immediate as with situations discovered with sensitivity, with people who are loved, hated, admired, despised, then that person's thought moves in fields that are other than those to which formulae and geometric figures belong. But, it may be remarked, experience in schools shows that girls do not have an "aptitude" for mathematics and even when they "want to" they cannot "grasp" the subject!

This may be so, but we understand what the fact actually means only when we know what "aptitude" and "want" and "grasp" really signify, and

ences to be more or less in agreement with the aptitudes for the subjects preferred, and this seems in fact to be confirmed by the psychological investigation of functions and abilities.

We come finally to a word on interest in a career. The general opinion is that the choice of a career runs parallel to the possibilities open to men and to women in our society, but it takes no account of the fact that, given a different pattern of social relationships, women would show entirely different preferences in the matter of choosing a career.

To us it seems "natural" that young men should show preference for a profession which demands responsibility and in which

---

in what relation these stand to the reality we call "taking an interest." We have as yet very little insight into this matter. Certainly there is such a thing as an aptitude for mathematical thinking, but in what this aptitude consists, we cannot say. It is probable that the problem has not yet been formulated correctly; so far, it has proceeded on the tacit assumption of a latent faculty that "awakes" at a certain age (and under certain conditions) and begins to manifest itself as active. This psychomechanistic view is wholly at variance with the modern insight into the development of the structure of existence.

If it is true that the little girl constitutes herself as *homo eroticus* rather than as *homo faber* because of her original basic dynamism and her encounter with the world, this establishes an "aptitude" which will make a mathematical interest less likely in her than in the little boy who sees himself as placed in *opposition* to the power of the world and therefore takes *flight* in thoughts and loses himself in formulae that no longer signify any material resistance but are purely intelligible.

As far as "wanting" is concerned, Gabriel Marcel has an enlightening thought to offer: "To want is not to contract, it is to expand." We need only to have seen how a girl can "contract" when faced with a mathematical problem, how she can become rigid, cling fast to the "given," and be unable to follow even the smallest step although in fact she wants to. Whoever knows something of living with neuroses, caught between a not wanting to be able and a being not able to want, and who understands how this can be so, will be able to understand something of the decided ineptitude of (the majority of) women for mathematics.

One more fact needs to be mentioned. The educational system and the text-books in use are set up in terms of the abilities of "normal brains," the "normal" ones being those that can stay with a train of thought in which *jumps* of a certain size occur. For ungifted girls, and for many boys too, these jumps are too big. If the jumps are reduced, and more and smaller steps taken from one point to the next, anyone who is a normal human being will be able to "grasp" mathematics, for there is in fact nothing very special about it to be grasped. For mathematics is a science which makes no demands whatever on experience, and does not call for any form of personal participation, but simply requires a logic which is identical with the minimum of common sense. Or does woman's mind perhaps work with uncommon sense?

they will be able to fulfill a function of leadership. In contrast, we find it just as "natural" that young women prefer indoor careers, and especially those that make personal contacts with other people possible. Specialized, scientific or constructive work attracts young men; young women prefer the kind of occupation that gives more scope to care, such as nursing, teaching and pediatrics. It is not surprising that these and similar professions are the ones in which we find most women engaged, especially when we consider, along with the types of profession calling for the greatest degree of "care," those that involve a fairly intense association with other people, for instance, journalism, sales, secretarial work, doctor's receptionist, and so on. The differences in interest in a career are constant to a fairly high degree and are maintained until late in the period of adolescence. The only development that can be noticed in the preference is that it gradually comes more and more under the influence of the actual relationships in society. The little boy wants to drive a locomotive, the little girl, perhaps, to become a gymnastics instructress; later on, this boy studies engineering and the girl takes up teaching, and thus, the general tendency of the preference of each in the matter of a career remains for the most part unchanged.

Aggression and Rebellion

Girls are less inclined to have a strong desire to dominate, or to show the related tendency toward aggression and rebellion. People are so generally convinced that this is the case that any girl who proves an exception in this matter is supposed to be suffering from some disturbance or to be one in whose basic makeup the masculine type prevails.

Psychology has been able only to confirm the general opinion. An investigation of young children carried out by Hattwick [21] has shown, convincingly, that little boys break or lose their toys far more often than little girls, and that they are much more inclined to attack others and to refuse to share their toys with others. Little girls on the other hand would rather refrain from playing altogether than cause a row, and are in any case more ready to give in.

[21] *Sex Differences in Behavior of Nursery School Children.* Child Development 8. 1937. p. 343-355.

In their conduct toward adults, little boys are more often disobedient and unwilling, while little girls like to be praised and willingly go in amongst adults. Other researchers too have shown that even very little boys are uncooperative, rebellious and troublesome, whereas the girls are much more inclined to try to adapt themselves socially. Boys more often get into arguments, and use their fists more often to back up their words, while arguments among girls are almost always confined to words and mimicry. The angry boy stamps and hits out, the girl scolds, makes a face and sticks out her tongue. Some elements of this kind of behavior remain well into adulthood, although the individual's conduct is gradually transformed as his personal development progresses. The full-grown man too is often more dominant and more "aggressive" than woman, but at this stage the characteristics appear much more in the form of a feeling of superiority and a kind of social aggressiveness.

Besides being more aggressive than girls, boys are also more cruel, more obstinate and less able to concentrate. This is shown in Cummings's investigation of school-children between the ages of 3 and 7 years.[22] Houwinck quite rightly remarks, in this connection, that the greater aggressiveness of boys at such an early age makes it probable that this is a manifestation of a *real* difference in "nature" between the sexes. At a later stage, we will return to this point and discuss it at greater length. The urge to dominate and to be aggressive leads to all sorts of rebellion. The little girl is more willing, more docile, more tender, more cooperative, she follows more easily, she is more obedient. All this we know from ordinary experience, and the literature of psychology confirms it. Undoubtedly, the powerful tendencies and associations that predominate in a girl from her earliest years are closely related to these characteristics.

No other psychological characteristic has been ascribed to woman with greater decisive emphasis than emotionality. Heymans writes: [23] "Now, as far as woman is concerned, there is agreement among the researchers on no other point to compare with their tremendous agreement on this, that woman reacts emotionally to a much weaker stimulus than man, and that she reacts emotionally to an equal stimulus much more strongly than man,"

[22] *The Incidence of Emotional Symptoms in School Children.* British Journal of Educational Psychology, 14 (1944) I, p. 151-161.
[23] *Die Psych. der Frauen.* Heidelberg 1924. p. 63.

and he goes on to quote a number of earlier authors, among them, Auguste Comte, who called woman "the affective sex," and Marion [24] who said, "Woman is practically never indifferent, passes never a minute without loving or hating something or someone, without having some heartfelt emotion."

Emotionality

Now all of this is wholly in accordance with the opinion that has been formed in every-day life all through the centuries. A number of modern child psychologists have shown that there is a greater degree of emotionality in girls, and have confirmed the opinion of Fröbes, who wrote in his well-known textbook,[25] "Girls are more easily moved than boys, they laugh and they weep more quickly, they have a greater fear of examinations, they are more nervous and more enthusiastic. Women love and hate, enjoy and suffer more, and more deeply. Woman grasps everything in an emotional way, and nothing is indifferent to her," and he holds that all of woman's typical characteristics can be understood in terms of this greater emotionality (and the greater degree of activity to which it gives rise).

The most recent and extensive experimental and statistical investigation has been done by Terman and Miles, and this too gives, as almost the only result, the fact that woman is more emotional than man. We will return to this investigation later. For the moment, we note only the fact that these investigators warn that caution should be exercised in the interpretation of the results of their experiments. For it is possible that woman chooses to be more free in expressing her feelings and that society concedes her the right to be so. This remark brings out once more the fact that the so-called establishing of psychological facts has a very limited value if it is done without any phenomenological insight into the situation of the "fact" which is being established.

What sense is there in speaking of the greater emotionality of woman if we do not even know what we really mean when we talk about emotionality? Is emotionality nothing more than sensitivity to impressions, is it irritability, or is it a lower degree of integra-

24 *Psych. de la Femme.* 1900. p. 98.
25 *Lehrbuch der exper. Psych.* II. 1929. p. 486.

tion, a looser structure of the personality? Is emotionality the live-liness of "inward" experiences accompanying perception, presentation, thought and action, or is it the experiences that arise as a result of the autonomic processes going on inside the body? There is a question which comes closer to the principle of the matter: are the emotions and the less intense feelings and moods based on "processes" going on in man, passively undergone but noticed by him inside himself, or are they intentional acts which mean something, which project a situation, and thus project a manner of existing in that situation?

Lersch [26] defines the emotions as "the experiences of need felt by those who are under the influence of a powerful stimulus, and the experiences of encouragement felt in accompaniment to the fulfillment of aim and intention," and agrees more or less with the view taken by earlier psychologists. Unlike this, modern psychology, basing itself on anthropological and existential grounds, develops further the line of Scheler's thought,[27] understanding emotion as an intentional act. Scheler himself considered that there were *"blosse Gefühlszustände,"* states of mere feeling, as well as intentional feelings, but as phenomenological investigation has progressed, it has come to hold the view that what Scheler would say of only certain feelings does in fact apply to all emotions, feelings and moods: "In the course of our intentional feelings, the world of objects reveals itself to us, but under the aspect of values."

The clear analysis and description of the intentional character of the emotions is an achievement for which J. P. Sartre [28] deserves credit, but he has entirely failed to appreciate their positive value for a "knowledge" of the world. In the first place, says Sartre, the experience of an emotion is identically the same as a sympathetic grasp of the situation in which one finds oneself. For the sake of clarity it must be remarked here that in the act of feeling (feeling

[26] *Der Aufbau des Charakters.* Leipzig 1942. In the new edition, published in Munich in 1951 under the title *Aufbau der Person*, the anthropological point of view is more clearly developed. Thus we read on p. 41: *"Es kennzeichnet die Situation des Menschen, dass ihm sein Dasein nicht, wie dem Tiere, einfach gegeben, sondern aufgegeben ist"*— a characteristic sign of the human situation is that man's being is not, as the animal's, simply given; man's being is a task.

[27] *Der Formalismus in der Ethik und die materielle Wertethik.* Halle 1927.

[28] *Esquisse d'une théorie des émotions.* Paris 1939. *Sketch for a theory of the emotions.* London. 1962.

in the sense of touching included) we do not intend to *note* the quality of things, as we do in objective observation, but we "let ourselves go" in such a way that we experience a modification of our being-in-the-world, and it is this modification of our being through the act of feeling that we generally call emotion. The motivation for "letting go" in this way is provided—at least to some extent—by the situation. We do not feel in a vacuum: when a man is afraid, he is always afraid of something, even if this something is the unnameable unknown; "emotion is a particular manner of apprehending the world." In the second place, noting that normal adaptation (to the world) takes place through rational and effective means and through the achieved pattern of conduct, *Sartre* holds that when normal adaptation becomes *difficult,* the world (to which we adapt) undergoes a transformation through the emotions. "All paths are closed to us, but still we have to act. And so we try to change the world, that is to say, we try to live it as though the relationships of things to their potentialities were not ruled by deterministic processes but by magic."

There is no conscious deliberation in all this; it happens spontaneously. But nevertheless emotion embodies the intention of grasping new relationships and thus also of placing new demands on the world and on ourselves. In principle it always takes place in the same way, whether in anxiety, in passive grief, in despair or in joy. "Joy is a magical aspect of conduct, trying to realize, through incantation, the total and instantaneous possession of the object desired."

Thus Sartre looks upon every emotion as something undergone, a spontaneous *degradation* of consciousness in its relationship to the world. Man casts himself into the wonderworld emotion discloses, and believing in its reality, he actually takes part in it through all his own bodily reality. Captured in the meaning of the emotion, man becomes wholly engrossed in the situation, and in this sense, therefore, man may be said to undergo his emotions. Now we might well say that extreme emotions like tremendous fright and anxiety, insane anger, overwhelming depression or intoxicating happiness, imply a degradation of consciousness in the sense that they actually do make man "blind" to many actual relationships and to many characteristics of people and things. Nevertheless, *these* very emotions, for all that they are extreme, do in a positive sense possess a value for knowledge. Sartre did not altogether fail to see this. The qualities discovered by emotion are absolute and substantial qualities of that which is real to us. The world *does contain* reasons for anxiety, and there *are* horrible and painful and delightful things in the world, and if a person does not know this, he will never be able to understand the world of man.

But then the only way a person can come to know this is by *really* undergoing the emotions himself. The more finely the life of feeling is differentiated, the richer the variety of qualities will be that one discovers in one's world, and the more numerous the occasions will be for a situation to provide motivation for an intentional act of feeling or emotion. Now supposing that woman's emotionality consists in her having a more delicate perception of nuance in her participation in the qualities of things and persons and situations, her greater sensitivity is the basis of a form of knowledge possessed by her but hidden from man whose existence is more rationally directed toward objective fact.

The important factor in the modern understanding of emotions is that they are no longer viewed as meaningless phenomena accompanying abilities and efforts, but understood as meaningful acts by which man directs himself toward the world and takes hold of the world in its concrete reality in a particular way. It is not possible to say what the significance of the emotional effect is in a particular instance, unless it is approached through a phenomenological analysis of the act, the situation and the whole pattern of behavior. When a woman melts into tears because, as she says, things have become "just too much" for her and she can no longer respond to them, it may indeed be that she has suddenly had the experience of discovering the inexpressible "vastness" and power of the world—as Alyosha did when he knelt to kiss the earth [29]— but it is also possible that she resorts to tears because she simply does not want to respond, or because capitulation seems to be the easiest way out of a difficulty.

We have had to dwell on the contrast between the classical and modern theories of emotional life in order to make it quite clear that there are two ways of viewing woman's greater emotionality, and that each of these ways differs in principle from the other. Woman's emotionality can be considered as an inborn "characteristic" that is quantitatively variable, or it can be considered as a mode of human existence and thus as a modus of woman's projec-

[29] Dostoevski, *The Brothers Karamazow.*

tion of herself and of her world. Since human existence is *always* a being-in-the-world *in the body,* the physical constitution of the body provides important and sometimes even compelling motivations for the quality, duration, profundity and extent of emotions.

Nevertheless, the meaning given to the actual conditions of being-in-the-body as experienced, is constantly related to the meaning given to external situations. It is only because of the constancy of the relation of the meaning given to bodily conditions to the meaning given to external situations (in all human existence) that it is possible to explain the *special* forms emotionality takes in woman. The difference between the emotional life of man and that of woman only seems to be a quantitative one. It may appear to be possible to measure and establish this difference as if it were merely quantitative (e.g., by investigating the reactions of men and women to the same stimulus), but in reality men and women differ in the very nature of their feelings, in their qualitative differentiation, in their depth, seriousness and authenticity, and also in their expression, control, and in the way they give meaning to the situation; they differ in their previous history, in the projection of the future, and in the way they view themselves; in short, they differ in the whole of their existence.

It is clear, from the words of Heymans quoted at the beginning of this section, that the position taken by the old psychology was incorrect in principle. It is simply not true that a human being reacts to "stimuli." A human being never receives a stimulus; he receives impressions that mean something to him or that image something for him in and through the way he encounters them, and this may be more or less emotional or unemotional.

We need only remember how a woman or even a little girl expresses appreciation or dislike—for instance, of food,[30] or persons, or in matters of disputed ethical points—to be able to understand that we are dealing with an emotionality that is not "stronger" than man's, but "of another kind" than his. Consider how different the workings of love, hate, anger, temper, anxiety, shame, scorn, etc. in woman are from the way they work in man; how differently woman reacts, and often how much less emotional

---

[30] Cf. Tussing's investigation, *A Study of Sex Differences in Food Likes and Dislikes.* Proc. Ind. Ac. Sc. 48, 1939; and Wallen's *Sex Differences in Food Aversions.* Journal of Appl. Psych. 27. 1943. p. 288.

her reaction, to great disasters, for instance in war, to personal suffering and to sickness. Long,[31] who describes the reaction to bombardments in England, praises the courageous behavior of women, but goes on to give an explanation for it that is in fact very widely accepted. "Their protective instinct for those they love is actually a shield against the nerve-shattering effects of warfare noises." Why not simply accept that emotionality is not an unchangeable characteristic? Experience in concentration camps, including those where women were held, has given convincing proof of this.

But the emotionality of women is always recognized by everyone as a *fact*. If we want to understand it, we must not look upon her so-called greater sensitivity as a "natural" characteristic. We must take it as a *second* nature, a cultural phenomenon. This means that the differentiation, the force, the duration, depth and the after-effects of emotions depend upon the history of the person, and thus, depend in part upon the scale of moral values.

The results of the very extensive investigation instituted by Heymans confirm this. They bring out most strikingly the existential background of the life of the emotions. We see for instance that girls in junior-high schools are more demonstrative, more touchy, more easily offended, more quickly inclined to tears and sulking, more easily discouraged, more anxious and concerned about examinations, more enthusiastic and more nervous. These judgments give an overall view of something that for the greatest part has come about because of the attitude the individual girls have adopted from their earliest years because of what was expected of them or tolerated in them and because of the means that were available to them.

But can this view be defined as one of a *greater* emotionality? Does not the girl choose to transform her world in an entirely different way, a "magical" way, precisely because she chooses to exist in a way that is entirely different from the way a man chooses to exist? If the answer to this question is affirmative, it would help to explain the tremendous difference between men's judgments and women's judgments on the matter of emotionality in men and women found in the answers given to the questionnaire on heredity

[31] *Bulletin from Britain*. No. 55, 1941. Quoted by Scheinfeld, *Men and Women*, p. 421.

devised by Heymans. A number of doctors (and members of other professions) were asked to detail their views of the members of a family well known to them, in the manner called for by the questionnaire. The ninth point raised in the questionnaire reads as follows: *emotional* (takes trivialities in a personal way; greatly delighted or deeply upset for small reasons), or alternatively, not emotional (less sensitive than others; tends to be cooler). Now it appears from the questionnaires completed by men that of all the people considered, 58.9% of the women and 45.9% of the men were judged to be "emotional," but only 39.3% of the women and 26.5% of the men were judged to be "not emotional." A quite different picture emerges from the questionnaires completed by women. Women represented 70.9% of the women and 48.5% of the men they considered as "emotional," and 20.3% of the women and 39.7% of the men as "not emotional."

From these figures it is clear that people in general undoubtedly consider women to be more emotional than men, but that women actually consider fellow members of their sex to be over-sensitive *more often* than men do. Now this shows that men and women do not mean the same thing when they speak of emotionality. And the whole problem rests on precisely what they mean by emotionality. What does emotionality *mean* to a countrywoman, a farmer, a stockbroker, or to the mother of a large family? According to Heymans, there is a greater intensity of desire and hope in woman. But there are equally good grounds for doubting whether this is actually so. Heymans also holds that women *want* to be affected more strongly by their feelings. "For this reason, women do not avoid, but rather seek out, those things which excite the emotions. . . ." This, again according to Heymans, is the reason why there is so much talk of woman's tendency to do forbidden things.

Truth and Honesty

Now, we do not want to try to settle whether this is correct or not, but it does show how uncertain the results of an investigation are when it is not carried out along with a phenomenological analysis. There is however a point which is even more important. On the grounds of common experience, Heymans himself could not do otherwise than regard emotionality as a factor of existence. Thus, if we can disregard his constructed theoretical explanations which are based among other things on a distinction between the extent and the degree of consciousness, the work of Heymans provides us with many striking observations. His investigation shows that women are more trustworthy than men, while the opinion commonly upheld in earlier writings says just the opposite. Heymans finds an explanation for this contradiction in the improvement of woman's social position. In general women exist on a higher moral level than men, in spite of centuries of the kind of oppression that encourages lying and insincerity: if, in spite of this, women are more truthful and more honest than men, "the natural disposition on which these qualities are based must be uncommonly strong in them." [32]

This conclusion is hardly a convincing one. There is no such thing as a natural disposition for untruthfulness or trustworthiness, but it is possible that Heymans is thinking of some sort of causal effect that emotionality or the extent of consciousness or other factors can have on furthering or arresting the development of these qualities. In any case, we must lay the very strongest emphasis on the fact that this psychologist, very exact in his work and

[32] Without further research it is not easy to say why woman should have a greater *sense of duty,* as Heymans says. Very likely it will appear, as in the case of other (pseudo-) characteristic qualities (such as zeal), that many motives lead to the choice of a meticulous fulfillment of duty, and thus that this possesses some other ethical and characterological significance. Woman is certainly *able* to have a sense of duty which is morally very deeply founded, but the thing that is called duty is very often simply the acceptance of a task through lack of resistance.

There are many factors in an existence projected in the feminine way that indicate that woman is likely to have a lower resistance to the general demands made upon a person and to the particular calls made upon her in a personal way. All weaker people are inclined to be indulgent; this is not merely an expression of their weakness, but also their "power" (and even a kind of "extortion"). On the other hand, the careful association with people and things that are nearby establishes a more direct and therefore more decisive obligation than that established in the free project of labor.

And, finally, woman lives "under the eye of others" more than man does, and she elects to identify herself with the mode of existence that others expect of her. Thus there can be many reasons for the greater application to duty that Heymans and others have remarked in woman. It may be an expression of anxiety, scruple, compensation for inferiority, resentment, demonstrative virtuousness, enforced carefulness—but it may also be the expression of the full value of a mature moral consciousness.

very careful in his judgments, came to the conclusion that the "physical habits" of a person are only *3% dependent on the person's sex,* roughly 10% on characteristics inherited through the paternal line or possibly through the maternal line, 30% on general historical conditions, and for the remaining 67% derived from the living experience of the individual. This conclusion varies more than somewhat from the popular notion that a woman is a woman in everything, and that a man is a man in everything!

Thus, there is no doubt that we do find in Heymans' work a very broad grasp of the irrefutable facts of experience and of their meaningful relation to human possibilities and to concrete existence, but even so we need constantly to take care to avoid taking up the same theoretical stand as Heymans took. He, for instance, presents the "physical habits" of a person as a *structure,* analogous to the structure of a plant or an animal. In this view, all the characteristics of the feminine psyche are equivalent to the inborn or acquired characteristics of an "object" which, like any other thing, is nothing more than the sum of its properties.

There is certainly some methodological advantage to the method of investigation Heymans followed. It provides descriptions of persons in such a form that they can be classed according to comparisons and statistically compiled. However, the disadvantage of this method is that the persons described are described as *others* see them, and so the results obtained are largely a reflection of the opinions and impressions and judgments of those who give the descriptions. The actual point of the disadvantage of this method is not so much the fact that people in a given cultural circle—such as doctors or teachers—hold an inconsistent variety of views about the nature of men and women. The variety of view, as well as the competence of those who hold these views, is, as Heymans thinks, compensated for "by the objective nature of the given situation of the acts."

The real point of the disadvantage is the fact that the "object," the person who is to be judged, is already pre-judged in the view of the observer, because the observer already regards this person either as a man or as a woman, and thus his pre-judicial view gives a particular determination in a special direction to the very meaning of the questions in the questionnaire. For this reason, the result of an investigation of this kind is practically always in full agreement with popular opinion.

The M-F Test

Terman and Miles [33] follow an entirely different method. This is already apparent in the name they give it: "attitude-interest analysis test." This is a test in which the person being tested answers the questions himself, without actually knowing the actual aim of the investigation, and thus indirectly and unconsciously provides answers about the degree of femininity or masculinity of his or her nature. Thus these American investigators work on the presupposition that there are innumerable and fluid shadings of variety between the extremes of male men and female women, and that the investigation must not therefore be aimed at discovering the characteristics of men and women, but of masculinity and femininity. Now, what is understood as masculinity and femininity is the idea of each that *actually prevails* as the pheno-typical idea of masculinity and femininity in a particular grouping of people in American society, the group actually chosen being that of "the intellectuals." The masculinity-femininity test (the M-F test) was standardized for this group. Thus, what appeared from a reading of the scores of the majority of both men and women in this group was taken as the "norm," and this "norm" was used to measure the degree of divergence toward the masculine or feminine in any particular individual, or in another group of people. Following this method, it should therefore be possible to discover to what extent a particular individual (e.g., a homosexual) or a particular group of people (e.g., athletes, or the students of a particular faculty) diverge from the "norm."

Houwinck [34] adapted and applied the M-F test in the Netherlands, and correctly remarks that this test designed by Terman and Miles is certainly not aimed at the essence of the psychological difference between man and woman, or between masculinity and femininity, but is limited mainly to an investigation of the *veneer* with which this essence is surrounded by any given culture. This "veneer" is a matter of superficial characteristics determined entirely by tradition, but its investigation is nevertheless very important if we want to achieve an insight into social relationships as they actually are. More than this cannot be expected of an investigation of this kind.

[33] *Sex and Personality*. New York 1936.
[34] Ned. Tijdschr. v.d. Psychol.; nieuwe reeks V. 1950. p. 242-262.

Of course one ought to be aware that the M-F test will not provide any other results. Therefore its inventors themselves refrained from any theoretical speculation on the "essence" of man and woman or of masculinity and femininity. But even though Terman and Miles in their research were moving in a field that actually lies outside the area of the problem that occupies us, we still want to pay some attention to their test, because its results show us what, in our culture, is in fact *regarded* as typically masculine and typically feminine.

The test consists mainly in lists of questions to be answered in writing, the questions relating to word association, general development, emotional and ethical reactions, interests and preferences, personal matters and opinions, and so on. The answers to the questions are to be given by selecting one of a number of possible answers provided. For example, to the question "are you afraid of intruders?," the possible answers are "very afraid; afraid; a little afraid; not afraid." In evaluating the answers, the first two are reckoned as feminine, the third as neutral, the fourth as masculine. The whole test consists of 450 questions, more or less. The masculine answers are called + and the feminine are called -, and so the total score of any one person will have a positive or negative sign. In the replies collected by Terman and Miles, the final scores of the men varied between +200 and -100 (averaging +52); women's scores varied between +100 and -200 (averaging -70).

To give some impression of the actual data obtained by means of this test, we may quote some of its results from the book *Sex and Personality*.

The book does not give any correlation of the M-F test to the typical physical characteristics of the sexes (such as shoulder-breadth, slightness of build). The authors were of the opinion that the number of cases they had actually investigated in this regard was too small, and that a much greater number would have to be done before such correlation could be made. It is however remarkable that the M-F score of athletes, both men and women, was far and away the most masculine. We get the impression that it is not the physical constitution, but rather the way an individual views himself, and his existential project in keeping with his view of himself, that actually determines his degree of masculinity or femininity, as masculinity and femininity are culturally understood.

And, in agreement with this, we find that the M-F score is also dependent on the person's profession or occupation. It thus appears that engineers (+77) have almost as high a degree of masculinity as student athletes (+92); by way of contrast, the scores of (American) clergy and artists (+10) are very close to those of women intellectuals and sportswomen (+10 to -10). Among the women, the remarkable thing was that stenographers, along with dressmakers and hairdressers (scoring -90), are more feminine than teachers (-70) and nurses (-64). Most feminine of all are the "domestic servants" (-104).

It is also interesting to note the influence of age on the scores obtained. Masculinity is greatest in boys of around 16 years of age (+73), less in boys of 14 (+35). From the 16th year, the score gradually descends; the overall average (+52) is reached in the 28th year; by the age of 60 the score is +10, and the neutral point 0 is reached in the 80th year. The pattern among women is quite different. The most feminine (-95) are the 14 year-olds; the least feminine point (-60) is reached at the age of 20 years more or less. From the age of 20 onwards there is a gradual increase in the femininity score toward -90 which is reached at the age of 50, and this remains constant between the ages of 50 and 80. These results too are quite in keeping with ordinary experience. Everyone is familiar with the way old men become a little "feminine" in their ways, and with the very marked femininity of girls at the time of puberty.

All these results appear to make the dependability of the M-F test more probable. Nevertheless, critical studies have shown that many of the questions, and even whole series of questions in Terman and Miles's test do not provide for a sufficiently clear differentiation. As an example of the critical evaluation of this test, we could mention the work of Houwinck. All this has moved others to devise other M-F tests, or to modify or shorten that of Terman and Miles. With refinements achieved in this way, it has even appeared possible to establish the degree of sexual differentiation in pathological cases, for example, in homosexuals.

Catherine Cox Miles describes a particularly interesting application of the M-F test [35] to the case of a pseudo-hermaphrodite who had been brought up as a girl. This case came up for clinical investigation and treatment when the person was 17 years old, and

[35] C. C. Miles, *Psychological Study of a Young Adult Male Pseudo-Hermaphrodite, Reared as a Female*, in *Studies in Personality*. New York 1942 (McGraw Hill), Chapter XI, p. 209-227.

examination showed that sexual organs of both sorts were present. It proved possible to restore complete physical masculinity by means of surgery. A psychological investigation of the case was carried out shortly after the operation, and repeated several months later when supplementary plastic surgery was performed. It appeared that the M-F test produced an unmistakably masculine score, although the influence of the person's upbringing as a girl was naturally evident. It is indeed a fact that cannot be denied that the specific attitudes of the sexes, especially insofar as these are measured by the M-F test, are predominantly determined by education and upbringing within a cultural structure in which these attitudes are firmly established.

Criminologists too have shown some interest in the M-F test. Walker [36] carried out an interesting investigation showing moreover that of all the criminals examined, burglars scored the highest masculinity ratings, while at the other end of the scale, the most feminine scores were those of the murderers. Convicts who proved rebellious and came into conflict with prison regulations obtained scores that were more masculine than the ratings of those who adapted themselves cooperatively. Burger, Nemzek and Vaughn [37] carried out an investigation of 120 male convicts, aiming mainly at discovering the influence of subsidiary factors on the M-F rating. It appeared that older criminals and those who came from an unfavorable domestic background were more feminine, while on the other hand the more masculine scores were obtained by criminals of higher general intelligence and those who had been convicted several times. Other factors, such as social standing, size of family, occupation and religion, seemed to have no influence on the M-F scores. If one considers the relation of all these factors to the culturally pheno-typical characteristics of masculinity and femininity we have mentioned, the explanation of all of this becomes obvious.

Smith's investigation [38] should also be mentioned. It has aroused considerable interest. Actually, Smith did not work with the Terman-Miles Test, but used the *Goodenough Speed of Asso-*

[36] *The Terman-Miles M-F Test and the Prison Classification Program.* Journ. Genet. Psycho. 59 (1941) p. 27-40.

[37] *The Relationship of Certain Factors to Scores on the Terman-Miles Attitude-Interest Analysis Test.* Journ. Soc. Psych. 16 (1942) p. 39-50.

[38] *The Relation of M-F Scores of Sorority Girls on a Free Association Test to Those of Their Parents.* Journ. Soc. Psych. 22 (1945) p. 79-85.

ciation Test to compare the M-F ratings of married couples and parents with those of their daughters. It appears that the girls with the highest feminine ratings are daughters of mothers with the most markedly feminine scores and fathers who are above average in masculinity. At the same time, Smith found indications that there was a tendency for the more masculine men to marry women who are strongly feminine. It would be interesting to check and verify these results and possibly even to extend the investigation by means of M-F scores obtained according to the Terman-Miles method.[39]

The shortened adaptation of the Terman-Miles M-F test drawn up by Houwinck produced credible results, although only a hundred individuals were investigated. In this connection Houwinck again remarks, quite rightly, that the masculinity or femininity measured by means of this (or any other) test relates only to the pheno-typical image of masculinity or femininity in a particular cultural sphere. This image is almost wholly determined by factors of milieu and education, and thus, by the traditional norms actually adhered to in that particular cultural sphere. Houwinck and Dr. Lena Jansen carried out an investigation of the students in the senior classes of schools in Limburg and East Brabant, and found that in non-coeducational schools, both boys and girls tended to be more feminine, while coeducation favored development in the masculine direction, especially among the boys.[40]

Perception and Personality

In recent years, experimental psychology has taken an increasing interest in the connection between perception and personality. In tests aimed at revealing this connection, it appeared that there was also a difference in the way in which men and women orient themselves optically. The difference between man's way of orienting himself and woman's way can be noted only in experimental situations in which the person's orientation is dependent on factors that can be quantitatively modified. For example, the person un-

[39] The results quoted here are taken from Houwinck (see note 34).

[40] R. H. Houwinck and Dr. Lena Jansen, *Masculiniteit en Femininiteit bij de Middelbare school-jeugd in Zuid-Oost Nederland*, Nedr. Tijdschr. v.d. Psych. 6 (1951) p. 439-445.

dergoing the test is placed in a darkened room, and asked to keep a line of light vertically while taking up a number of different bodily positions, or while a square outline of light projected into the room is moved from one position to another.

Witkin [41] and his assistants carried out a number of experiments of this kind, and obtained the following results:

1. Women in their orientation are more dependent on the structure of the whole field of perception. Women accept the field as a whole more passively, while men who are tested tend more to make an active analysis of it. Thus, the men tested were dominated much less by the field as a whole than the women were.
2. Men orient themselves in space by means of the observable position of the body which can be noted by physical sensation. Women relate their body as a visual datum to the surrounding visual environment, and pay little attention to the sensations within the body that make it possible to note the actual position of the body.
3. When the people tested are told to do a number of different things, for example, to adjust a line of light vertically in a dark room, or, in the dark, to move the chair on which they are sitting from a leaning position to an upright one, the results of the women's responses are much more varied than those of the men. The men reveal a greater stability. This comes from the fact that their perception is predominantly analytical, and so from the fact that they note particular details of the situation and particular impressions that arise from the actual position of the body itself.
4. Finally, it is to be noted that after a number of repetitions of the same experiment, women are able to achieve the same result as men, and sometimes a better result than the men.

Besides Witkin's experiments, a number of other recent investigations have shown that women are inclined to be less objective and less analytical in their perception than men, at least on first encountering an experimental situation. In this connection it is

[41] Witkin, H. A., *Sex Differences in Perception.* Trans. N.Y. Acad. Sc. 1949, 12, 22-26, and H. A. Witkin and others, *Personality through Perception,* N. Y. 1954.

interesting that there seems to be some correlation between a quick and accurate perception of detail and an interest in the physical sciences. Woman's tendency to submit to the total impression of an experimental situation in a more passive way is in keeping with ordinary every-day experience, which shows women to be more sensitive than men to "atmosphere" and "mood." It even seems possible to indicate by means of experiments that the sexual difference extends to the manner in which a person experiences his or her own bodily reality.

Prof. Van Lennep and his assistants have also made an important contribution to our knowledge of the factual elements of psychological difference between the sexes.[42] Their investigation was based on a statistical compilation of several thousands of original manuscripts written in response to the "four pictures test" devised by Van Lennep. This is known as a "projection test." Van Lennep's test subjects, practically all of whom were high-school graduates, were asked to write a story, taking their inspiration from four colored but fairly vague representations of people in various ambivalent situations. The investigation produced a number of results, from which we quote the following:

1. Women express themselves in the present tense more often than men do. On comparison of 10 age-groups (the first, 9 to 12 years; the last, 36 to 41 years), the use of the present tense by girls and women undergoing the test was seen to increase in regular proportion to the age of the writer, from more or less 15% of the youngest group to 40% of the oldest group. The use of the present tense by male test subjects shows an increase only from the age-group 20 to 25 years, and reaches more or less 30% in the oldest group. Van Lennep suggests that the increasing use of the present tense is probably related to a decrease in mental vitality, and thus the result of the investigation would make one suspect that vitality of spirit decreases more quickly in women than it does in men.

2. Girls and women make more frequent reference to bodily sensations (tiredness, pain, hunger, thirst, shivering from cold, feeling hot). In this respect there is no difference between boys

[42] D. J. Van Lennep and R. H. Houwinck, *Paper Read at the Symposium on Validity of Projective Techniques at the XII International Congress of Applied Psychology*, London, 1955.

and girls in the age-group 13 to 15 years, but in the age-group 26 to 29 years, mention of bodily sensations has increased in the women's test papers from 54% to 65%, and decreased in the papers written by men from 54% to 43%. The increasing incidence of mention of bodily conditions and sensations is in all probability related to the fact that a young woman takes more interest in anything that concerns her body; a young man, on the other hand, becomes less concerned with his body as he gets older. This result of the investigation is interesting, and is in keeping with the views that will be discussed later on in this book, in Chapter V, section 4.

3. Finally, it can be pointed out that Van Lennep's "Four Pictures" test manuscripts also give indications of woman's greater "youthfulness," which will be discussed in our chapter IV, section 2. Van Lennep set up what he called a "youth score," on the basis of a number of variables dependent on the age-group of the writers, grading the score on a scale of 0-12 points. In this way it was possible for him to grade the papers of the persons tested, and from the points given, to check whether the actual age of the writer agreed with or differed from the age-group to which he or she appeared to belong according to the writing itself. Following this method, it was found that homosexuals are "younger" than comparable groups of normal individuals. When girls and women were compared with boys and men, it appeared that in all of the six age-groups, from the 12-14 group to the 30-39 group, the "youth score" of the ladies was higher. This result is in agreement with a long-standing experience. Girls are more intelligent, and women are probably wiser, but nevertheless (or perhaps for that very reason?) girls and women are more youthful than boys and men of the same age.

Appreciation of Cartoons

One of my students, R. H. R. Dresen, has carried out an investigation into "masculine and feminine appreciation of cartoons" [43] Five categories of cartoons were selected, as follows. 1: *Innocent* (simple, harmless) funny drawings. 2: *Aggressive* (sometimes

[43] Doctoral dissertation.

gloating) jokes. The innumerable cartoons about aggression between husband and wife and about "wearing the pants" in marriage belong to this category. 3: *Lugubrious* jokes, cartoons with a cynical, painful or macabre turn. 4: *Sexual* cartoons, in which the main interest is centered on sexual matters. 5: *Absurd* cartoons, in which the impossible is presented as actual. Five examples chosen from each of these five categories were given to a number of men and women, all of whom had passed high-school at least and some of whom had had further education. These people were asked to comment on the cartoons, to rate them according to a scale of points, and to give an appreciation of the different categories. Dresen's investigation produced a number of interesting results, a few of which we can mention here.

1. There is in fact a difference between masculine and feminine reaction to cartoons, and it is an observable difference that is able to be demonstrated experimentally. In general, the cartoons seem to have been understood more quickly and appreciated more highly by the men. The cartoon drawing apparently is not given the same meaning in the masculine world as in the feminine world. Men are more "addicted" to them than women are; they are more inclined to look at the cartoons in the paper first, and unlike women, they tend to prefer funny drawings to verbal jokes.

2. Apart from this difference in the general attitude to cartoons, there are marked differences between the masculine and the feminine attitudes toward particular sorts of cartoons. It is precisely here that the difference in appreciation is both quantitatively and qualitatively most clear.

   The innocent cartoons are appreciated by both sexes, but more so by women than by men. On the average, this is the only kind of cartoon that the women find wholly successful. The quality of innocent fun found in them does not evoke any painful emotions to spoil their comic effect.

3. The greatest quantitative difference of appreciation between the sexes was found in relation to the aggressive, lugubrious and sexual categories of cartoons, and here too the qualitative difference of appreciation was found to be still greater than the quantitative difference. In this context we can speak of characteristic differences in masculine and feminine appreciation,

insofar as the reactions of men and women may be said to be typical of the masculine and feminine modes of existence respectively. Men give a considerably higher rating than women to these three categories, and it appears from their comments that they do so above all because cartoons of these types give expression to a "naughty" intent ("naughty" in two senses of the word: actually not permissible; but pleasant nevertheless, because the impermissible comically portrayed does not reflect the retribution to follow). Men find these types more pleasantly stimulating than the innocent cartoons, which in their view are inclined to be a little "weak," as long as they are not too crude (e.g., the aggressive type) or too malicious (e.g., the lugubrious type). In general, the men judged the sexual cartoons to be the most successful.

The women found the comic effect of cartoons diminished by the entry of any tendentious element. The more any cartoon served a tendency to make a direct appeal to the emotions, the less they found it to their taste. They felt too much involved, they sometimes identified themselves with the object being ridiculed, and so could not maintain the "emotional distance" necessary to be able to give the situation an ambiguous and amusing structure. This was most clearly evident in the case of the lugubrious category of cartoons. If they found cartoons of this category funny, it was because of the primary comical element of "the linking of disparates" rather than because of any "added pleasure," which in the men's opinion constituted the real "punch" of the cartoon.

4. The absurd category of cartoons forms a group apart, because in relation to them it is very difficult to speak of any typical masculine or typical feminine appreciation. Quantitatively, the men rated these cartoons higher than the women did, but it was not possible to detect any qualitative difference between men's reaction and women's reaction to the actual element of absurdity. There was a remarkable similarity between the ways in which men and women judged cartoons of this kind. Typical differences could be found only in relation to secondary elements of the situations represented by some of the drawings.

5. Taking an overall view of the results of the investigation, we notice that women show an actual preference only for the kind of cartoon that can be called *innocently humorous,* and that

men take more pleasure in the kind we could call *satirically humorous*. In *satire* there is a strong element of distance between the observer and the satirical object, and a strong tendency to view the object as relative. The object is more highly "objectivized" and made the butt of ridicule. It is "not the object of a smile or even of harmless hearty laughter; rather, it appears as something ridiculous and is laughed at" (Lipps). The object is taken "by" . . . taken by some weakness or other (note the expression: to take someone by the nose), and this is injurious to its true value (as someone so taken feels himself "trapped"). The satirically humorous attitude presupposes that the observer be at a distance from the object; it is a critical attitude. The fact that woman gives a lower rating than man to the satirical genre of humor is in harmony with what we will have to say about the feminine mode of existence (see for instance p. 487).

Sense of Humor in the Sexes

6. The fact that woman has strong affinity for the nearby and the concrete causes her sense of humor to be excited primarily by things that are "naturally" funny, amusing things found in the situations of daily life. Woman's sense of humor is much less inclined to be moved by the rather far-fetched situations unlike real life that we find in many jokes and cartoons.

For its part, the masculine sense of humor can equally well be understood in terms of man's particular mode of existence and relationship to the world. The basic masculine concern with the distant and the objective, and the way the male discovers the world as a resistance and as a means, not having any proper value of its own, are factors that promote a critical and aggressive attitude. It is precisely this attitude that predisposes a man to appreciate satirical humor (as well as ridicule and irony) in general, and jokes and cartoons in particular (especially the tendentious ones).

The basic personal dispositions of the male are directed for the most part to the abstract and the impersonal, and in keeping with this fact, the masculine sense of humor tends more to create a distance between a man and the humorous object and to relativize the value of the object than to make a man participate with sympathy in the situation of the object; masculine humor tends rather to "take by" than to "appreciate as." In a manner of speaking, man's sense of fun is much more a matter of the head than of the heart.

Naturally the contrast between the masculine and feminine sense of humor is a relative contrast—just as the difference between the masculine and feminine modes of existence is a relative difference: an individual woman is entirely capable of developing a masculine sense of humor, just as an individual man is capable of developing a feminine one. For the sense of humor is not an inborn characteristic, but a quality of the individual which is constituted in the existence of the individual and therefore is dependent on a number of factors, among them the individual's cultural circumstances.

This means that when we evaluate the results of an investigation, we have to take the cultural situation of the individuals investigated into account. If these belonged to a different level of society, or to a different country or to a different time, the sense of humor would be found to be different too, and there would be a different shade of distinction between the masculine and the feminine sense of humor. Nevertheless the fact remains that it is always possible to discover some difference between what is typically masculine and typically feminine in the sense of humor, no matter what the form of the structure of society, and that this difference reduces ultimately to the sexual differentiation of the mode of existence.

Taking an overall view of the older literature on the characteristics of woman's psyche, what we find is on the whole fairly disappointing. The older writers noted woman's emotionality, the direction of her interests and inclinations, that she is more sympathetic, that she has a greater power of adapting herself to circumstances, and that she takes greater care in the performance of duty. There is no attempt to answer the question of what her "psychological nature" actually is. Also, when we come to investigations concerning children, we find little that can help us gain an insight into this problem.

The reason for this is not only that the influence of the environment determines the psychological characteristics of the individual from his very earliest days, but also, and chiefly, the fact that investigators have approached these "characteristics" and tried to determine them as if they were "facts" in the sense of this word that applies only in the physical sciences. Modern investigators approach the matter differently. We have given three examples of their work above, and in each the investigation is aimed at discovering the total relationship of person and world. Witkin's results, and even more so those obtained by Van Lennep and Dresen, show that the theoretical and methodological principles we follow can and do give rise to fruitful experimental studies.

The standpoint defined by these principles will emerge more clearly in the chapters that are to follow. We will be paying attention to woman's mode of manifesting herself to the world and to others, and to the character of this mode of manifestation as expressive of woman herself. And then we will try to understand woman's personal existence, in terms of her encounters with the world, beginning from the first encounters of the child, the medium in which these encounters take place being the child's own bodily reality. But before we can take up this twofold task, we still have to discuss the way in which woman's nature is viewed in depth-psychology.

4. The Psychoanalytical View

> There is a conflict inherent in woman's existence. She
> has a brain and a womb; like an ellipse she has, as it
> were, two centres compared with the one centre of the
> man's existence, which may be likened to a circle.
>
> OSWALD SCHWARZ [44]

From the earliest of Freud's clinical studies, down to the latest
of the numberless psychoanalytical writings of our own time, interest has centered on the question: what essentially is the nature
of woman? Freud himself, at various stages of his long career,
answered the question decisively, and his answer was accepted and
developed by his orthodox disciples. In the more or less "schis-
matic" offshoots of the original psychoanalysis, we find all sorts of
divergent views regarding the nature of woman, but even so there
are a few fundamental points of insight that constantly recur. We
will not occupy ourselves at any great length with the foundations
of this important trend in psychology, and still less will we try to
trace its historical development and the different lines it has taken.

Freud's own view always bore the stamp of a naturalistic understanding of man, and today the biological point of view still has a
very great influence in psychoanalysis, even where it is not actually
the predominant influence. On these grounds, and for other considerations as well, the psychoanalytical school has been accused
of holding theories that lack depth, of reducing the life of man's
soul to set schemes, and of holding views on sexuality and eroticism that are based on distinctions made without phenomenological foundation. To a fairly large extent, the accusations are well-
founded. Nevertheless, this does not mean that the influence of the
wide-spread Freudian school of thought holds but little significance
for psychology.

The Freudian influence is comparable, in a way, with the significance Darwin's theories have had and the influence they have
exercised on all branches of the science of life. There is all the
more reason for making the comparison when we remember that

[44] *Psychology of Sex.* Pelican Books A 194.

Darwin too could be reproached for being too schematic and too superficial in his views. But still, an "incorrect" theory can lead to the discovery of many facts. Every narrow scheme a scientist draws up, projects an image with wider lines. Now if this image is in fact one of the *aspects* of the object of science, it can help to clarify many experiences. The history of the natural sciences leaves us in no doubt about this.

Freud's basic notion is an extremely simple one, and it most certainly does relate to an important aspect of human existence. For human existence presents itself as a history, a genesis and a differentiation. Along with this, the history of an individual person seems to be wholly determined by the person's basic bodily aptitudes and his milieu. To this irrefutable aspect of human development, Freud added the supposition that a person's *reactions* to his own bodily reality and to the influences of his environment are *also determined,* the determination in this case coming from inborn and elementary instinctual urges, for example, the *instinct for pleasure.* At first sight, this supposition appears to be just as little of a shot in the dark as Darwin's about the "struggle" for self-preservation and the survival of the species. There is however an important difference between the two. The biologist can confine himself to a description of objective natural events that can be observed, and he considers the forms and functions described in relation to the preservation of the individual and the species. Unlike the facts of the biologist's field, pleasure is known to us only as something of which a person is conscious. Therefore it is necessary to ask what pleasure *means* to a person, and it is possible to answer this question only by means of a phenomenological analysis of intentional acts, for that which is called pleasure is found among these acts, and this requires an analysis of the situations that motivate these acts and that are formed by them.

However, Freud and the majority of his followers say that pleasure is so universally "known," that it is quite unnecessary even to try to define it. For indeed it would seem to be perfectly obvious that a "normal" person "naturally" desires pleasurable sensations and wishes to avoid the unpleasurable ones. Circumstances—reality—however often get in the way of the fulfillment of these desires. Freud taught that the first source of pleasure the child finds is its own body; it experiences warmth and the satisfaction of hunger from its mother, the sensations of suckling, the provision of its needs, the caresses it receives, the touching of certain parts of its body, and so on. All of this is elementary and convincing. Thus, the child's first contacts with its own bodily reality and with the situations in the domestic milieu that promote or hinder its pleasure, determine the basic direction in which the life of the child will develop.

The way in which this basic notion is worked out is of secondary importance, but the notion itself deserves our closest attention, in view of the problem of the difference between man and woman. For there is in fact a difference between man and woman from the very beginning of life, and it is a bodily difference that is mainly evident in the anatomical difference of the sexual parts. Because of this difference, the milieu can influence the development of the child in different ways, mainly because a child's educators do not treat a girl in the same way as they treat a boy. Later in life the difference in development is accentuated more strongly, through the child's *reaction* to its own body and to the milieu, and above all to relationships with other people.

The Libido

"The differentiation of man and woman," writes Freud in his *Three Contributions to the Theory of Sex,* "begins already at a very early age. The differentiation is especially accentuated at the time of puberty, but differences are already present in the first years of life." Moreover, libido (which is to be understood as the "energy" of the erotic-sexual instinct in the broadest sense) is— according to Freud—actually more of a masculine characteristic, since it is an energy which subserves the biological purpose of masculine sexuality, and in principle this purpose is not dependent upon the consent of the woman. Thus it is not possible to speak of a special "female libido," but even so, this energy is also operative in the female sex from birth. It is present in girls as well as boys, and the energy is in principle independent of the object toward which libido is directed.

The second notion developed by Freud in his writings is that the sexuality of a girl is powerfully inhibited from a very early age.

The curb put upon it is to a large extent determined by education. Freud does not go into the question of whether and to what extent an aboriginal and inborn difference between the sexes gives rise to this curbing of female sexuality. That something of this sort does exist is suggested, in a certain sense, by the fact that the partially sexual urges of the little girl, which manifest themselves in a great variety of forms, are actually formed in such a way that preference is shown for predominantly passive manifestations.

The third notion, influentially prevalent in all of Freud's studies, is generally well-known. The "sexuality" of the young child passes through three different phases. The last of these phases, which occurs between the 3rd and the 5th year, is directed toward the primary sexual organ. When this becomes the erogenous zone of the libido, the anatomical difference between the external sexual organs gives rise to an important difference between the behavior of the boy and the behavior of the girl. During this phase, an infantile sexual relationship toward parents (or educators) begins to be formed in the way the sensations of pleasure are developed. We may note that this relationship does not follow the same course in girls and in boys, but for our purposes it is not necessary to go any further into this particular point.

Freud considered it to be of the greatest importance that there is a perfect continuity in the development of erotic experience and of the experience of the sexual organs in boys, throughout the latent period (from more or less 6 years old until puberty) and beyond it. The development of the little girl into the normal woman is much more difficult and much more complicated, "for it embraces two additional requirements which have no counterparts in the development of men." [45] The erogenous zone of a young girl in the last phase of infantile sexuality is entirely different from the erogenous zone of an adult woman. The first requirement to be fulfilled during the development of a woman is that the seating of sexual pleasure be removed from the one erogenous zone to the other.

We may ask why this is called a requirement, a task, whereas in the first few years of life the erogenous zones modify and change themselves, "automatically." The reason for calling this particular

[45] *Die Weiblichkeit*, in *Neue Folge der Vorlesungen zur Einführung in die Psycho-analyse.* (Gesammelte Werke, London, Vol. XV. p. 124)

removal a task is because it takes place at a time of life when the young girl is aware of her own initiative, and does not merely sense her body but also gives it a meaning. Moreover, according to Freud, the change of the erogenous zone implies and signifies a profound modification in the basic pattern of behavior, this particular modification being in fact the passage from "male activity" to "female passivity."

The second task or requirement the adolescent girl has to fulfill concerns her relationship to her parents. In the matter of this relationship to parents too, there is a much greater continuity in the development of a boy. A boy's mother is the first object of his love, and she continues to be the object of his love even in the so-called Oedipus complex, an ambivalent attitude toward the father, and often she remains the first object of his love throughout his life. For a little girl the mother is also the first person to whom she directs the vitality of her love, but when she gets a little older her father becomes the object of her love. This happens in order to lead on to the eventual binding of herself to a man, where the development has been normal.

"From a certain age onwards, the elementary influence of heterosexual attraction makes itself felt, and the young woman feels an urge toward man while the same law confirms the young boy in his belonging to his mother." [46] This would of course be the most ideal solution, and the simplest one, if we could accept it. It is quite clear, from experience of the psychoanalytical treatment of many women as well as from observation of children, that the transference of love from the mother to the father can go hand in hand with a whole series of experiences that are at the same time moral *"tasks."*

In order to be able to understand what these experiences are, it is not sufficient to judge them in terms of the data provided by the analysis of patients. For it is not only possible but likely that the analysis of a patient will reveal abnormal experiences in the patient's youth. Direct observation of the life of children will also not provide sufficient data, for the experiences in question here are impressions and feelings the child lives through inwardly, and seldom if ever expresses outwardly in words or in modes of behavior. Here then we find one of Freud's theoretical suppositions—which

---

[46] *Die Weiblichkeit*, p. 127.

can be called "brilliant" or "risky" according to whether one's appreciation of his views is approving or critical. Whatever the case, these experiences are not mere figments of the imagination; they are possible aspects of human reality in the child, and therefore we will have to give attention to them.

The difference between men and women, says Freud, is an anatomical difference, but, he says, this anatomical difference *must* have psychological consequences, and therefore it forms the basis of the whole of the subsequent personal development. Thinking along these lines, it was easy for him to connect the difference with the "active-passive" antithesis. In this context, activity means aggression. Passivity however does not mean allowing oneself to drift, but a positive striving after what Freud calls "passive ends."

Passivity is thus an active pursuit of passive ends. This takes place in association with the suppression of aggression. Thus, for a boy aggression means having a grasp on things and dominating, and this means pleasure. In contrast, the girl elects to be and constitutes herself as the one who is grasped and dominated. In cases of pathological development, this contrast leads to the contrast between sadism and masochism, pleasure in hurting and pleasure in being hurt. In the whole world and history of psychoanalytical thought, the paired concepts of sadism and masochism have fulfilled and still fulfill an important function.

Thus, Freud himself defined feminine nature very briefly as a *passive masochism*, and in emulation of him, one of his woman students, Helene Deutsch, defines it in the same terms. This passive masochism then is supposed to be "genuine" femininity. It would however be unjust to Freud to think that he took feminine masochism to be simply what it appears to be in every-day life, and did not attribute to it any richer or deeper content than it possesses as a type of sexual perversity. We find he does, in his description of how even the very little girl is by nature less aggressive as a rule and also less self-sufficient, and of how she is in greater need of tenderness and for this reason more dependent and more docile. Because of these characteristics, the little girl develops a premature sense of cleanliness, she is more lively, affective relationships are predominant in her, and, in Freud's view, she shows a greater development of intelligence at an earlier age. These differences between the sexes are extremely variable and they are not essential.

Discovery of Anatomical Differences

However, the ambivalent attitude toward the mother has a very profound influence and determines the direction of development in boys as well as in girls. This attitude is decisively conditioned, according to Freud's thinking, by an experience in the child which is regarded as a critical factor in its development. This factor is the castration complex. In boys this complex takes a different form than it takes in girls. On the basis of the psychoanalysis of very many patients, it is held to be proved that the girl discovers the anatomical difference of the sexes when she is still very young indeed, and that she gives meaning to the difference in two senses. In the first place, the little child thinks that the boy's sexual organ is in fact the reason for the boy's particularly privileged position in the society of children. In the second place, and following immediately from the first, there arises in the little girl the so-called "penis envy," that is, the unconscious wish "also to have something like that" so that she too may be granted her full value. Very many objections have come from many sides, that in the majority of children nothing of this sort can be found, and that most people cannot remember ever having been through such an experience. But these objections carry no weight with the Freudians, precisely because they are thinking of an *unconscious* wish and a meaning given unconsciously to the anatomical difference.

Even so, we cannot disregard the fact that the very possibility of making the discovery of the actual anatomical difference is wholly lacking in a large number of cases. It is therefore not possible simply to accept Freud's view literally as it is presented. And it is certainly not possible to accept his view literally if one wishes to make use of it to explain the important change that takes place in the little girl's attitude toward her mother, a change that is supposed to arise out of the experience of a lack which is looked upon as a maiming, a castration. For Freud holds that through the discovery of the fact that she lacks the male sexual appendage and the discovery of the *solidarity* with her mother that she has developed, the little girl holds her mother chiefly responsible for the fact that she lacks it.[47] This is taken to place the child in an ambiguous and retarded attitude of life, just as all ambivalence, disap-

[47] "The discovery of her castration is a critical point in the development of a young girl." *Die Weiblichkeit,* p. 144.

pointment and feelings of resentment are expressed primarily in a curbing or retarding of the attitude toward life.

The consequence, however, of this curbing of the life of feeling —Freud speaks of "sexual restraint"—is a reaction which can take various forms. It can take the form of an attempt to imitate the type of life enjoyed by the male sex, and so, to want to develop the self in the direction of masculinity (the so-called masculinity complex). A second possibility is that the reaction takes the form of a neurotic development in which all sorts of compulsive patterns of behavior and all sorts of anxieties can arise. A third form of the reaction is the normal one: the girl simply submits to the irrefutable difference, she accepts the feminine mode of existence, she overcomes the sense of disillusionment and the apparent inferiority which seemed to fill this mode of existence, and she sets positively about the development of an adult feminine life in all its dignity and value. Freudians discuss how these three modes of reaction are manifested, and how they are expressed in the games girls play, with dolls for instance, but from the point of view of our problem, the importance of all this is secondary.

What is the end result of the normal development? As Simone de Beauvoir correctly remarks, Freud's view of the final outcome of normal development is entirely dominated by the image that men have always formed of women. He is more sentimental than scientific when he writes, "Woman has little sense of justice. . . . this indeed goes along with the predominance of envy in the life of her soul . . ." [48]

There is more psychological depth in his explanation of the fact that woman is less inclined to involve herself in the affairs of the community. "We usually say that women have less interest in society and that their capacity for sublimating their urges is less than that of men. We can explain the former in terms of the a-social or dis-social character undoubtedly proper to all sexual relationships. Lovers find a sufficiency in each other, and even the family is opposed to being absorbed in wider connections. As to the latter, the ability to sublimate is subject to the most powerful individual variations. Yet I cannot neglect to mention an impression one gets time and again in analytical practice. A man of 30 years or so gives the impression of being a youthful person, and even of being an incompletely formed person, of whom we might expect that he

[48] *Die Weiblichkeit,* p. 144.

will make energetic use of the possibilities analysis offers for his further development. But a woman of the same age often disturbs us by her psychological inflexibility and unchangeability. Her libido has taken up definite positions, and appears to be no longer able to leave these positions for others." [49]

This rather lengthy quotation shows perfectly clearly how Freud viewed feminine nature. The girl is forced to react to her environment in a determined way because of her basic bodily aptitudes, and because the nature of her urges relates to these aptitudes. One consequence of this is her greater need for tenderness, and another is her jealousy. When the difficult process of development into an adult woman has been completed, the woman's personal potentiality for directing the energy of her instinctual urges to other objects seems to have been exhausted. This is the image of passively masochistic woman that Freud develops, and we have to admit that we meet with it all too frequently in our culture.

Nevertheless, even the psychoanalytical school regards this much more as the outcome of education than as the result of basic aptitudes—even if it is regarded above all as the consequence of the overwhelming power of sexuality in the broadest sense. The concluding lines of Freud's treatise on femininity are therefore a testimony of his great experience and wisdom: "But do not forget that we have been describing woman only insofar as her being is determined by her sexual function. This influence is certainly very far-reaching, but we do keep in mind the fact that, independently of it, the individual woman is able to be a human being." And this, indeed, is the very crux of the problem. How can the humanity of woman maintain itself in all its freedom, in spite of her being forced into a manner of existence that—according to Freud and all practitioners of depth-psychology—is confined to the libido as to the source of its energy by the aboriginal striving after pleasure?

Pleasure—Displeasure

What is actually known about these feelings of pleasure? We could look through all the writings of all the psychoanalysts, and still not be able to find any "canon," any clear information, on the feelings in question. As we have seen, the psychoanalysts regard all

[49] *Die Weiblichkeit*, p. 144.

pleasures as variations of "sexuality," without however making clear what sexuality means. But as long as we do not know, precisely and *properly* what pleasure in this *primary* sense of the word actually is, it will not be possible to explain why the two sexes follow different lines of development from the very beginning, for this aboriginal pleasure is taken to be the aim toward which the living subject—whether animal or young child—directs itself, through the immediacy of its very *first* encounters, long before there can be any question of "penis envy" or "castration complex."

The psychoanalytical view of feminine nature falls short for several reasons, one of them being that psychoanalysis, like the older psychology, has tried to divide the feelings and emotions under the headings of the antithesis: pleasure—displeasure. Thus the libido theory has had no lack of critics, particularly in regard to its having equated all the various forms of pleasurable feelings univocally.

In the young child—and in the animal—we can observe an alternation of rest and activity. A vital equilibrium is established, and when it is disturbed, there is no doubt that the disturbance is answered by an effort of the life-principle to restore the "indicated balance" (Goldstein). But it seems likely that the removal of a disturbance, from the subject's point of view, has the character of the cessation of an unpleasant sensation and not the character of a positive pleasure. But when rest is experienced as a positive pleasure, phenomenological analysis shows that it is experienced, not so much as the cessation of disturbance, but rather as the entry into a state of security. Rest has this in common with very many other forms of security, that it is chosen because it is pleasant.

What now of spontaneous activity? It is said that the child takes pleasure in activity—the "pleasure of function," in Bühler's terminology. This is more or less the case. The child manifests an urge to be in movement, and tries to realize the urge, and evidently takes pleasure in the resulting activity.

But what precisely does this activity mean? On the one hand, it means the abandoning of a present state of security, whatever form of security this might happen to be. For every activity implies breaking through a certain boundary, and every activity is the abolition of an existing situation. For this reason, an act of transcending lies at the basis of every human activity, inasmuch as this human activity is intended within a human existence. And then, on the other hand, the active subject, by its activity, places itself in a new spatial dimension, the dimension in which it runs, walks, jumps, hops, climbs, grasps things, makes sounds—the dimension of the action which it performs. Thus, every activity has a twofold meaning. Activity means, in the first place, the abandoning of a given security and, in the second place, the entry into a new dimension unfolded by the activity and discovered through it.

If, as the psychoanalysts point out, all rest has the character of "orgastic" pleasure, even in the new-born infant, it is obvious that every spontaneous activity will also possess orgastic characteristics —to think only for instance of the 'intoxicating' forms of activity in which we can see this most clearly.

However, in *each* situation, the feelings of pleasure have a *different* quality. There is a feeling of pleasure in having overcome a resistance, and another in having achieved something, and it is inadmissible to class them both under the concept of sadism. We can speak of classes of similar feelings only when there is similarity among the situations projected, and thus, only when the intentional acts projecting them are of the same kind. The concepts of sadism and masochism are meaningful only when they relate to neurotic and sexually perverse acts, and therefore only when they are used to refer to highly abnormal divergence from the normal attitude to the world. What in fact do an achievement of something and an overcoming of resistance have in common? The common factor consists in what may be called the passing of a narrow gateway, with the subsequent experience of ease and breadth of space. This however is the central characteristic present in the realization of every act of transcending. All acts of transcendence are developed out of the constraint of a spontaneous initiative, and must pass the narrow gateway of a realization which is in some sense a risk, in order to flow with satisfaction out into the world toward which the acts are, properly speaking, directed.

If we try to draw up a preliminary phenomenology of the elementary and universal forms of pleasure, paying attention above all to the characteristics pleasures have in common and not to the distinctive characteristics of each, we see that there are in any case *two* types of pleasurable feelings, one representing the meaning of projected repose and the other, the meaning of projected activity. In the first place, there is the awareness of "being-at-one-with." This could be called the pleasure of security. In the second place, there is the awareness of entry into a new dimension, an awareness of the removal of constraint, of escape, overcoming, transcending, an awareness of choosing to be oneself in one's own initiative. Following upon the most original and basic form of life and flowing from it, there is a joy of expansion, of freedom and independence, and equally a joy of security, of submerging, of being wholly absorbed, of "being-in-and-with."

But a question arises. Can we in fact understand the various forms of pleasure that are already evident in the little child in terms of these two basic types of pleasure? It is quite clear that the little child's efforts to achieve something or to overcome some resistance are intentional. Knowledge of this fact is not reserved to the psychoanalysts. Everyone knows it from personal experience, and every mother knows it from experience with her children.

Even in the animal world, the organism expresses itself spontaneously in grasping and chasing and catching. Besides this, we know very well that little children and little animals manifest an opposite but equally original form of behavior, allowing themselves to be held, submitting to and becoming wholly absorbed in caresses, in being stroked or nursed or rocked, in sleep and warmth and silence. These forms of security take on a particular importance when the little child first succeeds in the risky business of standing up and walking, and so gains in freedom what it loses in certainty and safety. The antithetical states of activity and repose, hunger and satisfaction, restlessness and contentment, alternate in every infant in arms, but as soon as the little child begins to walk, its primary situation has in principle become quite different and now full of danger.

The child might resist and overcome the danger "with courage," or it may seek refuge in the familiar and safe embrace of its mother. It can enter on the way of initiative and human independence, or it can choose to remain an infant, to submit to what others do for and to it. These two possible forms of behavior are opposite extremes. In between the extremes, is there not an area of actions and situations which possess their meaning neither in the awareness of the act nor in the awareness of security? Between the extremes there is in fact a large area of acts and situations that are ambiguous. There are dangerously safe situations, irritations that are somehow delightful; there is excitement in uncertainty, there are things that tickle and things that give one the creeps—there are all those situations in which the self is itself and yet not itself, situations which are sought in their ambiguity as a bond and a tension between the two primary forms of pleasure.

In the primordial eroticism (by which we understand the interiorly appreciated allure of the child's physical sensations), and, later on, in all sexual relationships, *both* forms of pleasure are continually bound up in an ambivalent tension which is elicited, preserved and satisfied by the reciprocal behavior of the participants in the relationship. It is precisely this ambivalence or ambiguity that in love-play sustains the actual quality of play.

The phenomenological analysis has to be pressed further with greater refinement of perception if this schematized image of the primordial forms of pleasure is to be filled out with greater richness of detail. But the preliminary antithesis of the polar unities of the pleasure of security and the pleasure of expansion does offer us the opportunity of a deeper insight into the primordial difference of the sexes. According to Freud and the Freudians, there is an inborn dynamism of an instinctual urge toward pleasure, the libido, and it is capable only of quantitative variation.

Freud understands a person's behavior as a reaction of a psychic structure to the environment that exists around it. This reaction produces feelings of pleasure or displeasure which are caused by physical stimuli and become the content of the consciousness. However, we need not look upon these feelings as things the subject undergoes, things which at the same time provide the *power* which moves and directs the subject's behavior. We can look upon these feelings as modes of existence in projected situations. The Freudian way of looking at them leads to an analysis of a supposed psychic mechanism and its reactions to a world already present and constituted. The other way of looking at them leads to an analysis of a subject's historical development proceeding from project to project, revealing that the subject itself in its development makes a world of its own of what it finds, and gives this world a meaning of its own.

In the Freudian way, the bodily reality of the subject is regarded as the primary fact. Later we will see that in the other way too, we must look on the bodily reality as the primary reality offered to the subject, but in an entirely different sense than that followed in psychoanalysis. Our existential standpoint also calls for an investigation of the shades of variation in the "treatment" of boys and girls from the very earliest days of their lives. The educational situation and the living relationships of children and their parents and of children among themselves, are determined by the meaning actually given to existence as a boy or existence as a girl. If one lot is provided with a security-environment and the other with an expansion-environment, this can elicit an imbalance of the primary forms of pleasure, and the imbalance can itself become the chosen meaning of the mode of existence in which the individual develops. However, the imbalance is never so completely to one side as to eliminate the other. Little boys and little girls are all human beings, and all human beings, even little ones, always manifest the initiative of directing themselves to the unknown, the new, the dangerous, just as much as to the known, the old and the safe.

We can now try to come to understand the psychoanalytical definition of woman's nature in greater detail, and in doing so will take our lead from Helene Deutsch, one of Freud's students, but one who, in her extensive study of the question [50] has disassociated herself to some extent from orthodox Freudian views.

Woman as "Passive-Masochist"

Helene Deutsch defines woman as passive-masochist,[51] by which she means that woman experiences *pleasure* in the form of subjecting herself, of undergoing things, of giving herself over into the grasp of others, of accepting unfreedom, patience and even suffering. Quite understandably, practically every woman objects to this opinion. But if we replace the word "pleasure" by the word "value," the description of passive masochism immediately takes on another meaning, one that provides much more clarity for an understanding of woman. But in doing so, we have departed in principle from the psychoanalytical way of thinking. If woman grants a quality of positive value to putting up with something, or to being subjected, or to being in a position of unfreedom, it may be that she does not merely accept all this because of the value she grants it, but that she chooses it and seeks it out.

[50] We follow the Swiss edition of *Psychology of Women: Psychologie der Frau,* Bern 1948. (quotations from the German).
[51] "We ascribe the role of a central core in the psychical structure of woman to passive-masochistic tendencies" *Psychologie der Frau* p. 255.

However, there is no more than a formal relation between the positive quality of a good or a value and the character of a sensation of pleasure. It is precisely the failure to make a distinction between these two concepts that leads the psychoanalysts to equate the thetic awareness of a value with the thematic awareness of a feeling (e.g., of pleasure), for it is clear that none of the psychoanalysts ever make this distinction. Because of this, there is a vagueness about their images that makes it impossible, using their mode of thinking, to arrive at any theoretical insight into human existence. Their concepts are indeed able to be used for practical purposes, but then, so were the concepts found in the mythological presentations of the brain in the older forms of psychiatry, even if these were perhaps not quite as useful.

But still, Freud and his followers have gathered a vast treasure of observations and experiences, and even though they speak in vague concepts and mechanistic imagery, it is possible to penetrate through their manner of speaking to the reality they are speaking about. In this way it also becomes possible to discover a stature of truth in the psychoanalytical view of woman's nature.

Thus we may ask, to what reality are they referring when they speak of woman's passive masochism? Helene Deutsch declares explicitly that passive masochism—which is, essentially, taking pleasure in pain—is for the most part the outcome of the dominating influences to which a girl is subjected from babyhood and which are later perpetuated in the dominating influence of a social structure designed according to the needs of the men.

But Helene Deutsch also says that the "central core" of femininity has biological, anatomical and physiological foundations too, and that this can be seen from the fact that even in the animal world the female individual is predominantly passive in sexual relations. Thus, this passivity is taken to be an inborn characteristic, natural to the female individual, and that it is phylogenetic, *i.e.,* it has its roots in the origin and evolution of the species. We ought however to remember that this passivity is a quality which in man is unlike this passivity in animals, in that the human expression of it is not confined solely to sexual relationships. How is this to be explained? An explanation seems possible only if we accept Freud's basic notion, that the sexual relation is the basic form of the general attitude of the subject toward fellow human beings and even toward the world.

Now if this is correct, it would indeed be possible to speak of a biological determination, not of course in the sense of an immutable disposing of woman's lot, but as an enticement, an invitation, an accomodation of nature itself which could be understood even as a compulsive motivation proceeding from her biological and physical reality. It could then be quite probable that the female child's pleasure in security arises in her the more easily because of the basic aptitudes and dispositions of her body.

Jealousy

Little children, though they may be very young, are human however, and thus the little girl discovers within herself the possibility of directing herself to what is new, toward transcendence, in the free initiative of her actions. But already at a very early age, the little girl experiences that "giving free and vital expression" to this initiative is the "privilege" of the boy. Helene Deutsch therefore has good reason to say that psychoanalysis has gathered evidence of many experiences that indicate that woman is not entirely satisfied with her own nature,[52] and we might add that the same has been found in child psychology. Thus there will in general be a ready tendency toward jealousy in the little girl, and the feeling to which it gives rise becomes a mode of her existence as she establishes herself in relation to the boy.

Particularly when the joy of security plays little part in her life, perhaps because she experiences little tenderness from others or for other reasons, a "lively" little girl is liable to grow jealous of the joys others can experience in their expansivity, in their ability to control things, to set themselves free, to give free rein to their initiative. Jealousy, it is sure, may easily lie at the basis of a woman's mode of existence. The causes of this jealousy are partly in her physical constitution and partly in the demands made on a woman even when she is still in her childhood. In our view, this jealousy is of a much more original and understandable kind than the jealousy which may occasionally be engendered by a girl's discovery of the anatomical difference between herself and a boy, although it is not denied that it *is possible* for this jealousy, once it

[52] *Psychologie der Frau,* p. 204.

is present, to be symbolized and concretized in a desire to possess the male sexual organ.

Jealousy with regard to the privileged position of the strong and dominant sex is related to the resentment which Scheler, [53] following Nietzsche, shows to have a predominant influence on the structure of ethical relationships. A person's resentment however does not merely project his own insufficiency and poverty in his desire for the abundant sufficiency of another; resentment is characterized precisely in the fact that the resentful person's jealousy is kept "secret" because the object of that jealousy is presented as worthless. The "sour grapes" attitude is typical of resentment; because they are out of reach, the grapes *are* "sour," that is, they are projected as sour.

A woman's jealousy with regard to the masculine mode of existence, and the jealousy of a girl with regard to the boy's mode of existence, may thus take either of two forms. It may be an uncomplicated and open-hearted desire for the greater number of possibilities open to the male, for more expansivity, for more freedom, or it may be a hidden, "sour-grapes" coveting concealed in a rejection of what is rich, ripe and attractive, and in a demonstrative insistence on the individual's own poor insufficiency. Scheler shows us this structure of resentment present in the typical attitude of the "bourgeois," [54] and, if we wish to understand correctly the so-called passive masochism of woman, a grasp of his phenomenological insight is of fundamental importance.

It is therefore incorrect to retrace and reduce the passivity of woman "to the sexual development of the little girl, above all, to a particular difficulty in this development (the genitalia-trauma)," as Helene Deutsch has done [55] (and as Freud does too). The passivity in a woman—if and when a woman is passive—comes of the woman having elected to be passive, and if she does, it is usually because of resentment. This passivity is not animal; it is a human thing, and *therefore* it *can* characterize the whole of a woman's existence. Thus the psychoanalysts, in our view, take a view of woman's "nature" that is incorrect in principle, and by way of illustrating this, we quote once again from the work of

[53] *Das Ressentiment im Aufbau der Moralen; Aufsätze* I p. 39ff.
[54] *Der Bourgeois und die religiösen Mächte.*
[55] *Psychologie der Frau*, p. 218.

Helene Deutsch: "This preponderance of passive tendencies expresses itself in the whole of a woman's instinctual life. To give but
one example: in women, the love of display becomes an exhibi-
tionism that is overwhelmingly passive in character—woman loves
to be seen, while the activity of seeing is more proper to man."
Now, if there were indeed a biological foundation for these passive
tendencies, how very "genuinely" feminine the peacock would be!

Psychoanalysts do make a distinction between feminine masochism and the moral masochism that is the consequence of a sense of
guilt and that involves a tendency toward self-punishment. Furthermore, feminine masochism is not the same as the conscious
sexual perversity of the masochist (who is usually a man). Every
human life, whether of man or of woman, is aimed at the diminu-
tion of displeasure and pain. This, says Helene Deutsch, is the
reason why people do not believe that there is such a thing as
feminine masochism. Woman does not wish for pain. She certainly
does not seek physical pain, and like any human being, she defends
herself against suffering. To understand the origin of woman's
masochism, it is necessary to follow the course of the life of a girl.
Thus, Freud says that feminine masochism is "erzogen," the result
of upbringing, and supposes a very strong influence on the part of
the milieu. The little girl is actually at her most neutral before the
time of her puberty. She is not then averse to her femininity,
neither does she have more than a very slight desire of masculinity
in the majority of cases. She has a balanced control of reality. But
when a girl enters upon her time of puberty, she sees herself placed
before two tasks: to set herself free from the past, and to overcome the difficulties of the actual present situation.

The past is represented particularly by the mother. For the
mother, to the little boy as well as to the little girl, is the means of
development, at least for as long as the child constitutes itself in its
dependence and in its security. But when the child reaches a certain age, the mother can become a continual impediment to its
initiative and thus a hindrance in the way of all the pleasure of
expansivity. Expansion demands the severing of bonds. It is indeed
the abandonment of security—that security which the mother always is to the child. This severing of bonds may become the reason
why love is suddenly changed into hate. One thing is clear. The
more strongly the child experiences the bonds as a hindrance to its

freedom, and the more powerfully an appeal is made at the same time to the child's conscience, the more inevitably feelings of uncertainty, very much like anxiety, will accompany the child's aggression against these bonds (psychoanalysts would say, the child's aggression against its mother).

The uncertainty is anxiety about the loss of love, anxiousness in the face of the unknown and about guilt incurred. How will the boy and the girl react to this situation at the time of puberty? Obviously, since there is no absolute division between the characteristics of the sexes but the tones of masculinity and femininity flow together and intermingle differently in each individual, the reaction may take any one of an immense variety of forms. But still, education, in which the traditional demands are maintained, will already have formed the girl in a particular direction, and puts pressure on her to choose an existence other than that of the boy, and to come to decisions that are other than his, for the boy after all has to do what boys are supposed to do. Girls are not "expected" to be like them; they are expected to choose to be passive.

Thus, when the child reaches the age of puberty, it is moved to constitute its personality in the male or the female form that is pheno-typical of our culture. Now, in this, the child separates itself from its parents, or rather, comes to place a lesser value on security. It is therefore quite understandable that the father, who in the little child's environment was the person who represented expansivity, should become, to the adolescent girl as well as to the adolescent boy, the one who represents the existence the growing child desires, the one who projects a human world in all the fullness of its value. The child wants to be a fully adult person, and the adult world is the world of the father. The adolescent girl as well as the boy continues to see the mother as home and refuge, security, the source of infantile satisfactions (in the terms used by the psychoanalysts), or, to put it plainly, they continue to see the mother as the one who represents helpfulness, and *therefore* as the one who represents the helplessness and attachment of the child, and *therefore* as the one who represents their dependence. All these define a social position which the child begins to see through and to reject when it reaches the age of puberty.

The process seldom involves any great difficulty for the boy. He, after all, is expected to untie himself from mother's apron-strings.

Helene Deutsch says, convincingly, that the boy tries to establish ties with his father and that the father on his part honors these ties. This is an "agreement among men," and free from the emotional complications of a rivalry with regard to the love of the mother. Both father and son stand as it were in opposition to her. "In the more active phases of his life, the boy is characteristically rather condescending toward his mother, he behaves protectively toward her and despises her a little, and it is interesting that the father in most cases shows himself well disposed to ally himself to the son in all this," and Helene Deutsch adds that a mother of delicate feminine sensitivity will accept and even encourage this, even though it may mean a certain loss of tenderness and affection to her.

Functions of the Ego

We can agree with this; it is an accurate picture of the life of a boy. In it, there is no attempt to make interpretations on the basis of supposed instinctual urges and the conflicts to which they give rise. The behavior described is purely human. If one wishes to go on and call the elements of this behavior "functions of the Ego," then Helene Deutsch's remark is very much to the point: "Our psychoanalytical thought finds it very difficult to understand these functions of the Ego, which play their rôle outside of any conflicts arising from instinctual urges." [56] For these reasons it is necessary to regard the supposed mechanisms of psychoanalysis as one-sided aspects of the reality, to see that the psychoanalytical view has only a relative value, and to find some other formulation of the truth it does contain.

This is certainly necessary if we want to see what "feminine masochism" really does mean. In a sense, Helene Deutsch herself shares our view, for she states that to accept an independent active tendency in the Ego—we call it the free human initiative—can be very helpful in coming to understand woman's passivity and masochism. Adaptation to the milieu is then not merely a passive submission, but an active inclination to influence and possibly to alter the situation.

Not only the boy, but the girl too directs herself toward her

[56] *Psychologie der Frau*, p. 121.

father when she reaches the age of puberty, because her human initiative leads her to suspect that there is joy in the expansive act. For the girl too, the meaning of adulthood is, in a certain sense, "separation from the mother." But when the girl tries to direct herself more toward her father, she is socially impeded in a variety of ways by both parents, but especially by her mother. An appeal is made to her womanly "nature." People are at pains to point out to her her fragility, to remind her of the place "everyone" expects her to fill in society, to remind her of her probable forthcoming marriage and motherhood. Thus much pressure is brought to bear on her, to seek the centre of her satisfaction not in expansion but in security. This is perhaps a more apt formulation of the reality than can be provided by the concept of "passive masochism" which is so liable to be misunderstood.

The psychoanalytical view of woman attaches no more than secondary importance to the fact that the girl's ties with her father can be of such variety that many forms of sublimation and substitution are possible (for example, her brothers may fill this role), or that she may develop a very boyish mode of activity which suddenly gives way to a so-called masochistic mode of behavior—seeking her delight in being subject or in being made to submit to others. None of this is essential, but only coincidental.

Accidental too is the relationship of boys and girls to each other, in whatever of the many possible forms in which this relationship occurs. It is not a universal and constant rule that the girl is accepted only if she takes as her own the role of victim. Her acceptance is however very often subjected to this condition; this is a known fact. (Remembering the games of his own childhood, everyone knows how girls were admitted to the boys' games, how they were treated roughly and went away in tears, and how they quickly dried the tears and came back to play again.) Remarkably enough, this kind of experience does give rise to the idea that the ones who do this are "genuine" little girls, in whom, thus, a masochism is an important factor.

The main point to notice is that aggressiveness is not tolerated in a girl. "The milieu," writes Helene Deutsch, "offers a prize, as it were a natural bribe, to the feminine Ego if it renounces all aggressiveness." [57] The prize, in actual fact, is the friendliness, the kind

[57] *Psychologie der Frau*, p. 229.

reception, the tenderness the girl receives from her father and the praise she receives from father and mother both.

And so we see that psychoanalysis makes no startling novel discovery: what it offers can also be known in other ways. When the psychoanalysts speak of the passive-masochist *nature* of woman, they are actually referring to the contrasting strength of the pleasure of expansivity in the boy and of the pleasure of security in the girl which, under the influence of the milieu, leads the boy to develop himself in one direction and the girl to develop herself in another. The outcome of the development will later find a marked expression in the sexual life of the man and the woman, but in some way it can already be seen in the erotic ties and the ties of tenderness that exist in the life of the child and in the outward forms in which these are expressed. The existential project of the girl calls for foresight and carefulness; she really looks ahead and thus there is a certain reserve about her, she holds back (from the impulsive, unconsidered action), and this reserve can easily be called passivity.

All security in the world is always threatened. But if expansivity is threatened it is at the same time provoked, for that which threatens expansivity is precisely the resistance that hinders it. This is why a masculine existence may *"easily"* be developed as an unlimited transcendence and why the man finds his pleasure and satisfaction in transcendence without limit. But when security is the centre of an existence, that existence is not merely threatened accidentally, but always threatened in its essence. For a threat to security cannot be answered by a deeper security, unless of course the deeper security is in that which cannot possibly be threatened, or which at least seems unable to be threatened. The psychoanalysts refer to this as sublimation.

The act of sublimation in a woman's existence is therefore wholly understandable in terms of the deepest basis of that existence and of the most fundamental characteristics of the feminine world. But sublimation in the case of a child is only apparent sublimation. For the child knows no security other than the security of particular situations, *all* of which may be threatened. A young girl may become reconciled to this negative characteristic of her world, and if need be, her reconciliation to it may be called masochism, but in her case masochism never means pleasure in pain, dependence, weakness, helplessness and so on.

Passive Masochism

But the woman who has attained to the full value of her adulthood knows a possible security that cannot be threatened, and this security lies in goodness, in truth, in God. If this is called a sublimated security, the word is not used in the sense the psychoanalysts give it. What then is the meaning of passive masochism—the supposed nature of woman?

The concept of masochism has actually a twofold meaning. In the literal sense, it is used to signify joy in suffering. But masochism can be given another meaning, using it to signify the discovery of a positive *value* in the acceptance of something that in itself has only a negative value and that for this reason is encountered primarily with displeasure. Of these two meanings, one differs in principle from the other. That suffering *itself* becomes a pleasure is something wholly and entirely different from the fact that a good (a pleasure) can be realized through and beyond suffering, the good in this case being able to be reached exclusively through the *acceptance* of an actual pain. The question is, whether this relationship of pleasure and pain can possibly be found in a pre-reflexive life, in the positional consciousness. Whatever the answer to this question, pleasure and pain can be so related in the reflexive consciousness, and innumerable ethical and religious images can be found which reflect a relationship between the acceptance of a pain and the acquisition of a value and a joy through that acceptance. Attempts have been made to define this relationship in terms of masochism and sublimation, but there is no justification for this.

For example, Helene Deutsch tells us that the imagination of a girl passing through the phase of puberty indicates that the structure of her personality is completely masochistic. That it does so, says Helene Deutsch, can be seen not only from the nightmares she suffers, but also from the fervor of her generally sorrowful longings and from the wish to be able to suffer for some (sometimes unknown) lover. Now it is clear that in all this no attention is given to the concrete reality of the girl's experiences, of her acts, or of the situations she projects, and neither is any attention given to their meaning, and all sorts of things that are essentially different are lumped together in one single concept.

We do not yet have a complete phenomenological analysis of

the imagination. Neither is it possible to perform such an analysis *ad hoc,* and the most we can do here is indicate the lines along which such an analysis would have to be directed. The empirical material for the analysis would in fact have to be taken from the expressions of the imagination of a girl undergoing puberty— would thus have to be sought in her diaries, dreams, day-dreams and behavior. But here the whole consideration would be centered on the fact that all human beings, including the adolescent girl, always give a meaning to their world and through this always give a meaning to themselves. When Helene Deutsch speaks of the young girl's *"schmerzhafte Sehnsucht"* (ardent and sorrowful longing), we ought to enquire into this precisely, to find why this particular form of vague transcendence toward an as yet unknown distance is "sorrowful" and why the girl chooses that it should be so.

That she does in fact choose it so certainly does not mean that she necessarily takes pleasure in sorrow; sorrow in her case may be experienced as a narrow and confining strait which forms the only access to a wider region of security. Helene Deutsch has also noted the frequent wish on the part of adolescent girls to suffer for a loved one, and this in any case is quite certainly something wholly different from a masochistic pleasure taken in pain. It is much more likely that the young girl discovers in her imagination the connection between love, sacrifice and suffering—a connection that has its basis in the deepest foundations of human existence— however nebulous her discovery of it may be. But still, Helene Deutsch usually has a sound judgment on the life of woman, in spite of her faith in the psychoanalytical construction. She remarks, for example, that a genuine pleasure in pain is a very rare thing in women. She sees pure masochism in the more strict sense of the word as a pathological phenomenon that may be found in hysterics and prostitutes and in types of sexual perversity that are more common in men than in women.

Even in hysteria, however, masochism is not exclusively a *pleasure* in pain; the hysteric is clearly also quite conscious of the values that are attainable through pain. An inaccurate view of masochism and hysteria has given rise to a great deal of misunderstanding. Passive masochism, which is supposed to characterize woman, takes on the meaning of a danger to her if it manifests itself in the form of an erotic sexual compulsion. For feminine masochism may easily degenerate into something pathological in sexual relationships. The borderline between the normal and the pathological is in all cases determined only by the achievement or the lack of achievement of harmony in the attitude toward society and among the basic tendencies of the individual's existence. Helene Deutsch is saying the same thing, for she, like all the psychoanalysts, speaks of "basic tendencies;" that is to say, masochism is but one tendency, while narcissism for example would be another tendency. We must not allow ourselves to forget, however, that a human being is not a mere conglomeration of tendencies; the human being always constitutes his own existence, and only in so doing, *gives himself* a particular mode of being, a particular structure of character and particular tendencies. There is not, in any sense, a concrete essence that precedes his existence.

Masochism and Narcissism

There is no doubt that *narcissism* is wholly and entirely different in nature from masochism. Narcissism is something by which a person gives a closed self-sufficiency to his own existence. In masochism this existence can be experienced as pleasurable only as something caught and held in the grasp of another, precisely because the person chooses to regard himself as *not* self-sufficient. Now, if it is held that these two, masochism and narcissism, must be brought into harmony in a woman if her life is to be normal, an enquiry ought to be made into the way in which this harmony is to be realized.

In the literature of psychoanalysis, we do not find such an enquiry. It is simply not enough merely to say that aggressiveness must be controlled, or that there must be a suppression or a sublimation of hate or anxiety, or that there must be an unfolding of warm tenderness, and so on. Any of these things may appear to be intended in particular cases, for instance when a person chooses to begin to exist on a new level, the level of self-sacrifice perhaps or the level of heroism. But if a person does this, he is not establishing an equilibrium among the tensions that were originally opposed to one another in him—the tensions that are so markedly opposed in the behavior of an infant. Rather, this person is "creatively" uniting his original tendencies in a higher form, and he does this as a personal achievement. But in this way the original tendencies lose their original meaning and are given a new one; we pointed out the new meaning given to masochism when we spoke of the positive value suffering can have as access to a higher good.

But the psychology of woman as presented by Helene Deutsch and others is dominated by the psychoanalytical way of thinking, and this is something of an entirely different order.

Woman is happy or unhappy "according to the measure in which she evaluates and assimilates her feminine masochism." [58] The superficiality of the thought is obvious. The quantitative interpretation of instinctual urges is here applied to masochism, and masochism is understood as nothing more than a tendency which can be strong or weak, and in either case is understood as a source of energy which is able to be used and transformed. Once again we must return to the fundamentals of human reality: energy is found as an *aspect* of every dynamic event, and the drama of human existence is a dynamic event and therefore displays the aspect of energy, but it is not the aspect of energy which constitutes the existence as human. In this, psychoanalysis is prolonging the misconception of the old psychology of the faculties.

We do not see what is essentially *human* in a human existence until we see and understand the structure of meaning in the situations of that existence and the structure of meaning in the acts which give significance to the situations. If this insight is lacking, we can have no more than a vague notion of the connection of events or an incorrect interpretation of them. Where this insight is in fact lacking, we find the kind of judgment that is actually typical of unscientific thought, but that nevertheless suffices, more or less, on the level of practical action. We have an example of this in: "Woman needs a certain measure of masochism so as to be psychologically prepared to take upon herself sexual functions which are painful. It is clear that in this situation the danger of an exaggeration and of a pathological distortion of the normal can easily arise." [59] But why should a certain measure of masochism be necessary? For, all things considered, the sexual situation—and not the sexual function—is given its structure according to the nature of love (and being in love), and in the intentional acts which signify the mutual union of two hearts, bodies and lives many elements are contained, such as courage, trust, the readiness to

[58] *Psychologie der Frau,* p. 252.
[59] *Psychologie der Frau,* p. 153.

make sacrifices, giving and receiving, respect, surrender, and many more besides. Does this not approach much more closely to the essence of a woman's existence and thus to the reality of her nature than the concept of passive masochism?

However, Helene Deutsch is not so shallow as to think that woman *desires* humiliation, pain, violation, and so on. Nevertheless it is central to her thought that narcissism and masochism are two elementary *powers* that stand in a particular relationship to each other in the psychological life of a woman and that determine her existence. She makes a basic mistake, and it is this: the nature of the person is confused and identified with the structure of the existence. For example, when a woman (or a man) by means of a particular act sets herself up as self-sufficient vis-a-vis the world, it is said that her *nature* or her character or "her real self" is self-sufficient or narcissistic. This may not seem to be any more than a minor bias in the view taken, but actually it has an essential bearing on the whole of the understanding of human existence. The old psychology—of which psychoanalysis is a part—could not see that a human being establishes his existence, and thus his concrete essence (his character), as a present reality only in a continuous act of establishing or discovering it, and thus choosing it, and thus the old psychology could not see that man is not determined like an object, a thing, but always exists in freedom, even if it is a *limited* freedom because nature in us and around us is a need to accept what the real world offers, and this implies a limitation of freedom. The psychoanalysts think in terms of a psychomechanical *determination,* meaning that external stimuli can work upon the interiority to suppress things or to evoke them or to strengthen them in it, and that there are various powers which may or may not counterbalance but which "favorable" circumstances (favorable to what?) can bring to a certain measure and harmony.

It is because she thinks in this psychomechanistic way that we can understand why Helene Deutsch regarded it as a discovery that anxiety about pain could be overcome by a powerful narcissism and that a powerful masochism could give rise to this anxiety. If the structure of the person is strongly masochistic, the chances of experiencing pain would be so great that the person would react with anxiety. Thus it is always a matter of action and reaction, whether proceeding from the environment or interpsychic, that, in this way of thinking, is presented as a system of knowledge. The psychoanalysts are always prepared to admit that they speak metaphorically. But every word evokes its world—and therefore these "mechanistic" *images* and the whole of psychoanalytic imagery cannot be a matter of indifference as far as the view of woman popular in our time is concerned.

It is very interesting to note how the psychoanalytical point of view is discussed in Simone de Beauvoir's study of *The Second Sex*. Simone de Beauvoir holds that woman defines herself by taking her nature into account and assuming it in her effectivity. We may find many things to criticize in her book, but we cannot fail to recognize that with one sentence of this sort she can evoke a much more accurate picture of the humanity of man (and of woman) than the literature of psychoanalysis is ever able to do. For the real issue does not turn upon a *nature* by which woman is defined; rather, it turns upon the manner in which woman assumes her nature, takes account of it, accepts it, and thus chooses it in her freedom. The fundamental point is not whether woman's nature is in fact more affective, weaker, more sensitive, more easily impressionable in the ordinary physiological sense that man's; the fundamental point is rather the *manner* in which woman accepts her nature, granting that it is like that.

In Simone de Beauvoir's view, the trouble with Freud's theory becomes obvious as soon as one realizes that Freud regards woman as nothing more than a defective man. There is a good deal of truth in this. If we read those writings in which Freud expounds his views on woman, we do in fact find them to reflect the traditional masculine judgments on feminine being. Admittedly, he does acknowledge, theoretically, that woman is human, but when Freud says that the whole of woman's existence is based on jealousy and envy because from her earliest years she knows that she is not a man, he is developing a point of view in which the full value of woman's humanness is simply ignored.

Anxiety and Conflict in Woman

Adler in a certain sense is much less inclined to take the same line. He rejects Freud's exclusively sexual criterion and places the social conflict arising from woman's attitude to the male protest in the forefront of the development of feminine existence. But both Adler and Freud actually recognize only one conflict in woman's life, and that is the conflict of tension between the desire to be a woman and the desire to be a man. Thus there are supposed to be two "tendencies" in woman: the tendency to develop herself as a woman, and the tendency to develop herself as a man. It is thought that the presence of these tendencies and their effect on the life of a woman can be established empirically by submitting patients and normal people to concrete psychoanalysis.

But as Simone de Beauvoir sees it, the choice open to woman is something of an entirely different sort. She presents the choice as one between autonomy and heteronomy; woman may choose to be independent and to establish herself in the primordial human freedom of choice, or she may surrender herself to alien powers and to an alien will.

According to Simone de Beauvoir, Freud regards *anatomy* as the determining factor in woman's lot. But this criticism of psychoanalysis is not altogether correct, for we have seen that although the psychoanalytical theory does proceed from the anatomical difference between the male and female primary sexual characteristics, it traces the development of masculine and feminine existence from the manner in which these anatomical differences are experienced. A very much more serious misconception lies in the fact that Freud sees this experience as nothing more than the most simplistic of contrasts between instinctual urges and feelings which may or may not be conscious, between pleasure and displeasure, satisfaction and envy, hate and love, and so on.

Clearly, the thing that is missing is an analysis of existence itself. Simone de Beauvoir attempts to provide one. She proceeds on the principle that existence is filled with an indeterminate anxiety. This anxiety is already met with in the existentialism of *Kierkegaard*, and he calls it the "vertigo of liberty." The very discovery itself of autonomy establishes existence in the mode of anxiety. Therefore every authentic existence—and only human existence can be authentic—holds back from itself, flees from itself. Because of this, human existence is always in a certain sense alienated from itself and seeks safety and security elsewhere than in itself.

One form of the flight from self is the search for an "alter ego," a double, in which the being of the self can be found, but found in a way that is no longer established in the dangerous autonomy of "ipseity," or responsibility, of being one's self.

Simone de Beauvoir says that even the little child tries to find itself in the glance of its parents. Primitive peoples try to find themselves elsewhere than in themselves, for instance in a totem, or like the Polynesians, in a Mana. Thus, no matter how dangerous their life may be in the world, their existence is safe in the Mana or in the totem. Civilized man constructs an inviolate interiority; he gives himself a name that protects him and that he bears but that also bears him through life. Existence is *fixed* in possessions, in work, in some refuge, in any one of innumerable possible forms, so that it may be held back from its fearful reality.

This insight into the essential nature of existence also appears to help toward an understanding of the existence of the child. For the child too seeks an alter ego, a "double," and it is Simone de Beauvoir's opinion that the little boy finds his in his sexual organ. This he encounters as a play-thing which is at the same time his own flesh, and he regards it as an "alter ego," a little person, a playmate. Remarkably enough he is not alone in this, for his parents and friends are inclined to look on it and point it out to him in the same light. Because of all this, the little boy is supposed to discover in a symbolic form in his own flesh the possibility of transcending the fearful loneliness of existence.

The loneliness of existence is experienced in every encounter, prescisely because of the autonomy of the individual and the freedom this gives, and the transference of the existence to the "alter ego" is an attempt to escape from its loneliness. This is the sense in which we must understand Simone de Beauvoir when she writes: "The phallus is the fleshly incarnation of transcendence." [60]

Simone de Beauvoir says that the little girl does not suffer from penis-envy, thus disagreeing with Freud, but that she lacks the opportunity of finding an "alter ego" that the little boy has. This leads to a very far-reaching difference. "She is led to make an object of her entire self, to compose herself as the Other; the question of whether or not she compares herself to boys is secondary. . . ." When the little girl does regard herself as a subject, her doll becomes her "alter ego" for the doll is herself and she

[60] *Le Deuxième Sexe,* I, p. 89. (Eng. Tr. Knopf, N. Y. p. 48)

herself is the mother. However, the actual form taken by the child's existence depends entirely upon the education the child receives.

The important difference between Simone de Beauvoir's view and the Freudian psychoanalytic view is this. Psychoanalysis explains existence in terms of the past, and thus holds that certain conflicts that occur when a person is young must necessarily lead to certain consequences when the person is older, whatever these consequences may be. On the other hand, the existential psychoanalysis proceeds from the characteristics of human existence, and thus, for example, from the fact that existence is always an autonomy-in-being and that it is always a being in fear of the possibility of being threatened, an exposed being, a being left alone with its own decisions.

The psychoanalysts hold that a woman is able to alienate herself from herself in two ways: either by playing at being a man (and failing) or by accepting a woman's role (and deceiving herself). The mistakes which psychoanalysis makes even in explaining the most simple facts are obvious. For instance, when a little girl climbs a tree, Freud says that she is trying to imitate a boy. Simone de Beauvoir—who as a woman is better able to know this fact—says this is not true; girls climb trees simply because it is good fun to climb trees. If a woman chooses an independent career, the psychoanalytical view is that she is sublimating her masculine tendencies. Simone de Beauvoir denies this emphatically, and says that it is a falsification of the history of woman as a human being. Psychoanalysis describes the little girl as attempting to identify herself with her father or with her mother, and thus as vacillating, leaning now toward the masculine and now toward the feminine, seeking a compromise between these tendencies. Simone de Beauvoir regards the young girl as wavering between the role of a "heteronomous object" and the acceptance of her freedom with all its dangers and anxiety. She sums up: "As we see it, woman defines herself as a human being seeking values at the heart of a world of values, and a knowledge of the social and economic structure of this world is indispensable . . . ."

What are the values that woman seeks? Are they nothing more than forms of erotic pleasure, or does she seek what is universally human as represented in her cultural world, and besides this, because of her own special dispositions as a woman, does she seek as well certain values that have a predominant significance in her specifically feminine human existence?

The definition of woman as a passive masochist provides no answer to these questions. To the extent that woman does correspond to this definition, passive masochism is a secondary "nature" which is freely chosen in woman's own existence, sought after in such a way that it can be given the meaning of nature, and also in such a way that it can have this meaning for woman's consciousness of herself, and no less for man's consciousness as well. We can therefore see that the concepts of passivity and masochism really have no clearly defined content, and that even in psychoanalysis they cannot be purely biological concepts.

Many psychoanalysts themselves are convinced of this. Thus for instance we can readily agree with Karen Horney when she writes that in her view "masochistic phenomena represent the attempt to gain safety and satisfaction in life through inconspicuousness and dependency." [61]

[61] *New Ways in Psychoanalysis,* New York 1939, p. 113.

IV

How Woman
Manifests Herself

Introduction

The way in which a human being makes himself to appear, or manifests himself, possesses a meaning, because the act of human appearing is always an appearing to another. When a fellow human being looks on our appearance, he understands it as the observable reality of our self. By this "self," he means our own special way of being-in-the-world and of being-in-ourself, seeing us as being in a situation for a particular purpose and in a particular mood or frame of mind.

The appearing or manifestation of a human being, then, means the existence of that human being in which his personality and his world have been formed. Each person knows the meaning of his own appearance, at least in part, and is also able to lay down what that meaning shall be by the way he projects it. Everyone knows that he manifests himself to another in some way. However, we never know completely how another will see our stature and our face, how another will regard our attitude or our gestures, how another will hear our voice; we never know fully how another will understand what he can observe of all these things taken as an indivisible whole through which the other thinks he can know us.

Our appearance, the way we manifest ourselves, "speaks" of and "bears witness" to our self, our world and our existence, our intentions and our feelings. Even if we do not wish to speak to others of these things, our appearance continues to speak of them. Thus, a person's appearance is both communication and means of communication; in fact, to some extent it is an invariably communicating means that a person bears in himself throughout his existence.

The outward appearance of a person is not only something that speaks to others; it is also something that calls for a response from others, and at the same time it is the response that the person makes to others. It is the expression of something in which the person, who is manifesting himself in a particular way, can agree, which others can *grasp* in a particular way and to which they can respond.

193

When someone looks at another, it is not an eye merely that sees the other. The looker is *present* in his glance; the whole of his bodily reality is present in the glance, and it is present as he himself is, and at the same time it is present in the way that he establishes himself as present in the glance, as friendly or as suspicious, for example, and probably also as feminine or masculine.

In her appearance woman manifests herself to everyone, and everyone perceives her *in* that appearance. We never fail to notice whether the person we are about to meet is a man or a woman, one of our own sex or one of the other sex. But we do not always notice the femininity in the woman we meet. Each sex has a categoric mode of manifestation in meetings with the same sex and in meetings with the opposite sex. It is quite impossible for a human being to banish the fact that he is a human being from his thetic-reflexive consciousness or from his thematic-positional consciousness. A human being is always aware that he is a human being, even when he is not thinking of it. In the same way, each man is aware, all his life long, of the fact that he is a man, and each woman is aware of the fact that she is a woman.

Now, the meaning, or the expressive content, of our appearance is certainly not determined by anatomy exclusively, although it is always based on our anatomy. In the first place, it is based on the anatomy because of the very general characteristics of the stature, the face, the limbs, the skin, the eye and the voice, all of which possess a quality which is highly expressive; for instance, they may be angular, weak, regular, large, balanced, rough, neat, fresh, or the opposite. The appearance does in fact have an expressive *content* because of these general characteristics; we speak of "content" here in somewhat the same way as we speak of the "gold content" of a coin, meaning the gold present in every part of it, determining the quality and value of the coin. Angularity of appearance, for instance, is something that can affect every detail of the whole appearance; it will apply not only to the various parts of the body, but possibly also to the pattern of the skin, the manner of movement, the quality of the voice, the way the eyes are used, and so on. The same may be said of freshness, regularity, and all the other general characteristics.

Besides these general characteristics, there are details of the anatomy that can give a particular meaning to a person's appearance. These are usually characteristics of the physiognomy, like a domed forehead, a hooked nose, or other features of this order, but other things, like the hands, the set or droop of the shoulders, and the line or hunch of the back, are no less important.

If we want to get to know the expressive content of woman's appearance—to get to know the feminineness woman manifests in her appearance, and to know the manner of existence of a person of the female sex—it will not be enough merely to confine ourselves to the architectonic structure of her features and her body. There is also the whole matter of mime and pantomime, which take on certain general characteristics in every group of people, and so it is possible to establish the general characteristics of these in "women" as well. The milieu calls forth a facial expression, a particular type of attitude, a basic form of the dynamism of gesture, a procedure in the manner of executing even the simplest of acts.

On the basis of tradition, a particular development of many things comes about: the manner of speaking, the way the eyes are used to regard people and things, the way a nod of the head can open a person to someone else, greetings, and handshakes. Expressive movements in the narrower sense, too, such as the expression of anger, anxiety, sorrow, joy, have a characteristic form in women that is not the same as their characteristic form in men, and this is connected on the one hand with the physiognomic build of each and on the other hand with the meaning each sex gives to various situations and with the way each chooses to act in each situation.

We will, however, not go into the matter of emotional expression, but confine ourselves to the expressive content of the feminine physical stature, features, look and voice, considering the notably greater degree of symmetry in the feminine manifestation and the image of youthfulness it presents, and then go on to try to understand woman as the manifested appearance of a mysterious interiority.

1. Stature and Features

A tender build of proportionate size, enclosed in beautifully undulating lines, in all parts fullness and softness. . . .

W. VON HUMBOLDT [1]

Woman always manifests herself as woman, to women as well as to men, but nevertheless it is always *in her humanity* that she manifests herself. Woman is thus a manifestation of the human in the mode of femininity. We look on her humanity and her sexual specification simultaneously, but this simultaneity does not imply a perfect balance. There is a tension and a visible dialectic in the ambiguity of this manifestation, and the observer plays his part in these, projecting, idealizing, identifying, hoping, loving or hating through his own intentional acts.

Experience shows that a male person very seldom appears in the light of a glorious masculinity to such an extent that he is no longer a human among humans—if a man appears in this way, it is usually to an immature schoolgirl with a "crush." But on the other hand, a woman is very often seen as "genuinely" or "typically" or "perfectly" feminine, in such a way that the image of femininity completely obscures the image of humanity. Naturally, if one views what is manifested more or less analytically, distinguishing its elements, the unity of the total image is broken and in all women one would note the erect stance, the frontal glance, the domed skull, the hands, speech, and all those things that are characteristic of the human being. However, each one of these elements can take on a masculine or a feminine aspect. When a stance is notably erect, its meaning is one of independence and opposition, and we find it *easier* to identify this with the characteristic image of masculinity rather than with that of femininity.

All the emphasis here falls on the fact that *we* find it easier, and by this "we," we mean a very limited group—the group of those people who are called "intellectual" (or civilized). Elsewhere, among a rural people, the "genuine" woman will very likely be the

[1] *Ueber die männliche und weibliche Form* (*Gesammelte Schriften*. I. p. 341).

"valiant" woman of the bible, standing with hands on hips and feet apart—like Henry VIII in Holbein's portrait—sturdy as a warrior on a wide open plain. But to our cultured—or decadent?—eye, the "genuine" woman is the one who has removed herself furthest from this sturdiness and independence and unflinching attitude. It is certainly possible to distinguish various degrees of decadence in the cultural form, down to the ultimate refinement of the mannequin who exaggerates femininity to the point of caricature. She stands as insecurely as possible, limply sagging, an "elevated serpent," but still in some sense achieving a certain elegance because of it, although she is far from any classical notion of grace. She moves on heels that are nervously high, designed to draw attention to her lability rather than to her human freedom.

If we are to discover, in general, what the expressive content of the feminine manifestation is, we must constantly be on our guard against an exaggerated and one-sided image of the manifestation and expression of femininity. It is necessary to adjust ourselves to the cultural appreciations common to all who approach civilized woman with sympathy, wanting to understand the way she manifests herself in encounter and in social relationships and wanting to discover her manifestation of herself in all the elements of her world, but for whom the being of woman has nevertheless become a problem.

The expressive content of the female stature and the female face is determined entirely by culture.[2] It is only in social relationships that physical facts take on a meaning. The meaning of woman's outward appearance has been formed above all under the regard of the other sex, and thus, according to the way she is seen by man. Woman's outward appearance is woman's answer to man's regard of her. A person's outward appearance is determined by the tacit and not so tacit demands made upon that person, and this is true of woman in a much greater degree than of man. The demands made on woman are made not by men only, but by women as well. One woman will see another woman in the light of the traditional points of view of both men and women "in general." The individual, naturally, is able to break free of this social dependence.

[2] When we speak of a high forehead, a small mouth, a smooth skin, round cheeks, a slender figure and so on, we are normally referring to the expressive quality of a person's appearance. It is not necessary for the terms always to be appropriate to the actual measurements of the person's anatomy.

For indeed, the awareness of self is understood, among other things, as an emancipation with regard to the opinion "people" might have of one. This holds true of every human being. Woman is human, and a woman too wants to form not only a personal existence but also her own particular manner of manifesting herself on the basis of her own aptitudes, education and status and of the scale of values she has adopted.

Physical Manifestations

Nevertheless, the individual differences all remain variations of what is "typical" of a group. Every nation, social stratum, profession, sometimes every district or village, has its own characteristic view of the manner in which woman ought to manifest herself. It may be true, as it is sometimes thought, that among rural workers and among laborers woman does not intend to evince any special expression, but simply to be "what she is"—worker alongside her man, sturdy, strong person and mother of her family. But we are making a mistake if we fail to see that "being what one is" also demands a particular manner of living and acting—not only a particular manner of movement and type of attitude, but also a particular manner of manifesting oneself in a physical way. As we have already remarked, the architectonic image is not often likely to be stabilized in a particular social stratum through the selective effect of the choice of marriage partners.

In spite of all individual and group differences, in our cultural sphere there is a general form of outward physical appearance which, as pheno-typical, is relatively constant, and it is possible to speak of a typical female body and a typical female face. The image of woman's body differs markedly from that of man's body by the roundness of its forms, the lower relief of the muscular pattern, the broader pelvis and thus the different proportion of the various measurements of the trunk, and by the greater smoothness and lesser hairiness of a thinner skin. Breast development is varied, but even so it is a very striking sexual characteristic.[3] The female arm is more rounded, less strong than man's, and the hand

[3] The central mass of the body, called the trunk—as in a tree—is "positioned" in a person's awareness. A man feels it to be more in his chest, his *rib-cage*, while a woman experiences it rather as in the abdominal region, around the *pelvis*.

This gives rise to entirely different experiences of the feelings and emotions. Certain basic anatomical structures are related to the way in which the person projects his or her body as expression and representation, in the same way as the basic structure of the face is related to mime.

In the man, the basic structure of the anatomy is in the chest and breadth of shoulder; in the woman, it is in the pelvis (thought of as a basin) and breadth of hips. This difference is manifest throughout all use of the body as a means of expression—even to the kind of diseases to which men and women prove to be prone. Compare the masculine ailments: heart-attacks, angina pectoris, with the feminine ailments: abdominal complaints, gall-stones, constipation and so on. Woman's life wells up from her (hidden!) innards; she thinks of them and speaks of them. (Man is inclined to do this only when *courage—coeur,* heart; strength: *vir-virtus*—no longer forms his centre and, *discouraged,* his centre is *depressed* to his belly. He then becomes acid, sour, and wears himself away in his own sourness).

The *chest* is related *as source and power* to expansive action, to excitement, to impulse and effort, through the heartbeat (pulsation) and the breath (inspiration) being in the chest. The abdomen does not play any part in the expansive act; rather, it is *stilled,* kept quiet. The *abdomen* stands in relation to the continuity of life, conservation (of nourishment), digestion, assimilation *and* to reproduction *as the space* in which these take place, these being *immanent* and to some extent alien events.

The midriff (diaphragm) clearly separates the two portions of the *trunk,* and each individual chooses to live as from above it or from below it, to live with animal vitality or with vegetative vitality, to live as actively directed toward the world or to live in passivity and subjection (to the species and to nature).

Emancipation and freedom mean, to develop the chest and forget about the belly.

There is no point of comparison between the female *breast* and the human *chest* or rib-cage thought of as the seat of human courage and the source of strength. The female breast is softness exteriorized, womanly "feeling" in its motherly ability and tenderness. This exteriorization may be very pronounced, even enormous, or it may be minimal. But each individual woman experiences it in her own particular way, and experiences it as her own particular mode of being-present and being-together-with, *relating* it to a *norm* and relating it to "the regard of others." The *norm* in this case is not a static, biologically efficient, aesthetically ideal *measure,* but rather, a socially determined value of expressiveness closely connected with other values, such as those attaching to femininity as desirable motherly tenderness, to youthful fullness and tension, to restrained intensity, or even to puritanical de-sexualization. To a woman, each one of these values—and there are many more than the ones we have mentioned—has the *meaning* of a *situation* which has been formed for her by her body. Thus there is a special (special to each individual) psychology of the breast. The central point in this psychology concerns the way in which each *individual* woman carries or perhaps puts up with this exteriorization of her own "feeling" (for it may be small, flat, budding, slight, normal, large, sagging), the way she displaces it or hides it, projects herself in it or rejects it, the way she is aware of it (at all times or sometimes) or forgetful of it.

is narrower, smaller, in its outward form less instrumental and less obviously adapted to the powerful grasp of labor. The features are proportionate to the bodily build. Woman's face too shows softer, less angular and less pronounced forms than man's, and its skin is smooth and hairless.

It is commonly thought that the most expressive parts of the face are the eyes and the mouth. To a certain extent, this is quite correct. Van Lennep and Strobl [4] however have shown us, convincingly, that there is an intimate connection between the expression of the eyes and that of the mouth and that *all* the anatomical parts of the face play a part in determining the expression of eyes and mouth. The nose, jaw, cheeks, forehead or the ears can all be characteristic of an individual. We have only to think of the slender, straight nose that since olden times has stood as the mark of a distinguished spirit.

There is a general opinion that a high forehead means great intelligence. The fact that man has a more strongly developed jaw and a more pronounced chin and nose than the woman is supposed to indicate his greater power of will. But very little value attaches to these widespread notions; they prove just as little reliable as Gall's craniology or Lavater's interpretations of the physiognomy. It is not unusual to find a person with a broad, high forehead who is quite outstandingly dense, or a man with a strong, square jaw who is an indecisive and gullible as a—well, as a woman.

However, the point that interests us is the question of why such interpretations of the physiognomy are so stubbornly entrenched, and why people are apparently so persuaded of their truth that they pay no attention to the "exceptions." Actually, this is not difficult to understand. A person is present in a particular way in each one of his physical parts. We find an indication of this fact in the accepted way of speaking about the contrast between the head and the heart, and in expressions such as "having an acute nose for something" or "poking one's nose into something" or "lifting up one's nose at something" or "clenching one's teeth" and so on.

The broad, high forehead shows a roomy skull; a person with such a head can hold much in it. A person who is worried and thus has much on his mind is inclined to rest his head in his hands or to

[4] *Psychotechniek als kompas voor het beroep.* Utrecht 1949.

press his hand to his forehead and rub it from side to side; one who is thinking deeply or keeping a close watch on something is inclined to frown. If complications in the "interiority" are visible because of the creases of a frown, a clear, smooth forehead is the frown's opposite, a sign of pure, balanced simplicity and rest, and if the clear forehead is also broad and high and arched, it may signify clarity and harmony and wisdom. Thus the expressive character of the forehead has been developed in terms of the certainty that the seat of the powers of reason and of all spiritual faculties in general is in the skull.

The interpretations we have mentioned are not based on this certainty; rather, this certainty is a light brought to bear on the architectonic appearance of the features and it is through this light that we have given meaning to what we see. There is for instance a general opinion that musicians usually have high, smooth foreheads. We do find that a person who believes this will be much more inclined to describe the forehead of a man whose picture is shown him as high and smooth if he is told that it is the picture of a musician. The following will make clear how very differently the features of one and the same face can actually be viewed. If we show a portrait to a person, saying that it is the portrait of a murderer, the parts and their relationship in the features of the portrait will *appear* to that person with a meaning that is wholly different from the meaning they would have for him if he were told that the portrait was one of a greatly respected and learned man. It is astonishing to experience how much the view of the image observed can change when the observer discovers that the image represents a person of some other category than he at first suspected.

Expressive Content of Features

These remarks are important if we are to understand the expressive content of the features and figure of woman. The meaning of what we see is determined by the sense generally given to a particular part on the basis of an attribution of meaning which is phenomenologically founded to that part, or perhaps on the basis of evident functional relationships. As an example of a part to which meaning is attributed on a phenomenological foundation, we could mention the forehead. It is easy to think of many examples of parts to which meaning is attributed on the basis of functional relationships.

The arm with muscles etched in strong relief shows power. Now, human power is not a physical concept, but it *is* rather the possibility of grasping hold and of striking out, the possibility of the spontaneous and of the reactive act in general. The strong and prominent jaw is not looked on an anatomical detail, but as the sign of brute animality—as for instance in drawings of prehistoric man—or as a representation of a mouth habitually and actively closed, teeth deliberately clenched—and in the light of our own dispositions, seeing this we experience it as the tension of a firm resolution to get something done or to take a decisive stand in the face of some situation.

A high forehead in the features of a woman sometimes "speaks" of high, noble, pure and spiritual dispositions, but in other cases it is a sign of out-and-out silliness. Which one of the possible expressions will appeal to us depends on the way we project the image of the features as a whole, and in this we are motivated not only by the static proportions of the face but also by the way the person *uses* her features in her mime and in her behavior as a whole.[5]

As we come to know a person differently (or better), so the expressive quality of that person's body and face changes. If a person holds the view that women are a different kind of being or are second-rate beings—passive masochists, dependent, anxious, weak or whatever—that person will *see* a particular total image of woman's manifestation and will give each part of it a particular meaning, and these will all be entirely different from the image seen by another who holds that women are a "higher" kind of being—patient, chaste, the incarnation of love, and so on.

We might be inclined to draw the conclusion that there is on the

[5] In Rilke's *Stundenbuch* we find the following lines on the forehead of a child. As I see it, they may equally well be taken as a poetic appreciation of a woman's face. The child's forehead is like *"ein Stein im Bach, gerunded von den Tagen, die nichts bedeuten als ein Wellenschlagen und nichts verlangen, als ein Bild zu tragen von Himmeln, die der Zufall drüberhängt heut drängt auf ihr sich eine Weltgeschichte von einem unerbitterlichen Gerichte und sie versinkt in seinem Urteilsspruch."* ("a stone in a stream, rounded by the days, signifying no more than the beating of the waves, and asking no more than to image the face of heaven looking down on chance, on fate, indicting it today with a whole world's history of inexorable judgment, and drowning it out in the sentence it speaks").

whole no constant content of expression in woman's manifestation. Yet the observable characteristics of woman do have a relatively stable significance, because in a given cultural sphere there is a relatively stable "idea" of what the genuinely feminine should be.

The human face as a whole often possesses general characteristics of the same kind as we have already noted with regard to the body: angularity, boniness, fleshiness, fineness of features, mobility, immobility. Thus it is not surprising that Kretschmer relates his well-known division of character-types not only to the build of the body in general but also to the features of the face.

We have already noted that of all the parts of the face, the eyes and the mouth are the most strongly expressive. This is actually true in a literal sense. The eyes and the mouth with their surroundings form two regions in which the physiognomic character and the ability for mime are the most strongly developed, and for this reason, these regions, even in terms of their anatomical appearance, call for a reaction from others. In their mobility the mouth and the eyes follow the nuances of the interior life. They are not merely an expression of moods and feelings; in a language of their own they are also an indication of what a person really wishes to say, whether on mature consideration or simply spontaneously. The wink and the pout are two well-known examples of this.

The eyes and the mouth are related in that they are able to open and close and to be directed, each in its own fashion, to one's fellow men. Even when a person is not in contact with others, the eyes and the mouth are situations of the person's own bodily reality having meaning in a direct sense as openings upon the person's interiority or as an opening out of the interiority—ways into and out of the "heart." The mouth and the eyes "speak" and "listen," and all know that this is possible. The act of seeing is not merely the reception of visual impressions; in seeing, one is directing oneself questioningly or communicatively toward what is seen, following it, noticing it, relating it to a context and agreeing with it or denying it.

In the words of Novalis, Louis Lavelle says of the mouth, "What is the mouth, if not an ear which is able to move and to respond!" [6] The act of listening is visibly expressed by the mouth as well, relaxing, opening, and—as in its first meaning, as *"animae*

[6] *La Parole et l'Ecriture;* (L'artisan du livre) Paris 1942, p. 69.

amphora"—allowing the "soul" to flow out so that the person becomes wholly absorbed in the speaker (or the music).

The eyes are more important than the mouth, not so much in the matter of expressing emotions as in the matter of expressing the person's mode of existence. We encounter a person in his world, and everyone's world is an optical one, and each person can vary from the next person in his relationship to his world, and each one's relation to his world is represented in his glance.

Our glance rests on the world or slides over it, penetrates it or stares blankly at it, congeals it or dissolves it into its parts. To be awake is to notice things, to be watchful is to be on the lookout, and to be vigilant is to look ahead. These activities are above all optical ones. In the manner of his glance, in the way a person is present, he is also able to conceal himself. Downcast eyes can reveal the phenomenological structure of the "ostrich tactic" or the phenomenological structure of the deceptiveness and self-deception of refusing to look at reality. A shrouded glance and drooping, long eyelashes, nervous blinking and the beady, birdlike eye, the steady, controlled regard and the predatory eye—all these are but a few of the variations that show us the richness of the expressive content of the region of the eyes and the coherence of its structure and the mime of which it is capable.

The chief morphological factors—those which are most important as far as expression is concerned—are the depth of the eye (more sunken or more protruding), the moistness of the eyeball, the width of the pupil and of the opening between the upper and lower lids, the color of the iris and of the eye's surroundings, the shape of the upper eyelid which may or may not droop, the eyelashes and the eyebrows. All of these factors play a large part in determining the character of the glance, which may be warm or cold, fleeting, sharp, nervous, surprised, innocent, and so on.

In studies of character, we seldom come across any reference to the eye or to the glance. It is generally supposed that the mode of the glance is entirely determined by the milieu, which is variable, and that the glance has no basic forms which relate to forms of character. However, in the contrast which he draws between the so-called basedoid and tetanoid types, Walter Jaensch points emphatically to the forms of the glance typical of each. The basedoid type shows a wide-open eye and the glance is more feminine, while in the tetanoid type the eye is smaller and more deeply seated and has a more masculine glance. But we cannot regard this contrast as having any general validity.

We remarked, by the way, that we come to know a person through the world that person projects. This comes about because, in our experience of the world projected by another, we play our part in the acts by which that world is formed. This generality applies to all the particular elements of the world of another, including his bodily figure and his features. For the figure and features of a person are elements of that person's world which are most properly his own, they belong most inalienably to that person, they are the parts of the world projected by that person which he animates the most fully by the meaning he gives them in accepting or rejecting the determinate anatomy and physiology of his natural body. No individual knows how he appears to another or how his voice sounds to another. He will not even be able to learn how he appears to another from a mirror, a photograph or a recording of his voice. On the other hand, there are a number of factual marks of the individual which the individual himself is able to experience in a way that is *related* to the way others will note these marks of his while experiencing them along with him. We have an example of this in the case of a feature that is "disproportionately" big, such as a big nose or large ears.

The Borderline of the Lips

Now with regard to the mouth, there is also something special, and it is this. The lips are experienced as the borderline between the "within" and the "without," and they also are observed as such by others. The mucous membrane is visible from the outside; this is something we find in man alone, and not in the case of any other animal (excepting new-born anthropoids). Thus, the *red color* of the lips is wholly and entirely a human characteristic. It is the moist, warm, mucous-secreting flesh of the inner world appearing on the outside, the natural animal interior exteriorly visible, accentuated in its contrast with the surrounding skin and the row of teeth, and it appears as the red color of warm, life-giving blood.

This is a profound basis for our sensitivity with regard to variations in the size, form and shade of the lips, and with regard to their freshness, ripeness, pallor and so on. It also helps us to understand why the expressiveness of the mouth is so greatly dependent upon whether it is open or closed and upon whether the lips are thin or full. At the same time, it bears repeating that a particular anatomical detail can never of itself possess and express one single given meaning. For instance, an open mouth is an anatomical detail. It can however appear to us as a mouth that is falling open or that has fallen open unthinkingly, as a child's does when it is interested in something or when it is asleep. Or it can appear to us as a mouth that is actively opened or held open, to receive and keep receiving, as when someone is listening attentively.

In this image of the mouth—and in that of the eyes—we find too a wonderful duality of activity and passivity, a duality which Lavelle calls "the substance of our I," "the union of activity and passivity is the substance of our I." [7] Whatever we actively do, we passively undergo in a certain sense as well. Within the closed circle of that which we do and at the same time undergo, we form the intimate reality of our existence.

It is this intimate reality that "speaks out" in the "language," not only of the features, but also of the bodily figure, the limbs, the hands, the quality of the skin. But it can speak out only to the extent that the physical has been viewed and accepted as meaningful, as "speaking." Such a view and acceptance can be formed only if we understand the figure, attitude and features of a person as the means through which that person exists in his world and in contact with his world, and as the means through which he meets us in his world. The body can then be understood in any of its possible movements, as it has been moved or will move itself. The face is then understood in the specific manner of its expression among all expression possible to it, and in relation to the whole of the body. The intimate reality of existence as the "substantial" unity of activity and passivity, is manifested to us as the indivisible unity of being and having, of bodily reality which is given (naturally) and bodiliness which is formed (humanly), in such measure that we will never be able fully to explain and justify our judgment of it. For this reason (when we encounter others) we are not judging a physical image; rather, we are taking part in a bodily manifestation.

After these introductory remarks, we are in a position to give

[7] *La Parole et l'Ecriture* (cf. note 6) p. 70.

some answer to the question about woman's manifestation of herself.

Woman is fuller, weaker, more rounded of figure and of face than man; she has a luxuriant growth of hair, breasts rather than a chest; she has a lap, and a sensitive hand, not a hand for coarse work.

It is obvious that these characteristics can have a *sexual* significance. There is however one thing that is always expressed in these characteristics, and that is always made manifest to the observer through these characteristics. That is the manner in which woman relates herself in the general context of the *erotic* to man, and not only to man. The quality of these characteristics manifests the intentional offer of what is soft and tender, and thus rounded, flowing, caressable—an offer of abundance which is gratuity and gracefulness. The very body of woman gives visibility to the act of her receptive self-giving; it makes the acts of tenderness expressed and tenderness needed visible to us. Although these acts give a specifically female definition to the human form of the fulfillment and experience of the sexual function, it would be wholly incorrect to think that the physical appearance of woman meant no more than sexual attraction.

Woman's physical appearance can mean sexual attraction. It can even mean a sexual attraction to such a powerful extent that the elements of her stature which are primarily erotic in expression merely form a background. How this comes about, and what alterations in the figure and the features—sometimes minimal alterations—can change something ordinarily pleasant into something powerfully desired: these are questions that belong, like the whole "art" of sex-appeal, to the field of applied psychology, and however interesting the theoretical problems covered by this field may be, we do not plan to enter upon it here.

We might do well to remark, however, that practical experience of human relationships, coupled with sensitivity and perceptiveness, often leads to a deeper insight than can be gained through schematization and judgments worked out at the writing-desk.

For instance, it is not possible to say that thin lips are typically masculine and full lips are typically feminine. Full lips have a meaning only in terms of the face as a whole. This is obviously so, and it is demonstrated convincingly by the fact that the expressive quality of full, red lips can be sensual and can also be sensitive; as Van Lennep and Strobl have shown, lips coupled with a particular expression in the eyes can have a clearly sensuous quality which disappears when the eyes take on a different expression. The ambiguity of the particular parts of the face makes it impossible to ascribe any particular expression to any particular part on its own. In actual fact, in living contact with others, we do not ever ascribe meanings analytically to particular parts of the features of another. Thin lips, for example, can mean a variety of things; they may be the expression of isolation, of a strong will, of resentment or of resignation, but they may also mean delicacy of taste, implied doubt, a critical or ironic attitude, or wisdom.

The Photographic Image

Thus, in order to come to some judgment of the femininity of a face or a figure, we have to look upon it in its entirety. If we do so, it is clear that an expression which is specifically feminine certainly does not depend on thin or full lips, a large or small mouth, for its femininity; we could rather say that in general rougher features, disharmonious proportions, and larger parts (such as nose, mouth, jaw, ears) are more inclined to give rise to an impression of masculinity. If we take a number of persons for purposes of a test, and show them photographs of boys and girls of a particular age-group (8 to 10 years), it is commonly thought that they will be able to tell the sex of the child from its features. But it appears that they are often mistaken when the photographs are partly covered, and they are not able to go by the so very characteristic styles of the children's hair.

It is however found that people are seldom mistaken about some photographs while they are very often mistaken about certain others. Some individuals too have a better "eye" and are more often correct than others. And insofar as the individual is able to justify his decision about the sex of the child represented, it appears that the decision is strongly influenced by "a certain something" in the expression of the eyes and by whether or not there is a roughness about the features. When one has made a mistake about the sex of the child in the photograph seen with the hair concealed, the change appearing to take place in the features when the hair is uncovered and then concealed again is quite astonishing.[8]

A static image is not enough to enable us to arrive at an assessment of the expressive content of a bodily figure or a face. For this reason, photographs are meaningful only if we are constantly able to compare them with our observations of the people they represent in real life. It is extremely difficult to view a stationary image as a phase in the coherent continuity of a movement or as the attitude preceding a movement and on which movement will follow. Good photographic material, and more especially well painted or drawn portraits and above all sculptural studies help us to approach this way of viewing an image, but experience does nevertheless show that some likenesses can be very like, and others not like at all.

It is not possible for a photograph to be anything else than an image from one particular point of view, but if it is a well-chosen one, it is still possible for the real character of a person to "speak" through it. The success of such a picture, however, merely means that it presents us with an opportunity to view the static image in a dynamic way, seeing the lips curve, the eyes alive and the hands full of life.

Balzac remarked, "Woman's virtue is intimately bound up with the right angle. . . . Grace requires rounded forms. . . . See the joy of a woman who can say of her rival, 'What an angular person she is!' " [9] Reading these words, we are reminded of the "techniques" woman has employed to hide or to accentuate those aspects of her face and figure that are thought to be sensuous. If it should be asked, but is there, beyond the roundness and tenderness and smoothness, some *general* expressive characteristic of woman's figure and face, we could obviously think of the distinction between man and woman that has been observed for as long as history can remember, and that is expressed by Aristotle in the thought that *the woman is closer than the man to the child*. This view has been preserved all through the ages. Even today it is easy to notice that there is a relationship between the features of a woman and the features of a child, and between the build of a

---

[8] The details are taken from a test carried out by Franka Klijnen, graduate student in psychology, and a report on it is to be published.

[9] *Théorie de la Démarche. Oeuvres complètes* XX. Paris (2me éd.) 1897, p. 591.

woman and the build of a child. We say, a *relationship;* it would be entirely incorrect to say that the woman is more of a child than the man. Woman is certainly not more of a child than man, and certainly not more childish than man; if anything, she is less childish than man. But still, in her manner of appearance in figure and in face, there is a certain parallel between woman and child. We will have to go into this more closely.

2. Youthfulness

> . . . Youthfulness. Youthful does not mean static. . . .
> no, her youthfulness again is an indefinable richness. Be-
> fore all things youthfulness is that lively play of forces,
> of which one may say that it is that fresh and abundant
> unrest of which one always and involuntarily thinks when
> one thinks of being in love. . . .
>
> KIERKEGAARD [10]

The figure and the features of the boy change more than those
of the girl when they pass through the time of puberty. It is possible to establish this objectively. Van Lennep, with the use of photographic material, was able to show that, between the ages of 12
and 18 years, the changes taking place in boys are much more
varied and much more accentuated than those taking place in girls.
Every-day experience confirms this. When he comes to the age of
puberty, the boy's muscles begin to stand out in stronger relief, his
form becomes more angular and his skin more taut and rough, and
his contours more coarse, not only in his face but also in his larger
hands.

Let us remain a moment with the comparison of these qualities: the rough and angular form contrasting with the form that is
smooth and rounded. It is interesting to note that the original
meaning of rough and smooth has to do with no more than the
observable qualities of a surface, whereas angular and flowing
have to do with the visible course of a line. However, the smooth
surface stands in proportion to the rounded form just as the rough
is in proportion to the angular. To our immediate view, the contrast of rough to smooth is at the same time the contrast of dark to
light. These are synthetic and not associative connections. What is
smooth is immediately taken *to be* light, fresh and cool. Von
Hornbostel has shown experimentally that clear connections do
exist between the various senses, thus between the sense of touch
and visual impressions and impressions of sound and taste and

[10] *Die Krisis und eine Krisis im Leben einer Schauspielerin.*

213

smell too, and that these connections are not based on experience and therefore cannot be formed associatively; rather, the connections come about because the various impressions themselves possess an intermodal relationship somewhere above and beyond their particular modal differentiation.

The connections between the various sense-impressions play an important part in the way we understand what a human face and figure are expressing. When we look on a form that is angular, the angularity does not *make us think* of a material that is more rigid and hard, that offers more resistance to forces working upon it from without. If this were the case (if one impression were associatively related to others), then the relationship between masculine, angular and rough would indeed be something that results from experience. In fact, however, it is not so. A rigidity and a particular manner of offering resistance appear to us directly *in* what is rough and angular, and we call this masculine, on grounds of an existential experience, surely, and not because we have experienced it discursively. In this material quality and together with it, we see the possibility of its being beaten against and of its being defended, and the fact of its defense.

Now, if we see the relationship between the female face and figure and the face and figure of the child as their likeness to one another in smoothness of skin and roundness of contour, there is a strongly expressive content in this very likeness itself. Nevertheless, we must be careful to distinguish relationship from identity. It is not safe to judge people on an impression. It is particularly dangerous so to judge them when we are adopting a traditional view in our judgment. Woman most certainly does not manifest herself to us as a child, or as a *"mas occasionatus"* (an incompleted man—St. Thomas), but rather as a person in the full dignity of humanity. Instead of saying that woman *is* youthful, it would be better to say that woman *preserves* youthfulness in her maturity and femininity, and thus that qualities of youthfulness are present in the female human stature.

The reality that is made manifest in woman is a youthfulness that has been raised up to the level of an adult humanity and a fulfilled femininity. Our common judgment is in danger of degenerating into a romanticism and into the traditionalism that is founded on romanticism; how much in danger, we can see from the social influence of the rather naïve expression: woman is more youthful than man. There is no doubt that in woman's own view of herself, there is a romantic dream of eternal youth; and again, in the idealized image that man forms of woman, the same thought recurs. We want however to free ourselves as far as possible from such idealism and romanticism.

We might ask, therefore, what youthfulness in manifestation really means. And to this we might answer that the youthful quality gives expression to a potent immanence, since it is something alive but without a very evident grasp on the world, something vital but without a demonstrative expansiveness as a self-transcendent being.

In youthfulness, in the smoothness and roundness of contour, this immanence is made manifest to us as the inviolate interiority enclosed in these; the immanence is made manifest to us as the appearance of that which is possible, of that which already exists in potentiality, as the flower appearing in the bud. If we talk about it in this way, we can notice that the words "inviolate interiority" are also an allusion to the form as being filled and rounded out from within. The smooth and rounded form can appear to us as the result of expansion within, as a flexibly supple substance undisturbed and unharmed from without, that has received its stature through its own inwardly enlivening tensions shaping it outwardly. And when it does appear to us in this way, it is precisely then that we find in it all those characteristics of the image of youthfulness that even on reflection we would ascribe to youthful being.

There is a connection between the image that appears and the view we take of the person who is manifested in that image, and it is remarkable how strongly this connection is "felt" when it is a woman who is being looked on. Paging through literature, we find time and time again the thought that something special is to be expected of woman. We are in suspense as to the possibilities that are to become actuality; will they be good or evil, will she be Mary or Eve? Pandora's box is nothing else than woman's own immanence itself.

At the same time yet another thought wells up out of the contemplation of woman's youthfulness. It is the thought of the ideal worth of the human being. Everyone, man as well as woman, holds that one or other of the highest human possibilities is able to be

realized in his own existence, but each one surely knows that this
is not to be found in the actuality of the encountered moment or in
the actuality of the work projected. There must be an immanent
potentiality, one that has not been posited intentionally but that is
able to be realized nonetheless. The human being is worth more
than the sum of all he does.

"Become as a Little Child"

We have remarked that this opinion is emphatically denied by
the existentialism that Simone de Beauvoir represents. No, this
writer would say, the value of man is the value of what he does
and no more; man indeed *is* what he does. In such strong contrast
to this, we hear the demand, the wonderful demand spoken to
every one, "to become as a little child." The most simple of heart
is just as able to understand this demand as the greatest artist. This
demand means that the worth of man is the worth of the youthfulness each has preserved and brought to higher perfection in his or
her humanity. And thus we find an obvious thought arising, but
one that is difficult to put into words. It is the thought that leads to
the respectful appreciation of the manifestation of woman in her
youthfulness.

The youthful being appears to us as one that is open in a special
way, not in the sense of an intentional openness, but rather as an
indeterminate receptivity, not yet hardened and not yet directed.
To be youthful is to be not yet fitted into situations, to be not yet
the complement of a projected world and a projected action. This
is an important point. It reveals the grace of youthfulness, but
reveals also the very well-founded thought that that which is most
essential to the human being is precisely the human's transcendence over nature. The animal stature is suited only to its own
special world, as the key is suited to the lock. Man on the other
hand is everywhere at home, or nowhere.

The philosophical anthropology that testifies to this and that
explicitates the indeterminateness of man is an anthropology that
everyone implicitly understands. For everyone knows that his
humanity lies precisely in his freedom, and that is to say that it lies
in the indeterminateness of his possibilities. In the appearance of
youth, and therefore in the manifestation of woman who displays

youthfulness in her outward characteristics, we encounter humanity—possibly as the *illusion* of an inviolate and inviolable freedom —but here we encounter humanity in a different way than we do in the male stature, the incarnation of motivated action.

As a third characteristic of youthful being, we note that it is *"pathic"*.[10a] Its pathic quality may be defined as the sensitive ease and immediacy with which it is able to be disturbed and moved emotionally. We have already remarked on this, while speaking of lability as one of woman's factual characteristics. Where youthfulness is manifested, this pathic quality too is expressed in the manifestation of youthfulness. For immanence and indeterminate openness are at the same time a sensitive receptivity for all possible influences from the world without, whenever these influences present themselves. If we want to know what we mean by the youthfully immanent, indirected openness in the feminine manifestation, it will become clear to us if we take a look at something decidedly *not* youthful. As opposites of the youthful, we could think of the masculine man militantly *determined,* or of being old, standing aside (from the vital flow of life), colorless and withdrawn into self, wearied, dull, weathered and broken down.

In the introductory part of the discussion of the features, we remarked that the eyes were the most important part of the face. A person's glance dominates the whole of his face; for this reason, the face is called the "visage." The glance does indeed have a powerful content of expression. Therefore, we would also want to enquire what the relationship between youthfulness and woman's glance might be. What is the meaning of the feminine glance, one that we might call "genuinely" feminine? As we have already said, we have to be very careful with the concept "genuine" in these matters. There are a great many things taken to be "genuinely" feminine that are in fact no more than a myth, or even less than a myth—nothing more than the vague and fleeting ideology of a very limited group of people or even of one author. But still, there are good grounds for our holding that there is in fact a "genuinely feminine" mode of the glance, and that it is connected with youthfulness.

[10a] Note that we return here to a direct derivation of the primary adjectival meaning of the word (pathikos: passive, from paskhō: I suffer), since the word "pathic" in modern English, according to several dictionaries, has become equated with "catamite," and means one given to cooperation in sodomy (Translator).

Glances

However easily our view may be able to be altered through the influence of traditional opinions, there remains an unmistakable difference between the adult masculine glance and the youthful glance, to mention the two extremes. Some time ago Lorenz,[11] in his theory of schematic presentations, was able to show that there are a number of schematic images of the human appearance to which a traditional moral significance has become attached. Thus, for instance, the eagle eye (think of the pose cultivated by the SS officer) was taken to represent the peak of masculinity.

We find schematic images of more or less the same kind in every one of the many stages through which the history of our civilization has passed, as we can see from the way these stages are represented in the art of portraiture. Works of art can show us that throughout the centuries, in the cultural history of Europe, a face has been looked upon as genuinely feminine when in its eyes there has been nothing of the tense, cold directness of glance that we have called the eagle eye. This is a negative characteristic. Taking a positive approach, we could say that the glance is typically feminine when the open eye is allowed to *rest* on things and *take them in*. The sharp, direct glance is a penetrating glance, implying a negation of what is seen and also manifesting the intention to see through what is seen, to pierce it with the glance; but the glance that rests on things and takes them in is one that *tarries* with what is seen.

In the implicit and intuitive view taken by the Western mind, this tarrying—this togetherness with the thing seen—is something that is genuinely feminine. The restful glance that dwells on what it sees, and which we regard immediately and without reflection as typically feminine, and which a woman would also regard as such, is undoubtedly not the same as the youthful glance, but still there is a relationship between the two. The tarrying glance that rests on things may very well be compared with the glance that glides over things and passes them by. There is no contradiction here. For indeed this gliding over the passing thing is a kind of tarrying with what is transient; it reflects a togetherness with the other (with what is seen, seen as the other) in that this "other" is lightly

[11] *Die angeborenen Formen möglicher Erfahrung;* Zeitschrift für Tier-psychologie, 1943, V, pp. 235-408.

touched in passing, and this does not imply a negation of a restful tarrying. But this negation is present in the glance that fixes upon a thing, or in the sharp and penetrating glance.

The intention implicit in the glance that fixes upon the transient thing is to hold it still and to place it as an object before the onlooker; the penetrating glance is a negation of tarrying with the thing as it is seen, because it is a seeking for something hidden, something behind the appearance of what is seen. The resting glance and the glance that glides over things are kinds of a glance that radiates from an immanence opening itself out and that testifies to a simple *"Mitsein,"* a "being-together-with" without any ulterior motive. This is why this type of glance is experienced as one that contrasts with the masculine glance.

The child's glance is however something clearly different from the feminine glance, as we have already remarked, and as we are now able to explain a little more closely. The thing that is lacking in the child is the real interiority that manifests itself in the glance, and for this reason we do not notice "reserve" in the child's glance. The child looking at something in amazement or admiration is certainly open; phenomenologically, we can say that through the medium of its glance the child finds itself in what it sees, but the child becomes so wholly absorbed in the thing it sees that it is actually not possible to speak of a "being-together-with"—the child, rather, "is lost in" the thing seen. The child becomes absorbed in the thing seen without any reservation. In contrast to this, the feminine glance resting on something is a glance that constitutes a contact between the onlooker as one and the thing seen as the other, the onlooker remaining herself and inwardly remaining in herself, and the thing seen being seen as established as present to her. Thus the reserved, restful glance expresses a "being-together-with," a communion.

Everything that passes as genuinely feminine is human, and everything that is human is able to be genuinely feminine. Therefore it is possible to find feminine characteristics in the glance of a man, but there too we would be inclined to call the glance a feminine one. Again, the relationship between the reserved, restful glance and the youthful glance can be so marked that the adult humanity of the woman fades into the background. Experience shows that there are no clear dividing-lines between one kind of glance and another, and that the glance that restfully glides over what it sees, giving powerful expression to an interiority, can very easily shade off into a dreamy glance that overlooks what there is to be seen. This, then, taken together with its relationship to the youthful glance, manifests the person as lost in self, in thoughts and dreams in which the real world plays no part.

The peculiar absence expressed in the dreamy sort of presence to things is sometimes taken to be feminine, but at other times, with a slightly different nuance, it becomes the look of a peaceful wisdom that, from ancient times down to the present day, has been represented in this way in portraits of men. Absence differs from reserve, and an attitude of holding back differs from both of them. In the phenomenological approach, it is necessary to distinguish the various ways in which a person can be present to something and become absorbed in it or not as the case may be. It is necessary to do this if we are to understand the forms of feminine existence; the ideological interpretation that people have given to the different modes of presence and absorption does not depend on the contingencies of situations but is typologically determined, in the same way as the type to which a child conforms determines the look of the child. Just as there are children who already have the look of adults, so are there also women who have a manly look. But to the extent that a woman has acquired a stable form of existence—and has projected this form of existence as "genuinely" womanly—her look will be constant and characteristic.

The feminine glance, which we have described as the glance that tarries and expresses reserve, can in any case be manifested only by a person of mature humanity, because a real immanence can be present only in a person who is able to transcend self. It is precisely this immanence, the immanence that appears in the reserve of the glance, that shows forth the full value and dignity of the personality, and through it in turn the personality shows that it is capable of transcendence, and that it chooses to transcend itself in the direction of youthfulness.

It is interesting and it is also amusing to note how fashion in every age finds means to lay particular stress on the typology of masculinity and of femininity as well. We need only remember the great beards and mustaches cultivated in imitation of the lion's mane. In the matter of the feminine glance too, fashion knows how to take the meaning possessed by the reality and caricature it. This hardly needs any comment. It is easy to over-assert the "simple openness innocent of ulterior motive" of youthfulness by means of artificially thinned eyebrows. Dreamy immanence as a way of being shrouded in shadowy mystery can be imitated with a little mascara. But let us not go into these problems of fashion.

3. Symmetry

Grace is deviation from the structural line.

R. BAYER [12]

There is yet another factual difference between the features of man and the features of woman that calls for our attention. The features of woman are less asymmetrical than those of man. This is a simple fact that can be established by measurement and statistic. But we need to take a closer look at the *meaning* of symmetry in general.

Automotion, or self-movement, that constitutes the animal mode of being (here we are not speaking of existence, for existence in the proper sense belongs to human beings alone), is primarily always a forward movement, a movement toward some goal. The animal is always on the way, and the animal's world is a world of here and over there. The structural polarity of the animal's world makes all besides what is here and over there a matter of indifference; it is all of equal value or of no value, it is all of importance or its being is not vital. The animal moves itself over some terrain or other, over the ground, or in a particular medium, the air or the water. In the animal's spatial context, therefore, there is an above and a below, an in front and a behind. The distinction between left and right has no meaning. If something appears to one side, whether it is a danger or some prey, the animal turns toward it or flees from it, and it becomes something before or something behind. Thus, the animal does not live with things that lie to the side.

Now, the organization of the body is always in agreement with the mode of life. Symmetry, as an image of the vital equality of the two sides, is a primordial principle of the entire animal world, and it is at the same time a reflection of the simplest form of the vital situation. If anything lies to one side of the animal's path, it can become a goal and thus come to be in front. It can also be some-

[12] *L'Esthétique de la grâce.* (Alcan) Paris 1933.

223

thing that poses a threat, and can be passed by or turned away from, leaving it behind.

Thus, in a literal sense there is a bio-logica, a logic of life, and it can be read in the pattern of two eyes, two ears, one mouth, and paired limbs. The head and face of an animal are symmetrical too. Insofar as the animal face shows an ability to mime, it expresses only approach and retreat, the individual opening to something or closing itself against something. The animal's stance, too, is symmetrical, even in mammals. Naturally, a horse or a dog can stand with one foot a little forward, or with the head turned to one side; this however is not a stance the animal "adopts", but rather a frozen moment in the continuity of its movement. It is a phase in a movement of orientation, the beginning of a particular action. Thus, it is an action in which the movement has been interrupted, or it is the initiation of an action; it is not, however, a genuine stance or attitude.

Now, there are picture-books in which animals are humanized, and advertisements that make use of the same technique. In these, the thing that strikes us is that one of the most elementary methods used to produce the anthropomorphism is precisely the introduction of asymmetry. For instance, an animal is pictured with the head turned slightly to one side, but with the eyes looking towards the other side and not turning along with the head. There is an ambivalence in all asymmetry, and as soon as this is imposed on an animal face, it becomes an expression of humanity. Max Scheler once said, "When a dog comes in and winks at me, the dog most decidedly is a human being bewitched." [13] Thus, an animal takes up a genuine attitude toward a situation only in the sense of an initial movement toward something or away from something, crouching down or raising itself up, opening itself or closing itself.

Even among the highest animals, of which the chimpanzee is an example, the matter is in the main no different. It does happen that an anthropoid might sit down in an asymmetrical position or perhaps rest its head on its hand. When it does this, the animal appears human to a remarkable degree. But the extent to which the animal, in doing this, intends to "adopt" an attitude, or just happens to sit or lie in the position its anatomy would indicate, is quite another problem.

However, no matter how asymmetrical the position of the ani-

[13] Conveyed to me verbally.

mal's body may be, the face remains symmetrical. Anyone who is experienced in the matter of animal behavior will know that the picture we have given of animal behavior is too schematic, over-simplified. For instance, an animal is well able to "hestitate," and its hesitation means that the situation does not present a clear meaning to the animal. The situation is ambiguous, but the question remains: is this an ambiguity in the human sense of the word?

In any case, we do see that animals sometimes adopt asymmetrical bodily attitudes; we can see this in dogs during a mock battle, in monkeys at play, and in the ambiguous situations we create for household pets in order to provoke quasi-human reactions in them —pretending to threaten, offering something but holding it back, speaking to them in half-questioning tones. In this sort of situation, for example, we might see the head partly averted while the eyes continue to look ahead and are not turned aside like the head, and so on. It appears to us as though the animal were adopting an attitude *with regard to* the ambiguity of the situation. This is one of the many examples of the human becoming visible in the animal; the *adoption* of an asymmetrical attitude is present in the animal world in the same sense as love, hate, jealousy, thoughtfulness, freedom and so on are present in animals—all these things are present "in appearance."

Symmetry is the pure expression of a being *somewhere* in such a way that the being-there is *free from ambiguity*. Thus, symmetry is the expression of being-together-with something, or of being-in-opposition-to something. Defining symmetry in this way, we can understand why asymmetry, as the project of an ambiguous existence in an ambiguous situation, is something that in principle is human. Now, why is this asymmetry so much more marked in the man than in the woman?

Symmetry as the expression of freedom from ambiguity can be noticed in a child too. Undoubtedly the child, just like a monkey, is able to adopt an asymmetrical bodily attitude whether it be sitting, standing or lying down, but the face of the child remains symmetrical. And, with regard to the child as well, we may take the asymmetrical positions to be positions that conclude a movement, or as attitudes from which a movement is commenced, or as positions which may be taken up in preference to others on anatomical and physiological grounds.

Thus too, as far as our understanding of the child is concerned, we do not regard its adopting of an unsymmetrical position as the adopting and intending of an asymmetrical attitude *toward* a situation which it is facing as an ambiguous situation. If a child should give the impression of facing a situation in that way, our inclination is, immediately, to say that the child is being "old fashioned" (not meaning "out of date," but behaving in the fashion of older people). For it is a quality of adulthood, not to accept situations according to the naïve simplicity of vital relations as these relations immediately present themselves. In adults, then, we find asymmetry not only in the bodily attitude but in the face as well, and this asymmetry is something that is positively intended.

Intentional Asymmetry

Now, we find this intentional asymmetry in men more often than we do in women. It would however be quite incorrect to draw from this the inference that asymmetry should be called a masculine characteristic exclusively, in exactly the same way as it would be incorrect to think that the woman is less human than the man.

A sociological explanation for the fact that the woman is less often intentionally asymmetrical than the man would be insufficient. There is no doubt that the conventions of our society still demand that woman should avoid a markedly asymmetrical attitude, because such an attitude is taken to give an impression of masculinity—although in this regard the conventions are less rigid than they used to be. Popular views that are determined by social and psychological factors are inclined to change fairly quickly; not many years ago, the most elementary asymmetry, such as sitting with the legs crossed, was regarded as a masculine attitude.

For our present purposes, however, we can leave aside the matter of these traditional views and judgments and confine our attention to the matter of expression alone. We can see that all forms of doubt and hesitancy in the structure of situations whether external or interior, and all ambiguity, whether discovered or intended or imagined, and every tentative advance that is at the same time a partial withholding, contain elements of meaning some of which are in contradiction of others, and require physical attitudes and facial expressions that will represent these contradictory meanings simultaneously. This kind of representation of contradictory meanings is realized in a person's adopting an attitude in which he is indeed present to things, but present in a personal way, and that is to say, present *with reservation.*

The phenomenology of the various shades of meaning that are possible in the attitude adopted has not been worked out to anything like a sufficient degree, even though it is of great importance in applied psychology, for the first thing anyone notices in another is the attitude adopted by the other. A child, for instance, can approach or retreat, accept a situation or reject it, react either positively or negatively to an invitation, and in all of this it is constituting connections and disassociations that are symmetrical in their origin and significance. But this is not quite the same as adopting an attitude. To adopt an attitude means to make oneself present, but not wholly present; thus, by the adopted attitude one is present with certain intentions and with the hidden motives in those intentions. It means that in a certain sense one remains oneself and remains oneself in a particular manner. The fundamental ambiguity from which all forms of ambiguity are derived is precisely this, that one is present to something and at the same time not present to it, which is to say that one is not naïvely, simply present.

We can gain a clearer insight into the question if we notice that there are certain situations which *demand* that one constitute oneself present in simplicity, and that one must comply with the demand if the situation is to be constituted as meaningful. In the presence of a superior (for instance, in military ceremonial), in the presence of a judge, in the presence of God, standing before a scene of great beauty (not before a painting which we are viewing critically), we do not adopt an attitude—the features and the bodily position show a symmetry.

An investigation has shown that among all peoples the attitudes of prayer are symmetrical.[14] The asymmetrical attitude means that the attitude has been *adopted,* and thus it means something else than placing oneself in a presence—in the way that the child is present to something—and prayer calls for a simple presence.

We will show, later, that the characteristic of dwelling upon things, and thus also of being more inclined to approach them or

[14] The report on this investigation, undertaken by W. Stoop, O.F.M., in Nijmegen, has not been published.

withdraw from them without any ambiguity, is a genotypical characteristic of feminine being, and not a phenotypical one. In woman, this characteristic is manifested in a much greater wealth of differentiation than in the child; but even so, woman departs from the childlike symmetry of face very much less than people do in the asymmetrical-ambiguous positions that are less constitutive of feminine being. Woman constitutes herself as more or less sympathetically interested, as more or less present, and in doing so she is actually rejecting the fundamental form of the *critical* attitude.

The critical attitude is essentially aggressive. It is not necessary to go quite as far as Hegel, who held that consciousness as such, from its very origin, meant hostility, because, in being conscious of something, that thing of which one is conscious appears as the "other" and therefore appears as relative in relation to the absoluteness of the conscious subject. This point of view is one of the roots of the existentialism of Sartre and Simone de Beauvoir. But to be conscious, to know, is not merely to be intentional and critical; it is also to dwell upon, to be *with* what is.

By the critical attitude, the other is decisively constituted as something relative. In this attitude, one does not take a situation *as* something, but one views it *according to* something else; one does not take things as they present themselves unambiguously, but as something suspect. All mistrust is hostility, and thus all mistrust holds things at a distance and signifies the intention to accept them only after having made distinctions and reserved exceptions. The valuable must be separated from the valueless; something else is sought behind appearances, and behind that, something else again. The meaning of what appears therefore always remains uncertain. The critical attitude is the expression of doubt-on-principle and of the fact that any admissions made are made conditionally.[15]

[15] Taking the line of his thought from Pascal's not very well-known *Pensée:* "Symmetry, speaking of the total impression taken in at a glance, (is) based upon the fact that there is no reason to see otherwise; and also based upon the human figure—whence it comes that one notes symmetry in breadth, but not in height nor in depth" (*Pensées et Opuscules.* Paris (Classiques Hachette) 1961, p. 330: éd. Brunschvicg, 28.) Binswanger remarks that in any notable departure of the left or the right side of the face from equality with the other side (as for example in paralysis affecting one side only), the distortion strikes us as frightening and occasionally is even repulsive, because, "built symmetrically as *we* are, we *feel* that a principle of life in the living stature is injured." And he goes on to say: "In

We are aware of the fact that our attitudes and our facial expressions reveal their meaning to another who is present, or would reveal their meaning to another if he were present. We almost always take the regard of the other into account—even in anger or deep sorrow—and it is for this reason that attitudes and facial expressions are so often judged according to some other affectivity than they actually represent. For they are more than merely a spontaneous expression free from deliberation; they are also a manner of manifesting an *ethical* standpoint. Some attitudes and expressions annoy us because they signify indifference or because they are disrespectful, and we reprove them in children and try to correct them in ourselves.

As to the place of asymmetry in this, we have only to think back on our experience of a school-teacher (or lecturer) who was oversensitive about "attitudes" and very ready to remark on them. Such a person could not bear any lack of symmetry in a child and regarded all asymmetry as disrespect and as a relativizing of the position he himself wished to fill *vis-à-vis* the child.

Traditions can be very instructive. The dignified, genuinely feminine seated position, to judge by all portraits from the classical period of our culture, was a position of strict symmetry. Nonchalant attitudes, as the word itself suggests, are more or less critical attitudes, for they imply a relativizing of what is encountered while the attitude is held. In the matter of amorous play, too, since this is so strongly represented in the relationship of the sexes, we can see, for instance, how people of flirtatious dispositions display the most impossibly twisted and asymmetrical attitudes

---

real or imagined *distortion,* which is the opposite of symmetry, we imagine we see something alien and hostile to life, something that disturbs life, and the name of this "something" is, the nearness of death. Furthermore, in the Rorschach Test, when so many schizophrenics, neurotics and depressives show such a remarkable tendency to complain about the symmetry of the ink-blot patterns ("All I ever notice is that the two sides are the same!"), it is *life* that they are actually complaining about." (L. Binswanger, *Bemerkungen zu zwei wenig beachteten "Gedanken" Pascals über Symmetrie,* Zeitschr. f. Kinderpsychiatrie, 1947, 14, Jrg. H. 1/2). Concerning the asymmetrical attitudes of criticism and doubt, we might well ask to what extent these attitudes themselves reflect a certain alienation from the immediacy of life. These attitudes need not of course go to the extent of being repulsive, but they can reveal, in the human face, how very much human existence is already in principle a transcendence over biological life.

and mime; this applies to "flirty" women, and just as much to men as well. The asymmetry in this case is not so much the expression of a rational criticism as of the desire to demonstrate and accentuate the ambiguity of the situation.

Asymmetry occurs, although perhaps to a lesser extent, in children who are disappointed, and it is also found to accompany irony, ridicule and contempt. We find an illustration of the asymmetry of contempt in the famous picture in Darwin's book on the motions of expression; this picture shows a woman sneering so as to expose the canine tooth on one side of her mouth only, as a sign of extreme contempt, an expression which in our day we seldom if ever see any more.

Asymmetry and Ambiguity

In all of these cases, the asymmetry represents the ambiguity which is present in the situation. It is thus not always a critical situation that is ambiguous, and the situations are certainly not always what we would call "typically masculine." There are indecisive, uncertain, labile relationships in which the subject does not intend much more than simply to be in the play of the situation in its unstable, labile structure. In these conditions, we find modes of behavior and expressions which quite surely do not show any sexual differentiation and can equally well be found in both men and women. In fact, in a lively conversation the most expressive differences between the sexes fade into insignificance, and we can note that asymmetrical poses appear in women just as readily as they do in men. In ordinary contact with others and in living dialogue with them, we do not always encounter the same constant view of the world and do not always respond to it in terms of the basic form of existence. Rather, we become involved in a situation whose meaning is constantly changing and which is constantly giving tokens of coming changes; a situation therefore which constantly presents another face to us and calls on us to present another face to it.

So it is not possible to say that all asymmetrical attitudes are masculine. It is not even possible always to understand the asymmetry in terms of what is human in the human being, for there are those attitudes which are the preferred attitudes of the physical organism at rest: for example, one leg supports while the other is relaxed, one hip lower than the other, and so on. It does however seem that there are no asymmetrical attitudes that we could call specifically feminine, even when we want the term to refer to nothing more than what is phenotypically feminine in our own cultural sphere. In hysteria, explicitly ambiguous relationships and attitudes are possible because of the inconstancy of the hysteric's views of the situation. However, one would not be inclined to call these typically feminine unless one wanted to maintain that hysteria is a peculiarly feminine type of illness, as an earlier generation used to maintain.

If we accept that the masculine intentionality is a transcendence in the direction of something distant and that woman directs herself more to what is nearby, we would still not have grounds for concluding that a greater measure of asymmetry in the masculine world follows from this. Rather, we would be inclined to draw the opposite conclusion. We would expect that the feminine world, as a world of nearby things, would give rise to a much more finely developed and critical feeling for shades of meaning. But it is in fact the distant object that appears much more as uncertain, unclear and possibly ambiguous. When a person is attentive to a distant object, for example, listening to a sound from far off, the features often take on asymmetrical lines, and the effect of these is to give a masculine appearance to the face. An experiment with photographs taken of people who were listening intently to a distant sound has shown that this is so. When these photographs were shown to the people with the hair and the clothing of the subject covered and only the face visible, the tendency was to judge that the women's faces were faces of men.

Our existence in the neutrality of every-day life, in the manner in which we live and move and get on somehow with all we have to do—existence in the form of the nameless "one" as Heidegger describes it—has the form of a kind of undifferentiated humanity proportionate to an indifferent world, because it lacks a decisiveness of choice and the definiteness of a being which is, for its own sake. One passes things by, accepts them, rejects them. And so people go through life, with a number of physiognomic differences that are actually not much more than habitual expressions determined by tradition, expressions which vary from one people to the next and from one social status to the next. Everyone is on the way; everyone passes by whatever happens to pass him by, and accepts what happens in its simple, unambiguous factuality.

In this form of existence, of the "herd," (of "one," of "people" as an anonymous generality), sexual differentiation as to attitude and movement is minimal. Man and woman are practically identical in the symmetry and asymmetry of their poses and of their mime. We need to make ourselves aware, again and again, that the question about the essential difference between man and woman can *never* be answered if we pay attention only to this most general and most neutral mode of existence. Essential differences, whether between individuals or between groups, whether according to social status or nation or age or sex, occur only when the *"Dasein"* of the individual person takes on the character of a *"Selbstheit."* That is to say, essential differences occur only when the person authentically constitutes an existence for himself or herself as a self—Heidegger having included in the meaning of his term the decisiveness, the resoluteness of human choice and the situations projected in the act of choice.

When a person is no more than "one" among the "herd," the person's face is usually almost expressionless. But when a person "comes into his own," is himself or herself, it is then that we really see the marked symmetry of the feminine face and the asymmetry of the masculine face. The art of portraiture reflects this in many different ways. There are however certain situations, as we have already noted, in which a person simply expresses his or her presence—in a respectful attitude before a judge, in admiration for something, or in the relationship toward God. In encounters of this kind, the differences fade once again, and all people are simply present as human beings. There is a line of development running from the uncritical child, through existence as a person in decisive grasp on the world, and on to relaxed, contemplative dwelling upon things in pure presence without ulterior motives, and in this line of development we can see the progress of the human quality of human being, from absence of differentiation, through the differentiation of the sexes and beyond this to fulfilled humanity.

There is a way of being present to self and to the given reality that coincides with a *relaxed* symmetry. This is the condition of being sunk in sleep, of being lost in reverie, of perfect wisdom. Some statues of Buddha display this wonderfully well. The expression of wisdom in them is an expression of being immersed in self, able to be disturbed by nothing in the world, being with the unchangeable being. It is very noticeable in the graphic arts that artists have represented this same serenity of expression in many a portrait of woman.

It is also noticeable that mystical contemplation, in connection with which a woman can be called the Seat of Wisdom, is not only an important cultural possession of our Christian civilization. The wisdom of woman is storied in all legends and tales. It is a myth; let us say, for the moment, that it is no more than a myth. It is a myth, possibly in the same sense as the philosophy of the cat, philosophizing on the corner of the table, is a myth—a myth to which the expression gives rise, for there are no myths produced without motive.

Simone de Beauvoir makes a mistake when she passes over myths as expressing nothing more than male dominance or as disguising the intent to conceal the truth. Of course, a myth is not pure truth, to the exclusion of all else, because a myth always arises from an interpretation of the expressive content of a manner of appearance. Although the cat, sitting in silence, is no philosopher, it is nevertheless the image of a philosopher—at least of some philosophers, who also prefer to remain silent.

So it is too with the wisdom of woman; although a woman may not in fact be wise, her relaxed symmetry can express in image a profundity of knowledge, of wise thoughtfulness come to the equilibrium of rest. What is it that lives in the legends and tales? The discovery that involvement in the world is actually the foundation of having come to rest within the self, present to self and to all that is. Genuine wisdom is, as it were, a presence to reality that is no longer a laboring presence, that no longer needs to take care, to distinguish and to criticize. This, we might even say, is second youth in appearance. It is the transcending of all transcendence. Human existence is stretched between youthfulness that lives and is lived and the withdrawal from intentional directedness that we call old age.

The feminine image of human existence appears in that of youthfulness, but in the uncritical symmetry of posture and features, it represents at the same time the withdrawal, that we call reserve, the intended *suspension* of intentionality directed to the world. The manner in which woman manifests herself expresses an existence not reduced to the pure vitality of youth, nor reaching the pure life of the spirit, that is not of this world. Between the two extremes of possibility open to man, lies the image of the being of woman as we know it, an image that, withdrawn from the restless labor of *"homo faber,"* relates both to youthfulness and to wisdom, and that, through the world of value and depth that woman projects, points to the one and to the other without however being an image of the one or the other.

The Image, the Manifestation, the Reality

We must make clear and careful distinctions between the image, the manifestation and the reality. At the moment we are concerned exclusively with aspects of the feminine manifestation. Sociologically, it is the manifestation rather than the reality that determines judgment and practical behavior. In every-day human relationships, we do not really see into the reality of a person; we take him as he appears, and as he manifests himself. Our critical judgment probably tells us that the cat is not a philosopher, but again and again it appears to us as a philosopher; only, in this case the appearance is fleeting and of no importance. But in the relationship of the sexes, the appearance is usually more important than the essence of the reality.

The meaning we give to the relaxed, youthful, symmetrical features of a woman depends on the meaning given to their opposite, the typical face of a man. Masculinity manifests itself in a face that is interested—in the sense of inter-esse: being in among the things that are. It manifests itself in a face that is intelligent—in the sense of inter-legens: reading between the lines. Masculinity is manifested in a face that is irritated, in the sense of being stimulated to aggressive and critical reaction. In our way of seeing things, the male is grasped by sight as the negation of the open, the symmetrical, the relaxed, the youthful, the image of wisdom.

In saying all this, we are naturally not speaking of men and women, but of the masculine and the feminine in humanity. Many portraits of men—the portrait of Goethe in his old age—show a relaxed symmetry, an openness, an everlasting youthfulness coupled with a mature wisdom in the features. As portraits, they are often more beautiful than portraits of women. But in both, those of men as well as those of women, the sexual contrast can fade into obscurity when the glow of perfected humanity comes to the fore.

Yet it is possible to notice an unintentional asymmetry that is typically feminine. Bayer [16] discovered in it the characteristic of gracefulness, and says that it appears as a "play of axial lines". "Grace is deviation from the structural line." Instead of the body having a straight median axis, we see the curving central line typical of so many statues of women in graceful poses, and the transverse axes upon this are not the same length on either side of it. When the head is held a little to one side, one hip placed a little lower than the other, and one knee and one elbow slightly bent, an undulating median results and the lines through the eyes, the shoulders, the breasts, the hips, the knees and the ankles do not form parallels but a pattern of angles on the median.

Nevertheless, the graciousness of this feminine attitude of the body (which we can see in caricature in fashion photographs and in mannequins) calls for an asymmetry of quite another kind than we see in the masculine assumption of a critical and ambiguous stance. "Genuine" feminine asymmetry is not ambiguous but harmonious; it does not express several contradictory meanings together, but one undivided *unity* of meaning. Feminine asymmetry is a rhythmic proportioning of the parts within the whole, a melodic play of lines. In this regard, we should call it an *immanent,* intentional and demonstrative asymmetry, in contrast to the asymmetry of transcendence manifested in the masculine assumption of an attitude toward some person or some situation.

Symmetry as the enacting of "here I am" is also a symmetry of transcendence, while there is a pseudo-immanence about the symmetry of the animal in the same way as there is an immanence about the symmetry of youthful and feminine features. In artistic representations of feminine grace, we cannot fail to notice that any asymmetry of the features is carefully avoided. We find too, therefore, that a feminine quality is given to the male image when the head is positioned a little to one side but there is no asymmetrical mime on the features, or when the hips are held one a little lower than the other, thus causing the axial lines of the male exterior to form a rhythmic undulation such as we may see in many statues of the Greek classical period.

Finally, we may remark that the attitude of the coquette—which

[16] R. Bayer, *L'esthétique de la grâce.* (Alcan) Paris 1933, pp. 580ff.

is regarded, with reason, as far more a feminine than a masculine attitude—also displays a marked asymmetry. Neither does this contradict our view, that asymmetry is more marked in the man than in the woman. As we have already said, asymmetry is something that is common to all human beings; it must be so, for it is the representation of the ambiguity with which the human being is able to involve himself or herself in situations. There is, however, a difference in principle between hesitancy and doubt.

In the coquettish approach, a woman does not face another person with any intended ambiguity or critical doubt. There is of course the intention to establish herself in presence as simultaneously giving and withholding, but it is a hesitancy that qualifies this manner of existing in a situation. We can observe the same kind of thing in a young child, and even in an animal, but in these cases the hesitancy is not coquettish. Coquetry, properly speaking, is constituted only by the fact that the hesitancy is adopted as a means of giving demonstrative expression to the erotically sexual elements of typical feminity, the expression taking the form of a pretended offer of hesitant submission, of cautious approach and regretful withdrawal.

The gracious, immanent asymmetry of which we have spoken remains the basic pattern in all of the innumerable variations of combined approach and withdrawal and of all shades of significance in the relative positions of the head, the trunk and the limbs adopted in order to express the traditional forms of passive willingness, active enticement, of allowing oneself to be grasped and held, and of wanting to be left to go free. This does constitute a specifically feminine form of asymmetry essentially different from that of the critical, masculine attitude, precisely because it displays a constancy of graciously feminine, immanent selfhood together with the ambiguity of the modes of conduct.

4. Voice

> The beauty of the voice is made of flesh and blood, and
> it seems to us as though the sound of a woman's voice
> brings us not a picture of her but the very essence of the
> woman herself.
>
> P. MANTEGAZZA [17]

In the introduction of this chapter, we remarked that the voice
too forms part of a person's immediate manner of manifesting
himself or herself, and that it also has its own content of expressiveness. The clear voice of a woman must undoubtedly be reckoned
to belong to the sphere of the youthfulness that is manifested in
woman. The voice too is bodily reality constituted as presence; it is
an expression of being-in-the-world in and through the body, an
expression of being present to things in a particular way.

We know from experience that the voices of little girls and little
boys do not differ much, but that when children reach the age of
puberty the difference becomes marked because the voices of the
boys become heavier, lower, more sombre. The light, high, clear
voice of the woman represents an easy development from the voice
of the young girl. A boy's voice goes through difficult changes; it
"breaks," passes through a crisis, and its tone sounds falsely for a
time. There is a saying, that at this stage the boy "has a beard in
his throat": somewhere in the depths of him he is becoming a
man. One would think that these changes could be explained in
terms of the anatomy of the larynx. There are some grounds for
thinking so—to the extent that there is always an accommodation
of the physical reality to that reality which is specifically human. The
larynx of the growing boy does change. But the question that
interests us is whether the larynx changes because the voice is
changed, or does the voice change because of changes in the structure of the larynx?

Among all peoples, the female voice is higher than the male

[17] *Die Seele der Dinge,* Leipzig 1911, p. 88. (The quotation in this case
is a translation of a German translation of Mantegazza's original, which I
have not been able to trace. (Tr.)).

237

voice. Among animals—apes, for instance—hardly any difference in voice according to the sex of the individual can be noticed.

The height of our voice is determined by the level of the note which is dominant in the way we cast our voice in speaking. It is certainly not mere happenstance that there is a certain proportion between a person's manner of existence (the character of the person) and that person's voice. Of course, the agreement between a person's voice and character is not so unambiguous that it is possible to tell from the voice what the person will look like. Efforts to describe people, going by the voice alone (for example, as heard on the radio) have been spectacularly unsuccessful. Furthermore, it is not always possible to tell whether the voice heard is the voice of a man or a woman. But still, one thing is clear: the clear voice has a youthful sound, and this itself projects a certain image of the person to whom the voice belongs. In the tonality, the tone-level and the timbre of the typically feminine voice, we can detect a relationship to the youthful voice.

When we try to find words to describe this relationship, it becomes clear that the decisive factor is not the tone-level alone. There is a special quality of clarity, of lightness and freshness in the voice, and a quality of vivaciousness too, but this, remarkably enough, can be heard in the voice of anyone, when the person is in the appropriate mood. One finds the best examples of this in the voices of boys when they come to the age of puberty. This is the time when a boy's voice can break. He is able to speak in either of two ways: he can still produce the voice of a child, and all of a sudden begin to talk in the quite different voice of a man. And then, we are occasionally able to notice a characteristic of the voice that Werner tells us is common among primitive peoples—that when speaking of great and weighty affairs they use sombre and heavy sounds, but for joyful, pleasant things the tone of the voice is higher. In a way, we all do this. The gulf between the primitives and ourselves is not as great as we are accustomed to think.

There is a certain lightness in the feminine voice, taking lightness here to refer to the expressive quality of its sense. The melodic continuity of a woman's talking is light and playful, a quality that appears much more easily in the higher registers than in the lower. But there is also another way in which we can distinguish between the heavy voice and the light voice: we take the terms here to refer to "weight" or "gravity." The more grave a person is, the more sombre his voice will be; the weightier the personage, the heavier the voice. The effects of this correspondence are surprising. It is simply not possible to chatter lightly in the grave and dignified voice of a Dutchman—a voice better suited to "yarning." Light chatter is possible only in the higher tones of the feminine voice. Chatter *must* ring clear, and must already in its tonal movements possess a melodious grace and wealth of expressiveness that has nothing to do, strictly speaking, with the meaning of what is said. This is genuine chatter. Now, it is said that women chatter more than men. The sense in which this is said is usually derogatory, and it is perhaps intended also to imply, with irony, that woman is more childlike, and childish, than man. These views have come to be part of the traditional notion of woman, but it is so easy to see through the judgments they contain that there is no need to analyze their affective origins.

I do not know of any exact data on the quantity of chatter in which women and men indulge, or, for that matter, girls and boys. No importance has been attached to the matter, perhaps with reason. Nevertheless, if we ask educators, teachers and the like for their views on the comparative quantity of chatter, we find them all giving the same answer.

Chatter is decidedly not the same thing as a great deal of talk; rather, it is a kind of uninhibited talking. Chatter is actually a breaking free from the structure of conversation. It is, in other words, a break through the confinements of the structure of dialogue, of question and answer, of imparting information. The chatterer displays an expressive spontaneity together with an unmistakable delight in what can be observed, in thoughts, in suppositions, or simply in the presence of others chattering for the sake of chattering. And so the chatter of a group of girls or women bears some relation to the chirping of a flock of starlings under the eaves.

Piaget described the chatter of children as a collective monologue. It is conversation without any listening to the other participants, and thus it is a continuous interruption of the discourse of others without there being in fact any continuity of discourse to be interrupted. In chatter, therefore, interruptions in the strict sense do not occur: it is only to the non-participant that one chatterer seems to interrupt the other. The chatter that breaks out among girls after an enforced silence, after school, for instance, and the chatter among women after a meeting or at an exuberantly friendly gathering, is unmistakably related to the chatter of children, and also has the characteristics of a collective monologue. It is the expression of a primordial delight taken in the very expression of delight. But it is not merely this alone.

The chatter of women is not time given to spinning yarns—it is men, precisely, and not women, who fall so easily to yarning—women's chatter is communication without any motive beyond the pure motive of communication via the vocality of the voice. This chatter is a form of being-with-someone without specification of motive. It may be said, therefore, that this chatter cannot be called conversation because the participants, in speaking, do not project a definite meaning in their words, but then we ought to remember the relationship this chatter bears to the type of pseudo-conversation that takes place between people in love. Here too, there is no question of a definite meaning in the words used. Lovers repeat "sweet nothings" *ad infinitum*—a collective monologue where the sound of the words is a pure means of communication projecting nothing more than a *being*-together; the words have none of the intentionality of a conversation.

These are simple facts which, in our cultural sphere, really reveal an unmistakable, phenotypical difference between men and women, and it is precisely to these facts that we must pay careful attention. For it is in fact most difficult to find any real difference between men and women. There are any number of relative differences which we are all too ready to regard as essential.

It hardly needs to be said that chatter is not something inborn in girls and women; it is developed spontaneously in the existence of a person, on the basis of an aptitude which at first sight seems to have nothing to do with it. Thus, chatter too is a genuine cultural product, just as all human characteristics are products of culture.

We have yet to say a word on the clarity of the feminine voice. We have already seen how well a comparison with its opposite can bring out for us the expressive character of the phenomenon of clarity. The heavy, sombre sound of a man's voice growls and rolls like thunder. Ponderousness, imposing words, threats, aggression—these all prefer the obscurity of the sombre sound. And then again, we speak of a voice being deep. Here too, we need to note the facts carefully. There is a special quality in the expressive contents of a voice that leads us to say the voice is deep rather than that it is heavy. The deep voice, as we hear it, testifies to a depth of thought, of intention or of feeling. Now there is certainly some relationship between depth, obscurity and menace, but the three differ from one another in very important respects.

In certain circumstances every voice becomes deeper. The high-pitched voice is usually not deep, but superficial and shallow. The voice of the child becomes deeper, begins to express a greater interiority, when the child reaches the age of puberty, and this applies to girls as well as to boys. There are phenomena in this connection which still have to be given a thorough investigation, not only theoretically but by practical means as well, such as comparative analysis of recordings of the voice.

What is it that the depth of a voice expresses? Is it the glow that is brought forth from the interiority of the person, the resonance within that matures the voice and gives it its quality of depth? Is depth of voice a witness to the ontological relationships of a person, relationships to the foundations of existence? Does the depth of a voice perhaps express its relationship with love, the inscrutability of authentic human existence as *"Wirheit,"* we-ness—love and existence as *we* that, when it does enter into people's lives, gives their voices such an inexpressible, indefinable depth? Is this also the reason why the voice always becomes deeper in all sorrow and disappointment and indignation? This is the group of problems that surrounds the light but still full, not heavy but still deep voice we can *sometimes* hear in woman: the voice that is able to achieve a harmony with stature and features and in this to make the perfection of humanity present to us in the mode of feminine being.

The possibilities contained within this feminine humanity are revealed to us in some sense when we listen to an eminently deep but still clear voice—a voice like that of some Spanish *danceuses*. It is certainly not a passive masochism that appears in a voice like this; such a voice manifests rather a strong self-assuredness won through arrival at a secret understanding with authentic existence in the conquering power of love. The kind of woman who manifests herself in this voice is, to take the words of a Valencian song, a woman "to whom the flowers bow down when she passes".

The voice that comes from a person's depths is not a sombre voice, but one that through its clear transparency reveals the rich shades of tone and color and all the suppleness of grace that belong

to youthfulness when youthfulness is the soul of femininity. Such a
voice is as full of power as the submission of a faithful lover and
as light and happy as every creative gift. It is a voice in which a
woman can show pride without any ponderousness or aggression,
the pride that goes along with the most delicate, tender, never-to-
be-satiated feeling for what really is in all its luxuriance of form.

5. Interiority: The Mystery

> Consider the lilies of the field, how they grow; they do not toil. . . .
>
> MATTHEW 6,28.

When we were considering the intuitive notion of femininity, we came across many expressions mentioning woman's inscrutability. There is not any judgment on woman that is repeated quite as often in ordinary, every-day life as the statement that it is impossible to understand her, whether applied to women in general or to one woman in particular. Experience apparently compels people to see woman as sphinx and chameleon, secretive, changeable, the incalculable dreamer, the dark abyss, or the shining light—in any case, as a being that bears values hidden within itself, or that obscurely has no value within, a being of inscrutable purposes that veils more than it reveals.

There is a common basis to all the experiences that come to be expressed in this way. It is the certainty built up in the immediacy of observation and living contact that the masculine appearance and masculine behavior can be understood, unlike woman about whom there is always some mystery. Philosophers as well as poets have been struck by this. Even Immanuel Kant, who had so little patience with anything irrational—and, incidentally, whose shallow, bourgeois views on woman we have already met—wrote in his *Anthropologie:* "The man is easy to fathom, the woman does not betray her secret." [18]

If we leave all these sayings, in all their superficiality, aside, and pay attention directly and without any preconceptions to the manner in which woman manifests herself, we find that it is in fact *possible* to encounter woman as a mystery. But it is possible to encounter her in this way only in certain circumstances, and therefore it is necessary to stress the fact that such an encounter with the mysterious interiority of woman is a *possibility*. Something that is a given fact is never a mystery; it can become a mystery to us

[18] Reklam-ed. p. 271. The quotation continues as follows: "even though she preserves the secrets of others very badly, because she is so talkative."

243

only through taking on a certain kind of relationship to us. We must try to determine the meaning of this more closely.

Whatever enters into our presence has a certain meaning, a meaning determined by the knowable relations which the given object contains within itself, as well as the relations contained in the connections of the object with other factors in the situation, with ourselves, with the past and with the future. Thus, we can speak of internal meaningful relations of the object and also of its external meaningful relations. If we are able easily to perceive these relationships, whether by direct observation, or through the certainty of our judgments or through the clarity of our ideas, then there is nothing mysterious about the object and neither can it be puzzling in any way. If one part of the meaning of the object is not directly knowable, but the object appears before us in such a way that we can draw a *possible* completion of our knowledge of it from that part of its meaning which is directly knowable and so come to a more complete insight into its meaningful relationships, then we can say that the object as it appears to us presents us with something of a riddle, something we can formulate as a problem.

However, there is a further possibility, and it is this. Starting from what is knowable about the object as it appears before us, we can discover with great certainty that over and above this there must be a greater wealth of meaningful structure in and about the object, but at the same time discover that in principle this is *not* knowable. It means that in this case we do not have to do with a riddle to which a solution can be found but that cannot be solved by us because we do not have the means of solving it. Here, rather, we have to do with something that goes beyond the level of the problematical, beyond the riddle, in such a way that its meaningful relationships cannot be revealed by any human means of knowledge. As an example of this, we could take the existence of evil in a world created by the all-powerful, infinitely good God; this is not a problem, not a solvable puzzle, but a mystery. Speaking of the difference between problem and mystery, Gabriel Marcel says: "A mystery is a problem that encroaches upon these (its own) proper data, making its own data problematical, and because of this, passing beyond itself, even as a simple problem." [19]

In an encounter with another, it is possible to abandon our

---

[19] Gabriel Marcel, *Position et approches concrètes du mystère ontologique*, Louvain-Paris (Vrin).

being-for-ourself and to lose ourself in that which comes into our presence. To the extent that we do this in a particular encounter, we take part in the being of the other, the encountered, and therefore, in the "ontological mystery." There is in this an immediate certainty that we are in the presence of a mystery: "the thought, or more correctly, the affirmation of the meta-problematical is the affirmation that it is indubitably real, as real as something the existence of which I cannot doubt without contradicting myself." [20] If the encounter and the participation in the being of the other perfected in the encounter are the conditions upon which it is possible to encounter something as a mystery, it means that the something so encountered must in fact be something that has a *"Dasein,"* and that it must therefore be more than merely a sum of characteristics and relationships forming part of discursive knowledge.

We could say that as far as discursive knowledge is concerned, there are puzzles, which may or may not be solvable, but there are no mysteries. The mystery arises only in the field of essential knowledge. We can go even further, and say that all essential knowledge brings us into confrontation with mystery, and that essential knowledge confronts us with mystery the more clearly, the more deeply it penetrates into the reality of actual being.

There are a number of ways in which it is possible to encounter woman, in which an awareness of mystery is the distinctive mark of the encounter, the encounter being one with an independent and meaningful being existing as fulfilled and closed within itself, *immanently* possessing a meaning which it cannot abandon since this meaning cannot ever be the object of a discursive knowledge.

A remarkable characteristic of every *form,* let us note, is the fact that in our perception it is experienced as something mysterious. For we are never able to indicate a cause that makes the form to be what it is. The form simply is, as it appears in its intrinsic regularity; Goethe correctly called the law of form a *"geheimes Gesetz,"* a mysterious law. The more organic a form is, the more clear it is that the law determining the stature of the form is a mystery which does not reveal itself to us or give up its secret to us. On the other hand, if an organism does not appear to us as a unity of form but as a mechanical interconnection of parts, there is no mystery about it. Mechanical organization poses problems, and

[20] Gabriel Marcel, 1. c. p. 62.

may to some extent be beyond our grasp, but it is always possible to solve the puzzles it poses if we take the trouble to gain a sufficient analytical knowledge. But not even the most extensive analytical knowledge will ever provide the means for explaining a stature or form. Every form testifies to its own meaning, the meaning it contains within itself as *proper to itself* and not reducible to anything beyond itself. We come across the stature of a form *in* the world, but the world does not provide *means* to enable us to understand the stature.

Stature in the World

We can encounter every human being as a stature in the world. The human being, however, is never a static, silent manifestation. The human being is always doing something, and in encounter with him, we take part in his behavior. We can understand what the human being does, just as we can understand the behavior of an animal, in terms of causal and purposive relationships to the world outside. Human life, which we share the living of in encounter with others, appears therefore as something we can understand. We can take a human being as he is sometimes taken in psychology, as a closed form with an interior structure entering into interaction with the world through this structure, and he will appear to us as a problem—probably as a very complicated problem —but a problem that can be solved, and not a mystery.

However, we can take a human being in another way altogether, as will happen when we discover the vegetative or autonomic aspect of the human organism. The human being then appears to us as an open, incompleted indeterminateness, but nevertheless as a stature.

In the sphere of lower nature, an organism is either vegetable or animal. But in man, this division of lower nature appears to be healed, elevated and bound in a higher unity. For human existence, as a *spiritual* existence, is at one and the same time a closed form and an open form; it displays the functional and structural aspect of the animal stature and the demonstrative values of being of ecstatic growth, a neutral stance *vis-à-vis* what is alien to it and an assimilation of what is not proper to it, rebuttal and receptivity, a being-involved involving care and submission without care, a purposefully directed activity and an idle inactivity. Through this submission, this docile receptivity and this complete lack of resistance, pure *"passio,"* the human spirit displays the freedom of transcendence and besides this, also displays an image of being-in-life, immanent and blooming, bearing fruit, easily moved, strongly rooted.

On this level the human being appears as having meaning in itself, and for this very reason appears as a mystery, for all the richness of self-development *essentially* exceeds the idea of a rational purposiveness and because the static (non-dynamic) elements of the human stature or form exclude all possibility of functional and causal relationships of a kind that can be seen and understood.

The human being usually appears in his concrete bodily reality as a closed form, just as the animal appears as a closed form. Man stands in himself, as himself, as distinct from the other. Through his bodily reality, its definite limits, and his independent being (being-for-himself), the human being always assumes a standpoint. Thus, he *stands* in the world as distinct from the world though related to the world, which because of this becomes *his* world.

It is not difficult to see that intelligible behavior is something that is more markedly manifest in masculine existence than in feminine existence. The man intends continually to exceed the limits of his own existence. He loses himself in a series of actions, adapts himself to the environment. It is through his activity that he overcomes the world. The aspect of "genuine" masculine being is the aspect of *activity;* although it is a condition of this activity that it should be a closed form, its manner of being closed appears to be that of the machine. It is always *possible* to understand this kind of activity; it is never a mystery. The man becomes mystery only in his achievements, in the initiative of his actions, in his creativity.

The *plant* appears to us as a *growing* stature, as increase. Its very form is a denial of being-for-self as well as of being-in-itself, because of a twofold indeterminateness. For it cannot be said that the plant is present to itself, and neither can it be said that it is present to something else outside of itself. Therefore we spoke of a pseudo-immanence with regard to plant life.

The realization of being-as-a-woman within the concrete reality of human existence always takes place in the medium of the natural; hence, we find ourselves once again obliged to pay attention to the natural in woman and to the comparison of this with living nature.

Now, in order the better to understand the mysterious interiority of woman and the relationship to the pseudo-immanence of vegetative life, we can point to one of the physiological foundations for the differentiation of the sexes: the difference between *tension* and *relaxation*.

Perfect relaxation is possible only in sleep. It is significant that aesthetes all through the ages have remarked that when a person is asleep, the outward appearance of the person takes on a more feminine quality. If we look at a picture of a sleeping man or a sleeping woman, or even of a meditative Buddha with completely relaxed features, we are always struck by the absence of anything specially masculine. Atonicity, the absence of tension, expresses a lack of directedness; tension, on the other hand, always expresses the adoption of an attitude. An attitude is always, intentionally, an attitude-toward something, a relationship. The tensed glance, like the "eagle eye" of a certain earlier generation, is the symbol of masculinity, of a fully deliberate assumption of a position, of an intentionality directed toward something at a distance. But atonicity, being in a relaxed state, is the expression of an existence without intent. It is not merely negative, however, but also the expression of something wholly positive: a presence to self, an interiorization. This, too, strikes us when we see a person asleep.

The *image* of the sleeper is the image of one who has abandoned self but at the same time as the appearance of an inward reality that has taken on an independence, withdrawn as it were from all the world's changeability and uncertainty, constituting itself now in complete mystery, because the existence now appears as not directing itself *toward* the world. For existence is an understandable existence as long as we see it as directed toward the world, as long as we can see that the person is doing this, or will be doing that, and therefore are able to take part in the person's intentional relationships. We understand the existence, we understand the situation and we understand the act. Apart from all this, we know of the "thing," that which is not an existence in the proper sense, but simply is what it is, "in itself" but not "for itself." The sleeper appears to be an "in itself for itself" whose being is no longer a being-toward-the-world, but still manifests itself as human, with a mysterious interiority which appears to be a world of its own, conscious in its absence, neither in the world nor having knowledge of the world but simply tarrying in its presence to itself.

This image is the image that we find in the myth of the mystery of feminine being, and that we now find once again in the essence of relaxation. The graphic arts express this very well. From ancient times down to the present, when an artist wants to represent that most perfect of all women, the mother of God, he projects into his drawing a rest, a relaxation and an immanence that nothing and no situation can disturb. Suffering and suffering in sympathy disappear from the features as they do from the face of one who sleeps. The wonderful beauty of Michelangelo's Pietà lies in this, that here the Mother holds her dead Son without any emotion, in a perfectly relaxed and interiorized existence that is not an existence toward this world, nor even toward this death.

Now, in every myth there is an element of truth. At any rate there is more truth in a myth than Simone de Beauvoir wanted to recognize, but nonetheless, we have to be very careful with the interpretation of myths. One conviction however seems to press itself upon us, and it is this, that spiritual being, in the mode of femininity, can reach a degree of perfection that goes beyond the highest level of human existence, a degree of perfection in which human existence returns to the origin of life itself, to the plant, where there is nothing but growth, immanence, promise and fruitfulness —like the lilies of the field, which do not labor nor have any cares, but appear in pure and perfect beauty.

Femininity and Sleep

Schiller had already pointed out the mysterious relationship between femininity and sleep, and it was Kierkegaard who noticed that the image a woman presents is accentuated in a certain way and takes on a greater perfection when she sleeps. "The Venus (asleep) remains essentially, wholly beautiful; indeed she is probably most beautiful thus—and yet, sleep is straightforwardly an expression of the absence of spirit." [21] Kierkegaard holds, for the same reason, that man "when asleep, is the less beautiful the older

[21] Kierkegaard, *Gesammelte Werke* V. 1923, pp. 60ff.

he is and the more his individuality is imbued with spirit; the child, on the other hand, is most beautiful when asleep." The man, when asleep, is ridiculous or pitiful.

One of the most outstanding poets-in-prose of our own day, Max Picard, showed a fine awareness of this mystery when he wrote, "There are women's faces that seem, in wakefulness, to be looking out from a sleep within". . . . "The face of woman is a face asleep, so much so that many of its movements are like the movements of a sleeper." This same interiority may be reflected in woman's voice, the interiority of sleep and dream. Max Picard says, when a woman speaks softly, it as "as though she spoke softly so as not to disturb the sleeper in herself". . . . "She speaks all her words to the sleeper within herself; it is as though she first tests her words so—and then only, speaks them out aloud." [22] This is certainly a caricature of the image of a normal woman, although perhaps one that stresses the nobler lines of that image. It is certainly not an image of the concrete woman, simply because there is no individual woman who is all perfect, just as there is no all-perfect man. There are only human beings, and in these human beings there are feminine qualities and masculine qualities, both occurring in each individual of either sex in different proportions. The idea of the eternal and absolute woman, and the idea of the eternal and absolute man, are ideas that cannot possibly be realized in the concrete reality of existence.

In the aspect of woman's femininity there appears to us the outcome of having transcended the animal level, and also of having transcended the need for all initiative, and because of a mysterious relationship between the beginning and the end of creation, it appears to us as though primordial life—plant life—comes to its ultimate fulfillment in woman. This is the appearance of woman's mysterious interiority made manifest. This mystery, this interiority, is not just an idea, and still less is it a "myth"; rather, it is the visible fulfillment of all that is fruitful and of all that grows, and at the same time it is the visible fulfillment of all that is not merely mechanical and of all being that consciously and freely is not absorbed in directing itself to the outer world.

There are yet other ways in which woman appears to us as

[22] Max Picard, *Das Menschengesicht*, Zürich-Leipzig (E. Rentsch) 1941, p. 224.

mystery. She manifests herself not only as living, immanent order silent about its own inner reality, or as stature in the balanced tension of its harmoniously united parts, but also perhaps as plenitude, presenting to us in herself an undefined, unconfined possibility of luxuriance and bliss. The image of the man appears as but one moment of the flow of his history in time and space. It is the image of a moment in which we meet something of the man's history, but not in such a way that this something of his history is statically, concretely present.

No; in the masculine stature it is restless life that becomes visible. It becomes visible as an event taking on this stature, in its restlessness dissolving the stature to one dynamic moment in an onflowing existence. The existence itself, as past or as future, always lies outside of the image of the man as he appears to us; the person, as he appears, is a pointer to this existence outside of the appearance, and so gives the existence an objectivity in which it is always knowable to us.

But the *appearance* of woman is not like this. Her appearance, however much in movement, is static, because she appears as the unchangeable, on which the eye can *rest*—this woman, here and now, complete in her being, as she is. The transcendence which is her humanity is not manifested as a visible supersession of this living being which we meet. In this, we look upon her as "lily of the field," and the mystery of woman that we encounter in this way is the mystery of a transcendence that is not visible as transcendence, and so lets us see only an abundance, the fullness of life-in-being. It seems not to be in this world, it does not project a world through intentional choice, and it is not subject to the world because it does not encounter the world as other. In this mode of encounter with woman, the world of woman appears *in* her and *with* her.

The static is always a mystery, the dynamic is always a puzzle. The woman and the flower are what they are, as though they were not made but revealed by the unfolding of something already there. It is not a history and a future that appears in them. In looking upon them one enters into communion with their self and thus with their mystery, because one enters into the presence of a stature that does not signify any becoming.

It is not possible to pause before a plant, still less before a flower, without being led to wonder at the mystery of the abundance, the life without awareness, unfolding itself out of itself in luxuriance and without "labor."

Thus we encounter the plant as a visible "idea"—much more so than we encounter the animal. In the plant we see much more clearly the "mysterious law" of its static, stately stature. If we compare the mystery of woman to the mystery of the plant, we find an indication of the possibility that the eternal idea, the unchangeable *"eidos"* of femininity will appear to us in the encounter with woman. Animal being, because it is a being in a world of changing situations, must appear as *specified* at each moment, and thus must appear in the particular act which renders the being here-and-now, present in this situation. In contrast to this, the plant—and woman —appears to us as stolid, unmoved, intending nothing; in appearance a mysterious, inward, unchanging world of its own, immune to every situation. A man, through the mediacy of his relationships, through distancing himself from situations and through becoming involved in situations, is always a "persona" and thus always masked; [22a] he always appears in the role of a profession or occupation, as representative of a people, a milieu, an age-group.

But a woman *can* appear as *woman,* in somewhat the same way as a flower is this kind of flower, always unchanged, without a succession of differing attitudes or expressions, ageless in appearance. Woman, appearing in this way, *conceals* nothing, just as the flower conceals nothing, and it is precisely this that appears as her mystery. Perhaps we can best formulate the plant-like aspect of the human being in Hegel's words: "The spirit of nature is a hidden spirit. It does not appear in the form of spirit; it simply *is* spirit to the spirit that knows it. It is spirit in itself, but not for itself."

Woman as Mystery

We are not now concerned with the question of why this aspect should be possible in woman. But we do want to pause a while

[22a] The allusion is to the derivation of the word "person." In the classical Greek and Roman theatre, the actor wore and "spoke through" (*per-sonare*) a mask shaped to indicate the role or character (*"persona"*) adopted (Translator).

before another problem: to what extent is the mystery of woman something that is discovered only by men, and discovered with the greatest conviction by men who adopt the "romantic" view?

In all likelihood an investigation would reveal a far greater number of men than women among those who see woman as a mystery. Many women are inclined to say that there is nothing mysterious about woman—although not all women are inclined to say this, as the words of George Sand we quoted in an earlier chapter will prove. Among the women who see no mystery in woman, the most outspoken are those who have a part in public affairs or who take an interest in them. The traditional, middle-class housewife, and the woman whose main aim is to maintain herself in the sphere of sexual attractiveness, have a need to present themselves more or less as a great mystery. Both are likely to say to a man, "You can't understand. You have to be a woman to be able to understand." But the fallacy of this is transparent. Anyone who knows something about *human* existence knows of the way a person can try to project a certain image of himself in order to maintain his social position, and knowing this, can see through the motives of a woman who tries to display her mysteriousness through an irrational and therefore unintelligible preference for a particular tablecloth or for the latest fashion. There is no mystery in this, from any point of view.

Such motives are transparent to any man not captive in sexual serfdom but with sympathy enough for woman to be able to meet her as his fellow human being. They are perfectly transparent to the working woman, too; she perhaps is able to see through her fellow woman more clearly still. For she knows of all these pitiful attempts to present oneself as a great mystery, to some extent from the experience of her own inclinations.

Because of the humiliation and bitterness of these experiences, the emancipated woman is even more inclined than the man to take a certain ironic delight in stripping the mask off a woman who likes to pretend to be mysterious. We can see Simone de Beauvoir doing this. Only those women who are truly *free*—and these are chiefly the older ones, who have passed through and beyond all the misery of unfreedom, or those who have been objectively successful in a chosen career, or those of a deeply religious life, and through such lives have truly *developed* a love for their fellow men (and women)—only these free women discover how poor and counterfeit that pseudo-mysteriousness is, into which so many women fall. They can recognize (as anyone can who judges objectively) woman in her humanity, and also in her irreducible femininity.

In the ordinary life of society, men and women meet each other as fellow human beings. Everyone has a place, exercises a profession, does something, fills a role, has his own or her own judgment and feelings, and another can understand all of these. The image of a woman is a human image when it appears as the expression of a past and future of her own. For the woman too is involved in situations, makes decisions based on motives, has memories and makes plans, has intentions which are clear and intentions which are hidden. She manifests herself as a character, as a temperament, as a type, and as a person and a personality, but always, also as a woman.

It is quite certain that this means, mainly, nothing more than that she is a human being with particular qualities that are "natural" to woman. It also means, however, that in this concrete woman there is the possibility of discovering the idea of femininity. But this can only be done if we disregard all concrete actuality and all that is circumstantial, and when we do, the aspect of femininity in woman that appears is precisely the aspect we have called her mysterious interiority. Not only a man can discover this; a woman is equally well able to do so. This mysteriousness is genuine, and founded in the being of woman. The fact remains that the man is more inclined to look on woman in such a way that she appears to him not only as a human being, but also as the incarnation of femininity.

It is not difficult to understand why this should be so. We would however be mistaken were we to imagine that the female person manifests herself as mystery to the sexual glance. On the contrary: desire is blinding, and he who gazes with desire does not understand but is caught up in the subjective reality of his own affectivity and cannot penetrate to the meaning, the *"eidos,"* of the image he sees.

Thus, if a man is to encounter woman as a mystery, he must transcend the sexual sphere. A man sees the mysteriousness of woman in erotic encounter with her; the erotic glance does not only discover this mystery, but constitutes it. And if a woman is to encounter woman as a mystery, it would be necessary to transcend the sphere of human relationships in general. Transcendence of the sexual is easier, because we might almost say that in a man's view a woman is always either desirable or undesirable. Now, since this category (desirability-undesirability) of affective encounter is the *opposite* of the pure approach of love, it is always possible for the man to leave the former and pass over into the latter. But if a man has become *accustomed* to look on a *particular* woman in her humanity and to understand her as human (in the way that *every* woman always looks on other women), it is just as difficult for him as it is for a woman to perceive the idea of femininity and, through this perception, to discover the mystery of woman's interiority. However, everyone finds it easy with regard to his or her own mother, or with regard to a woman who has been accepted as a mother.

We can now see why it is that *far more men* than women have discovered woman as a mystery, and through the course of history have added innumerable expressions to our cultural heritage bearing witness to their discovery. We have yet to see whether this discovery is more striking, more emphasized, in the "romantic" attitude than elsewhere. The question has a methodological importance. For the romantic view is usually regarded as powerfully emotional and subjective, and thus valuable only to the arts and not of any value for a knowledge of truth. In science and in philosophy the word romantic has a derogatory tone, and even in the every-day sphere it means very little more than the sentimentality of the adolescent fanatic and the idealizing imaginations of some poets. If it is only in the eyes of *such* people that woman is a mystery, the idea has no scientific value at all.

The Romantic Approach

However, when we speak of the romantic attitude, we mean something quite different. If we are to see a stature as a unified whole, and in this stature to see the *"geheime Gesetz,"* the mysterious law, constituting it, it is first of all necessary to abandon the analytical method. Thus, the whole reality of eidetic intuition is implicitly contained in the romantic approach, eidetic intuition being a regard for the pure phenomenon without factual questions about reality; an insight into the image as it appears leading to awareness of the structure of meaning within the image.

Thus, we could regard romanticism as an undisciplined phenomenology, and in this case it is true that the romantic approach is a required condition for the discovery of woman as a mystery. The "simple" person can make the discovery, because his approach to images and statures has the same originality as his approach to concepts and judgments. However, with regard to the factual characteristics of woman, the unscientific judgment of the "simple" person is not enough. We need a methodical discipline in order to come to know them better and with greater certainty. In the same way, the romantic approach to living statures is not enough; it needs a methodical clarification in order to bring it to the level of a valid, phenomenological insight.

There is a valuable accompaniment to a phenomenological investigation to which we ought always to be attentive. It is found in the intuitive spontaneity of language, especially of language as developed by the poetic art of the centuries. The psychologist's task is a wide one, and it is part of his task to find what the poet means and bring it up to the level of full consciousness, to discover the deeper senses of the word as it is used in the artist's spontaneous *"finesse d'esprit"* in order to lead man back to the inexpressible reality of appearances.

Let us take an example. Goethe, when an old man, once said to Eckermann, "Woman is like a silver bowl in which we lay our golden fruit". Now this can be interpreted in many ways. It is for instance fairly easy to find a psychoanalytic explanation of it. It is also possible to see the image Goethe conjures up as the outcome of a connection between his aestheticism, nourished on the ancient arts, and his platonically chivalrous love for Frau von Stein. But let us try yet another way. The image, "woman as a silver bowl," is apparently trivial, but let us look at the dimension it takes on when we consider it in the light of woman as mystery, the mystery of plant-like being, brought to perfection as in a flower. On the surface there would not seem to be much relationship between a flower and a bowl. But, if we do not stop when we have glanced at the bare facts, and thus, if we do not confine ourselves to what is coincidental and concretely determined, we can see that the *special* characteristic of both bowl and flower is that both are a dialectic unity comprising an openness and a closed form. We then understand this unity as the idea of a structure which presents itself as open and therefore transcends itself in the direction of a fulfillment.

A flower has a heart, a depth, an inwardness, and this is its mystery: the call of its perfume, the promise of its fruit. A bowl is something man has made. It has no heart, but it is intended to contain something and thus its meaning is to contain something. This is the objective purpose of the bowl, but in the aesthetical and phenomenological view this objective purpose becomes a possibility given within the phenomenon itself and this possibility is at the same time a reference to its own fulfillment. To the sensitivity of a cultivated taste and to an awareness of the beauty of matter and form it is obvious that the crystal goblet *asks* to be filled with a noble wine; it is obvious that the cool, expectant, precious silver bowl *asks* to hold the sunniest, most perfect riches, the "golden fruit" of which Goethe speaks.

The richness of an image-evoking word can never be exhausted, for every meaning means something more in its turn. Goethe, Novalis, Carus, Kierkegaard, Rilke, Verlaine, Valéry and many other poets have, in the deepest moments of their sensitivity, had insights into woman and there is no counting the images they have composed in trying to set down what they have seen. Each attempt follows the path of the imagination, moving from what can be seen and touched and defined to the mysterious interiority within this, to the *heart* of woman, the heart that *can* sometimes shine out through her bodily reality. There is a mystery in woman, but it is not found in her manner of being in the world and with the world, for this manner is historically and socially determined, and neither is it found in a woman's reciprocal relationships with other human beings. Men and women of every period and civilization have had and do have a grasp of "the feminine," and it is no mystery but rather a *familiar* image excluding all mystery and intended to be something very clear.

But if anyone *pauses to ponder* on an appearance of this image, to ponder on what is usually called something typically feminine, even if simply on a well-dressed, fashionable young woman, he will find it possible to penetrate through all masks, all outward appear-

ances, to the mystery of femininity. For a woman, in her sexually
specified bodily reality, does not exist *primarily for the man;* she
exists for herself, as she herself bears witness. She does not dress
herself in nylon underwear to please men; she does not redden her
lips and powder her shiny nose because she thinks of these things
as a means of attracting others. However much fashion may vary,
and however silly and pitiful a particular fashion may make a
woman appear, woman always makes use of fashions to find new
ways of demonstrating and concealing the mystery of her own self.
When she says she wants to be as beautiful as possible, she is
making no reference to any aesthetical norm. When she speaks of
taking care of herself, she is not speaking in terms of any objective
hygiene. And when she says that a woman must live up to the
demands of good taste, there is no point in asking who the con-
sumer might be whose good taste establishes the demands.

There is a paradox in this. Woman does not want to be "con-
sumed," she does not want to be regarded as "useful for a purpose," and yet, in the hidden profundity of her positional consciousness, she regards herself as the dependent of everyone else,
of other women as well as of men. Women are seldom inclined to
reflect on their own existence, and the "civilized" woman usually
chooses to be herself in being a demonstration of femininity without knowing what femininity really is. The reason why we so often
find her anxiously trying to keep up with the fashion, in dress, in
the style of "doing" her face and hands, in the poses and gestures
she adopts, is precisely this, that she does not know what femininity really is. Jean Paul holds that clothing, to the woman, is
"the third organ of the soul," [23] and this may well be true of those
women whom we call "women of the world"—their number includes the simple neighborhood type got up in her Sunday best.

Let us not miss the significance of the expression, *"of* the
world." Every individual is *in* the world; all share a *"Mitsein,"* a
togetherness-of-being. Thus for men as well as for women there is
a tradition, a fashion, that constitutes and testifies to the individual's roots in his social position. But male fashion is very seldom
intended as a demonstration of masculinity, and practically never
intended as a constantly variable image of masculinity concealing
the real masculinity beneath. If male fashion is employed in this

[23] *Levana* IV, 4 S 96.

way, it is usually something confined to the more primitive phases of culture.

What of the woman who is not a "woman *of* the world" and not wholly "taken up" in an attempt to be what is thought to be genuinely feminine in the popular estimation? She may either conceal her own specific femininity beneath her humanity in a determined and resolute adaptation to situations, or else she might be one who experiences her femininity very deeply and manifests this in her mode of appearance. In these cases she is not a woman *of* the world; she is a woman *in* the world, but one who at the same time transcends the world through a mode of existence such as that of love (reaching above and beyond the level of the world, as Binswanger says), as selflessly disinterested as a flower—although of course a flower is only an image for such an existence.

In manifesting her femininity, woman however brings about a realization of *"Dasein als Wirheit"* (of authentic human existence as togetherness with others) that is more profound than the realization of it an intentionally conscious man could achieve, even if the woman manifests her femininity in loneliness.

Genuine loneliness is not desolation nor isolation nor abandonment by others. It is something that can be experienced only where there is a real possibility of companionship, and it is precisely this loneliness that gives a person that immanent, silent dignity in which all intentionality is suspended in the awareness of the absence of the reality of that "golden fruit" which the world can never provide.

That manner of being alive, of living being, that we have called the pseudo-immanence of the plant, can be recognized in *every* human being, because there is a certain proportion of femininity in every human being. In the same way, every human being is able to be lonely, through the intentional consciousness of a positive passivity and deceptivity which is, quite simply, the consciousness of the presence of an absence, of the possibility of receiving and of being-together in the mode of *"Wirheit,"* as *we,* and not I in isolation. Women have cultivated this more than men have, and thus woman is more disposed toward it, and therefore the more *genuine* her loneliness, the more clearly she manifests her mysterious interiority.

There are two forms in which this is more marked than in any

other: dreaminess shrouding a youthful, feminine appearance; and
the dignified resignation of old age. Both images are moving, precisely because of their inscrutability, their ineffability, their mystery.

The Mystery of Feminine Beauty

In this, we are coming close to the *mystery of feminine beauty*.
Feminine beauty is grace, gratuitous, gift, and Kierkegaard says,
"The Lord gives it to his own as they sleep." The beauty of a
young, developing woman does in fact appear to be something that
comes into being through the mysterious creative power of unconscious nature, as Venus comes from the foam of the sea—a *"mira-
cle"* that Botticelli tries to help us to see. No-one, it seems, has
penetrated more deeply into the mystery of this beauty than
Dostoevski, who has one of his brothers Karamazow say,
"Beauty is something terrible, something terrifying . . . terrible
because it cannot be defined." And Prince Mishkin is disturbed in
the same way by the beauty of a woman because it is an affront to
his "sober" humanity, it makes him dizzy, just as it does to Dimitri
the violent one, to the angelic Alyosha, the sombre Ivan, the vul-
gar Fedor.

For these men—for all who are inwardly and intimately bound
up with the mystery of feminine beauty—the power of a woman's
beauty is frightening, its depth like the scent of a flower that overcomes and intoxicates the senses. But this beauty is not objective;
just like the scent of a flower, it arises as a force only in encounter
and in resonance between persons, and this precisely is the reason
why it calls attention to the mystery of *nature,* nature to which the
human being is subject. Why are we human beings overcome by
the *scent* of a flower that, after all, is meaningful only to the insect
that fulfills a certain function for the flower in the *harmony* of
nature? Why is woman beautiful, where her beauty is pure "luxuriance" and transcends all meaningful purpose and *can* even
mean an intoxication, a threat, a temptation, a disorganization, a
"frightening" loss of freedom?

The most likely way of arriving at an answer is probably to be
found along the lines of Kierkegaard's sensitive and penetrating
study, published under the title, *Krisis im Leben einer Schauspielerin* (Crisis in the life of an actress). It *is possible* for the

beauty of a woman to increase with the years, through a "meta-morphosis," a transformation of her natural beauty into a higher, more ideal and more ennobled form. A woman who has passed through her *crisis* and given up her primary beauty—her primitive beauty, because it is her natural beauty—and does not frantically try to prolong it by all sorts of cosmetic tricks, attains to a manner of manifesting herself in which the real meaning of femininity is at last revealed in all its perfection.

The depth of her mystery is now no longer that of plant-like unconsciousness, but the mystery of the spirit, the mystery of re-ceptivity as free self-giving in which communion with being, with reality and with truth is at last possible. It is not the "woman of spirit" in whom the mystery of having transcended the limitations of earthly reality is made manifest; we can see this only in the "spiritualized" woman, in the quiet dignity of the woman of ripe maturity, the "old" woman. This beauty—we see it for instance in Rembrandt's aged mother—is no longer a danger, no longer frightening. It is silent, it is the quiet mystery of an interiority, still mysterious, but shining out through the outward reality of the woman's appearance.

In the feminine stature, the human being appears as a mystery through a twofold reality: the reality of nature and the reality of spirit. It is possible for this mystery to be revealed in a man as well as in a woman, for the man too is able to participate in that existential mode of humanity to which woman is called by her "nature." This mystery of nature and of spirit finds a possibility of expression in the plastic pliability of the female body that cannot be found in the more rigid material of the male. The muscular masculine form points toward a possible goal, an efficiency, just as the masculine face expresses an intentionality. Feminine form and features do not display an efficient directedness; they have a demonstrative value of being. The feminine form manifests an inscrutable *luxuriance,* the highest and most fundamental principle of nature, and therefore manifests also an equally inscrutable *eros,* for luxuriance is *eros* in the mode of joy and fruitfulness for their own sake alone, and not merely as means to some goal beyond them. The more differentiated and intensified this twofold expres-sion of the mystery of humanity in the feminine stature, the more clearly this mystery appears in the woman, through nature as lux-uriance, and through spirit as *eros.*

All writers on woman, including Simone de Beauvoir, have argued that woman is in bondage to nature. They try to explain this bondage in terms of the greater vulnerability of woman's body, the fact that her existence is a dependent existence, the biological determination of the sexual in her. There is truth in all this, but in the phenomenological approach we can also see in woman a relationship with the "lowest" level of life, the unconsciousness of growth, and see it as a participation in the purest demonstrative values of the being of nature: a relationship with the flowers, the "lilies of the field," not living to labor but free of care to bloom today and tomorrow to fade.

The mystery of nature, of unconscious beauty and obscure originality, of overwhelming *eros*, of grace and luxuriance, is a mystery of which Goethe was deeply aware when he closed his hymn to nature with the words, "Her crown is life. Through it, one comes close to her." The crowning perfection of nature is surely found in humanity, and within humanity, in femininity. Thus the crowning perfection of nature is love, love in the community and indeed only in the community; and so, through the disinterested approach of love, one comes close to the essence of woman.

One might perhaps think that nature is predominant in woman while spirit is predominant in man. Klages, as we have already seen, tried to defend this point of view, and there have been a vast number of writers who have argued that the spiritual faculties, particularly will-power and reason, are greater in men than in women. If woman is seen as "an ovary with some overgrowth," man is seen as the incarnation of spirit. Nietzsche says, "Volition is man's nature; the nature of woman is willingness."

If spirit were in fact nothing more than mere dominion over nature through will-power and reason, then woman would indeed participate in spirit to a lesser degree than man. But spirit is that by which the human being is able to transcend, to "surpass," himself or herself, to transcend his or her own natural will and reason. This transcendence is possible only through *agapē, caritas,* love, one drop of which is more than an ocean of will-power and reason (Pascal).

At the same time, this love is wisdom, acceptance and sacrifice. Thus, Theodor Haecker could write that woman is *more perfect* than man, because "of her very nature she is the more loving creature, she offers the more." It is not within the capacity of the

human being, however, to achieve perfection within the continuity
of natural existence; perfection is achieved only through a crisis in
which the "old man" is laid aside and *eros* transformed into *agapē*.
This metamorphosis, rebirth, sanctification, spiritualization, en-
noblement—all these and other names besides are given to the
same reality—is a possibility in every human life, and it is not
something which is specifically feminine. But nevertheless, it is the
mystery of the interiority of woman.

We do not in any sense wish to identify a mode of manifestation
with the reality manifested, and thus emphasize the word "expression" when we refer to the *expression* of resignation and remote-
ness, and to the expression of compassionate approach, in a
woman "after her crisis." It is never possible to know exactly to
what extent a person really is what that person appears to be. But
when, in the spiritual beauty of an old woman of great dignity, we
meet the mystery of disinterested love at its greatest perfection, we
are at the same time encountering the very meaning of feminine
existence itself.

Sociological Effects

Let us now take time to consider the sociological effects of feminine inscrutability.

There is "the problem of woman," not because women are held
in subjection, but because there is a *mystery* about femininity. This
is why the "problem" has always existed, and will continue to exist
as long as human beings ponder upon their own existence. Naturally, the problem of woman takes on special characteristics in particular countries and in particular social circumstances, and this is
comparable, to some extent, with the problem of slavery or the
problem of labor or the problem of anti-semitism or the color problem. Nevertheless, the subjection of a slave class or of a dependent
minority, while it is a problem, is never a mystery; on the other
hand, the suppression of women is, precisely, a mystery. It is not
possible to explain it in terms of particular sociological causes.

Freud and the Freudian school (Helene Deutsch, for example),
as we have seen, speak of the passive-masochistic "nature" of
woman, but Simone de Beauvoir has a deeper insight into the
reality, and quite rightly asks why woman should project such a

"nature" in our society, granting that our social relationships are what they are. Simone de Beauvoir, however, does not provide any conclusive answer to her own question.

It is not possible squarely to maintain a comparison between the suppression of women and a problem such as that of the subjection of a dependent minority-group or that of racial prejudice which is fundamentally emotional. The defects of the comparison become obvious when we take note of the fact that even with the greatest of effort the so-called dominant male is able to preserve only the *appearance* of independence. There is of course a very familiar and ready explanation for this. Its terms are: sexual enslavement. But is this in actual fact the reason why the "dominant" male's schemes go awry, the reason behind excuses like *"cherchez la femme,"* or like "there must be a woman behind this somewhere"?

Woman attracts an awareness of herself as a dangerous abyss, as an intoxicating perfume, as the playful luxuriance of flowers, as maternal security, as the perfection of moral courage in sacrifice. Most people consciously or unconsciously take this kind of view of woman, and the popular mind is summed up in an expression like Richard Curle's "women are at the *root* of *all* human affairs." In this, we are coming close to the actual effect of feminine inscrutability on society.

Woman is at the root and origin of human reality; she is close to the hidden source from which it draws its nourishment. But still we may ask, how is this to be understood? On the one hand we try to answer the question by pointing to the mysterious quality of the expressiveness of the way woman manifests herself, and on the other hand we find that everyone somehow or other vaguely suspects that precisely because of what she essentially is, woman stands apart from the "mechanism" of the rational world and outside the web of intentional activity, and because she is outside it all, she fulfills a function in society which she alone can fulfill.

While we are considering the "problem of woman," we must be careful never to forget that *every* human being has had a *mother,* and that it is the mother who in principle brings about the realization of human possibilities in every individual. In every phase of the collapse of our existence, in every disorganization and every experience of being lost, we, all of us, seek the security of the "eternal mother," the origin and the final destiny of every one of us.

Woman can prove to be a narcosis, a danger, a seduction and thus the evil of *being lost;* she can prove to be an evil in this way, not only to man, but also *to herself,* through living an "ingrowing" sort of life, reflected back into herself, auto-erotically and narcissistically. This too is one of the aspects of her mystery. But woman can also prove to be a *salvation* to everyone, man as well as woman, crushing out evil, giving birth to caritas, to love, to goodness, in this world.

The mystery of woman as a bloom, as a "silver bowl," as a luxuriance and a beauty, as spirituality and love, is always a mystery in the medium of her humanity. It is a mystery that is the *foundation* of her existence. Therefore, if we are to come close to it, to understand it a little, we need to share in her deeds, to learn to appreciate the finer meanings of her attitudes and her gestures, when these spring forth and unfold from the intimate heart of her own self as she really is. How is it possible to do this? The great poet, Rilke, gives us some idea.

The Mirror Image

Rilke sees a woman standing before a mirror

> "lightly pouring her weary movements
> into the liquid, clear glass
> like aromatic spices
> into a draught to bring sleep,
> and she makes herself smile,
> quietly, within." [24]

It would naturally be absurd to try to *explain* the image this verse evokes. But it is perhaps a most strikingly close approach to the mystery of the interiority of woman. Dissolving her tired movements and all the immanence of her smile in the mirror, clear as a mountain stream, she makes her own image into a sleeping-draught, a drink that will turn the image into a *dream.*

Combing her hair, powdering her cheeks—these gestures before

---

[24] *"Wie in einem Schlaftrunk Spezereien*
Löst sie leise in dem flüssig klaren
Spiegel ihr ermüdetes Gebaren
und sie tut ihr Lächeln ganz hinein."

the mirror become dreamy. They become dreamy because the mirror-image, giving reality to the "narcissistic" possibility in the woman, lends an ambiguity to the whole situation in which the gestures take place. Ambiguity enters into the situation because she *sees* her own movements; their obvious intentionality dissolves, they become gestures, even to herself. The familiarity she experiences in this encounter with herself makes her smile, inwardly. This smile from within is felt in her lips, her eyes, and at once becomes visible to her in her own image in the mirror, which absorbs it, along with her movements, as the soothing drink absorbs the herbs. Before the mirror, the woman is seeking her own being, her own essence, modelled for her by the past, the dream of herself, of man, of all mankind.

She who stands "at the *root* of *all* human affairs" is not placed within the world of transient actions and kaleidoscopically tumbling structures of situations. The human being is always in the world, but femininity gives this being in the world a mode of transcendence, of reaching above the level of the world, and yet, through femininity, what is human is still "present to itself" and— for that very reason—"far away," present to its origin and to its destiny; here, and at the same time remote.

Feminine humanity is *always* before the mirror, which dissolves away intentionality and along with it the stability and the reasonableness of masculinity and the world of masculinity. Woman, inside the home and outside it, fulfills a function which is unambiguous, not irrational, not a dream. She does this, not only in the more primitive cultural spheres, but also in our own highly differentiated, technologically structured society.

Even before the mirror, acting objectively, woman is a human being, wanting something and doing something. Happily, this is so. Woman exists, and *must* exist, as a human being. But the question remains: she is human, but does she at the same time constitute a presence of human-being in the mode of feminine-being? Granting and understanding that she does, it must also be granted and understood that there are two modes of existence, a masculine mode and a feminine mode, and thus, that there is also a feminine mode of being-for-self and a feminine world as well as a masculine world.

V

The Manner of
Woman's Existence

Introduction

We have examined the attempts made to define woman's nature, and we have discussed the manner in which she manifests herself. We turn now to a consideration of her manner of existence.

The discussion of the problematics of feminine being has already made it clear that woman exists as a human being, and that all the possibilities inherent in humanity are open to her, as a woman, as well. We know that existence can be understood only as a being-in-the-world in the body and by means of the body. Human existence in any other condition would be unintelligible. If, therefore, we are seeking the deepest grounds from which that existence that is specifically woman's existence must necessarily flow, we must seek these grounds in woman's bodily reality.

But what is meant by the term "bodily reality"? In this context it means something other than, and more than, the entire whole of those structures whose nature can be objectively determined by anatomical and physiological study. When discussing the way woman manifests herself, we had already to refer to the phenomenological content of expressiveness in the animated bodily reality of a person, and the meaning of this bodily reality then appeared as an interiority made manifest outwardly—and this itself led to the discovery of a number of characteristics of existence in the feminine mode.

However, if our enquiry is aimed at discovering the most general and fundamental characteristics of one or other particular manner of human existence, we have to seek these characteristics in the basic scheme of the world that belongs to that manner of existence, and in the basic structure of the behavior relating to that world.

The basic structure of behavior relating to the world belonging to a particular manner of existence is called the specific *dynamics* of that manner of existence. For the way a person moves is in fact the general *manner* in which that person grasps and understands the actuality of all the things he encounters, the manner in which he lives with them, gives meaning to them and, doing all these things, projects the basic character of his own world. Thus the characteristics of this dynamism differ from one person to the next; they differ according to nation and social status and professional or occupational standing, and they differ also according to the sex of the individual. As we shall see, this dynamism is already established in the child, through its basic aptitudes, together with the establishing of the basic scheme of the child's world. But this takes place in such a way that the subsequent influence of the milieu can bring about a confirmation or a transformation of the inborn type of dynamism as well as of the world to which it relates.

One might well think that there must be some other—and better —method of coming to know woman's manner of existence. In particular, could it not be approached through the study of woman's world as it is, in all its diversity from the masculine world?

What really belongs to the typically feminine world? People have been trying to answer this question for centuries. We have come to the conclusion and are now convinced that woman can count all that is human as belonging to her world. But, one might object, why then does she persistently choose not to absorb all that comes with "technology" into her world? Why does she so readily accept all her little domestic occupations? Why does she attribute to almost every single thing a value that is different from the value man gives it? Why is her world more human than objective and businesslike?

Psychology can give no satisfactory answer to these questions. The supposition that the direction of woman's interests is *entirely* determined by her socio-economic relationships gets us nowhere.

And so, we now want to try to come to an understanding of woman's world, in its difference from man's world, by taking as our starting point the characteristics of feminine movement. We will look at the basic physical aptitudes of the little girl, and from these try to grasp the meaning of her *original* world. We will also try to see the way in which the development of her dynamism takes place, what course it follows, and then try to show that of all wholly mature human activities, the activity of *taking care* is the one that is most in accord with the feminine manner of movement and the one that best represents the meaning of woman's existence and so, the meaning of her world as well. We will also come to see that her being-in-the-world so as to *care* for it determines woman's relationship to her own body. And finally, we will try to see how the activity of taking care is manifested in its most perfect form in woman's aptitude for motherhood.

1. The Dynamics of Feminine Existence

> Man, he lives in jerks. . . . Woman, it's all flow, like a stream, little eddies, little waterfalls, but the stream it goes right on.
>
> JOHN STEINBECK [1]

We cannot come to understand the difference between the sexes by considering only static images of men and women and the expressive content of these images. However, even where the image observed is a static one, it is always possible in some way to see through its stillness and behind it to find indications of a certain manner of movement. When we look at a photograph or a painting, or when we have just a momentary glimpse of a living person, we see more than a given, defined configuration, a whole formed of its lines and surfaces. We see more than this, because every line suggests a manner of movement to the eye, and every surface is a field of tension and rest.

Klages in his time had already pointed this out. It is the total, phenomenological aspect of the static image, and Klages was able to find very simple examples to help to throw light on it. Look at a landscape, for instance: the course of a river, the line or the curve of a road, the raised finger of a steeple, the swift fall of a hillside—in all of these things as we see them, we see an aspect of movement by which we in turn are moved, and in our own being moved, immediately understand all the more the quality of virtual movement in what we perceive.

Something of the same sort takes place when we look on the figure or the face of a man or a woman. Even when we look at a motionless image, its seemingly static proportions suggest something dynamic to the sight, through the smooth flow or the jerky angularity of its lines. But when we can observe a person *really*

[1] The Grapes of Wrath.

273

moving in his own particular manner, the characteristics of the movement are revealed to us very much more clearly than by any image. For then we see a dynamism, expressed by the altering contours of the figure, a dynamism being unfolded as a stature of movement in a sequence of time.

It is in the field of music that we are most familiar with dynamic shapes or statures. In the quality of a tone of voice, quite apart from the words being pronounced, we encounter a stature of movement characteristic of the person to whom the voice belongs, a dynamic form in which the person announces himself, presents himself, in a way that is special to himself. To some extent, we have already noticed this, while thinking of the voice as one of the ways in which woman manifests herself.

The characteristic qualities of each person are formed gradually during the course of the person's existence, and, since each person belongs to some group, there is at the same time a gradual formation of the characteristics of the group. These group characteristics may be the peculiarities of a nation or of a particular social status, but within each set there is always a concurrent differentiation of the group characteristics according to sex.

There is no doubt that a particular person's dynamic image develops from that person's inborn aptitudes and in accordance with them. However, these aptitudes do not invariably dispose a person to conform with the typology of the group to which he belongs. It is possible to come across someone belonging to a particular race who is by no means a perfect representative of the dynamic image of that race. There are many individuals belonging to some or other status or occupational group—farmer, seaman, soldier—whose appearance is somehow not wholly "true to type." There are even schoolmasters who do not look like schoolmasters. There is a reason for this. In every group, there is a typical manner of acting, of doing things, but it does not necessarily follow that every individual in the group will conform exactly to type.

From all of this we can gather what is meant by the dynamic image proper to a group, or proper to a sex, and when we now go on to speak of the dynamic image of woman, this is the sense in which the term is to be understood.

Thus, when we study woman's manner of movement, it is in order to discover that special quality of the movement that constantly recurs in all of her activity, the quality that defines her movement as movement in the specific feminine manner and gives the dynamic expressiveness of her movements its specific feminine characteristics.

There are many words in common, conversational use that describe a person's habitual manner of movement. We speak of someone as hasty, calm, sluggish, bold, well or ill mannered, solemn or dignified and so on. Each of these words is used to signify a manner in which someone moves, and the intention implicit in the word is that once this particular dynamic image has been genuinely recognized in a given individual, one knows in advance how that individual will go about opening a newspaper or carry on in a conversation—the words are used to mean that the manner of movement they describe is so characteristic of the individual that we can tell, in general, how that individual inhabits the world, how he conducts himself in relation to other people and in relation to the things about him. Travelling in a train and having an opportunity quietly to observe a stranger's movements for a time, it is sometimes quite entertaining to discover how very likely he is to do things just as we expect he will do them.

Each person's dynamic image is so characteristic of him or of her that domestic animals quickly get to know a person from this alone. A dog does not need to see who is coming; it recognizes its master or the milkman from the sound of the footsteps alone. There are minute peculiarities in the gait and rhythm of each individual, and from these alone the dog can tell who is approaching the house, even if a number of people are coming and going at the same time, or can tell whether that one among the many is coming closer or moving away.

If we try to observe movement that is typically masculine or typically feminine in such a way that we ourselves take part in what we are observing, we begin to discover the basic forms of the movement—the forms that recur in every particular action. Naturally, this discovery is not the discovery of the "eternal" feminine form or the "eternal" masculine form, as though there were eternal forms of movement established unchangeably for all time. Human movement is not determined by nature; it is developed according to culture. Thus, we must add a further qualification to the meaning of the term, the "dynamic image" typical of a particular sex.

The term, in our context, means the image pheno-typically characteristic of that sex in our cultural sphere.

It is possible to ask whether the genesis of development in the
child does not provide an explanation for the fact that there are a
typically masculine and a typically feminine dynamic image. For
the moment however we will leave this question aside, and concentrate on trying to see and understand what these images are.

Difference of Dynamism

Throughout the centuries, people have noticed that the dynamics of the female sex are not the same as the dynamics of the male
sex. This difference of dynamism is the actual origin of the notion
that the difference between male and female pervades all things, a
view that has been formulated in many ways and is always present
in one or another current expression.

As Feuerbach says, "The difference between the sexes is a
difference of marrow and bone, present everywhere in everything,
infinite, a difference of which we cannot say that it begins at this
point and ends at that point. I think that what I perceive now I
perceive both as man and as woman." Clearly, Feuerbach did not
set out to formulate a phenomenological typology in the strict
sense, but let us take his words in this sense nevertheless. Understanding them in this way, they do not mean that there are two
sorts of human being, one sort being different from the other in
every respect; rather, they mean that in our cultural sphere human
existence has become differentiated in two main directions, a male
direction and a female direction, in such a way that a very constant
dynamic image has become the specific image of each direction,
and that each of the two specific types of dynamism have given rise
to a particular manner of perceiving and acting, a manner of thinking, a manner of feeling, called masculine or feminine, each manner relating in its own different way to its own different world. It is
this difference of dynamism that we are trying to see and identify.

In order to be able to do this, it is necessary to pay careful
attention to very simple movements. Every movement expresses an
intentionality with a twofold aspect. In the first place, the intentionality is directed to that which the movement itself is intended

to achieve. Thus, it is directed to what is being done, whatever this may be, whether seeing something or grasping hold of something or saying something or addressing someone or persuading someone of something. The first direction of the intentionality is to some given act.

In this aspect, the intentionality is not reflexively conscious; its motivation is exclusively positional. For it is not possible simultaneously to do something *and* to reflect upon the doing, in the strict sense of simultaneity; reflection might take place *during* the doing, but the meaning of "during" implies interruption and essentially excludes the meaning of "simultaneous with." The actual, objective performance of an action is possible only when a person becomes involved in a situation directly and physically—real action is possible only to the extent that a person becomes wholly absorbed in the concrete situation. It is very likely that reflection plays a part in constituting the totality of the situation, but reflection alone can never produce as much as one wiggle in a little finger.

In the second place, every human action expresses a general intentionality that is entirely different from the positionally motivated intentionality of the concrete action. For in every action, the human being has and expresses the non-reflexive intention to establish himself or herself as present, determining the "shape" of his or her presence by the concrete nature of the action, even to its smallest specific detail. It is this particular individual who speaks, argues, takes hold of this thing, goes somewhere, and it can be no-one else who is doing these particular things in this particular way. In this regard some would speak of the existential consciousness or others of a self-consciousness that can never be lacking. But, whatever terms are used, the fact remains that each person makes himself or herself known in accordance with the way he or she as an individual chooses to exist in the world and in accordance with the way each one finds himself or herself placed in the world. It is this second kind of intentionality that is revealed in the constant dynamic typology of a person's movements.

And now, what difference is there between the way a man moves and the way a woman moves?

The masculine and feminine types of movement are so characteristic that they can be detected even through an otherwise "perfect" disguise. It is sometimes said of a particular man that his movements are typically feminine, or of a woman that hers are typically masculine. We are able to form this kind of judgment of another and express it with a certain intuitive certainty, because we have already formed our own idea of the dynamic images of the sexes. This idea is not explicit, and neither is it a-prioristic; it is formed spontaneously, without reflection, from our experiences of the way in which men and women manifest themselves in our own circle.

In order to become objectively aware of the image of movement and to differentiate consciously between its masculine and feminine image, we have to observe and compare movements in which the sexual difference is as obvious as possible. This is an application of an elementary and universal principle of the phenomenological method. For we know that there are some phenomena in which the characteristic we want to investigate is present but not clearly manifested to our observation. For instance, if it is general animal characteristics we wish to investigate, we do not begin immediately to observe the infusorians, for in these animal species the general characteristics of animal life are much less clearly manifested than in other species. Thus we always look for examples in which the essential subject of the investigation is most easily and clearly observable. Later, after we have a clear image of the subject from study of clear examples, it will be possible to find what we are looking for even where it is not so obvious, where it is masked and shrouded by other factors.

The dynamic typology of the sexes is most clearly evident in all those actions in which the process of doing the thing done is not subject to any pressure from the needs of the situation. In such actions, the person is able to be free to some extent from the need to specify his or her intentionality, and thus the action becomes much more of an expression of the person's own mode of existence. It is far less easy to detect elements of the typical dynamic image of an old-time seaman when you make him sit down and write a letter than it is when you ask him to spit into a cuspidor. Certain actions have become so characteristic of the mode of existence of a group that they do in fact clearly reveal the typical dynamic image of that group. On the other hand, there are certain actions, such as the performance of production-line labor in industry, that conceal anything characteristic of a particular group. In industrial labor, all parts of the situation are wholly unambiguous, and there is no ambiguity in the changes that take place within the situation. This imposes a uniform manner of movement on all who take part in this labor, whether they are men or women, farmers or mechanics.

There may be a difference between the way a man hammers a nail into the wall and the way a woman does it, but this difference does not arise only from the special dynamism of each; it is determined by other and wholly different factors as well. The way a person hammers a nail is determined by the amount of practice the person has had, by the person's inclinations, by the person's self-confidence, by the decisiveness of the person's actions, by the person's sensitivity to "the regard of others," and so on. Neither, then, do these actions provide us with examples that are wholly suitable to our purpose, for they do not reveal exclusively the dynamic image of masculine or feminine movement or the difference between them.

Walking

But let us look at the action of *walking*—not walking with the purpose of getting somewhere, but walking without aim, free of any specification imposed by the situation, and thus, a walking that takes place in the pure spontaneity of the urge to move, in which the person who walks has a self-awareness in the walking and so also establishes his or her presence in the walking. When someone moves in this way, simply for the sake of walking, without taking thought of the action or having an aim to achieve in it, all expression of emotional condition or mood fades into the background. This kind of expression would be in the forefront of the expressiveness of the action if the walking were to take place under powerfully emotional conditions—or if the action were "theatrical" in any way—for then the manner of the walking would be determined by the structure of meaning in the situation, and the action itself would express mainly this structure of meaning. But we want to look at the action as free from any pressure from the situation.

If, then, we look at men and women when they are walking simply for the sake of *walking*, without any specific intent, we are able to notice a typological characteristic in the motion that is not very easily described in words. This is not surprising, for the eye is much more sensitive than our command of language. It does not surprise us when, for instance, an orthopedic surgeon looking at a person's gait can immediately notice some minute aspect of it that is not normal, but be able to say no more about the *gait* than that it is "not normal."

Someone whom we know very well has only to introduce some tiny alteration in his usual movements, and it will immediately strike us as "strange." But we will not be able to find the exact words to describe the strangeness, any more than the surgeon can find the words to describe the precise abnormality of gait, as an abnormality in the quality of the movement (distinct from an anatomical abnormality). Nevertheless, we now have to try to find words to describe a typology of motion, since it is a function of words to give direction to our attention.

To some extent, the essential difference between the masculine walk and the feminine walk relates to the division of the action as a whole into its natural components, in this case, into steps. But the difference also relates to the manner in which each single component, each step, is carried out. If we ask people chosen at random to tell us what is the difference between the way a man walks and the way a woman walks, we are very likely to get the reply that the difference lies in the length of their steps.

As a static measure, the length of stride is in fact usually longer in the man. But it is clear that many factors determine the length of stride and that it is certainly not determined by the sexual factor alone, and still less by the sexual difference as it has been constituted in the existence of an individual. The length of the stride is very largely a secondary characteristic, and is often an outcome of the intentionality underlying the action, expressed in the stride. However, let us return to the essential difference, and look first at the manner in which each separate step is carried out.

In a man's walk, it appears that the movement of the foot speeds up toward the end of the step. It appears so to the eye alone, and there is no doubt that in all cases where it does appear so, objective measurement (e.g., by means of slow-motion photography) would confirm that there is an increase in the speed of the movement toward the end of the step. We can take this as a typical characteristic of the masculine gait, and call it an *accentuation of the final point* of the individual steps.

This puts us onto the tracks of a very important characteristic of the basic structure of masculine motion. Since the end of a stride is actually a pause, it would perhaps be better to speak of an accentuation of pauses. It is possible to evoke a memory of the masculine gait in the imagination by the sound of a repetitive knock, for the movement in each case shows a clear division into separate and clearly distinct parts. Each part is closed off by a final point which, phenomenologically, dominates the whole movement of that part and determines the meaning of that movement as a whole. When the sound of the masculine gait is imitated, its characteristic timing is that of the march.

It is not possible to give a similar imitation of the sound of the feminine gait, simply because the feminine gait does not have this accentuation of the pauses or of the final points. For the moment we can only describe it negatively, as non-masculine, although the lack of accentuation does give it the positive characteristic of a more even, more flowing continuity of the whole action. Generally, too, the feminine gait consists of smaller strides, because longer strides automatically give the pattern of effort and the forward swing of the leg such a compass that a masculine accentuation can easily begin to predominate. But still, a short stride is not essential to the feminine gait. What is essential is that there should be no accentuation of the pauses and no speeding up of the movement of the step toward its end.

Thus, feminine movement is more moderate, more flowing. However, what is the *meaning* of a flowing movement as distinct from an angular or staccato movement? In a flowing movement, such as the undulation of a wave, every moment of the movement has an intrinsic relationship to present, past and future. This relationship must be understood in a strictly formal, phenomenological sense; there is no point in asking in what concrete connections the relationship consists. In contrast to the flowing movement of an undulation, the angular movement displays a direct course toward a terminal point, and then a sudden change of direction toward a new terminal point. The parts of the movement are straight and there is no variation in their meaning. The quality of angular movement is measure rather than rhythm.

Returning now to our consideration of the dynamic typology of the sexes, we can describe the contrast between the masculine and feminine ways of movement like this: masculine movement is constantly being brought to a *stop*, but feminine movement *goes on without stopping*. Here I would note that the angularity displayed by the static image of the masculine form and the more rounded shapes of the feminine form are in fact no more than the appearance in the static image of the same dynamic typology that can be observed so much more clearly in the actual movement of the two forms.

Once we have been made aware of the difference in the example of walking for walking's sake, it becomes easier to detect the same difference in all every-day actions, in the gestures men and women employ, in the rise and fall of their voice, in any of the numberless dynamic processes of human life. The masculine performance of an action is always *divided* into parts, each part having a marked termination. There is, moreover, a clearly accentuated *end* to the action as a whole, called the goal, end or final aim of the action. The goal of the action is the definitive moment of the whole action, giving meaning to all parts of the action preceding the achievement of the goal, and giving meaning to the action as a whole. In a masculine movement, therefore, the termination or sometimes the final aim that gives meaning to the whole can be recognized as present in anticipation in each part of the movement. There is therefore a masculine quality in every movement that is abrupt or angular or undeviatingly straight or very emphatically aimed at one given point.

This may be said not only of human movements, but of movements in nature as well; the pounce, the snatching bite, all predatory activity displays the characteristic of masculine dynamism, even when executed by a female animal. The roll of thunder or the fall of a rock from a mountainside, accentuating divisions of the fall as it crashes off of one boulder after another with gathering momentum—these are much more closely related to masculine movement than to feminine.

This does provide us with some description of the dynamic typology of the sexes, but it does not yet go far enough. We have to try to penetrate further, and understand the pattern of effort or *impulse* which determines the inner meaning of every action. To do this, we have to try to share in the intentionality which determines the visible aspects of the action.

Resistance and Circular Function

Every movement becomes masculine in the character of its expressiveness if the impulse that brings it forth, and thus the intention behind it, is aimed at a resistance to be overcome. Masculine activity is in fact born of the experience of resistance. Of all the variations of intentionality manifested phenotypically in masculine action, the basic theme is always resistance and the overcoming of resistance. In a repetitive movement such as walking, the accentuation of the final points or of the pauses means, quite simply, that at each phase of the action the remaining spatial distance to be covered is experienced as a resistance to be overcome; in the completion of each step, a new obstacle is projected. Thus, each masculine act arises anew from the situation and is directed toward the situation. Therefore, the character of masculine activity is powerfully *reactive*. Man goes ahead one step at a time, his distances are bridged little by little. As each step is aimed to reach its own particular end, each succeeding part of the whole masculine movement requires a new impulse.

Here again there is an obvious difference between flowing movement and movement that is angular and staccato. As Klages remarked, there is a "surge of impulsion" in the flowing movement. In the feminine movement, impulse rises and falls gradually in an unbroken line with the perfect regularity of the movement of a wave. In staccato movement, the impulse is characteristically noncontinuous but broken in a frequent succession of end and renewal; the present impulse does not grow out of the preceding one in continuity with it, but is given a new point of beginning in the positional awareness of the meaning of the situation.

This means that the expressive quality of feminine movement will be entirely different from that of masculine movement. Feminine movement does not arise from a sudden impulse and a reactive attitude, but grows from a tendency. The tendency may of course be enticed into activity by a situation, but whether it is or not will depend upon the tendency being of such a kind that it responds inwardly to the enticement. Thus, *there is always a formal bond between woman and her environment, established in a relationship that is maintained by the very manner of her movement and never resolved by her movement.* The masculine relationship to the situation is resolved in the execution of the masculine movement. There is no resolution of the relationship to the situation in feminine movement; the relationship is preserved by the movement itself, for the impulse toward a given end itself develops the energy for a movement in the opposite direction, in the same way as the crest of the wave itself develops the energy that will produce the subsequent trough in any rhythmic continuity of undulation. According to Klages, the flow of the wave is the archetypal image of rhythm.

Thus the predominant characteristic of feminine movement is that its function is circular. The meaning of a circular function can best be illustrated by the example of touch. When an object is touched, the sensations of touch elicit further movements of touch. The person moves the object and the object moves the person; both person and object are movers as well as moved, and the two are united in an unbroken circle of movement. In a similar way, feminine movement and all feminine activity flow in an endless circle: woman is mover, as present-in-herself, and she is also moved, as together-with-the-world, and neither state ever puts an end to the other.

It might be said that feminine movement, of itself, possesses no end. The meaning of this would be, that the intentionality of the movement as such is not aimed at one particular end and therefore has no definite termination. Naturally, feminine movement comes to an end "de facto," just as the action of touching an object comes to an end at some point. But this termination is always more or less "critical"; it is not implicit in the movement itself. These are all very important, elementary differences between masculine and feminine dynamism.

In the masculine dynamism, the intention establishing the meaning of the movement is the final aim and terminal point of the movement. But feminine movement is brought to a termination by a crisis; its termination constitutes a crisis. The concept of crisis is essential for an understanding of the relationship between the human being and the world, for it indicates the possibility of a total amorphousness into which an existence can fall, to rise up once again, renewed, through a "mutation in stature." [2]

Yet another aspect can be discovered in the feminine dynamic. As we have seen, this manner of movement constitutes a connection between woman and her environment, the connection indicated in the circular functioning of her movement. Now, there is a certain relationship between this and all manner of *playful* contact. For in playful contact too, there is a reciprocal union of moving and being moved. All play is play with something, with an object of play, and the object of play itself plays with the player in some sense. Thus an uninterrupted reciprocity of contact is established in which response to enticement is itself a new enticement to response. Thus, a continuity is set up in which there is a complete absence of intentional terminal points.

The rhythmic regularity of the feminine walk has brought some special qualities of feminine motion clearly to the fore, but there are others which it does not reveal with the same clarity. These special qualities can be seen a little more clearly in woman's way of dealing with things in every-day life. We discussed the expressive quality of youthfulness in the chapter on woman's mode of manifesting herself, and we find that there are characteristics of the feminine dynamism that lend emphasis to this youthful quality in woman's appearance.

The basic pattern of feminine dynamism gives rise to pathic relationships [2a] which, because of their reciprocity, can never be directed purely toward one given goal. These relationships pervade feminine existence from two aspects: from woman's own special manner of movement, and from the typically feminine world (the existence projecting its own world through its movement, and the world in turn ever eliciting new movement on the part of the existence). Thus there is an inward necessity in all pathic and playful connections by which they become concrete and necessary connections with nearby reality.

These connections can be established between a girl or woman and other people in her immediate circle, or they might arise between a woman and the things round about her, and thus form the foundation of those activities in which a woman is occupied from

[2] V. von Weizsäcker, *Der Gestaltkreis,* Stuttgart 1947.
[2a] Cf. footnote 10a, Chapter IV.

day to day. In either case we can see how the special characteristics of the dynamism involved give rise to actions which in their concrete form are experienced as typically feminine actions—the chief reasons for which we have already seen in our section on the psychological characteristics of woman's nature.

It is easy to name any number of occupations that characteristically call for the action to be very definitely directed toward a given point or which call for the action to be divided clearly into a succession of particular steps. It is equally easy to recall examples of actions in which the movement is predominantly a continuous flow and which are rhythmically repetitive, carrying on until stopped by some external circumstance or until the inner urge to move dies down.

Perhaps it will be remarked that this kind of contrast between types of action is in agreement with the typology of masculine and feminine dynamism we have developed, but that it does not appear possible to maintain the contrast when it is checked against objective facts. When the real performance of actions by men and women is recorded and analyzed, we find that there is definitely no constancy of difference between the patterns of masculine and feminine action that would agree with the difference of dynamic typology we have described. But this is not surprising. We have not said that everything a woman does is done in a feminine way. There are numberless actions which are "neutral," not specified in their execution by a sexual differentiation.

Sexual Differentiation

In the first place, sexual differentiation might be lacking in an action because masculine and feminine are both characteristics of humanity and both occur in human individuals whether they be male or female. Men are able to develop a markedly feminine manner of movement, just as women are able to perform a typically masculine action. In the second place—as we have already seen—the situation itself often requires a particular dynamism. Many occupations impose a particular manner of execution on the action, and men and women both have to conform to the requirements of the occupation, although their conformity in most cases still leaves room for slight variations arising from their own personal dynamism. Woman is capable of any profession or occupation, with the possible exception of the very heaviest forms of manual labor—but then, the majority of men are wholly incapable of this kind of labor too. On the other hand, those occupations usually considered to belong to women can all be carried out by men.

Nevertheless, a specifically feminine form of movement or a specifically masculine form of it does appear as soon as a person is free from the pressures of any situation, and the more completely a person is free from any pressure and able to "let himself go," the more clearly will his movements manifest a specific type. We can see it for instance in the idle handling of an object or in other very simple things that are done without any special thought, like buttoning a coat or greeting a friend with a wave of the hand. The popular judgments formed in our social relationships are in fact based on the way these insignificant gestures are seen to be carried out. In them we find the reason why we hear remarks like, "what manly mannerisms that woman has," or "what a peculiarly effeminate thing for a man to do." But then, we so frequently see examples; a manly man looks at his wristwatch with a jerk of his cuff and his elbow sharply bent; when a lady-like woman looks at hers, her movement is gentle and flowing.

We can approach the difference between the masculine and feminine ways of moving from still another point of view, by looking at the content of expressiveness in the movement as such—present in every human movement—and at the degree to which the movement goes beyond what is strictly necessary.

There is an important difference between an action and an expressive movement. The action gets its meaning from the end toward which it is directed, while the expressive movement contains its meaning within itself. From this, we might be inclined to draw the conclusion that action is the main characteristic of masculine activity while expressive movement is the main characteristic of feminine activity.

The contrast, however, cannot be formulated in this way, for action and expressive movement are both divided according to a sexual differentiation in the manner of execution. There is a masculine and a feminine mode of the expressive movements which reveal moods, emotions and affectivity. All explosive movements of expression, taking the shape of abrupt and angular gestures and containing elements of reaction to situations—sudden, loud laugh-

ter, outbursts of anger—are of a predominantly masculine character. Expressive movements developing slowly on enticement from
the situation and sustaining a continuity of contact with the situation—the quiet smile—are predominantly feminine in character.
Thus, it is not the contrast between action and expressive movement that parallels the contrast between masculine and feminine,
but rather, the contrast between the presence of a connection between the manner of movement and the movement's content of
expressiveness on the one hand, and the absence of such a connection on the other. What Schiller termed "sympathetic movements"
are characteristic of woman.

In any person's activity, there is generally no economic reduc-
tion to the minimum necessary movement; one is much more likely
to be able to observe an excess of movement. If we exclude those
movements that have become as automatic as it is possible for
human movements to be (such as simple repetitive operations on
an assembly-line), every human movement is essentially different
from a mechanical movement. The human movement possesses a
certain "richness" over and above its functional aim. This richness, which is displayed by even the most straightforward action
aimed at the simplest purpose, is variable. It might be developed in
a manifestation of gracefulness. We have discussed feminine gracefulness at length in another place.[3] Here, we need say no more
than that the graceful movement has, from the earliest times, always been regarded as specifically feminine. Schiller expresses it
very well: "The gentle feminine build is quick to receive an impression, and quick to let it disappear again. Stable constitutions
get under way with a rush, and if strong muscles are drawn tight,
they cannot display any of the lightness required for grace. . . . The
tender fibre of woman bends like a slender reed before the lightest
breeze of emotion."[4]

This thought takes us back to the connection between dynamism
and the build of the body, between graceful luxuriance of movement and femininity. But at the same time it draws our attention to
the relationship between woman's dynamism and woman's world,
the relationship that explains the foremost of woman's psychological characteristics: her greater affectivity.

---

[3] *Algemene Theorie der menselijke houding en beweging,* Aula 175, p.
587ff.

[4] *Ueber Anmut und Würde.*

2. The Original World of Woman

Girls dress themselves much more efficiently and earlier than boys, due to a better fine motor coordination and especially a more flexible rotation at the wrist.

GESELL [5]

There is a reciprocal relationship between the basically feminine type of dynamism and the feminine world. Even when the "genuine" girl is very young, she displays a typical dynamism. We learned to know this typical dynamism as the way a movement is carried out when it comes spontaneously, without deliberation and without any pressure from the situation, and also as the pattern of impulses formed and elicited by the situation. Femininity is thus a *mode* of the physically determined human being-in-the-world: a *manner* of touching, grasping, handling, approaching, withdrawing, glancing-at and glancing-away and looking "inward"; a particular *manner* of the movement of thought, of the rise and fall of emotion, of making decisions and of carrying them out. Because the specific difference is something that lies in the *manner* of action, expression and gesture, the sexual differentiation is something that can be established empyrically.

The feminine dynamic type, therefore, is *one* of the ways in which the human being can project a properly human world, developing it out of the actuality of the discovered environment, and in this way giving the projected world one general and all-pervading meaning—no matter how much that world may vary according to the contingency of the structures of situations. We are not thinking now of the mood or climate or brightness of the projected world. In other words, we are not now concerned with *how* this world strikes us or how it appears to us. We are now concerned with the nature of this world's *dynamic* "response" to the "word" the human person addresses to it—for the world's response must be dynamic, on account of the correspondence that *must* always exist between action and reaction. We are using the notions of word and response in order to bring out the fact that

[5] *The First Five Years of Life;* London (Methuen) p. 248.

every human action—whether deliberate or undeliberate (unconscious, so-called) or "inward" (virtual) action—*every* human action projects a meaning, and also that human action *can* project a meaning *only* because of the wealth of meaning already contained in that toward which the action is directed.

It is not as though the feminine dynamism projected a feminine world and there the whole matters rests. In turn, the projected world presents itself as a world encountered *in this particular way,* and thus, like environment again, makes new calls on the feminine dynamism. This is the reason we spoke of a reciprocal relationship between the basic dynamic type and the basic pattern of its appropriate world.

It should be noticed that this dialectical relationship between human being and environment, a relationship determined to some extent by the given physical reality of the human being, does not bring about a world projected and encountered as a world that is intelligible to the consciousness. The world that arises in this way is accidental and knowable in a non-rational way. However, *human* reality requires a *real* transcendence of all that is accidental, and therefore requires a real transcendence of the physical, for all that is physical is accidental.

Human existence is a call to the absolute, to reality and truth, and freedom is the required condition for such a call (as de Waelhens says). J. Wahl says, very rightly, that "all existence is choice." The existentialists may be extremely emphatic in insisting that being-in-the-world is always a being-in-the-body, but nevertheless they all agree that *"Dasein,"* human existence, is human in the strict sense only through consciousness, taking consciousness in the sense of an implicit awareness of one's own existence in its transcendence. In other words, existence is *human,* properly speaking, only through implicit knowledge of the *existence* of the possibilities open to one.

Now this insight into human existence is perfectly correct, and it leads to the conclusion that the only possible sense of *"Dasein"* is that of a human existence which is universally *human* in the strict, generic sense of human, and in consequence it is not strictly permissible to speak of a specific feminine (or masculine) existence or of a feminine (or masculine) "soul."

From this, it would follow that the notion of a feminine world, or of a feminine manner of existence, actually has nothing to do with what is *human in the strict sense* in the total reality of woman, but relates merely to the way humanity happens to be manifested in this coincidental form of the human bodily reality. This being the case, we could also speak of the "existence" and the "world" of a blind person or of a cripple or a paralytic, but our meaning would be much clearer if we used terms like "form of life" and "milieu" rather than "existence" and "world," since the concept of existence is to be taken in an ontological sense exclusively and not in an empirical sense.

No essential definition of existence is given in the notion of being blind, any more than one is given in the notion of being a soldier or of being a butler. No essential knowledge of such forms of being is possible; we can know them only as coincidental, in a way that is analogous to the way we refer to particular animal species as "variations on a theme" in nature. A fish does not "exist" in an ontological sense, because the fish does not choose; it does not project its own watery world, but fits into the given water like a key into its lock.

We hold, however, that the human being is not an animal; even with regard to the physiological reality of the human being, it cannot be said that the human being is animal, at least not without qualification. Inasmuch as the human being exists in the world through the body, the human body forms a part of the human world—although in a special way. The body is not merely coincidental to the human being, but humanly meaningful, through the way a person regards the body and gives meaning to it. Thus, there may be real grounds for speaking of a feminine world, where the term "world" would refer to everything that "belongs" to her bodily reality as meaningfully projected by woman herself.

Spirit

But there is yet another line of thought that makes it possible to speak of an original world of woman. To find out what this might be, we have to take a lead from the classical intuition that the outward shape and the motor aptitudes of the human body are *not* accidental. It goes without saying that the human body, like the animal body, is suited to its appropriate "mode of life" even to the minutest detail, but, unlike the animal body, the human body is suited also to the spirit.

Kierkegaard once wrote, "The idea of human being is spirit, and one must not be misled by the fact that one is also able to move on two legs." [6] And yet, could we not regard the *two*-legged stance, the upright stance, as an *essentially* human value, a *pre-requisite* condition for the realization of human spirit in its freedom.

Erwin Straus has published a penetrating phenomenological analysis which draws attention to the fact that the upright stance leaves man's hands *essentially* empty, and the significance of this fact has fundamental bearing on spiritual existence.[7] If we are really to come to understand the human being, it is not enough to fall back into the speculative and romantic way of thinking, and try to gain an insight into human reality by drawing conclusions from the "idea" of man's physical stature and from the abstract concepts that derive from this idea. Neither is it possible to gain any complete knowledge of human reality if we concentrate exclusively on conscious being in its intentionality, ignoring the whole sphere of things or non-conscious being. If we do this, we begin to see conscious being as a transcendence to which there is nothing to give determination or limit or direction, a transcendence "condemned to liberty." If human reality could be understood in this way, Sartre would be right when he says that man is no more than a "useless passion." [8]

It is much more fruitful to proceed from both the intentionality of consciousness as well as from the *determination* of consciousness that arises from its rootedness in being. For the human being cannot conceive of *himself* as other than someone who *is,* and this means that he can conceive of himself only as someone who *is together with* all that his consciousness is conscious of. Thus, the essence of human being is not merely "being for itself," but also, and primarily, conscious being that is conscious through "being in a situation."

De Waelhens contrasts the fundamental thought of Merleau-Ponty with that of Sartre, and shows that existence is to be under-

---

[6] In *Entweder-Oder.*

[7] E. Straus, *Die Aufrechte Haltung;* Monatschr. f. Psychiatr. und Neurol. Vol. 117, 1949, p. 367.

[8] *L'Etre et le Néant.*

stood, not as a "consciousness bearing witness to," but rather as a "consciousness engaged in." [9] Being-in-a-situation has a twofold ontological aspect. On the one hand it means directing oneself intentionally, with meaning—which Sartre would term *"s'éclater vers"*, a "bursting toward." But on the other hand it is at the same time a being together with something, meaning that one discovers oneself alongside of something other than oneself, or that one is "exposed to. . . . influence," as Gabriel Marcel has shown.[10]

A situation is really an element of a human world, and therefore a meaningful situation, because human existence is *essentially* a being in two modes at the same time: being in the mode of giving (giving meaning), and being in the mode of receiving (receiving meaning). In principle, consciousness is the possibility of onward movement in the free projection of meaning, and this possibility is always manifest in human existence. Therefore, the ontological aspect of "being together with something" is always qualified by a certain negation which excludes that "something" from the reciprocal unity of giving and receiving. By this exclusion, the "something" does not remain simply "that which I am with," but becomes something *other* than myself, and so is constituted as a *resistance* opposing the intentions of the onward-moving transcending consciousness.

Any human being who wants to do anything always has to realize his plans in a resistant world. Insofar as this world is encountered as "material," its resistance is encountered as a relative value, for the material serves a purpose in the realization of a projected form. Thus, material reality is a resistance and at the same time a means in the empirical sense too, but it appears empirically as both resistance and means only because on the ontological level it "exists" as resistance and means in relation to the human being and his intentions. The appearance of the world derives its meaning and its functional sense from human intentions exclusively, for it is encountered primarily as other, as resistance, as non-value. At the same time the ontological aspect of human existence as "being-with-the-other" necessarily reveals a (relative) value in the other by which it can serve the *intentionality* as a *means* toward the achievement of an end.

Thus, insofar as the world is intelligible to the human being, it is

[9] Introduction, Vol. I (2nd ed.) *La Structure du Comportement.* P.U.F.
[10] *Etre en situation. Recherches Philosoph.* 1936-37.

primarily a world of resistances, for the human consciousness which is expansive, intentional, free and unlimited always encounters the world primarily as a resistance and must always project it primarily as a resistance. The world of relative values is a human world in a *secondary* sense, for the world encountered in the expansive self-movement of the human consciousness, besides appearing as a resistance, *also* reveals itself as material and means and functionally useful.

The world *can* reveal itself in this second way because human consciousness is *not an absolute,* but is anchored in being in such a way that the existence of consciousness takes the form of a being *together with* something other than itself, where this "other" is what it is independently of human consciousness. This "other" embraces all things apart from the human consciousness itself. All things have a value as they are *in themselves,* an *essential value* distinct from their value as material and means *relative* to the human consciousness. This essential value is revealed only where the intention is to open oneself to receive it; given the presence of an intentionality projecting things as *resistances,* their essential value must remain hidden.

Resistances and Values

In actual experience, many things can "strike" us, bind, hinder, draw, distract or hold us (as for instance the sight of some object can do). Any ordinary experience of this kind can prove to be a restriction of freedom because it means that our intentions are directed (restricted) toward some object outside ourself and, insofar as this is a restriction of freedom, this is seen as a resistance that must be overcome in order to realize a value which we project as being "beyond" the experience itself. As we have said, it is possible to view the resistance under the aspect of its usefulness, and in this way the primary human world, the world of resistances, becomes a world of relative values. Wherever the human being encounters the world in terms of his *practical behavior* (desire to do something, to act, to make something, to arrive somewhere), *he constitutes the encountered world as resistance and means, thereby causing its essential value to remain hidden.*

We discover the world of essential values only when we are wholly free of practical intentions and enter into a state of being-*with*-the-other, not in the sense of an active adaptation, but in the sense of an adjustment of *ourself,* a conforming, coming to a standstill in the silence of the listener and the contemplative on-looker, or, however we do it, with the intention of ourselves *becoming* the key to the locked meaning of things as they are in themselves, before our intentionality gives them a meaning in relation to us.

This implies the definite choice of a contemplative *tarrying in the presence of* things, which means that the expansive restlessness of intended intentions is *suspended* for a while and that there is a pause in the onward movement of our own plans toward their realization. Thus we are able empirically to observe two basic forms of behavior: in one, the person stands still in the presence of something, in contact with it; and in the other, the person is on the way toward a projected goal. One means that the whole self is "here"; the other means that the self, while appearing here, is already "somewhere else." Empirically we have knowledge of two worlds: the world of essential values, and the world of usefulness or of pragmatic values.

All this is contained in actual every-day experience. We have presented it here as a distinction of ontologically fundamental categories, because whenever the *human being* is conscious of something (the other), in his consciousness that something is present as *opposed* to him and at the same time as *with* him *in* his existence. In consciousness of one's own restlessness, one encounters a world of resistance and projects a world of relative values; in consciousness of restful tarrying (the suspension of expansive rest-lessness), one fulfills the condition of intention required for the world to reveal its essential values.

When human existence is fully realized as a being-in-the-world in the body and through the body, it cannot be other than an existence with intentions. That is to say, the human being, as human, must "think"; he must view what he views in a particular sense. But when the intentions imply a view that is the negation of the view that the world is something *together-with* the human being, the world is constituted in the mode of "the other," and viewed as a resistance and a non-value.

To the *homo faber* the world must become a useful material that can be taken *according to* its usefulness in order to be given an integrated form by being used. This is one mode of being-in-the-world, and it defines a relationship of man and world that is the basis of all pragmatic *labor,* whether of thought or of any other activity intended to achieve a practical goal—and this includes the kind of activity that is often called "taking care" of something, but which is in fact not care for the thing as it is, but an effort intentionally to re-form or alter it in some way.

But a human being can project his *own* existence without intending to have any *practical* intentions, but with the intention of suspending the restless urge to transcend the encountered world. In this case, the intention is to remain *with* what is, not taking it *"according to"* something (such as its usefulness), but taking it *as* something in itself. This is another mode of being-in-the-world: *"Dasein"* essentially in the mode of *"Wirheit"* (all the emphasis on *"we are"* rather than on *"I am"*). According to Binswanger, this would mean an existence outside of the dimension of the intentional and consequently outside of the dimension of a *projected* intelligibility. In this view, the things encountered in actuality would not be encountered as coincidental, but would present themselves as *meaningful in themselves* through (in the sense of *à travers*) the meaningful manner of their appearance as perceived by the intentional consciousness.

To such an existence, things are not merely material with a functional value; they are not "other" in the sense of something projected as relative in the given situation. Binswanger describes this kind of existence as "in the world reaching out above the world," and in this existence the human being is in principle together with all that is, as it is, and thus together with the essential value of being as being. This existence unfolds as an immutable *stature* (*"Gestalt"*—the whole being more than its parts) and an absolute *quality* in the "grace" of a *"revelation"* that takes place in a reciprocal unity of giving and receiving.

Thus we have existence with intentions and existence without intentions, and being is encountered as a relative non-value (resistance, means), and also as a value in itself. According to Binswanger, these two modes of existing and encountering may be understood ontologically as the two basic forms of *"Dasein,"* or of authentic human existence. All human existence participates in *both* forms: we never find the personal existence of one individual entirely defined by one only of these two forms.

In the concrete reality of life, we can point to certain factors as the limits to which these forms can be realized. The highest limit of existence without intentions is *fulfilled, disinterested* love. The other limit, approached by existence with intentions, is existence in the mode of absolute transcendence over the encountered world in the intentional production of meaning and form, where there is no love but where all that is encountered is *taken* as material, formless and valueless in itself, and used in order to *produce* something.

Again in actual life, and especially in anything like creative art (which includes scientific work as well), material reality will always be encountered in both ways: as useful, and also with love for its own essential value. Art tends ultimately to present things to us in their own essential being. As Heidegger says, "Art makes the truth come forth." [11]

A suspension of intention is the required condition for an encounter with being in which the being will reveal itself, in its essence, as a stature and quality complete in itself. Being reveals itself in this way through the receptivity of the restful, sustained, interested glance and listening ear. But this suspension of intention and this receptivity are not in any sense a *passivity* like the passivity of soft wax taking an impression. Even if we were to agree with Binswanger that there is no intentional structure in an authentic human existence insofar as it is characterized by a contemplative awareness of the essential value of things, as awareness of "we, together" rather than of "me versus other," it would still remain true that an *act* of sustained, contemplative interest is the necessary basis of such an existence.

Human existence is always existence in a world that is a world both of resistances and of values. In a certain sense we always project the world of people and of things according to our own intentions, but in another sense this is also a *given* world since it gives itself to us in manifesting itself, and we *receive* its qualities, its statures, its meaning and its value in the kind of encounter with it that we can achieve only when we suspend our own practical intentions.

[11] *Holzwege*, Frankfurt 1950, p. 64.

Existence

Quite apart from the correctness of Binswanger's views on the two forms of *"Dasein,"* if we ask how it is possible that the human being, as an *existent being,* originally encounters a world of resistance as well as of essential values, it is clear that the question must be answered in terms of the *bodily reality* of the human being. In discussing this, we take as our starting point the classical (and in a certain sense dogmatic) view we have already mentioned, according to which the human body is not coincidental, but is objectively an organ of the spirit. Spirit is being that knows *of* being and that knows of being-*with*-other-beings, and consequently, spirit is, in principle, being in the freedom of choice, project and decision.

Existence in the body is always existence *within* one's own limitations, but at the same time this is an existence which transcends itself in the direction of that which limits human being. Self-movement is inseparably connected with sensation, and self-movement can be understood in an a-prioristic sense as establishing the foundation of transcendence in bodily existence and thus as the necessary condition for constituting a world. Self-movement is spontaneity, and therefore from its very origin it is expansive (and aggressive), for the "other," such as it is encountered in reality, is primarily *resistance.* There is however another equally original characteristic of self-movement: through the affectivity of the senses and through the aggressive expansiveness as *controlled* by this affectivity, the self-movement can become *adaptive* movement, and in this kind of movement existence develops as an existence in a world of qualities, of statures, and thus of *values.*

According to its basic dynamic form, self-movement maintained in primitive, spontaneous expansiveness and aggressiveness is the physical *equivalent* of intentional consciousness freely projecting a world and producing values. Adaptive movement, as conformed and conforming *itself,* is the *equivalent* of consciousness that conceives of itself as in-being-*with*-the-other, finding in this the source of the discovery of values that are already there.

Expansive movement and adaptive movement are expressions of two different acts. The act expressed in expansive movement is the act of an intentionality directed toward unlimited transcendence; this act is the decisive projection of a history in meaningful continuity (in "selfhood") and of the self as dominant (in dominion over nature). In this act, therefore, *homo expansivus* constitutes himself as *homo faber,* the producer of values. The other act, expressed in adaptive movement, is the *suspension,* the negation, of expansive intentions, and as such is the required *condition* for non-intentional encounter and thus for human existence (*"Dasein"*) in the mode of community ("we," "Wirheit"). This act, therefore, constitutes *homo eroticus,* who will become *homo curatious.*[12]

It is not difficult to understand how a particular dynamism constitutes a world and a manner of human existence which in turn demand that particular dynamism. For instance, the world of things becomes a world of resistances to the expansive dynamism, and because it is a world of resistances, it calls forth an expansive reaction. In this particular type of interaction, human existence develops a more and more pronounced *masculinity.*

An adaptive dynamism does not elicit any resistance, and leads to the discovery of quality and stature, to encounter with things as they are, and thus to the discovery of value. This discovery, however, is never complete; there is an inexhaustible wealth of value in being that never ceases to *elicit* a meditative and tarrying contact with being, which of course calls for the appropriate dynamism. In this type of interaction, human existence develops more and more pronouncedly in the mode of *femininity.*

No individual existence in the concrete is exclusively masculine or exclusively feminine—it is not possible for an existence to develop so entirely according to one mode that it lacks all trace of the other. Masculinity and femininity *are both possibilities of human existence as such, understood in terms of consciousness which is necessarily intentional and equally necessarily a "togetherness" with other being.* Masculine and feminine define two modes of being-in-the-world, and both are able to be realized in every individual because every individual possesses a twofold basic form of dynamism, although the proportion between the masculine aspect of this dynamism and its feminine aspect is different in each individual.

[12] We are not using the term in the sense in which it is used by Heidegger, who applies "curativus," care, precisely to the *practical* activity of *"besorgen."*

The foregoing ontological consideration provides us with a basis upon which we can try to understand the empirical facts concerning the fundamental differences between men and women.

If we consider those physical differences between boys and girls that can be objectively established, one of the things we notice is that the boys are inclined to be stronger and that their wrists are less flexible. The stiffness of the boy's wrist comes from an innervation of the muscles of the wrist that tends to make them more rigid. As expression, this represents a more emphatic inward irritation. However, the sturdiness of build, which is to be experienced as a position of greater independence, is also essential to a dynamism which is expansive and aggressive, this dynamism being attributed to the higher proportion of male hormones in the body.

The dynamic image of the little boy is simply the overall impression gained from observing "typically boyish" behavior in all sorts of circumstances. Through the sturdy abruptness of his movements, the little boy encounters a world of resistances; these resistances "irritate" his expansive aggressiveness and he tries to overcome them.

According to all the data available, it is also a typically boyish characteristic immediately to try to use whatever objects are found for some purpose. This is not difficult to understand, for the object encountered is experienced first as a resistance because it is a hindrance to movement, and by the very fact that it represents a hindrance, the primary *vital* spontaneity and expansiveness becomes constituted as an *intentionality* whereas, prior to the hindrance, it was no more than a consciousness of *onward-reaching* movement and not a consciousness of a *determined* goal to be reached. Experience of resistance is coupled with an existential experience of the self as reacting to the resistance in a masculine way, and these experiences lead the "typical" boy to project *all things* as *possible resistances*. From the very beginning, this determines a typically boyish, obstinate grasp on the world.

As the existence becomes more differentiated, particular goals present themselves more clearly, and movement becomes activity and resistances become useful material. The original world of resistances becomes a world of relative (pragmatic) values. But since this is a functional world, everything in it is regarded as there *to be used* for something else, just as resistances are regarded as there *to be overcome*. Thus, to an existence experienced in a boyish way, insofar as it is experienced in this way, the world is principally something to be transcended intentionally: *it is not a world with which one tarries; it is a world without any value in itself.*

Self-Movement and Touch

Through her proportionally more feminine dynamism, the little girl discovers the feminine world in a quite different way. The basic dynamic form here is adaptive, as we have seen, and it gives rise to self-conforming movement. It has become sufficiently clear that in this kind of movement the "other" is not encountered as resistance but as *quality* and *stature* and therefore as possessing an essential value in itself. It might be remarked that this is true only where the encounter is through the sense of *touch,* for this more than any other sense perception is bound up with the dynamic movement in a functionally reciprocal process. In fact, if there were no original unity of self-movement and touch, there would be no difference between the masculine and the feminine mode of life. For there is no sexual differentiation of sensation as such. Moreover, considerations based on "sensation as such," viewed as separate from anything else, are inadmissible. The phenomenology of sensation, and the concrete facts of the generic development of sensation, show the very close connection of *all* forms of sense perception with the basic dynamism of self-movement.

Experience confirms the conclusion we can draw from the above considerations. The typically masculine mode of being-in-the-world constitutes the human being as "worker," and it constitutes his world as a world of resistances and of means. The typically feminine mode of being-in-the-world constitutes the human being in a *"Dasein als Wirheit"* (to quote Biswanger's formulation); it constitutes the human being as a "loving person," as the *"fellow creature"* of all beings appearing in their own quality and stature. In principle, the world of woman is a world of essential values revealing themselves and being revealed.

However, there is only *one* kind of being called *human,* and each example of the kind can differentiate existence (although not completely) in two directions through the experience of being in the world in the body, and as this is done, two different worlds are more clearly manifested. And since all are human, it is not surprising that no concrete individual human being is wholly and entirely either masculine or feminine.

For centuries people have been aware that there is an area of overlapping between the (impossible) extremes of pure masculinity and pure femininity; real people always have some qualities of both. The older a person becomes, the more evident the overlapping is in that person, for as a person lives on, he or she must necessarily encounter both worlds: the world of resistances and means, and the world of essential values. Every woman is able, as 'homo faber', to be active, to work, to produce something. And every man, we might add, possesses the freedom to dwell on the essential value of things.

On the one hand, the structure of situations in practical life demands that things be taken *according to* some consideration other than the value of the things themselves, and in this the expansive form of dynamism is developed. On the other hand, every individual of either sex develops the adaptive form of dynamism as well, taking things *as they are,* and adapting to the milieu.

But still it is perfectly certain that there is an *inborn* difference between the little boy and the little girl, and that this difference relates to the dynamic type predominant in each.[13] Even though the inborn difference is small, its consequences are vast, all the more so in our cultural sphere, where education fosters and encourages the boyishness present in boys and the girlishness present in girls as much as it possibly can.

We come then to the conclusion that it is possible to speak of woman's "original world," in two senses. In the empirical-genetic sense, there is an original feminine world because there is an in-

---

[13] Confirmation of this is provided by an investigation (not yet published) undertaken by one of my students, M. C. H. Van Den Heuvel-Bastiaan. She has gathered and studied data concerning the pheno-typical difference between boys and girls during the first year of life. Observations were carried out on 214 babies in consulting rooms. It was arranged that the babies be clothed in a diaper so that the sex of the child would not be obvious to the observer. It was found that the difference between boys and girls was chiefly apparent through the pheno-typically distinct motor abilities of the infants. The "typical" baby girl moved quietly, was chiefly interested in nearby objects, tended to play with parts of its own body and clothing, and focussed its glance on close rather than on distant things. Baby boys had a more outgoing movement and tended to be interested more in their surroundings than in their own body. They moved more by grasping and pulling and focussed more inquisitively on distant than on nearby objects.

born dynamic difference between the sexes. Besides this, we may also regard woman's world as founded in her being as a person, in her *"Dasein,"* in her existence.

The two aspects which the bodily reality confers on the one and only humanity are in agreement with the two aspects of the *essence* of consciousness: the aspect of intentionality, and the aspect of being anchored in being.

3. Care for the World

She does not do anything as we do. She thinks and
speaks and acts quite differently.

MICHELET [14]

The broomstick, therefore, will be one of the attributes
of Hercules.

ALAIN

Taking the dynamic image of woman, we first traced its dynamic
characteristics, and then noticed that these same characteristics
appear spontaneously in the very first days of the child's life.
Thus, it is possible to understand the differentiation of the sexes in
terms of the expansive and the adaptive forms of movement under
the influence of education and milieu. We have also tried to understand these two forms of movement, as human forms, in terms of
the essence of consciousness, consciousness being both intentional
and at the same time anchored in being. And now we come to the
question of how the inborn sexual differentiation of the human
dynamism develops in later life, under the continuous influence of
the milieu, so as to give rise to acts which are characteristically
acts of one sex or of the other.

It is obvious that the original dynamic differences of the sexes
do not determine human development to such an extent that even
in widely differing cultural milieux the development of a masculine
and a feminine type would follow such a course that it would
necessarily produce pheno-typical images more or less the same as
the images of European men and women. Investigations among
primitive peoples have shown that development under educational
requirements and social conditions that are different from ours can
be wholly different from the development that leads to the emer-
gence of what we know as typically masculine and typically feminine existence.[15]

[14] *L'Amour;* Paris s.d. p. 50.
[15] Margaret Mead, *Sexuality and Temperament.* Also, *Male and Female,*
London 1950.

305

However, when we consider the course of development as it takes place in our own cultural sphere more closely, it becomes quite clear that a very large number of activities in daily life are "sexually" distinguished. These activities embrace those of children and those of adults. Some belong more to the masculine type of dynamism, and others belong more to the feminine type. The distinction is easy to grasp if, for example, we compare embroidery with football. Our conventional judgments of typically feminine or typically masculine occupations are controlled by an immediate awareness of the manner in which these occupations are carried out—by an awareness of the pattern of impulses necessary in these occupations. The appreciation of one occupation as the very thing for a girl, and of another as the very thing for a boy, is derived wholly and entirely from the different pheno-typical images of the two sexes that we already possess.

But we must ask whether there are not elements present in the development of the woman and of the man which, if one may say so, are implicit in the "nature" of their basic dynamic differences. The phrase "implicit in the nature" of these differences, is intended to refer to the fact that in all intentional activity the human individual is constantly renewing a grasp of his or her own physical aptitudes and "making use" of these aptitudes as the basis of personal development as this development proceeds according to the type fundamental to his or her sex.

In the first place, development of this kind takes place in a context of the opposition of the sexes. The image that members of one sex project of the other sex is formed in ordinary encounters between boys and girls and men and women. Members of one sex respond to the opposite sex in such a way that their response is in keeping with the image of their sex that the opposite sex has formed. Encounters between the sexes take place concretely through the medium of words, glances, voice, gesture, touch (handshakes for instance), and also through shared occupations. There is a certain reciprocity between the sexes in whatever way the encounter actually takes place. The reciprocity exists even where the reaction on one side to an action on the other is purely negative, as for example when boys and girls are playing together and a boy happens to give a girl a "shove," to which she responds by doing nothing.

For this reason there can be no validity in an attempt to project the pheno-typical image of woman as if from the point of view of a "neutral" observer. In a scientific approach one rather tends to try to be "neutral," but it must be emphasized that this attempt is necessarily invalid. An observer is certainly able to give some description of observable behavior, just as one is able to describe the psychological characteristics of men and women as they appear in our cultural sphere. But at the same time we should remember that the description is very far from the total, concrete reality. Heymans, after an extensive investigation and a meticulous statistical analysis, in his book on the psychology of women, concluded that "woman is more emotional, she has a slightly narrower range of consciousness, and she has a greater sense of duty" than man, and goes on to remark that this certainly does not agree with the *actual image* of woman. He says that this is inexpressible, just as anything known in actual encounter is essentially inexpressible. Moreover, the only way in which it is possible to get to know the pheno-typical image of a person is in actual *encounter* with that person. This holds true of the knowledge of one person, as Van Lennep has shown very clearly [16]; it is equally true of our getting to know a group of persons, whether the group be men, or women, or any other grouping whatever.

When one meets another person, even if one looks upon that person as a mere thing, one still expects to receive certain impressions. The impressions one expects to receive of another always have to do with the way the other will react or respond to being looked at. Therefore there is always a reciprocity of encounter in all meetings between two people. Even if one of them is trying to be merely an observer in the most objective way possible, there is still at least this minimum of encounter, truly reciprocal, although reduced. The manner of the encounter is of course very different where the *contact* between the two is not intended merely to establish a relationship of observer and observed between them.

One element of contact between men and women in daily life that we need to consider a little more closely is the handshake. The handshake is very often used without any motive other than to give concrete expression to the traditional greeting. It hardly needs to be said that when we offer our hand to someone, or when someone

[16] *Gewogen, bekeken, ontmoet.* Den Haag (M. Nijhoff) 1946.

offers us a hand in greeting, there is always a reciprocity of giving and receiving. This does of course not mean that the giving and receiving will always be equal on both sides. If we read Van den Berg's study of the way a schizophrenic shakes hands, we are struck by the peculiar inauthenticity of its manner. The schizo-phrenic's handshake gives the impression of being inhuman; it can even be disgusting to experience, and it alone suggests immediately that the individual so afflicted is somehow outside of the human community.[17]

What is the nature of a handshake between a man and a woman? There are very many possibilities. There are women who have a firm grasp and there are men with a soft, weak one, and there is no counting the shades of difference between these ex-tremes. Nevertheless, it is a fact that men generally have large hands and that women have smaller hands, and that the larger hand is the stronger. And this is not all. Not only is the muscular strength of the man's hand generally greater, but the manner of his *grasp* is different. In a masculine way the man will always experi-ence his own bodily existence as a decisive grasp on the world, and the masculine handshake represents one moment in his ever-present existential consciousness.

Simone de Beauvoir had a very clear insight into this and its implications. Not only does she say that lability in woman is a symptom of her autonomic nervous system simply speaking, like blushing or being frightened easily or being quickly tired. She also says—and here the fact that she herself is a woman must lend greater weight to her words—that there is an uncertainty in the way woman experiences her own bodily reality *in itself,* as a means of action, and she explains that this uncertainty comes from the fact that she is actually a citizen of two worlds: the human world in which one takes a firm grasp of reality and transcends oneself; and the world of "nature" in which all sorts of things just happen, a pseudo-immanence which she cannot help noticing in herself in such a way that she is continually being called back out of the world where existence means initiative and a firm grasp on reality.

This constitutional uncertainty in woman plays a part in shaping the manner of her handshake. The large and powerful hand of the

[17] J. H. Van Den Berg, *De betekenis van de phaenomenologische of ex-istentiële anthropologie in die psychiatrie,* Utrecht 1946 (Dissertation).

man enclosed the smaller hand of the woman, but the man exercises *moderation* in the use of his strength. The woman, whose soft, fragile hand is being grasped in the man's hand, feels this moderation, and she knows that the man knows that she knows that he is exercising moderation. There is not a single but a double cycle of reciprocity. It brings about a tacit agreement, a dialectical attitude, in the relationship of the sexes.

The man on his part feels the woman's hand is less decisively offered, less "grasping," and through this he experiences the woman as a more reserved person, as one who is less expansive and less aggressive, but above all he experiences her as *less open, less uncommitted.* She is less uncommitted, because in general a direct and immediate (transcending) grasp on the world has more openness and less of that cautious carefulness that sometimes proves to be the mother (not the father) of neat little cabinets of porcelain ornaments. Woman experiences the experience of the man, and the man experiences that the woman is aware of his experience in her experience.

This is very far from being a complete analysis of the simple phenomenon of a handshake between a man and a woman, but still it serves to open a methodological perspective on an entirely new kind of social-psychological investigation. We take as our starting point some elementary every-day occurrence in which people come into contact with one another in some way, and try to understand the forces of opposition, union and order that constitute the particular form of encounter in that occurrence. This was the reason why we needed to consider the matter of shaking hands.

In the concrete reality of a fully mature human existence—inasfar as we know it—we can see the same fundamental distinction of dynamism that was evident in infancy and childhood being manifested in all possible forms of adult *play.* It is clear that the adaptive dynamism is wholly congruent with fussing over little dolls and pretty little clothes for them, with bouncing a ball up and down, and so on. It is also clear that the experience of resistance and the development of expansiveness and aggressiveness is characteristic of boyish games like cops and robbers. All these childish games are still outside of the sphere of a mature human reality, but there are clear indications in them of what is to come.

Work and Care

Now, in the medium of the full maturity of human existence, the distinction and contrast of the sexes is revealed and can be known in the distinction of two acts: the act of *work* and the act of *care*. For the moment we will take in that these two acts are wholly distinct. Both are maturely human acts in an essential sense. They are performed in a chosen relationship to the world, in an existence not merely following the course of "the way people are supposed to live," "following the herd," but of which selfhood is the existential characteristic. These acts reflect the decisive acceptance of personal responsibility for the situation and for the existence and activity projected in it.

Comparing and contrasting work and care, we notice that work means an activity that proceeds from an intentional act in which the consciousness is directed toward a proposed goal, this goal being independent with respect to the occupation or activity itself. In this kind of activity, the world is understood as a system of means provided for reaching the proposed goal. Work presupposes that the one who works directs himself toward a particular end, result or goal that itself lies outside of the work as such (outside of the actual occupation) but to which the whole of the work relates. The fact that the reality of the encountered world is taken as a means for reaching the proposed goal, indicates that it is not taken as it is in itself and as it is able to appear, and thus, that it is not accepted in its own essential value.

The essential value of the encountered world is relativized; things are taken according to what the worker regards as their usefulness. By applying his concept of usefulness, the worker distinguishes between the useless, resistance, suitable material, instruments, connecting links that are necessary and those that are coincidental but helpful, making all these distinctions whenever his work gives him occasion to do so. As far as present reality as such is concerned, the worker as a worker intends simply to pass it by. Thus, he constitutes his own existence as an involvement in the projects of his work and in whatever the actual reality of the world can offer in the way of useful material. His existence, constituted in this way, is constituted as autonomous, as prospective, as aimed at distant goals, as expansive and always as aggressive.

Compared with this, the structure of care is not at all like it. As a human activity, care is the expression of a consciousness intentionally directed to the concrete presence of values discovered, preserved, recalled and multiplied or deepened through the decisiveness of an existence definitively chosen in the mode of togetherness, *"Mitsein,"* community. Thus, in the activity of care a person does not merely discover values; they are discovered in the decisive and definite awareness or consciousness of the fact that his or her own existence, as a care-ful sojourn with things, preserves, recalls and intensifies these values not only in themselves but also for itself as a personal existence. This takes place in meditative tarrying, dwelling upon things as being *with* them, and it also arises from a docile, adaptive dynamism, although this dynamism in itself is not the same thing as care.

Care is something that can be realized through the adaptive dynamism, but it is not within the dynamism itself. For the person who cares needs an adaptive dynamism in order to follow, to listen, and so come to know the essential and the possible values of the objective reality, and this activity will be experienced as a participation in being together with the objective reality. But all of this becomes *care* only when the person decisively takes upon himself or herself the burden of all dangers to the values of things as well as the task of realizing those values that remain possibilities, in the faith that all hidden values have the possibility of being realized.

The world of work is a world of resistances, and it forms existence through an alternation of tension and relaxation, constituting existence as solid, hard, strong, firmly grasping the world—this is an existence of 'I can, I must, I will', an existence of difficulties overcome and of courage. The act of work as such constitutes an ethos and a pathos at the same time. Work therefore is not merely a particular way of doing something; it is a normative manner of behavior, in terms of which existence chooses to be morally structured. Now the object of work is essentially something non-human, the reason being that the human is human only when it is not something to be worked upon—human reality in one cannot be made, constituted or formed under the grasp and control of another.

There is an intrinsic logic in all this from which it follows that work must constitute existence in objectivity, in cold efficiency, in knowledge that is rational and empirical, and therefore also in loneliness, without the human relationships proper to genuine community of life, *"Mitsein,"* understood as "togetherness through love." *Homo faber* knows human reality in terms of the relationships of right and duty, which form a necessary moral framework for the possibility of work. All work tends to intensify the masculine qualities of an existence; we can observe this in the women of primitive nations, in the laboring classes of our own society and in the older class of farming families. Working women can appear to be very masculine in their manner. This is accounted for not only by the poorer social and hygienic conditions of their lives, or by "sun and wind and rain," but especially by the work itself, for when work forms an existence, pheno-typical image of that existence shifts toward an emphasis of what we know as masculine.

The matter becomes clearer still when we observe the effeminateness or at least the shift toward feminine characteristics often evident in men who do not work. The pheno-typical image of the non-working man shows a clear shift away from the masculine toward the feminine, whatever the reasons for his not working— economic status, or custom (among some peoples), or culture (in certain periods). Naturally there are still other factors which can determine a man's existence and appearance, and these must not be underestimated. Warriors for instance do not work but they do wage war, or again, a Don Juan does not work but does undertake campaigns and adventures—real or imaginary. Although not work, the occupations of such people provide motives for forming a world of material, means and resistances and for an expansive and aggressive dynamism, and there is a formal relationship between this and the world of work. Work is not a matter of maintaining a certain level of keenness and of being busy. The essential matter in work is the structure of the intentionality determining the whole pattern of the dynamism.

And now, what of care? The world of care is a world of actual values encountered and of possible values educed and called forth by the presence and activity of the person who cares. In this, existence is constituted as accommodating, as attentive, not as obstinate but as docile. As to the existential quality of non-obstinacy, the word itself already suggests what the reality must be. An existence which is not obstinate gives up the opportunity of realizing distant practical goals simply on its own initiative without any consideration for the things that will be encountered on the way to those goals. This existence is not primarily defined by "I can, I must, I will," but by "it is fitting, I may," for this existence is docile, obedient and gentle.

A World of Value

The world of care is a world of value. The act of care is full of the ethos and the pathos that we call femininity. The object of care is above all the human reality, or whatever presents itself as human. Neither is it difficult to understand why. For care is developed in adaptation and accommodation, in adapting oneself to a value in order to dwell upon it as it is insofar as the thing encountered manifests itself to our knowledge as an interiority appearing outwardly (which in phenomenological terminology we call the hidden possibilities of the thing). We all know that it is in fact possible to speak meaningfully about the interiority, the inner reality, of something (a child, a work of art) without being called upon to give a rational justification of what is said or without explaining why we are moved to say it.

The phenomenological interiority of a thing means all that is not superficial, all that is not tangibly definable and evident on the surface, but nevertheless appears in every encounter with the thing, for "in every being that presents itself in encounter, there is this peculiar contradiction of presence, that it holds itself in concealment at the same time." [18] Care is something that can be carried out only in encounter, and the more deeply the encounter takes place on the level of essential values, the more genuine the care will be. The presence of even the most elementary intentional act in the sense of making something happen, even in the most favorable circumstances, detracts from the genuineness of the care. Where there is any of this kind of intentional activity involved in the encounter, we do not have care in the strict sense, but care of the kind exercised by the gardener for his flowers; he does allow them to grow according to their own nature, but by his labor produces the conditions he considers most favorable for their growth.

However, the development of authentic existence in a human being is not the same kind of thing as the growth of a plant. Thus, when the object of care is the human reality, the meaning of care is

[18] Heidegger, *Holzwege*, p. 42.

in principle quite different from care for a plant or for an animal or for a garden or for a cultural object. It follows, then, that genuine care is something quite different from those activities that are so often confused with care, such as nursing, for instance, or treating things carefully or making arrangements, which, as we all know, are looked upon as occupations reserved by preference to women. If there is to be genuine care in the strict sense, the one who cares and the one cared for must be established in presence to each other in the mode of *"Wirheit,"* in personal togetherness, in the call of one heart to another, which has nothing to do with sentimentality but is essentially a real call to the other in the freedom of each for each to realize self human beings.

This mode of togetherness is not discursive, it expresses no ulterior intentions, it is a spontaneous unity entered into without any considerations of individual interests, and it is constituted through an act which makes great demands on the individual, demands that are very difficult to fulfill. It demands the conscious suspension of all inauthentic care, the suspension of the labor of nursing, to heal, of treating, to conserve or of arranging, to improve the object of care. For in such activities, the ultimate basis of performing the acts is a confidence in an objective nature. In authentic care, things are not done out of confidence in an objective nature, but out of a love free of all self-interest, out of pure trust in the essential value of the other, out of faith, in the highest possible mode of human togetherness.

The Line and the Circle

This distinction between work and care *can* lead to very far-reaching differences between the masculine and the feminine worlds, but before we follow this line of thought further, we ought to look somewhat more closely at the concrete acts of work and of care. Work is masculine in character in that there is an accentuation of pauses in its procedure. The pauses are points of rest at preliminary goals within the process of work. Care, which is feminine in character, does not manifest a line of procedure. Within the act of care *as such* there is no directedness toward a goal to be achieved, for the act is intentionally directed toward the object of care as it is, in its own value. *The object giving rise to care is the centre of a sphere of care.* Care encircles the object of care, establishing for itself a continuity without beginning, pause or end and maintaining this continuity as long as the object remains the central pivot of the intentional direction of the act of care. The act of care terminates when its object is no longer present as giving rise to care; it does not terminate of itself, like the act of work, when a proposed goal is achieved. Thus, the encircling continuity of the movement of care ceases through the cessation of its centripetal force. In a formal sense, work can be represented as a line, and care, as a closed circle. We have already noticed, in the phenotypical images of the masculine and feminine dynamism, the same general characteristics that we discover in the mature reality of work and care in the strict sense of the words.

The essence of work is such that work always produces an alteration of form. But it is possible to produce an alteration of form only by taking control of given forms and overcoming them. In a literal sense work is always the production, the making, of something—even where nothing, apparently, is made, as in a work of demolition, for instance. When the human being is called *"homo faber,"* *"homo"* has the sense of "man," masculine. Thus, Alain writes in one of his *Propos,* that "the masculine spirit never ceases to compose"—as masculine, the spirit of man cannot do other than make something, put something together, produce something, create something.

Work is *always* creative, and therefore always contains an element of originality. Obviously the originality in work is reduced to a very minimum where the work is "automatic," mere repetition of customary acts. Where work possesses the full dignity and maturity of human work, it always possesses this in the sphere of expectancy and surprise. The very resistance of the world itself is full of surprises. This means that improvisation always belongs to the essence of work. Moreover, the reality that we call the formation of culture is in fact nothing else than the outcome of the element of improvisation present in all work; culture is produced when improvisation takes the shape of a creative intervention in the course of nature, giving new form to the natural course. *Homo faber* produces culture and forms history.

Work is always adventure, because of the element of expectancy and surprise in it. And this leads to the knowledge that work is an unexpected combination of strength and weakness—a strength realized in the productivity of the work, and a weakness realized in the moments of surprise encountered in executing the work. The strength, already expressed in the *ability* to work, is a power that arises out of the intrinsic necessity of the situation, the necessity to overcome resistances and to apply means. Nevertheless, work also demands at the same time an obedience to what are called the "hard facts." This will bring a little more clarity to what we said above, when we said that the ethical structure of the masculine world is built up in the concept of duty.

To this we can now add that it is built up in the concepts of commanding and of obedience, of power and weakness. The exercise of command and the exercise of obedience both very definitely impose a duty and both very definitely demand an ability. These correlatives, "I must" and "I am able," duty and ability, qualify the whole of human history, and human history is therefore always the product of *"masculinity."* Note that this does not mean that history must always be made by *men,* for every human being can work, and women are human beings. However, a phenomenological analysis of the masculine dynamism and of work, such as this analysis, does lead to the understanding that human society must be built upon the ethical norms of commandment and obedience. In order to exist together in society, human beings have to submit to these norms, but it is not only they who submit. The worker's world itself takes on the aspect of a number of particular "things" that command each other and obey each other and therefore are necessarily related to each other in submission to the same norms.

Here we have a view of the world and the ethos of work, but the world and the ethos that follow from the essential reality of authentic care are of quite a different sort.

Care, which grows out of an adaptive dynamism and is nourished by it, encounters the world as value and as the source of values, and therefore as unfulfilled with respect to *its own* possibilities. Care remains with things and dwells upon them where it finds them presenting themselves as needing care and therefore as asking to be cared for. Thus, the person who cares, insofar as his care is authentic, does not merely wait with expectancy like the gardener we mentioned; he waits also in the belief and in the trust that by the very fact of his being together with things and by the fact of his care for them, values will be realized that otherwise would remain hidden.

Therefore care, as it is manifested in feminine existence, is not the same thing as being discursively *occupied,* continually busy about one thing and another. Perhaps there seems to be a peculiar contradiction between our view of woman and woman as we actually see her. In our view, she is dynamically adapted to a *care*-ful dwelling upon things and with things. If we think of actual women, at least in their own most characteristic milieu, it might seem that they dwell upon nothing but are always restless, always busy. Even so, there is no real contradiction here. The apparent contradiction arises from the ideas we usually associate with the word "care." It seems to imply a notion of long duration, and that the act of care is directed to an object of care that needs care for a fairly long time.

In actual fact, the object of care, calling for care, is anything that is encountered, not as a means to an end nor as material to be given a new form, but as something unfulfilled because alone and at the same time unfulfilled because of the possibilities in it that could be brought to realization through the presence, the hand, the eye of someone who cares, even if the encounter is only for a brief moment. It is only through the fact of care that a few little flowers being arranged take on their high aesthetical value, and the same can be said of anything being arranged, placed, lighted, cleaned etc. so that *"it* will appear to advantage," which means simply that its own value will be appreciated.

"To Conserve and To Protect"

The world is thus a world of values to the feminine act, even when the act tarries only very briefly on a thing, and the value of the thing itself is all the greater because of the act. Nevertheless, authentic care can be fully realized only when its object is a human being, and above all a child. Alain therefore says, "The feminine function is to conserve and to protect the human form" (and shows in this the same sensitivity of perception that once before has helped to clarify our own insight). By the "human form" he means not only the stature of the human being but everything in the world that is encountered as human because it relates to the human mode of existence—for instance, the human dwelling-place, its furniture, all the objects which in our culture are directly for our use, and thus all things which, though not human themselves, are related to human beings and therefore fill out and support the 'human form'. The objects that do this more than any others are all those that belong to the milieu of the household.

In all she does, the (good) housewife is caring for human being, whether directly or indirectly. "Human reality (is) therefore the province of femininity, and the inhuman the province of masculinity", Alain adds, after the observation quoted above. The inhuman is the province of the man. This of course does not mean that man's concern is exclusively with the things of nature, but refers to all things and all concepts that are objects of the rational intellect that takes an objective view of all it knows, not knowing objects as *asking for care* but as material given into his grasp and needing to be worked upon if it is to have any cultural value. It would not be right to interpret the distinction between "human" and "inhuman" in this context as meaning that the male world of things and concepts is entirely emotionless, nor would it be right to look upon emotionality, as we have found it discussed in the literature of psychology, as a characteristic of woman arising exclusively from her adaptive dynamism and her aptitude for encountering things and dwelling upon them in the exercise of care.

Care is *one* mode of participation in the qualities by which things are related to human reality; in work, there is *another* mode of participation in these qualities of things, different from that of care, but no less significant. The rational activity involved in work is directed toward the objective relationships of things. Of this there is no doubt. But the goals of work and the resistances work has to overcome are emotionally "loaded" to a fairly powerful extent. In contrast, the sensitive dwelling upon things that is essential in care is actually *not* affective, *not* emotional, because it is not dependent upon the variable contingency of the situation; care is inspired and borne out in the knowledge of one heart for another, containing what Pascal calls "the reasons of the heart."

In Pascal's writings we find the thought that the heart is a source of knowledge of a special kind. It is a clear source of knowledge. It is also a powerful one, deriving its strength from a purity and strength of feeling that does not belong to the category of the emotions like anxiety, anger, or desire, but is an appreciative participation in an inner value. We all know this feeling, and call it attentiveness, admiration, affection, respect, tenderness, confident trust and expectancy, and all sorts of names that have to do with loving. This is why man, from ancient times, has known the connection between care and selfless, disinterested love, and also the reason why we can anticipate where this analysis of care will lead and say right away that, while work is outlined in the ethos of duty and obedience, care belongs in the ethos of love which is the ethos of sacrifice.

Love as such, strictly speaking, is not an act, and thus it is not an emotional attitude and relationship established on the motivation of free initiative. In Binswanger's work we find an extensive explanation of the thought that all intentional relationships lead to a togetherness in being in the form of *"liebende Wirheit"* (which may be translated as love changing the *I-thou* relationship into the *community of Us*), and that this togetherness in being is a knowing and being known that transcends all intentionality.

The same may surely not be said of care. Care as such exists wholly within the world. Care is an act that is performed; it is a tension that is maintained; it is an expectancy that is cherished; it is a tenderness that is intended. But nevertheless the act of care is always an act of togetherness without specific intentions, an act of heart to heart knowledge, and the "light" of this knowledge comes from the authenticity of human existence as a being *together with* others.[18a]

Since it is not possible to dwell upon something unless that something establishes itself as present to us, the object of care will always have a certain formative influence upon the person who cares. Thus there is a reciprocal action of the person on the thing and the thing on the person when a person constitutes his (her) existence as a caring involvement in a world in need of care, and it establishes the basic pattern of woman's "way of life" as conceived throughout the history of our present culture.

At this point, we want to see whether and to what extent the difference of the sexes in terms of the basic dynamism is manifested in the animal world as well. We want to see, in other words,

[18a] *"Daseinsform als Wirheit."*

whether the expansive and the adaptive types of dynamism appear already on the natural level, and whether the acts of work and care that flow from them have their natural counterpart.

Rilke once said, "it runs as the welling water runs," [19] meaning that dwelling upon an object actually has no place in an animal's existence (*apparent* existence, for it is not existence in the same sense as human existence). The life of an animal is determined by its nature, and in it there is neither any possibility of genuine work nor any possibility of genuine care, for work and care become possible in reality only because of the fact that the human being is able to take up an attitude toward himself and toward all that is in being with him in which he himself can shift his presence out of the given centre of his world.

The human being is able to choose to work and to choose to care only because of this ability to project his presence. Genuine work, as we have seen, presupposes achievement, and genuine care presupposes disinterested love. The animal can in fact do things, but its doing is not an achieving. It can answer a call, but it cannot apply itself disinterestedly to anything. Since there are many apparent images of human existence to be found in the animal world, we can also find many examples of pseudo-work and pseudo-care in animal life.

Animal "Work" and "Care"

The animal that goes about its business, seeking food, building a nest, looking after its young, is never anywhere *present* in the real sense of the word. It is following the needs of its own nature and of its situations. But still, there are some aspects of its behavior that image the act of care, that are care "in appearance." In the popular way of thought, these aspects of animal behavior are very often held up as examples to women.

The most popular example is taken from the behavior of the mother animal toward its young. The outward pattern of behavior here is the same as in the attitude of authentic care. The mother animal even presents a striking *image* of care, but whereas the human being who cares chooses the act of care freely as a response to something that calls for care, even if it is a motivated response,

[19] *Duineser Elegien* (8th elegy).

the behavior of the mother animal is not free but necessitated animal behavior. The animal is closed within the situation in which it lives. It cannot ever rise above the situation and neither can it take up an attitude with regard to the situation as distinct from itself. The mother animal *must take care of its young*. It cannot take care of them. Thus, the essential aspect of the human act is lacking.

We can say, therefore, that the animal never directs itself toward a goal on its own initiative and that it can never direct itself toward any value, but that work and care are objectively present in the animal world "in appearance," as images of genuine work and care. In living nature, all sorts of things happen as though in a human way. The bird builds its nest as though the building were an achievement. The parent animal looks after its young as though it loved them. In all these things, we encounter nature as a prefigurement of the essentially human reality; in these things, nature itself gives an indication of possibilities contained within the reality of life that will find their full realization only on the human level.

If we understand nature in this way, there is no question of a genuine distinction between masculine and feminine on the natural level; the distinction is one that can apply only on the human level. Of course, a difference of the basic dynamism is found on the animal level as well. The female organism is more supple and more mobile. A female chimpanzee can learn to thread a needle, but so far no male chimpanzee has been able to learn it.[20] The male animal is more angular, more sturdy in his movements, as we can see if we watch a ram or a bull. But on this level the difference is an initial one, and it remains an initial difference, never developing into a real differentiation of existence, existence being exclusively human and thus spiritual. *Being, in the mode of genuine masculinity and in the mode of genuine femininity, is always a spiritual form of being*. Therefore the distinction between the sexes is complete only in ethical differences (not in natural or anatomical differences). This is something we have already noted, but there is still more to be said on the point.

When we find the concept of masculinity expressed in a human existence—it may well be found expressed in the concrete existence of a woman—the masculine reality appears as the *ethos* of

[20] Quoted by A. Scheinfeld, *Women and Men*, p. 81.

the interconnection of duty, obedience, courage, effort and will-power realized in concrete achievements (thus, in work).

In the element of caring, in feminine existence, we find the moral requirement of selfless love, self-giving and sacrifice. If we were to conceive of masculine existence as an existence realized in work exclusively, without seeing that the *ethos* of duty is anchored in a love, such an existence would be nothing more than perpetual restlessness, an onward movement from one goal to the next, from one project to the next, always on the way, plodding step by step in a perpetual flight from self and from all actual being. Masculine existence would then in fact correspond with the definition of it with which Sartre concludes his theorizing in *Being and Nothingness:* "man is a useless passion."

Nietzsche expressed the uselessness of a restless existence in the idea of a perpetual rotation, "a turning cog"—a meaningless passionateness to do and to start doing again and again. Camus sees it as an "absurdity," for which he finds an apt illustration in the myth of Sisyphus, the Corinthian king who was condemned ever to roll a great stone up a hill only to find that it must roll down again every time he reached the top. If masculine existence were like this, its *ethos* would consist in the fact that man, condemned to silent obedience, to meaningless reality, would always have to be resigned to the everlasting repetition of work.

But the idea of femininity certainly contains another, different, moral ideality of existence, an ideality that is able to be realized in the conscious return of spiritual existence to its own origins, to the life that rests in *"Dasein als Wirheit,"* that dwells upon the value of existence in togetherness, and that reaches out above the intentionally projected world. We must add, however, that this ideality can never be realized in a pure state in this world.

Closed within this world, the human being finds that pure, selfless and disinterested love can be reached only if approached through hard work. But this ideality does provide an *image* of existence as rising above the limitation of "being cast into the world," and this is why there is, somewhere in every one of us, a kind of nostalgia, an indirect longing for human existence in the immanence of a hidden interiority, a togetherness in being which transcends the harsh reality of the world. Every experience of love gives rise to this nostalgia. It finds a constant source of nourishment in every form of religion, insofar as religion means a return to and a relationship with the source of life itself. It is not difficult, then, to understand why we so often hear remarks about the connection between religion and feminine existence. Or we might say that whereas the masculine aspect of human existence is wholly secular, wholly mundane, the feminine aspect of human existence is in principle an aspect of transcendence over the mundane world.

Now it is time to return to ordinary, everyday, actual examples of work and care, and to examine the structure of meaning within such acts as actually performed by real people. The first thing we notice is that there is no such thing as a masculine act of work that does not contain an element of care, for although the act of work is always directed toward a distant goal, it is never able to reach that goal without some dwelling upon present, nearby reality, even if it lasts only for a brief moment. Even in the purposeful stride, the onward movement of one step after another requires the foot to rest on the ground at every step, and the ground is encountered as it is in itself; one feels whether it is hard or soft.

In a somewhat similar way, every genuine worker using his material takes care of his material and takes care of his tools. Of course, this kind of care is functional, it subserves the work, and therefore it is not authentic care, and neither is it alone sufficient. Nevertheless, it is a kind of care, and it is even a necessary *condition* required for the performance of the act of work.

Grades of Work

Now there are "grades" of work, the lowest of which is simple manual labor in the narrowest sense. As we move into the higher grades of work, the element of care in the work takes on a proportionately much deeper value. When we come to the level of work which is "spiritual," progressive, creative and formative (the kind of work that in our culture is called spiritual achievement), it is very clear that the work itself must be pervaded by the feminine element of dwelling upon and caring for the reality that is being formed in the creative work of forming it.[21] We ought to note,

[21] Why then are there so very few women of outstanding genius? Dostoevski says (in the novel "Die Sanfte"): "There is no originality in woman—that's the truth." But why is there no originality in woman? Is

however, that the word "work" is also applied to occupations in which the whole of the "work" is controlled by the situation and not by the human being occupied in it—the worker himself becomes part of the situation and gives form to his existence by accepting the situation. A concrete example of this can be found in the manual operations involved in purely technical labor. In such operations the essential idea of work as such is lacking, since there is no question of the presence of an intentionality aimed at reaching a goal through the overcoming of resistance by means of the work done.

Such occupations have a goal, but the goal is to earn a living, and this has nothing whatever to do with the actual process of the activity called "the work." The source and continuity of the urge to carry out this kind of occupation, or the *ethos* of this kind of occupation, is not found in any goal or achievement proper to the "work" itself, but in the sociological structure of the life of the person who occupies himself in this way. The same applies to the

---

there some condition lacking in her nature that is required for creative genius to arise? Some have tried to show that the absence or rarity of genius in women is the result of their circumstances, the education traditionally accorded them, and their position in society. Against this, others have argued that women have practised the arts of music and embroidery and cooking for centuries upon centuries without having been able to produce anything better than good reproductions—some exceptions excluded. One thing is certain: for every creative achievement, in whatever cultural field, the first thing necessary is that one must transcend oneself entirely and not feel obliged to dwell upon nearby familiar reality. This of course is not enough to produce an achievement of *genius,* for genius requires not only an exceptional ability and an outstandingly productive imagination, but also a "mania," a "possession" which includes a form of freedom that means a passing beyond the confines of all traditional modes of existence without the one possessed *seeing* that these confines are being passed. Creative genius breaks through the confines, not only of traditional encounter and contact, of traditional thought and understanding, but also of the most fundamental patterns of relationships in the existence of other people, of "creatures." Anyone who looks back, becomes solid, immobile, like Lot's wife. To be "creative" is essentially to get away from "being created," and in principle therefore it means a rejection of bonds, obedience and duty. Woman is a little less prepared for this; Heymans as we have seen noted her greater sense of duty. Why she is so, we can understand in the light of the quality of her existence in the world. This is something that can sometimes be seen even in the way a woman plays a piece of music or goes about baking a cake—there is such a cautious carefulness in her approach that she will not permit herself the slightest variation from the score or the recipe book.

element of care that seems to be present in technical labor. We hear it said that the factory worker constantly needs to care—for his machines, that they are in good order, and so on—but to what extent does this have anything to do with the "human reality (that is) the province of femininity", which we have already seen to be the proper field of the activity of care?

Driven to its extreme, the technical kind of labor does not make "work" heavy or wearying as much as it makes "work" *hard,* in the sense of compelling the worker to become as hard as a mere thing, a machine. The activity of taking care is controlled by the situation and does not proceed any longer from the person's free and loving attention to the object of care.

It is in no sense part of our present task to enter into a critical or sociological discussion of factory labor. We are undertaking a psychological study, and psychology is interested in the human being and in human existence. From the psychological point of view, therefore, it is very necessary to distinguish between work that is authentic and labor that is mechanical to the extreme. However much authentic work may be motivated by the situation, it always proceeds as an intentional act and its end is always a genuine achievement. In purely technical labor, the worker becomes part of the machine (so well illustrated in the Charlie Chaplin film); the laborer's movements are not determined in the freedom of his own initiative but rather by the total mechanization of the situation in which the laborer is captive.

The problem of whether factory work is more suitable for a man than for a woman is one of the many practical problems arising in this context which we simply pass by. But we must recognize that an analysis of the work-situation and of the care-situation is of the greatest importance in the attempt to solve any of these practical problems.

So far the main direction of our discussion has been from possibilities toward their realization, but we cannot leave this topic of investigation without some thought for the opposite direction. The chief point arising here concerns the *pseudo-care* concretely manifested in the human world. Women are given a particular kind of work to do, and the work is called "taking care." It may be the work of a nurse or a governess or a teacher. Naturally, care and taking care are present as real possibilities, but very often, although not always, the social situation is structured in such a way that nothing is left of these occupations other than a wearying labor of very uncertain outcome, in which the object, that could be an object of care, perhaps becomes nothing more than a material object to be worked upon. Masculine and feminine dynamism are inborn. Masculine and feminine existence have to be achieved.

Every individual human being possesses both basic dynamic forms, although in different proportions. Every individual human being in his or her life develops masculine and feminine aspects of his or her behavior and his or her world. The earth, that in the labor of plowing it is a resistance to the farmer, can easily become an object calling for care as soon as that labor is done. This is only a random example; not only the earth, but the whole of "nature" is there to be worked upon and to be cared for. This applies to human nature as well. The occupations of country life are often looked upon as an integration of the masculine and the feminine modes of existence. To some extent this is true, but we really need an exhaustive and detailed study of the relationships of the sexes in the context of work in different cultures and cultural periods, and in the various groupings of our own society, and, still more important, a study of the way the masculinity and the femininity of each individual in a particular group are related to each other in characteristic proportions—but such a study has yet to be undertaken.

Before concluding this section, we want to return to the remark made at the beginning of the chapter, that the original or basic dynamic differences do not lead as of natural necessity to the kind of distinction between the masculine and the feminine worlds that we know in terms of our Western culture. This fact is demonstrated very clearly by some of the results of the outstanding research done by Margaret Mead among a number of tribes in the South Pacific and in New Guinea.[22] She spent years on end observing primitive tribes in these regions with the specific aim of discovering what the feminine temperament—the "natural sex temperament"—might be, and of discovering to what extent cultural influences have a bearing on the way woman manifests herself. Her research led her to the conclusion that biological differences between men and women (from the primary sexual difference up to and including the very least of the secondary sexual differences) have *no bearing whatever* on the social and psychological characteristics of men and women. Within certain very broad limits, men and women are able to be whatever they want to make of themselves.

[22] *Sex and Temperament in Three Primitive Societies.* 1935.

The "Dominance Factor"

Margaret Mead however does *not* agree with the view of Mathilde and Mathias Vaerting, that the whole pattern of social relationships is determined by the "dominance factor," the male lust for power. The whole of our Western civilization with its patriarchal structure does of course display a clear dominance of men over women. But Margaret Mead's work proves that there are communities in which the contrast of the sexes as dominant and subjected *does not exist,* and shows that it is possible for society to be structured in such a way that the contrast would be entirely lacking. It is very enlightening to learn what characteristics other peoples can regard as genuinely, typically feminine, and what they can regard as genuinely, typically masculine.

For example, there is a tribe in the Philippines that holds that "no man can keep a secret." The Manus say that "only a man likes to play with babies." The Toda have a saying that "housework is too holy for a woman to do." The Arapesh maintain that "a woman's head is stronger than a man's head." All popular notions of this kind are important *factors* in determining social relationships.

The following provides a clear example of the effect of one of these popular and accepted notions. Among the Mundugumor, whenever anyone is born with the umbilical cord looped around the neck, they say that the baby will grow up to be able to paint very well. One consequence of this view is the fact that all who are *not* born in that way are shy about painting, feel intimidated, lack *self-confidence* and never attain to any virtuosity in it. All so-called typically feminine and typically masculine characteristics arise in more or less the same kind of way!

If we take the trouble to examine the characteristics so very frequently idealized in our own society as *truly* feminine and as *genuinely* masculine, and to bring a little common sense and a little humor to our investigation, we will find at the roots of them all a wisdom of exactly the same kind that makes the Mundugumor identify the artistic temperament by the position of the umbilical cord at birth.

Margaret Mead compares three tribes, the Arapesh, the Mundugomor and the Tchambuli, all of whom live within a very short distance of one another.

The Arapesh are poor, live by agriculture and keep pigs. The men and the women *work together,* they lack aggressiveness and are easily satisfied, and the men and the women all behave with the same, typical "motherly" tenderness toward each other and toward their children. The children are suckled for a very long time, and when they need to be comforted they turn with equal readiness to a man or to a woman. The men are very feminine. Sexual life takes a secondary place. Men and women are all very gentle. Their whole society is somehow analagous to that of the peasant families of Northern Europe.

The Mundugumor live a short distance from the Arapesh, but quite unlike their neighbors they are highly aggressive. They are head-hunters. Both men and women are very vehement, easily aroused to jealousy and suspicion. They have intense sexual relationships, and motherly tenderness is almost totally absent, even in the women. They are a *rich* people. Women do *all* the work, including climbing the coco-nut palms, and they are very aggressive toward each other. There is no family life but a sort of "rope" relationship connecting father to daughter to daughter's son, or mother to son to son's daughter and so on. Mothers have practically no mother-love, suckle very briefly, and the children brought up in this way are hot-tempered and aggressive. Again unlike the Arapesh who have no taboos, the Mundugumor have innumerable laws and prohibitions. Their education is Spartan, their sexual morals are rough and incest is the normal thing. Anyone, man or woman, who is gentle is despised.

The Tchambuli, who live close to the other two tribes, are a gentle people, but the women are the dominating sex (in which regard their civilization is the opposite of ours). The dominant position of the women, however, does not derive from established *right;* it is simply *customary.* The women are robust, practical, impersonal in their outward behavior and generally "business-like." They undertake all the work. In sexual relationships, the woman is the aggressive partner. The men are impractical, passive, emotional, playful and coquettish. They devote their time to art, to carving wood, to dancing in their decorative costumes. They are treated with amicable tolerance by the women, who look upon them as overgrown children. In spite of all this, their society has a patriarchal structure (with bride-barter and other similar elements).

Margaret Mead comes to the conclusion that the observable

difference between the masculine and the feminine derives from a particular "social conditioning." The circumstances of the society in which a child grows up determine the child's form of existence. The same child in other conditions in another culture would develop as quite another type.

But what is the position in the sphere of what we call the *higher* cultures? In the tribal cultures of New Guinea the types are relatively simple and they show little differentiation. In the higher cultures there is a much greater differentiation of types, and there are many variations within any one type. This is due chiefly to the needs of the social situation. We also know of a kind of "social conditioning" that has nothing to do with the sexual differences as such. For instance, in our Western civilization we have the standardized type of the "ideal butler," we form an ideal of "bedside manners" for the doctor, and within some of the religious groupings of our culture there is a particular social determination of type (the Quakers are an example). Margaret Mead comes to the conclusion that "types" are formed wholly by social conditioning. Is it in fact right to assume that the differences between men and women arise in exactly the same way? As far as we can see, this matter is not yet absolutely certain.

It is quite true that we normally *require* a little boy *not* to be frightened while we do not mind very much if a little girl in the same circumstances *does* get frightened. Without doubt this has a fairly profound influence on their personal development. Thus, there are always some types of temperament that become standardized by education. Margaret Mead's conclusions bring an important light to bear on the whole matter, and they have a special importance with regard to our understanding of our educational approach. She notes:

1. Among primitive peoples, there is no teen-age problem. The girls do not have to wait and to choose. In our civilization, every girl goes through a "Cinderella" period, a sort of daydream about the possibilities of being chosen.

2. Among the primitive tribes of Samoa, no demands are made on children growing up. One never hears a child asked to do this or that "because mother (or father) want you to do it so very much." No moral pressure is brought to bear, and there is no anxiety, no suppression and no neuroses.

3. In Samoa, there is no special rule for any individual and neither
   is any individual excepted from the general rule. For instance,
   all children go to bed at nightfall. There is no such thing as the
   problem of "but the little girl next door is allowed to stay up
   later than me." In our society this kind of thing is often the
   basis of resentment or vanity, of assumed superiority or inferiority. This gives rise to a form of depersonalized dependence
   which is more grave than personal dependence. In this, Margaret Mead touches a very important point. In our social relationships, and particularly in the relationships of sex, the
   simple fact that something is permitted or prohibited can prove
   a source of vanity or anxiety in later life.

4. In primitive cultures, there is no such thing as a "double
   standard," not only with regard to sexual freedom but also
   with regard to what might be called helpfulness toward others,
   the sacrifice of time and energy "even if the whole thing is
   really futile." In our society there is a much heavier demand
   on women than on men to give their own time to doing something for someone else. The heavier demand begins to be made
   even upon the little girl. The demand is presented as the girl's
   "duty," and her reaction to it may be resignation and it may
   be bitterness. There is nothing of this in a primitive culture.
   Margaret Mead says that there is one thing we could well
   learn from those we regard as more primitive than ourselves:
   it would be intelligent to moderate the way we contrast the
   sexes and to give more recognition to personal differences. There
   is no sense in trying to make all little girls as passive as possible,
   and to make all little boys into soldiers. There are two things
   we have constantly to take into account: the great *plasticity* of
   the human being, and the powerful influence of the milieu.[23]

[23] A good deal of criticism has been levelled against Margaret Mead's
work. Among others, R. Thurnwald (Amer. Anthrop. 38, 1936) says that
the facts do not always support her theoretical interpretation. The differences
in temperament are clearly there. Along with cultural influences, these
differences lead to a definite division of labor. Margaret Mead replies
(Amer. Anthrop. 39, 1937) that she does not want to deny the fact of
differences in temperament, but that she does want to point out that "those
temperamental attitudes which we have traditionally regarded as feminine
can so easily be set up as the masculine pattern in one tribe and in another
be outlawed for the majority of women as well as for the majority of men
that we no longer have any basis for regarding such aspects of behavior as
sex-linked."

4. Woman's Relationship to Her Own Body

> . . . The whole of our society lies in the skirt. Take the skirt away from woman, and bid farewell to coquetry; passion too will disappear. All her power is in her dress. . . .
>
> H. DE BALZAC [24]

Dwelling upon something in care for it presupposes a particular mode of presence: presence to oneself and, at the same time, *as oneself*, presence to and with the other. On the other hand, the activity of work regarded precisely as work presupposes a transcending of one's own bodily reality: one becomes wholly absorbed in the occupation and one projects oneself into the goals set up in the act of work. We have already considered these two points. Each represents a relationship of the human being to himself, but on closer consideration it is easy to see that concrete situations in ordinary life can elicit other relationships besides these, including relationships that are the opposite of these.

In these two relationships, as modes of existence, we have seen two modes of the decisive, responsible determination of human existence or, to use Heidegger's term, two modes of "selfhood," *"Selbstheit."* But the adaptive dynamism, and to a still greater extent the erotic dynamism, can be thought of as carried through to the point of a personal co-existence with one or more other persons, where this dynamism would also mean a *giving up* of selfhood, of the responsible determination of one's own individual existence. Binswanger says that every form of love implies that the one who loves comes to form *one* image (*Einbildung*) with the one who is loved, and this unity of the image of the two itself implies a forgetfulness of self, however much it may also mean that one *rediscovers oneself in the other*.

Let us look first at the human being's relationship to himself in the context of work. Work is a process of imparting form, and this

[24] *Théorie de la Démarche; Oeuvres complètes* XX. Paris 1879. p. 594.

presupposes that the material worked upon is present to the worker as a resistance. The very word "resistance" indicates that in this activity the worker projects his own existence as a being in itself, and moreover, that he projects it as a being in the initiative of the responsibility demanded by the work itself. Thus there can be no doubt that the relationships involved here are complex and in a certain sense ambiguous. Therefore it is not very feasible to draw any firm and decisive conclusions about the human being's relationship to himself if we argue from the "idea" of work alone. This comes from the fact that a person can be present to himself in a number of ways.

Literature provides many examples of narcissism or of self-satisfaction in men and in women in every possible variety of circumstance in real life. The narcissist or the self-satisfied person experiences his own body in a peculiar way, as something which he *has* and also as something which *exists* as other in relation to himself and in relation to other people. Narcissism and self-satisfaction do not make work and care impossible, but they do subtract from both work and care those essential characteristics through which these activities can become fully mature acts in the ethical and the human sense. It means that we have to look for other points of view from which to be able to understand, in general, the meaning of the relationship of a human being to his or her own body, and we need to understand this before we can understand woman's relationship to her own body.

It seems to me that there are four aspects from which we could approach this important problem:

1) We could proceed from the fact that every human being, precisely as a human being, is able to take up a certain distance with regard to himself. This would be to proceed from the anthropological point of departure.

2) We could pay attention to the constitution of the body itself in sickness and in health, and so to the reality of physical existence in its biological and physiological aspects, and see how this reality can be taken up into the projection of an existence as human.

3) We could proceed from the sociological determination of a person's relationship to his own body, which is to say, we could proceed from the *regard of other people,* for it is in the body that everyone is seen, approached and contacted by others and through

their regard for him thrown back upon himself and made to experience his own bodily appearance and reality in a particular manner.
4) We could proceed from the genetic-psychological point of view,
i.e., from the person's relationship to his own body as it is formed
in the very earliest days of his life, and which—at least to the
psychoanalytic way of thinking—will have a decisive influence on
the course of his later life.

We have already seen something of the last of these four lines of
approach, having included it in our critical discussion of the psychoanalytical explanation of woman's nature. We have also to
some extent seen the second and the third of these four lines of
approach, for in discussing woman's existence and the way woman
manifests herself, we needed to pay attention to her physical constitution and her sociological relationships. This is why we want
now to examine woman's relationship to her own body in terms of
the first of the four aspects mentioned above, and proceed from the
distance a human being is able to take up with regard to himself.

In this, we take as our starting point the fundamental thesis of
philosophical anthropology, that the human being is never natural
in the sense that the animal is natural. The human person is never
simply what nature makes him: he is not conterminous with this
body, this temperament, this character and these aptitudes. In the
concrete reality of a human existence, all these characteristics and
bases of characteristics are manifested as things to which the person himself gives a particular meaning in relation to his own existence. This view is certainly not the outcome of the latest developments in the philosophy of existence.

Plessner, in 1928, expressed these same thoughts, as it were in
principle, in his book, *Die Stufen des Organischen*. In a more
recent work by the same author, we read, "A person's own body is
accidental to that person. . . . and he remains conscious of the fact
that it is accidental, whether he becomes master of it or not. Whatever he *has*, he can be—or not be." Whatever the human being
possesses in the way of bodily reality, he can take up a great
variety of attitudes with regard to it. Recall that we have already
noticed that a physical deformity can make a great difference to
the projection and development of a person's life. This should
make it quite clear that, although the accidental nature of the body
may be the lot that a person has drawn in the lottery of life, it

becomes truly his own lot only through the way he assumes it into his own existence and through the way he himself accepts it.

This self acceptance is necessary before the person can become present to himself and before he can take up a position with regard to others, seeing them and knowing he is seen by them. But while a person is accepting his own body and all that belongs to it in the way of temperament etc., as a part of the whole situation that comprises his own existence, he is at the same time constituting himself as a member of a particular group. A human being can never accept himself alone. He always accepts himself as the representative of his equals. Therefore, in the manner of his acceptance, there is always a projection of the image that *traditionally* belongs to the group to which he decides to belong, and this means that the same traditional image is always present in the person's own projection of himself.

It was not mere happenstance that made Plessner return to these thoughts and develop them further in a study entitled *Anthropologie des Schauspielers* (Anthropology of an Actor), for he wanted to make it clear that an actor's peculiar manner of existence can be understood only in terms of what is universally human. Now it is a universally human phenomenon that a human being figures, appears, in a certain rôle. . . . "and he can figure well or he can figure badly. But the figure belonging to that rôle is fixed, and that is what he has to be."

Like an actor accepting a rôle, every human being accepts a rôle in assuming his own bodily reality, and it is the rôle of the group to which he knows that he belongs. This we can see most clearly from the fact that the acceptance of the group-rôle comprises acceptance of the group style of behavior, and this is expressed in elements like the manner of the gait, the way of speaking, the gestures and so on that are characteristic of that group. It comprises acceptance of something else besides: the group style of dress. In his book *Der Mensch und die Religion,* Van der Leeuw writes, "The whole of anthropology is contained in clothing." It is so, for if we try to name the essential marks that set the human being aside from all other beings, we may think of the upright stance, the domed skull, the frontal glance, and so on, but the list is incomplete without this further item: clothing. Clothes make the human being human. When a man loses his clothes he loses everything: his dignity, his regard, his humanity, himself. It is not surprising, therefore, that every large group in which people grow and to which they decide to belong has not only a particular style of behavior and a particular way of regarding the bodily reality, but also a particular image.

Historical Determination

The style of behavior and the style of the clothing are historically determined. The historical determination of behavior and clothing always applies in the case of every human being universally and without exception, and *therefore* it applies to women and to men. Every human being experiences a sense of shame at being stripped of his clothing. In a "primitive" whose normal clothing consists of no more than a single girdle or little piece of cloth, the principle of shame is just as strong as it is in modern man; in everyone, it is shame at the loss of human dignity. Though we can say that the whole of anthropology is implicit in the phenomenon of clothing, and that clothing fulfills the same essential function for every human being, we still have to ask whether the men and the women of *our* culture experience this in exactly the same way, or perhaps in different ways. In this regard, what is the difference between the sexes?

Scheler once said that "woman experiences her own body constitutively. . . . she feels herself in it and knows herself in it," and in another place he said that man takes his body along with him "like a dog on a leash." According to Scheler, then, the man's position with regard to his own body is one of a peculiar distance from it, and in this he is distinctly unlike woman, whose position with regard to her own body is that she always knows herself as physically present in it, and it is in the body that she constitutes herself as present. It must be recognized that this particular distinction of the sexes is made in terms of a given cultural group at a given period of that culture, and insofar as it is a valid distinction, it is clear that the attitudes involved in it have been developed gradually in the individuals of the group from their earliest childhood.

Many authors of psychological works have remarked on the distinction between the demands made on girls and those made on boys from the very beginning of their personal development. In the demands made on little girls, the emphasis is on "this is how you must be" (or negatively: "you shouldn't be like that"), which in practice means the same thing as "you must adopt this particular manner of manifesting yourself in the body." In the demands made on little boys, the emphasis is on "this is what you must do." No wonder, then, that we find a psychoanalyst such as Von Hattingberg defining woman as "simply being there" (*nur da zu sein*).

It is well known that this manner of thinking makes itself felt throughout the psychology of the sexes. There is an element of truth in it. Simone de Beauvoir for instance points out the fact that puberty is a clearly determined event in a girl's life, in that it is defined not only by others but also for the girl herself through the changes that take place within her and produce clear physical characteristics, which mean that new possibilities (like nubility) are suddenly present within her, without the question having arisen of her having had to do anything herself. The girl grows up "in spite of herself."

The boy, on the other hand, is grown up when he is able to *do* what men do. When he chooses his father's career, goes along to work for the first time, goes onto the land or goes to sea, joins the army, or begins to take part in cultural activity of any kind, then he is no longer a child. There are of course some cultural groups that surround the advent of male puberty with mystery and connect it with a ritual of initiation, but a question remains as to whether, even in these cultures, male puberty has the same original significance as female puberty.

In terms of this anthropological approach we can draw the preliminary conclusion that there is a secondary "nature" in every human individual and that every human being is related to his or her own body in a particular way which is historically determined. But we must immediately qualify this conclusion and say that with reference to our own culture, the individual's relationship to his or her own body takes one form in men, and generally a different form in women.

Now we might expect that the "simply being there," which relates to the demonstrative value of being, would actually belong immediately to the context of an expansive dynamism such as we find in the male organisms of the animal world. Think of the peacock. We have already seen that it is the males who usually bear the manes, the antlers, the bright colors that reveal purely demonstrative values. Perhaps it is possible to trace the evolution of these demonstrative values much further, from the animal world through primitive human culture right up to modern man. Among primitive peoples it is usually the men who take to demonstrative decoration of the person. In our own culture, there are not a few men who like to appear as very dignified or as highly colorful characters, even though they strive after this *inwardly* and not by means of their clothing, which is usually rather dull.

There is a fairly widespread notion that the French Revolution brought about some profound changes in masculine psychology, and that the men who now keep to soberly dull and conservative fashions in their dress have a different and much more human self-awareness than the dandies of the *ancien régime*. We would have to be very cautious in any credence given to such a notion. Women's fashions however are very colorful, and with all their accessories and styles of make-up they vary according to social status and country and season, many times a year, the standard of beauty being set by whatever happens to be "the latest." This fact is usually taken quite simply as a confirmation of Scheler's view, that woman relates herself constitutively to her own body, and thus, not in the same way as man relates to his. But this is certainly an over-simplification of the real problem. We do not have sufficient empirical data to be able to deal with the problem of clothing in anything like a satisfactory way. For the present we can do no more than take one or two points that are open to further investigation.

Clothing

In the first place, we can consider a very simple element of the whole question: women wear skirts and men wear trousers. This difference between male and female attire did not exist in the beginnings of our civilization, during Roman times. Both sexes wore the tunic. Some writers have found a very profound significance in the wearing of a skirt, but this is quite unnecessary. It would probably be easy to find a straightforward, practical, historical reason for the origin of trousers and skirt as distinct modes of dress. Nevertheless, once these two modes are established, it is quite certain that they reveal a primary distinction between the way men manifest themselves and the way women manifest themselves, and that they reveal this distinction in a visible way, and that this repeatedly leads to the renewed projection of all kinds of mysterious suppositions. Every mode of dress peculiar to a particular group strengthens group-consciousness, whether the group be a military regiment or a coven of primitive witch-doctors, a women's social club or the people of a village or the inhabitants of a region. As well as strengthening the group-consciousness, uniformity in dress also strengthens the individual's consciousness of his or her own physical appearance. Every fashion, even if it is only a new fashion in ties for the young man-about-town, arises as demonstrative attire and never as purely utilitarian garb.

In the second place, every fashion strengthens the individual's self-awareness and consciousness of the body as something visible to the eye of another, giving rise to a pseudo-immanence. By this we mean that it gives rise to the individual's choice not to transcend himself, but simply to figure in the role of a being complete and enclosed within itself. This is a pseudo-immanence, since authentic immanence is existence proceeding from an irreducible initiative, from freedom and from consciousness of being. Pseudo-immanence is nothing more than the pretence of an authentic existence *for* oneself presented in the image of an actual existence *in* oneself, and therefore it manifests only an apparent interiority.

As there is no genuine interiority manifested in the individual's appearance, the individual becomes a "mystery" to another, taking on an "importance" and an interest in the eyes of the other which are the stronger the more the individual is self-satisfied in his pseudo-immanence. If even the manifestation of a pretended interiority falls away and the individual is content to appear in the image of a "thing," an object, that simply is what it is in itself, then, from the aspect of fashion, the individual is no more than a window-dummy, a "model," the caricature of a human being.

In the third place, fashion is always the uniform of a group, but through an illusory act of choice it is taken as personal attire. One of the chief consequences of fashion in this respect is the *care taken in grooming oneself*. It would be wrong to assume that time and effort are devoted to this personal grooming chiefly with an eye on possible criticism. Theoretical investigation and practical experience both confirm that a person's efforts at taking care of his or her appearance, even in early life, are directed primarily toward the person's own consciousness of self, toward the "moral sup-

port" (to use a term favored among English authors) that can be
derived from several sources, one of which is clothing.

What exactly is this "moral support"? It can best be understood
as support and motivation for self-esteem, for a measure of confidence in oneself, for a feeling of having escaped dismal nonentity
and being somehow important. Self-awareness is cultivated in this
direction from a very early age, more so by girls than by boys.
People express their consciousness of their own value in simple
symbols, and these at the same time tend to strengthen this consciousness. The starched white pinafore without spot or crease
can so easily be a symbol of infrangible purity or cleanliness. In
some pedagogical situations, the importance of some group attire
of this kind can be very great. One of the more experienced sisters
running the Catholic home for backward girls at Udenhout told me
that they had found perfectly clean, white aprons to be one of the
most successful means in aiding the backward children to develop
an awareness of their own personality. The symbolism visible in a
thing like those aprons is experienced so immediately that it needs
no explanation. We could go so far as to say that white is an
"archetypal" symbol of unassailable purity, and that when white-
ness and smoothness are combined (as in the lily, or in polished
white marble), they form a similar symbol of simplicity and so
also of clarity.

We can understand, therefore, why we attach importance to
white collars and white cuffs. For while the whole of the attire is
significant, a more particular significance is usually attached to
those parts where the head joins the body and where the hand joins
the arm (whence collars, necklaces, cuffs, arm-bands, bangles and
so on). In these areas, limits are set to those parts of the human
being that remain unclothed. Fashion is therefore *primarily* a matter of self-respect, and not of vanity. And what we say of fashion
in general is also applicable to the uniform attire of a closed group,
like the habit of a religious order, and sometimes may apply to the
working clothes of other groups as well, like overalls or nurses'
uniforms.

It is not true that woman's clothing is designed exclusively
under the influence of man's regard, under the eye of the *dominant*
male. It is true, as Adler points out, that every attempt to dominate will elicit a compensatory strengthening of self-awareness on

the part of the supposed subject. It is probably also true that the (lustful) glance of the male had something to do with the primordial development of the most primitive female attire, the loin-cloth and its derivatives, though this attire is ambiguous in that it draws attention to what it conceals. But as culture progresses clothing develops along with it, and attire in its higher, not yet degenerate forms is intended specifically to enable human beings to transcend these primitive motives.

Although we hear it said again and again that feminine attire is intended chiefly to enhance "sex appeal," women of experience and high mental development categorically deny that this is the general rule. Their denial is confirmed, and the "sex appeal" theory proved wrong, by two facts. Firstly, more often than not just as much care is taken of garments that will never be seen by others as of those that are seen, and these hidden garments are just as important as the outer ones to a woman's self-confidence. Secondly, and even more significantly, practically all exchange of negative criticism and positive appreciation takes place within the group itself—takes place in this case among women alone—and this means that women themselves determine their standards and that these are not determined by the way men look at women. When a woman does experience a man's critical regard, she experiences its meaning in *her own* way and relates it as *she* experiences it to *her own* existence. Thus we can see that the cultural phenomenon of clothing offers much opportunity for silliness and even for tragic degradation, but more importantly, it offers great opportunity for a fine sensitivity of spirit and for pure delightful fun.

These problems however really do require a much fuller collation of the details of sociological and historical situations and a more extensive phenomenological analysis of the empirical facts. Let us then leave them, in the hope that the above considerations will have been enough to open some new perspectives on the problems.

Constitution of the Human Body

We want now to return for a moment to the second of the four aspects of approach mentioned at the beginning of this section, and consider the *constitution* of the human body as such. Note once again that man has an awareness of his body that comes to him through his consciousness of the possibility of taking a grasp on the world. The body is experienced as a means for doing something, a means through which the man has a certain power at his disposal and through which he is able to enter into combat.

This is a general experience to which there is no exception, even in the matter of sexual functions or in the constitution of the organs relating to these functions. They too form part of the possible action of which the man is capable. One of the chief merits of Simone de Beauvoir's work lies in the fact that, in spite of much of what she says being tinged with resentment, she could and did point out so clearly that woman experiences a certain lack of sureness in her grasp on the world. If we may depart to some extent from the terms of her own explanation, we might say what Simone de Beauvoir says in this way: in all forms of encounter, woman experiences herself less as one who grasps than as one who is grasped or who is graspable—but we must note that the terms "grasped" and "graspable" are intended in as abstract a sense as possible. This means that *woman possesses her own body as the means whereby she can be taken or whereby she is taken.* Here again, we are using the word "taken" in a particular sense, the sense Binswanger intends when he speaks of *"das mitweltliche nehmen-bei-etwas"* (to take something "by" or "on" or "according to" something else, inasmuch as one exists in the world together with that which is taken).[25]

Perhaps the meaning will become clearer if we concentrate on the sense of "take" in the following phrases: we take someone on his word; we take someone according to his own gestures or behavior; he can be taken by or through his weaknesses, his inclinations, his passions. In the general sense of this formulation, the "being taken" by others that is experienced in encounter with others constitutes a fundamental human relationship to those others, and this relationship exists prior to and apart from any question of dominance and subjection in sexual relationships. If we consider this relationship, established in the human mode of "taking someone by or according to something," and compare it with the reciprocal relationship of "heart to heart" knowledge in which there is an equality of presence in togetherness and in contact, we can

[25] L. Binswanger, *Grundformen und Erkenntnis menschlichen Daseins*, Zürich 1942. p. 300ff.

begin to understand that there is a vulnerability (a graspability) in woman that is much more profound than the vulnerability resulting from the "comparative weakness" of her physical constitution.

The meaning of all of this can perhaps best be made more clear if we consider it in terms of an experience that is very likely to occur in anybody's life. The experience we are thinking of is the experience of being "caught in the act." Sartre describes it very well, drawing the example of someone who, peeping through a keyhole and deeply absorbed in what he sees, suddenly feels a peremptory tap on his shoulder. The experience that seems to overwhelm one at such a moment is a profound experience of being defenseless, of being "taken," "caught," "trapped." The same kind of experience is frequent in adolescents. They are not yet entirely at home in the adult world, but an adolescent will begin to do something that he wants to view with wholly serious intent and then suddenly feel that others are looking on, unmasking his intentions, aware of his clumsiness. The adolescent is *unable to forget* his bodily reality, because the state of the physical constitution during adolescence compels the young person to regard the body as one that is not yet wholly adapted to the adult world and to give it meaning as a means still inept for adult ends.

There are analogous constitutional grounds for woman's unsureness, vulnerability and "impracticality" that make her experience herself as "taken" and as "graspable." The peeper through the keyhole can never become wholly and entirely absorbed in the view, but always remains somehow conscious of his own situation. The adolescent can never give himself so completely to any situation that he ceases to be self-consciously aware of himself and so can never quite transcend his own body. Woman's case is like these, as long as she inhabits her own body as a private world separate from the greater world, as a body not perfectly adapted to the greater world—because she does not live entirely in the world of others while she experiences her own body in this way. If human beings are to encounter one another in untrammeled freedom and perfect equality, there must first be an organic solidarity in their life together in *one* world. For, when all inhabit the same world in the same way, no *part* of one renders him defenseless before another, and no one has a special "vulnerable spot," a characteristic unsureness of expression, through which he can be "taken" or "grasped" by another.

Woman's relationship to her own body is determined by the meaning she herself gives to her own body. But as long as a woman somehow feels herself to be a stranger in a world made by men, or in other words, as long as she cannot look upon the world as *one that she herself has made,* she will not be able to determine the meaning she gives her own body on her own free choice, and neither will there be any *obvious* meaning that she must give it. As long as she cannot look upon the world simply and straightforwardly as *her own,* there is an ambiguity in her "consciousness," her "knowledge" of the world and of herself and she stands somehow outside of the world, looking in upon it, like one who peeps through a keyhole. Women often find themselves in this position, and the reason for this lies mainly in an education deeply influenced by popular and traditional views. But the nature of woman's own constitution has something to do with it too, for her physical constitution invites woman to give her own body a meaning that is different from the meaning man gives to his.

Along with all this, we might recall once more the greater liability of woman's physiological functions, her comparatively smaller capacity for physical endurance, and the fact that her strength is less than man's, but at the same time it must be remembered that she is able to give a profound meaning and a positive existential value to this weakness. Paul's words come to mind: . . . "power is made perfect in weakness." [26]

[26] 2 Corinthians 12, 9.

5. Motherliness

> Fidelity corresponds to a situation of care and concern, and this is quite naturally feminine . . . The deft fingers of fidelity weave the threads of the web of life; fidelity stays at home, a Penelope weaving her everlasting tapestry, while courage hunts the wild boar or voyages among the islands.
>
> WLADIMIR JANKELEVITCH [27]

We have already noted the fact that woman's "nature" indicates the possibility of motherhood. It is just as much an objective fact that man's body possesses within itself the possibility of making a man a father. But these human possibilities can be brought to realization in a *human* sense only when the individuals in whose "nature" they are contained freely and deliberately choose so to realize them. "Nature" determines nothing, prescribes nothing, and reveals no vocation. At one time it was seriously maintained that man, by his "very nature," is polygamous, but if the physical capability of polygamy constitutes a "natural vocation" for the human male, it still does not mean that there is any reason why he should follow it.

Time and time again, in all sorts of different ways, we hear it said that woman *ought really* to become a mother because she is *capable* of bearing children. This point of view is wholly character-istic of the rationalistic and "constructive" way of thinking. Ac-cording to this line of thought, which is very widespread indeed, motherhood is the *"natural"* destiny of woman, and any woman who fails to reach this destiny is at best deeply to be pitied and often somehow worthy of scorn. This point of view is stubbornly entrenched in the popular mind; the fact of its present persistence certainly derives from a good deal more than merely the after-effects of Hebrew and Oriental socio-psychological and religious factors influencing earlier stages of our culture.

In spite of the Christian and humanistic traditions, both of which defend the humanity and therefore the freedom of woman,

[27] *Le Masculin et le Feminin,* Deucalion I 1946, pp. 173, 176.

the point of view persists—for several reasons. It is founded to some extent on the projected dominance of masculine existence, sexually defined in that the *only* role really conceded to the female human being is the rôle of mother. It is founded to some extent also on the excessive value placed on the idea of technical efficiency, which leads to a state of society in which the human being is valued in terms of his or her productivity. Now, since woman generally speaking is only a second-rate force in the ordinary affairs of society and can be employed only in an auxiliary capacity, it is more efficient to channel her productivity into the only line that man cannot manage by himself, and have her produce children.

The evaluation of the human being in terms of productive efficiency seems to find some confirmation in the theoretical view of man derived from a naturalistic biology. In the human species, as in a predator species or an anthropoid species, the females are supposed to fulfill their function by caring for the preservation of the species and bearing offspring, while the males are supposed to fulfill theirs by providing leadership, and by acquiring and defending the territory in which the species will hunt or carry out its search for food in other ways.[28]

These are the main influences at work upon the modern popular notion of woman's "place" in human society, and they are, obviously, no more than simplistic presentations and pseudo-scientific reasoning rooted in a technological culture. Alongside of these, the *primordial symbolism* of woman and mother, common to all peoples (which some say goes back to Pelasgic times in prehistory, and which Klages connects with Bachofen's idea of matriarchy and

[28] A more competent and profound study of the social life of animals shows that the male certainly does not always supply leadership in animal society. F. Fraser Darling gives an exceptionally good presentation of the facts in his study, *A Herd of Red Deer* (Oxford Univ. Press, 1937). After showing that the male does take the leading role in the herd, he says: "The patriarchal group can never be large, for however attentively the male may care for his group he is never selfless. Sexual jealousy is always ready to impinge on social relations leading to gregariousness. As Hobhouse (1913) has said: 'The principle of force is the very antithesis of the principle of social ethics'; and I contend that the matriarchal system in animal life, being selfless, is a move toward the development of an ethical system. The governing male cannot keep more females than he is physically able and he will not allow other males to mix with his group. . . . Matriarchy, which entails separation of the sexes for the greater part of the year and relieves the male wholly of parental care, is a decided social advance which helps the species toward survival" (p. 93).

explains at great length), exercises practically no influence on modern popular thought.

The occident in our age of technological thinking knows nothing of the *"magna mater"* or of the symbolical relationships of phenomena. Western civilization holds firmly to the belief that truth can be attained only by strict adherence to what it calls "objective" *facts* and acknowledges only an etiological relationship between these facts. The meaning of the human being is to be sought through the things human beings do and are able to do. There can be no sense in asking whether human being might not have a "deeper meaning." The answer to the question, "What *is* woman?" can be given only in reference to woman's specifically female actions and to the indications of the possibility of specifically female action.

"Objectively" speaking (in the technological way of thinking) there is only one *specifically* female action, and that is, giving birth to a child. This is why we all say that the girl becomes a woman as soon as she becomes nubile, *i.e.,* fruitful, but a boy becomes a man only when he has learned to work, and thus to control the means at his disposal and to produce or achieve something.

Now, of course it is obvious that *woman's physical appearance* relates to motherhood. However, woman's *manifestation of herself* through her physical appearance does not express actual motherhood (biological production of a baby); it expresses *motherliness*. Motherliness is a manner of being, a particular quality of the human way of being-in-the-world, a form of human existence which has been meaningfully developed on the basis of a biological aptitude under the influence of the milieu.[29] Motherliness, therefore, is not something that is inborn in a woman.

It is an amazing fact that woman alone, quite unlike the female of any of even the highest animal species, develops the physical appearance of a mother even if in fact she never becomes a mother —and as far as I know there is no explanation of why this should be so. It cannot be explained in terms of the biological basis of heredity. We know of course that hormone production at the time of puberty leads to the development of the secondary sex charac-

[29] "When I speak of motherliness I have in mind two ideas: 1) a definite quality of character that stamps the woman's whole personality; 2) emotional phenomena that seem to be related to the child's helplessness and need for care" (Helene Deutsch, *The Psychology of Women;* Vol. II: *Motherhood.* N. Y. 1945. p. 17).

teristics (breasts, etc.), but this does not give the reason why the course of this development in the human being should be so singularly different, so unique. But if we accept the general premise that the human body, however natural its origins, is designed for human existence and adapted to the needs of human existence, we can also see that the appearance of woman's body is in accordance with the possibilities of the feminine mode of being-in-the-world.

Motherliness

For this being-in-the-world in the mode of *care* does in fact reach a fulfillment in motherliness because, through this particular quality of the human mode of being in the world, all that is implicit in every act of caring is brought to realization in the meaningful unity of a number of acts and in the *"Daseinsform"* of pure love. These acts are the acts of bearing, enduring, conferring tenderness, permitting and promoting growth and protectively encouraging it, the act of wholly unselfish giving, and above all the conscious awareness of values realized *through* the approach to "the other" in the mode of care.

Motherliness is comprised in the activity of care and may be called the fulfillment of the activity of care. There are no authentic grounds for holding the view that the quality of motherliness arises from the sexual and reproductive instincts of the human female.

There is no doubt that it is possible for the quality of genuine motherliness to be expressed in actual motherhood, in the love of a mother for her child. But it is well known that the "natural" affective protectiveness of the mother for her offspring, like the instinctive care of the female animal for her young, is not a realization of motherliness in a genuinely human sense. When we human beings look at animal life, we normally experience what we see in our own human way, and this is why we talk about the mother animal "loving" its young. But this customary way of speaking reveals a customary failure to distinguish between animal reactions necessitated by nature and human responses, elicited by nature, but freely and deliberately chosen by the human being.

The essence of motherliness is human, spiritual, *universal,* and it possesses a structure of meaning that is already implicit in authentic feminine intentionality as the projection of a world and a relationship to the projected world.

Genuine love of mother for child is possible only when *motherliness* exists *as the humanity of the mother's existence,* and this motherliness has a much more general function than simply to be manifested in motherhood. Woman's motherly aspect means much more than the quality indicated and prepared by feminine youthfulness in the playful dwelling upon things and values in accordance with the feminine mode of existence. The youthful forms, of features, voice, glance, gracefulness, resilience, playfulness, pathic relationships, as we have seen, are able to be transformed in the adult woman into a truly mature humanity, but the development is taken much further in motherliness. Motherliness, as a general mode of existence with other people and with the world, transcends youthfulness—one might almost say, "transsubstantiates" youthfulness—in such a way that the outward appearances of feminine youthfulness serve to establish the presence of an entirely different and deeper quality of existence.

When considering the manifestation of youthfulness in woman, in feminine reality, we saw that youthfulness did not mean childishness and how the youthful quality could be manifested in the balanced strength of an adult existence right through to an advanced age. The same can be said of motherliness, for this quality can be manifested right through a woman's mature life and its manifestation does not depend upon the accidentals of bodily build and features or of age and circumstances of life.

We want to illustrate this by means of the phenomenon of *tenderness,* the most characteristic of the expressions of motherliness. Kunz gives an excellent description of tenderness, contrasting it with the masculine phenomenon of aggressiveness.[30] In essence, tenderness consists in a mode of conduct directed in the interests of an object requiring tenderness. This mode of conduct can be expressed in many ways, in words or deeds, in glances or gestures. The object of tenderness may be found in the "outside" world or in the "interiority" of the "tender" person. It may be another person, an animal, a plant, a landscape, the softness of a springtime, a work of art, a memory, or a mood—all such things can give rise to tenderness. But whatever the object, it is always one that "asks"

[30] H. Kunz, *Die Aggressivität und die Zärtlichkeit,* Bern 1946.

for tenderness because of its own softness, fragility, its appealing defenselessness.

Kunz writes: "The childlike . . . and its correlative, the motherly, together form the sphere which is the origin of tenderness," but we should not take this to mean that the original meaning of tenderness is confined exclusively to the *real* mother-child relationship, or even that the genetic origins of the quality of tenderness lie in this relationship.

Thus, when the feminine disposition inclines a woman who in fact is childless to seek and discover and satisfy herself with all sorts of "objects of tenderness," she need not be seeking them as some sort of *"substitute"* for the missing child. She may perhaps be seeking a substitute, but this is not specifically human. The same kind of behavior can often be observed in animals, and it reflects the dependence of the purely instinctive behavior of the animal organism on the pattern of sensation. But on the animal level there is no possibility of genuine tenderness. People of course do speak of the tender care of the mother animal for her young, and even see a tenderness in the way a lion "caresses" its mate, but as we have seen, this is because no distinction is drawn between the animal and the human. Animal tenderness is tenderness only in an analogous sense, the behavior observed seeming to the human being to express the quality of tenderness.

Every aspect of human reality can be matched with images taken from nature, but it does not mean that reason and will, freedom and love, are present in nature as such. The human being is rational, possesses a power of will, is free and can love. These aspects are present in nature *in appearance*. And since the human being participates in nature, even the images of the spiritual aspect of human existence can appear in the physical or natural aspect of the human being.

Thus, it is possible to see that "mother instinct" as well as natural images of care, tenderness and love can actually appear in the physical relationship of mother and child in the context of motherhood, without these instincts and appearances being in any way the expression of the spiritual acts of authentic, human existence. Everyone knows that the expressions of stimulated impulse and desire are very often and quite incorrectly called love. In a like manner, motherly tenderness is not always present in *every* act of cuddling a baby or displaying affection or embracing a child.

Tenderness is constituted as a *human* act by the intentionality expressed in the tender gesture, word or glance, when this is the intentionality of being present in a *personal* way personally occupied in the human activity of care through the realization of motherly warmth and softness, protection and self-giving. In this, care is given a new aspect by the introduction of the element of the delicate softness of its physical expression, which is adapted fittingly to the *defenselessness* of the *object* and which testifies to the way the person is moved by such an object.[31]

The simplest concrete example of the structure of this tenderness can be found in the relationship between a mother and the child at her breast, a relationship revealed in the quiet intimacy of their physical togetherness. The motherly caress, the warmth of the cherishing embrace and the movement of the little hands on the tender flesh are the classic examples of all expressions of tenderness.

Some have said that this fondling is a restrained expression of sexuality, but, as Kunz too has said, this is an unjustifiable assumption. There is no doubt that fondling can sometimes be a sexual gesture, but when it is, the fondling takes place with the intention of obtaining sensual pleasure. But not all joy and happiness are the same thing as sensual pleasure, and likewise, neither is all tenderness or all fond caressing something sexual.

The physical togetherness established in these may well be and often is intended and experienced as the giving and receiving of *presence*. Our gentle gesture and soft word, gentle touch and soft, caressing glance, bring the object in its *own* gentleness into our presence, the object revealing its own loveliness and sweetness only *in* our caressing it and its own defenseless fragility only *in* our gentle, careful handling of it. The discovery of a world of softness, sweetness, fragility, is not open to adult appreciation only: even the little child begins to discover such a world, in its "motherly" attention to dolls, little animals, plants and other objects, approaching them in the mode of its adaptive dynamism.

There is the same quality of reciprocally directed experience in

[31] Rilke draws a very evocative picture of the exceptional quality of care in a mother. Writing of the anxious hours of silence in the house at night, he says that the mother, knowing from her own childhood the terror of the silent dark, of creaks in the floorboards and things on the wall, by her own calm movements and loving smile kindles a light—is a light—to restore all good and familiar and simple things (R. M. Rilke, *Ausgewählte Werke,* Zweiter Band, Insel-Verlag 1950. cf. p. 68).

the caressing comfort of any appreciation of beauty—in good music, a harvest moon, a pleasantly furnished room. *One who caresses is at the same time caressed,* the gentle glance itself discovers gentleness in what it sees, and the motherly approach *elicits that childlike response* that is waiting as a potentiality in all people and even in the world itself, ready for the right approach that will bring it to life.[32]

Motherliness, which is expressed in the defenselessness and tenderness of the physical appearance of woman and which is comprised in the context of her youthfulness, therefore has a meaning that is capable of being revealed *in every facet of woman's existence.* To imagine that the quality of motherliness is confined to woman's readiness to accept actual motherhood, or that it implies only the promise of giving and receiving sensual pleasure, is in the first place a complete failure to recognize the true value inherent in the quality. In the second place, actually to hold such a view is a total betrayal of all that is specifically feminine in the sphere of human existence.

Because femininity contains the ideal of youthfulness, it preserves for human existence the dream of a "golden age" and the memory of its origins in the proverbially playful *Logos.* Femininity likewise contains the ideal of motherliness, and because of this, firmly anchors and establishes in human existence the possibility of genuine, tender love.

Two Modes of Human Existence

Once again we have to be careful not to forget that human qualities can be realized in human existence as such, and human existence can be achieved by every human being, whether man or woman. It may well be that the clearest and strongest connection is between motherliness and motherhood. It may also be a fact that the female physical appearance is capable of giving the clearest expression to a motherly existence. But this must not lead us to accept a radical division of human beings according to the

32 Just as a thing does not "caress" the tongue unless the tongue itself caresses that thing. The sensual delight in this consists in the discovery of subtle qualities of flavor through the intentional act of subtle, sensitive tasting.

anatomy of sex. We have to remember, as with the distinction drawn between work and care, that we are speaking of two modes of human existence, possible to every human being, and understanding the quality of motherliness should help us to understand this more clearly still.

When discussing work and care, we remarked that both acts, as possibilities of the human being, could be realized in either sex. We can now call motherliness tender love without the danger of being misunderstood, and we must stress that it too can be manifested by both sexes—that in some men it is in fact very evident, and in some women, rather weak.

There are two reasons which would explain why this should be so. The first is the peculiarity of the individual's aptitudes. The second, more important reason is the influence of education and of personal development as determined by actual circumstances of life and especially by the accepted scale of values. The most important factor in personal development and education, in this regard, is the particular form of love experienced in childhood, and to what extent the revealing power of motherly tenderness in the approach of others to the child elicited and unfolded a tenderness in the child itself and in the child's own world. Upon this factor will depend whether or not a person is able to say, in entire and heartfelt agreement with Alain, "Maternal love is . . . the model of all our loves." [33]

Alain's statement might seem incontrovertible. But we ought to be aware of the fact that the dominant trend to-day in psychology, specifically in the psychoanalytical field of psychology, is to deny the originality of motherliness and of the expressions of motherly love. Psychoanalysis accepts only one basic impulse, the libido, directed exclusively to achieving pleasure, and autonomically manifested in sexuality, whether the childish sexuality of early life or the forms more characteristic of later years. The thought intended in Alain's words is precisely the opposite of the psychoanalytical point of view, because motherly love, tender protective love for the still developing, still defenseless existence, is not only the first love a human being learns to know and respond to, but it is also the "model" upon which sexual love in later life—even the *"amour sauvage, terreur des mères"*—is controlled, as long as

[33] *Les idées et les âges.* Paris (Gallimard) 1927, p. 237ff.

there is any attempt to include this sexual love within the sphere of human relationships. Alain says, "It is interesting to see that lovers both at the same time imitate both motherliness and childlikeness, often in the same gesture being protective and submitting to protection."

Desire, and the sexual love that is based on desire, can be one-sided, unrequited, and therefore "unhappy," because they depend upon choice. Motherly love, on the other hand, can never be unrequited because it is not a love that chooses.

"Preferring What One Has"

The mother does not choose her child, she receives it. Thus, Alain says that "the perfection of love consists in preferring what one has," and he adds the penetrating observation that "this rule is a rule for the spirit." Now motherliness, as we in fact see it manifested in the feminine mode of existence, expresses love *in dwelling with tenderness upon what one already has—upon what is with one.* And there is no reason why the concept of "what one has" or "what is with one" should be limited. Genuine motherly love can extend to *everyone* and *everything.*

Alain notes that the love of desire—which is neither spiritual nor tender, though it counterfeits tenderness as a means toward the satisfaction of desire—is paradoxical in that it is a matter of choosing what will give pleasure, "but this is not to love; moreover, it is not even really to choose, for the only thing that matters is the meeting. . . ." Meeting, in this context, is not human encounter, but coincidental encounter in a situation which provides occasion for instinctual urges to become operative, even if they become operative in a slightly different way than in the animal. The content of encounter in the human sense is entirely different. It does not signify anything accidental or coincidental, but the giving and receiving of a gift. . . . "Love is the attitude of knowing that the *essential* may now be possessed in the form of gift." [34]

It is upon this that motherliness, as a characteristic of human existence, is concentrated. Motherliness holds vigil and waits. It is only in this sense that we could say that motherliness is passive

[34] Romano Guardini, *Notizen zu einem Bilde von Dantes Persönlichkeit,* Die Schildgenossen. Jhr. 18. 1939, p. 229.

and receptive, and it could be seen as something prefigured and prepared in the openness of youthfulness and of existence free from selfish intentions. Thus the motherly quality may be called the feminine fruitfulness of this youthful quality of being. But it is more than this. Motherliness, as the basis of every *"amour de pure grâce,"* of all totally selfless love, is not blind like desire but clear sighted, able to discover and bring forth value in the object of its love. Motherliness is creative.

To help ourselves understand this more clearly, we turn once again to the example of actual motherhood in which motherliness can be manifested clearly. The child is the outcome of the mother's giving. The mother gives her own nourishing blood, her warmth, her protection, her milk, a multitude of tendernesses. The child in a sense is a response to these gifts; by being, it makes response to the mother's giving. In Alain's image, the whole living body of the infant at the breast is a hymn of praise to the sweet abundance that feeds it. Mother love conferred upon the child makes the child grow. Growth is the child's physical answer to the mother's cherishing love. But when tenderness is lacking, the child's growth is defective. Kunz points to a phenomenon well known to medical specialists in child-care, sometimes called "hospitalism": "When little children do not receive a motherly tenderness in their upbringing—though for the rest they may be very well cared for—they develop more slowly and with much more difficulty than those who grow up in a protective maternal atmosphere, and the mortality rate among them is higher."

From this point of view as well, motherliness and its expressions of tender love are exemplary of a wholly selfless, unselfish love, for ". . . the gratitude of the child at the breast is gratitude for all the generosity and heroism of the purest kind of love," as Alain says.

Perhaps the word "gratitude" is not well chosen. The infant's response to its mother's love is not thanksgiving. No reciprocity of *love* ever takes the form of thankfulness. Every response to love is the realization of a value hidden until revealed in the response—and this is something already present in the act of care. Love, as Binswanger says, is "creatively productive." It is a willing promotion of value in its object,[35] because it is intentionally directed

---

[35] M. Nedoncelle: "une volonté de promotion." cf. *Vers une philosophie de l'amour* (Aubier) Paris 1946.

toward an elevation of the value of its object.[36] But it is not possible to produce or promote or elevate a value in something unless there is confidence that the value, though not yet apparent, is potentially there, and unless there is perseverance and "fides" (meaning both faith and constant fidelity) in the one who tries to promote or produce or elevate. Now we notice all these things in the inner structure of meaning in motherliness, and through the human quality of motherliness, they pervade all forms of pure love, including the love of a man for a woman and a woman for a man. By this, even the animal aspects of sexual "love" can be ennobled, restored fundamentally to grace and fidelity, and can express genuine love in the primordially human sense.

Binswanger, both philosopher and psychologist, has shown that investigation into the essence and meaning of love is the same thing as investigation into the essence of human reality. We do not now want to enter into a discussion of this whole matter, but simply to recall one thought he puts forward. He writes, "We acquire an ontological understanding of human existence as masculine and as feminine primarily through the correlation between "We" (*Wirheit*) and "I" (*Selbstheit*)." [37]

Decisive acceptance of responsibility, self discovery and the discovery of things, becoming aware of oneself and things, and grasping hold of them in whatever way, using them as objects there to be used—all this is in fact masculine, denotes an "I", a *Selbstheit*. Presence in the mode of "we", '*Wirheit*', as a being together without self-interest or intention in a giving and receiving that is reciprocal and *not* one-sided, is feminine.

But let it be noted once again: the masculine and the feminine are modes of existence that can be realized in the existence of every individual, whether the individual is a man or a woman. Thus motherliness is not a quality confined to women alone. Motherliness and the tenderness it comprises can be present in a man and can be operative in his relationships to other people and to the world—although this motherliness can appear as the *fulfillment* of existence and as *the* expression of the mode of manifestation only in a woman.

Nevertheless, concrete experience of life and theoretical discus-

---

[36] Cf. Scheler: *Wesen und Formen der Sympathie.*

[37] L. Binswanger, *Grundformen und Erkenntnis menschlichen Daseins.* Cf. his footnote on p. 94.

sion both indicate that a woman can carry out the activity of care without any motherly tenderness, but with a completely masculine decisiveness and a *resolute* intention to be present to self and to the other that excludes any other possible quality of togetherness. We might perhaps think that in this case, the act of care could better be called the act of work. But the name we give it is not important.

The thing that we must understand very clearly is the connection always present in every human being between the person's acts and the person's modes of existence. We have made a distinction between them, but only for the purpose of gaining an insight into the characteristics of feminine acts and the feminine mode of existence, and the fact that we have done so must not in any sense lead us to imagine that in any concrete existence the acts and forms of existence are ever quite distinct. When we are dealing with real people, all we can ever see is more or less of a predominance of the masculine or of the feminine, whether in the present "structure" of an individual's personality, or in a particular phase of an individual's life, or in an individual's attitude toward a given situation or toward another person.

Motherliness is contained in youthfulness, and youthfulness is contained in motherliness. Care, in one respect, involves the reality of work, and in another respect it involves the openness of youth and the tender quality of motherliness and also of the tender, defenseless being.

But once we have succeeded in giving an essential definition of the quality of motherliness and become able to recognize it in the feminine mode of manifestation, we ought to be able to understand that it is purely a human phenomenon, an *asexual* quality that is essentially universal and independent of actual motherhood. When we do, we can understand that the quality of motherliness is constitutive of *human* existence in the spiritual manifestations of human existence as well as in the vital expressions of life. We can see that motherliness, as a respectful, careful togetherness in selfless giving, fostering, nourishing, cherishing and caressing, is always the power that everywhere *elicits* the unfolding, the realization of hidden potential, of what is good, tender, fragile or subtle, whether in human beings or in nature or in culture. This is what happens in human relationships of friendship and love, in real education and in loving work.

The Woman

This is what is happening in all *art* and also in all pursuit of knowledge, for art and knowledge take their rise in admiration and appreciation and love for being. This is also what is taking place in the self-development of the personality, in the growth of clarity and precision of the mind, in the budding discretion of sensitivity of emotion and feeling, in the subtlety of careful distinction, and last but by no means least in the rounding out and perfection of faith, the restoration of the image of God in man, when we call in the aid of a *motherliness most free of all desire and therefore virginal*, the Woman, representative before God of the defenseless humanity of us all.

But still, the quality of motherliness in human existence is not fruitful on its own, without the masculine element, without understanding the world in its hardness and in its resistance, without the act of work directed, not to being-together-with, but to goals at a distance yet to be reached. The same may be said of every *woman:* as concretely existing in the world, she cannot perfect her existence in femininity alone without a masculine element.

In masculinity the human being projects a world of hardness, of stubborn resistance, of a mass of reality that is simply "there." In femininity, the human being projects a world of softness, without resistance, insubstantial—a world of what might possibly be "here." But while we should bear this in mind, we should at the same time be careful not to forget that these projections presuppose a world that permits them—a world to which all human beings, men and women, are *subject.*

Therefore, if a human being is to achieve the full dignity of a mature existence, both of these projections are needed. Every person, whether man or woman, needs both visions, both forms of being, the masculine as well as the feminine.

We need an example to bring this out more clearly, and the best is perhaps the example of the too feminine and too motherly woman. Her existence gets lost in a chaos of pathic connections without any ability to distance herself, to take stock, to objectify. She has no sense of reality. The tender quality of what should be her love becomes wholly absorbed in a display of tender gestures, possibly in a kind of egoism that is blind to the real other and sees only itself in the other, because there is no reserve, no withdrawal into the loneliness of self—for without reservedness and withdrawal, neither the self nor the other can be seen in their own reality, and thus there cannot be any real community between them. Love, in such a woman, lacks all power to create values, it degenerates into an uncontrolled and passionate emotional dependence and becomes idolatry; it is blind to reality and degraded to the level of illusion, of romantic sentimentality and of pseudo-motherliness.[38]

Love and the quality of motherliness are always full of feeling and emotion, but when a woman lacks the wisdom of the masculine element of "common sense," she tries to wield her own emotion and feeling as though they were magical powers and the only world she can project is the dream-world of unreality. The perfect quality of motherly love, which Alain so perceptively denotes as a "preference for what it has," points to strong *sense of reality,* but there is no sense of reality in any projection which is entirely undeliberated and exclusively sentimental. This is the reason why there is always some measure of vague uncertainty in every emotional relationship, and why, sooner or later, the uncertainty comes to be recognized as a doubt as to the genuineness of the reality and value of the emotionally "tinted" image.

The too-motherly woman is not a good mother; the too-feminine woman is just as incapable of real love as the too-masculine man.

The woman who over-cultivates the feminine and motherly aspects in herself and neglects the masculine, fails to reach her human destiny. She finds herself continually threatened by disillusionment and disenchantment, and like Don Quixote at the end of his road, she comes eventually to the painful discovery that the world is not under a magic spell after all. An end like this brings only the melancholy of lost illusions, the pain of a fall into effusively emotional flight. All that remains is the need to make the

---

[38] Cf. Binswanger p. 683. Genuine togetherness in existence, "Wirheit," is a "dual mode of human existence," and it is possible to achieve it fully only in encounter with another, in which the other is known as a "thou-self" in a way that brings out the reality of "my-self" and makes me aware of it. ". . . if it is *true* encounter, or in other words, if it is encounter "in reality," I do not lose the knowledge that *I am* while knowing that I forever belong to *our* being-together-in-love; such encounter is *creatively productive* (of experiencing understanding) and equally *creatively receptive* (of understanding experience); it is both *masculine* and *feminine.* Genuine "Wirheit" is always both masculine and feminine in a double sense: the togetherness-in-being itself is both masculine and feminine, and each one of the parties to the togetherness is both masculine and feminine."

effort to begin to come right when resignation is hard, when there is a bitter humor in the situation, when interests turn out to be fleeting distractions. This is perhaps what was in the mind of Madame de Rémusat when she penned the romantic sigh: "Even in the very midst of her happiness, woman is instinctively aware of suffering."

It may still be, nevertheless, that expressions like the one we have just quoted are intended to refer to the general relationship between the femininity in woman's mode of existence and sorrow. In this connection, we might be reminded of a number of attitudes prevalent in society—perhaps even of the "sublimation" of the uncertainty of a *wholly* unmasculine and therefore immaturely pathic existence, or simply of the fact of the greater vulnerability of the more feminine existence.[39] However, we could also consider the indissoluble connection between love, sacrifice and sorrow,[40] and we would in this way be more likely to come to an understanding of the very heart of feminine existence.

From an analysis of the content of expressiveness in woman's physical appearance, we found that youthfulness is a feminine characteristic. A typically feminine existence reaches its *fulfillment* only when it achieves itself as a genuinely *human* existence one quality of which is motherliness. This existence is always, necessarily, an animated, bodily being-in-the-world and a being in relationship with other people. This existence presupposes an existence *for self.*

It is never possible to understand a person's relationship to other human beings in any other way than in terms of an insight into that person's consciousness of himself. A person's consciousness of self is composed of his actual experience of existence as formed in all situations through the person's relationship to his own body, and also of the way the person wants to be and chooses to be, the way he wants to present himself to other people and to himself.

Thus, it is clear that a woman is motherly in a genuine sense only to the extent that she constitutes the characteristics of her animated bodily being as *her own* characteristics, *choosing* these characteristics to define the relationships she herself will assume in the midst of the web of social relationships she discovers round

---

[39] Cf. Liepmann, *Psychologie der Frau,* Berlin 1920.
[40] Cf. my *Over de Pijn,* p. 179ff. and elsewhere.

about her, and *choosing* them also to define her own relationship to herself. For every human being is able to take his or her own self and body and inward world and make them the subject of emotional experience or of consideration and reflection, and human beings can do this in a number of very different intentional ways. A person can see himself as admirable or as despicable, he can want to analyze himself or disregard himself, to accept himself as he is or protest what he is.

The relationship that constitutes a person with regard to himself also determines the person's position in the community of which he is a part. Conversely, social relationships can have a powerful influence on a person's attitude toward himself. Thus, a person's relationship toward himself is constituted of many component elements. One of the most important factors is the person's positive or negative appreciation of his own body as he experiences it as a means of action and of self-expression.

Another factor, equally important, is the person's awareness of the way others judge and evaluate his physical appearance and the way he manifests himself through his body. One's experience of one's own body gives definition to one's conscious awareness of all that one is "able to do"—it defines the power we possess over our body to employ ourselves in active effort or to rest in relaxation, and also the power to express or to conceal the way we are affected emotionally.

Moreover, in everyone's experience there is more or less of an awareness of the "dignity" of his or her own stature, attitude, manner of movement, voice, face, hands and attire. No one sets this dignity up as a representation or a visible image over against himself, and neither does anyone confront himself with this personal dignity of the body in a conceptually formulated definition. Every human being has an immediate and irrefutable experience of the value of his or her own body, since the body, in a human existence, is always present to the human being as the medium through which the human being becomes involved in situations or is able to become involved in them, and also as the medium through which the human being is subject to the world's influence and through which he is able to influence the world. In the words of Merleau-Ponty, the body is experienced as "the vehicle of being-in-the-world." It is "through the world" that I am aware of my own body. My body is the *central point* of my world, an "unperceived term" toward which my world converges like the radii of a sphere.

Woman is human, and so her female body is the central point of woman's world. Motherliness can appear as the fulfillment of woman's existence, then, only because the world is centered upon her body as the nature and manifestation of motherliness. Woman's own awareness of herself is comprised in this relationship between woman and the world, and in this awareness she is also conscious of her *freedom* to be able to be tender, "meek and lowly of heart," like any good person.